MULTIMEDIA COMPUTING

The word "multimedia" is often associated with specific applications from entertainment to Web design to video to music. This textbook presents emerging techniques in multimedia computing from an experiential perspective in which each medium – audio, images, text, and so on – is a strong component of the complete, integrated exchange of information or experience. Humans are the best functioning example of multimedia communication and computing – that is, we understand information and experiences through the unified perspective the combination of our senses offers. The goal of this book is to present current techniques in computing and communication that will lead to the development of a unified and holistic approach to computing using heterogeneous data sources.

The authors introduce the fundamentals of multimedia computing, describing the properties of perceptually encoded information, presenting common algorithms and concepts for handling it, and outlining the typical requirements for emerging applications that use multifarious information sources. Designed for advanced undergraduate and beginning graduate courses, this book will also serve as an introduction for engineers and researchers interested in understanding the elements of multimedia and their role in building specific applications.

Gerald Friedland is the director of audio and multimedia research at the International Computer Science Institute, a research laboratory affiliated with the University of California, Berkeley.

Ramesh Jain is a Donald Bren Professor in information and computer sciences at the University of California, Irvine, where he is doing research in EventWeb and experiential computing for developing and building social life networks.

Multimedia Computing

GERALD FRIEDLAND

International Computer Science Institute, Berkeley, California

RAMESH JAIN

University of California, Irvine

CAMBRIDGE
UNIVERSITY PRESS

32 Avenue of the Americas, New York, NY 10013-2473, USA

Cambridge University Press is part of the University of Cambridge.

It furthers the University's mission by disseminating knowledge in the pursuit of education, learning, and research at the highest international levels of excellence.

www.cambridge.org
Information on this title: www.cambridge.org/9780521764513

First published 2014

Printed in the United States of America

A catalog record for this publication is available from the British Library.

Library of Congress Cataloging in Publication data
Friedland, Gerald, 1978–
Multimedia computing / Gerald Friedland, Ramesh Jain.
   pages   cm
Includes bibliographical references and index.
ISBN 978-0-521-76451-3 (hardback)
1. Multimedia systems.   I. Jain, Ramesh, 1949–   II. Title.
QA76.575.F76   2014
006.7–dc23   2014002250

ISBN 978-0-521-76451-3 Hardback

Additional resources for this publication at http://www.mm-creole.org

Contents

Preface . . . . *page* xi

Acknowledgments xiii

1. **Introduction** 1

    Organization of This Book   3

    Recommended Reading   4

2. **Multimedia: A Definition** 6

    Communication in Human Society   7

    Evolution of Computing and Communication Technology   8

    Why *Multi*media Computing?   10

    Multimedia: A More Formal Definition   13

    Recommended Reading   13

    Exercises   14

3. **Elements of Multimedia Computing** 15

    Experience and Information   15

    Objects and Events   17

    Perception   18

    Perceptual Cycle   19

    Challenges in Multimedia Systems   21

    Semantic Gap   22

    Context and Content   23

    Recommended Reading   25

    Exercises   26

4. **Introduction to Sensors** 28

    Types of Sensors   28

    Properties of Sensors   31

    Digitization   32

    Recommended Reading   34

    Exercises   35

5. **Sound** 36

The Physics of Sounds   36

Observed Properties of Sound   38

Recording and Reproduction of Sound   39

Microphones   39

Reproduction of Sound   41

Production of Sound   43

Exercises   49

6. **Light** 51

What Is Light?   51

Observed Properties of Light   53

Recording Light   54

Reproducing Light   58

Perception of Light   60

Color Spaces   61

Light Production   64

Recommended Reading   64

Exercises   66

7. **Multimedia Documents** 67

What Is a Document?   67

Evolving Nature of Documents   69

Stages in Document Creation   71

Basic Elements of a Multimedia Authoring Environment   75

Representation of a Multimedia Document   77

Current Authoring Environments   78

Recommended Reading   79

Exercises   80

8. **Multimodal Integration and Synchronization** 82

Multimodal Integration   82

Sensor Integration in Multimedia Computing   86

Introduction to Synchronization   86

Content Synchronization   87

Temporal Synchronization   88

Synchronization Levels in a System   90

Specification of Synchronization   90

Deadlines   91

Spatial Synchronization   91

Recommended Reading   93

Exercises   94

9. Multimedia Systems 95

Components of a Multimedia System	95
Different Configurations of Multimedia Nodes	99
QoS and QoE	99
Different Modes of Media Delivery	99
Live Video	103
Emerging Systems	105
Recommended Reading	105
Exercises	107

10. The Human Factor 108

Principles of User Interface Design	108
Privacy	116
Security	118
Safety	119
Recommended Reading	120
Exercises	122

11. Fundamentals of Compression 124

Run-Length Coding	124
Information Content and Entropy	125
Compression Algorithms	128
Weakness of Entropy-Based Compression Methods for Multimedia Data	138
Recommended Reading	138
Exercises	139

12. Lossy Compression 141

Mathematical Foundation: Vector Quantization	141
Perceptual Quantization	144
Differential Coding	147
Recommended Reading	153
Standards	154
Exercises	154

13. Advanced Perceptual Compression 156

Discrete Fourier Transform (DFT)	156
Discrete Cosine Transform (DCT)	158
The Convolution Theorem	160
JPEG	161
Psychoacoustics	164
MP3	168
Perceptual Video Compression	170
Recommended Reading	171
Exercises	172

14. Speech Compression 174

Properties of a Speech Coder 174
Linear Predictive Coding (LPC) 175
CELP 182
GSM 185
Recommended Reading 186
Exercises 187

15. Multimedia Information Retrieval 188

Databases 189
Structured, Unstructured, and Semistructured Data 191
Classic Information Retrieval and Search 192
From Information Retrieval to Multimedia Information
    Retrieval 198
Content-Based Retrieval 199
Recommended Reading 205
Exercises 207

16. Signal Processing Primer 209

Sampling and Quantization 209
Levels of Computation 210
Thresholding 212
Linear Operations 214
Nonlinear Filters 216
Filter by Example 220
Graphical Filters 222
Notions for Visual Filters 222
Edges 226
Segmentation Using Split and Merge 228
Recommended Reading 230
Standards 232
Exercises 232

17. Multimedia Content Analysis 233

From Monomedia to Multimedia Content Analysis 234
Setup of a Multimedia Content Analysis Experiment 236
Features 238
Supervised Learning 248
Unsupervised Modeling 260
Error Measurement and Evaluation 262
Final Remarks 266
Recommended Reading 269
Exercises 270

18. Content Analysis Systems 272

Speech Activity Detection   272

Large Vocabulary Automatic Speech Recognition   273

Optical Character Recognition   275

Speaker Recognition   276

Speaker Diarization   278

Face Detection and Face Recognition   280

Acoustic Event Detection   281

Visual Object Recognition and Tracking   282

Multimedia Content Analysis Systems   286

Recommended Reading   287

Exercises   288

19. Content and Context 290

Connecting Data and Users   292

Content and Context   293

Context-Only Image Search: Commercial Systems   297

Device Parameters   297

Recommended Reading   302

Exercises   304

20. Future Topics 305

How to Predict the Future   305

Future Topics in Multimedia   306

Recommended Reading   315

Exercises   315

Index 317

Plates follow page 50.

Preface

The project to write a textbook on multimedia computing started a few years ago, when the coauthors independently realized that a book that addresses the basic concepts related to the increasing volume of multimedia data in different aspects of communications in the computing age is needed.

Digital computing started with processing numbers, but very soon after its start it began dealing with symbols of other kinds and developed computational approaches for dealing with alpha-numeric data. Efforts to use computers to deal with audio, visual, and other perceptual information did not become successful enough to be used for any applications until about the 1980s. Only slowly, computer graphics, audio processing, and visual analysis started becoming feasible. First was the ability to store large volumes of audiovisual data, then displaying or rendering it, then distributing it, and later processing and analyzing it. For that reason, it took until about the 1990s for the term *multimedia* to grow popular in computing.

While different fields have emerged around acoustic, visual, and natural text content that specializes in these data types, multimedia computing deals with documents holistically, taking into account all media available. Dominated by the availability of electronic sensors, multimedia communication is currently focused on visual and audio, followed by metadata (such as GPS) and touch. Multimedia computing deals with multiple media holistically because the purpose of documents that contain multiple media is to communicate information. Information about almost all real-world events and objects must be captured using multiple sensors as each sensor only captures one aspect of the information of interest. The challenge for multimedia computing systems is to integrate the different information streams into a coherent view. Humans do this every moment of their lives from birth and are therefore often used as a baseline when building multimedia systems. Therefore it's not surprising that, slowly but surely, all computing is becoming multimedia. The use of multimedia data in computing has grown even more rapidly than imagined just a few years ago with the installation of cameras in cell phones in combination with the ability to share multimedia documents in social networks easily.

It was at this point that we felt that most of the books introducing multimedia to students and practitioners discussed technology from a perspective that has now become obsolete. We wanted to introduce multimedia from a more current, yet sustainable, perspective.

In this book, we adopt a holistic approach in introducing the field of multimedia computing. Instead of introducing multimedia based on the media types (image, audio, video), we present multimedia as a fundamental and unique discipline that takes advantage of all media available to solve problems. This results in a unified introduction to the field by focusing on the fundamental techniques and mathematical foundations of multimedia computing as a process in information extraction from diverse types of signals. For instance, the book introduces lossy compression by presenting the principles of quantization and differential coding, before showing how these principles are applied to compression of image, audio, and video.

Having said that, covering all aspects of different types of signals used in multimedia computing in a book is not practical. This would require covering large parts of mathematics, physics, physiology, psychology, electrical engineering, and computer science aspects of different types of signals and related topics. We therefore decided to adopt a different approach: introduce the main concepts in a "capsule" form and provide pseudo-code for algorithms such as ADPCM encoding or the Paeth Predictor. We decided to include many research papers, blogs, and books giving details and detailed perspectives on different topics under further readings. We will keep these updated in a companion Web version of the book at http://www.mm-creole.org. Advanced and detailed literature references are provided that allow the reader to explore the topics beyond the coverage of this book.

We want our book to be used as a textbook for advanced undergraduate or graduate students in computer science and computer engineering. Students in other areas might also benefit, but they must have good preparation in programming, data structures, and data management. Many computer science, computer engineering, and electrical and computer engineering programs offer a course in multimedia. This book is targeted to be suitable to support these classes.

We intend to make this a "living book." Based on reader feedback, development of new methods and technology, and emerging applications, we will keep updating the book. As we are finishing the last words for this version we are well aware that this will not be the end of the project.

We therefore hope you enjoy reading this book and start engaging with this exciting field and, while you do, don't hesitate to contact us to participate in the evolution of this book.

Gerald Friedland Ramesh Jain
Berkeley and Irvine
November 18, 2013

Acknowledgments

A textbook project is a long one and requires significant efforts by several people. This book would not have been possible without the encouragement of many colleagues at ACM Multimedia who reminded us, year by year, of the necessity of this book. These include especially Klara Nahrstedt, Balakrishnan Prabhakaran, and Abdulmotaleb El Saddik. Moreover, we want to thank the various students who provided us with feedback during the course of this project. We want to thank our editors Lauren Cowles and David Jou at Cambridge University Press. Furthermore, we want to thank Joan Taylor for editing early versions of our nonnative English creations that we dared to call text. Last but not least, we want to thank our families, the Friedlands and the Jains, for bearing long weekends and nights of work.

1 Introduction

Clearly everybody knows the word "multimedia," yet when people think of it, they usually think of different things. For some people, multimedia equals entertainment. For other people, multimedia equals Web design. For many computer scientists, multimedia often means video in a computing environment. All these are narrow perspectives on multimedia. For example, visual information definitely dominates human activities because of the powerful visual machinery that we are equipped with. In the end, however, humans use all five senses effectively, opportunistically, and judiciously. Therefore, multimedia computing should utilize signals from multifarious sensors and present to users only the relevant information in the appropriate sensory modality.[1]

This book takes an *integrative systems* approach to multimedia. Integrated multimedia systems receive input from different sensory and symbolic sources in different forms and representations. Users ideally access this information in experiential environments. Early techniques dealt with individual media more effectively than with integrated media and focused on developing efficient techniques for separate individual media, for example, MPEG video compression. During the past few years, issues that span multimedia have received more central attention. Many researchers now recognize that most of the difficult semantic issues become easier to solve when considering integrated multimedia rather than separate individual media.

In the early days of computing, science fiction writers envisioned computers as robots that would effectively use audiovisual data. Later, people dreamt of systems that could organize audio files, images, and video. Now people want to share perceptual experiences independent of time and distance. Within the next few years, most of the data stored on computers – in terms of storage size and bandwidth requirements – will be audiovisual. Therefore, the fundamental media for computing and communications will also be audiovisual and will increasingly include tactile components.

Handling multimedia content requires incorporating concepts and techniques from various disciplines – from signal processing, from communication theory to image data-

---

[1]   In this book, we use the notions of sensory modality and media interchangeably, defined as data generated from one particular type of sensor.

Figure 1.1. Multimedia is like an elephant. Looking at it from a limited perspective leads to many completely wrong characterizations.

bases, and from compression techniques to content analysis. Multimedia computing has consequently evolved as a collection of techniques from different disciplines.

Because of the diversity of types of information and the evolution of technology, application development, as well as multimedia research, has evolved in a way like the elephant in the fable about the elephant and the six blind men (see Figure 1.1). In this fable, each blind man has a limited perspective. In real life, people impose limitations of perspective in many ways and hence – though naturally endowed with multiple sensory and cognitive faculties – functionally behave like these blind men portrayed in the cartoon: each engineering and research discipline perceives multimedia from its own limited viewpoint. This has resulted in a skewed development of the field, where multimedia is perceived as multiple monomedia fields.

We (humans) use our five senses (sight, hearing, touch, smell, and taste) together with our abstract knowledge to form holistic experiences and extract information about the world. Multimedia computing aims to develop communication techniques to share holistic experiences from multiple sources and modalities of data and to extract useful information in the context of various applications.

This fragmented perspective of multimedia has slowed progress in understanding and processing multimedia information, although the hardware used for processing it – ranging from sensors to bandwidth – has advanced rapidly. Multimedia computing should leverage correlated and contextual information from all sources to develop holistic and unified perspectives and experiences. It should focus on full *multi*sensory experiences rather than partial experiences, such as listening to an audio-only sports commentary.

This book presents emerging techniques in multimedia computing from an experiential perspective in which each medium – audio, images, text, and so on – is a strong component of the complete exchange of information or experience. Humans are the best functioning example of multimedia communication and computing – that is, we understand information and experiences through the unified perspective our five senses offer. Our goal in this book is to present current techniques in computing and communication that will lead to the development of a unified and holistic approach to computing using heterogeneous data sources.

By describing the properties of perceptually encoded information, presenting common algorithms and concepts for handling it, and outlining the typical requirements for emerging applications that use multifarious information sources, this book introduces the fundamentals of multimedia computing. It serves as an introduction to engineers and researchers interested in understanding the elements of multimedia and their role in building specific applications.

ORGANIZATION OF THIS BOOK

We organized this book to present a unified perspective on different media sources for addressing emerging applications. The chapters in this book are organized for linear reading even though the reader may choose to skip some of them. Often, we are not able to explain a topic in full detail; in those cases, we provide pointers to literature. Our main goal is to present concepts, techniques, and applications that will be useful in building integrated multimedia systems. The nature of the field mandates that this includes not only concrete algorithms, but also high-level concepts and strategic knowledge that illustrate the big picture of the problems to be addressed. We believe that the holistic viewpoint presented in this book is essential for understanding, using, and communicating emerging applications in multimedia.

Chapters 1–3 Defining Multimedia Systems

Evolution of technology related to communication and computing has resulted in fragmentation and limited perspectives in multimedia computing. The current stage of the multimedia field brings to mind the parable about the six blind men and the elephant; we therefore track the evolution of the field briefly and then define multimedia systems and discuss their main elements in these chapters. The big picture concepts in these chapters will help us discuss all elements concurrently in the subsequent chapters without losing the whole-system perspective.

Chapters 4–6 Nature of Perceptually Encoded Information

Like humans, multimedia systems gain information and experience through a variety of sensory and other sources. Understanding the relationships among data, information, knowledge, insight, and experience is crucial to being able to use these sources judiciously. We discuss basic elements of information and data source types, mostly focused on but not limited to audio and visual data, in the context of multimedia systems. These areas are well established and many other sources provide details on every aspect of representation and processing. Our goal here will be to present the essential elements from those areas and direct readers to sources for more information.

Chapters 7–11 Fundamental Properties of Multimedia Applications and Systems

Once multimedia data is acquired through sensors, it needs to be transmitted, stored, and reproduced. Users often use production environments to edit and create multimedia presentations out of the raw sensor data. In this part of the book, the fundamentals concepts of multimedia systems and applications will be discussed.

Chapters 12–15 Compression

Multimedia data is usually continuous time-dependent data that is significantly more voluminous than other data. Often, though, a system's input, processing, and output elements are at different locations. A large volume of data must therefore be communicated to different locations. The cost of these communications, as well as storage, must be reduced using data-compression techniques. The field of data compression has matured and been largely implemented in industrial products because most of these techniques have responded well to multimedia systems' needs. When working with multimedia data, it is therefore almost inevitable to think about methods to handle compressed data. This part of the book presents fundamental algorithms and ideas and provides sources for the reader to go into further details based on her interest.

Chapters 16–19 Organization and Analysis of Multimedia Content

Most multimedia systems are for collecting, processing, creating, and storing data to extract information and knowledge from it. Most applications of multimedia systems are for accessing, sharing, and using this data, information, and knowledge. In a data management system, structuring techniques are used to index and organize data for efficient access. Organizing multimedia data for search and navigation has been a challenge. Even organizing individual components such as audio, images, and video presents difficulties. During the past few years, the types of sensors used, as well as the volume of data acquired, has continuously increased, making this problem even trickier. This part of the book introduces techniques and approaches to structure, index, and access multimedia data.

Chapter 20 The Future of Multimedia

Multimedia is a very dynamic and ever-changing field. Therefore, we end this book with an outlook and with techniques that can help with finding a strategy to predict the development of multimedia computing that allows the readers to position themselves in the big picture.

RECOMMENDED READING

The story of an elephant and six blind men has been used many times by different authors, most famously by John Godfrey Saxe, to bring an ancient viewpoint from India. This story illustrates how a limited perspective may lead to erroneous understanding of a complex object or concept. James Gleick's book *The Information* is a very good exposition to the nature of information both from a mathematical and from an evolutionary perspective of information. Current multimedia systems have now evolved to the stage where, for the first time in history, those working with such systems can seamlessly combine different modalities. Another very good read for students of multimedia is Samuel Hayakawa's *Language in Thought and Action*. This book explains how languages evolve and is very insightful.

Further Reading

James Gleich. *The Information: A History, a Theory, a Flood*. New York: Pantheon Books, 2011.

Samuel Ichiye Hayakawa. *Language in Thought and Action*. Harcourt Brace Jovanovich, 1978, Orlando, Florida.

John Godfrey Saxe. *The Blind Men and the Elephant* (retold).

2 Multimedia: A Definition

Only a few inventions in the history of civilization have had the same impact on society in so many ways and at so many levels as computers. Where once we used computers for computing with simple alphanumeric data, we now use them primarily to exchange information, to communicate, and to share experiences. Computers are rapidly evolving as a means for gaining insights and sharing ideas across distance and time.

Multimedia computing started gaining serious attention from researchers and practitioners during the 1990s. Before 1991, people talked about multimedia, but the computing power, storage, bandwidth, and processing algorithms were not advanced enough to deal with audio and video. With the increasing availability and popularity of CDs, people became excited about creating documents that could include not only text, but also images, audio, and even video. That decade saw explosive growth in all aspects of hardware and software technology related to multimedia computing and communication. In the early 1990s, PC manufacturers labeled their high-end units containing advanced graphics *multimedia PCs*. That trend disappeared a few years later because every new computer became a multimedia computer.

Research and development in multimedia-related areas has been around for much longer. Research in speech processing, speech compression, and speech recognition was fueled first by telephony and then by digital sound applications. Image and video processing and compression have also been active research and development areas because of digital photos and video.

Before 1990, much of the research in audio and video compression, storage, and communication was driven by broadcast and consumer electronics related to entertainment applications. During the 1990s, combining these sources in a computing environment emerged as a clear possibility. As a result, research in all areas of audio and video received significantly greater emphasis.

In the following, we describe the historic evolution of communication to relate it to current multimedia computing. The current technology in multimedia computing and communications is only a stage in the evolution of humans' desire to share their experiences and to extract knowledge from those experiences. A clear understanding of the goal of multimedia computing helps in developing efficient approaches to deal with it.

COMMUNICATION IN HUMAN SOCIETY

The ability to effectively communicate complex facts and interrelationships is one of the main features that distinguishes humans from animals and has been a major force in human evolution. Communication lets us share experiences and create, maintain, sustain, and propagate knowledge. This innate desire resulted in several influential inventions that determined the progress of human civilization. Communication across space allows participants to exchange information independent of their current location, and communication across time allows observers to experience an event over and over again without having to be there at the exact moment. Mankind's quest for communication of experiences across both time and space is one of the defining foundations of multimedia. A third factor is the desire to communicate to as many people as possible, thus duplicating communication easily. Communication thereby becomes invariant to the number of addressees in space and time. As Table 2.1 shows, human civilization has seen many influential inventions related to communicating experiences across space, time, and addresses.

Human communication exists in many forms, including facial and body gestures, olfactory signals, and of course spoken language. Out of these, spoken language is the most capable of conveying the most complex facts, that is, the information density is very high. For most of humans' existence, though, spoken language only consisted of analog sounds uttered with the speech-producing infrastructure in the throat. Eventually, people realized that experiences were important and that they should somehow store these events for sharing with others. Initially, drawings and paintings would preserve these experiences, but they were not precise enough to unambiguously convey complex facts, and they were too cumbersome to produce. This resulted in the invention of written language as a system for representing language to share experiences. Bulky preservation techniques such as stone tablets gave way to more practical storage devices and writing methods. Next came the development of paper and ink, and still more people began using the stored experiences that others had painstakingly recorded.

Then came one of the most influential inventions in our history: Gutenberg's movable printing press. This invention enabled mass communication for the first time and revolutionized society. By making creation, storage, and distribution of documents more manageable, this technology resulted in easy sharing of knowledge in society. Our current education system, our reliance on documents (such as newspapers) as a major source of communication, and on libraries as public, government-supported institutions dedicated to storing knowledge, stem from that one invention that appeared more than five hundred years ago.

The telegraph, which allowed instantaneous communication of symbolic information over long distances, began to bring the world closer. This invention signaled the beginning of the global village. Telephones let us return to our natural communication medium – talking – while retaining the advantages of instantaneous remote communication. People could experience the emotions of the person on the other end of the connection – something symbol-based methods of writing and the telegraph could only hint at.

Radio ushered in the wireless approach to sound and popularized sound as a medium for instantaneous mass communication. Movies and television took communication a

Table 2.1. Communications-related inventions in human civilization

Invention	Resulting Application	Invariance
Spoken Languages	Natural communication	None
Written Languages	Symbolic record of language	Time
Paper	Portability	Time and space
Print	Mass distribution	Time, space, addressee
Telegraph	Remote narrow communication	Space
Telephone	Remote analog communication	Space
Radio	Broadcasting of sound	Space, addressee
Movies	Recording of sight and sound	Time, space, addressee
Television	Broadcasting of sight and sound	Space, addressee
Recording media	Recording	Time, space, addressee
Digital media	Machine enhancement and processing	Time, space, addressee
Internet	Personalized reception	Time and space (sometimes addressee)

step further by combining our senses of sight and hearing and making communication more natural. It was the first medium that let us experience with more than one sense and as such was able to more effectively key into our emotions. Video communication's popularity is clearly due to its use of our two most powerful senses working in harmony.

Storage and distribution technologies, such as magnetic tape, allowed the storage, preservation, and distribution of sound, again bringing us closer to natural experience. Video recording enhanced this experience and advanced experience sharing to the next stage. Digital media further improved the quality of our experience by making it possible to copy and share information with controllable loss in quality. Finally, the Internet took information availability to a new dimension, providing us with experiential accounts of an unprecedented variety by combining different media appropriate to the message to be communicated.

EVOLUTION OF COMPUTING AND COMMUNICATION TECHNOLOGY

The changes in the landscapes of both computing and communications have been overwhelming during the past few decades.

Just a few decades ago, a computing center was one of the most important buildings on a university or corporate campus. Access to this building, particularly to the "holy" room in which the computer operated, was highly restricted. A computer occupied several rooms,

Table 2.2. Comparison of early computers with those of a typical handheld in 2011

Computer	Processing unit	Operating system	Core memory	Secondary memory
1960s-era computer (IBM1620)	Could not do arithmetic, used look-up tables	No OS; human monitors controlled everything	60 Kbytes	2M characters
Handheld Experiential Computer (iPhone 4S) in 2011	Dual Core A5 Chip, 800 MHz	iPhone OS	512 Mbytes	64 Gbytes

Figure 2.1. A 1960s-era computer at NASA.(Source: U.S. National Archives and Records Administration)

if not floors, of a building; needed air conditioning; and required a specialized and trained staff to interact with it. These computers cost millions of dollars. Figure 2.1 shows a popular computer from the late 1960s and early 1970s. Table 2.2 lists important characteristics of the IBM 1620 computer, which is from that era.

Progress in processing, storage, networking, and software technology has changed computing beyond anyone's expectations. Today, most people carry computers in their pockets that are several orders of magnitude more powerful and sophisticated than the 1960s-era computer. Table 2.2 compares a current handheld to the early computer. Although the newest handhelds are more powerful and sophisticated, they cost several thousandths of what the older version cost, are easy to carry, and are much less affected by climate. Moreover, just about anyone can operate them, using them to solve everyday computing and communications needs.

Communications technology has experienced a similar overwhelming transformation. We've already discussed the historical perspective. Here, we focus on short-term technological improvements in one medium.

Consider the telephone. In its very early incarnations, the telephone had limited use. Only a few people could afford to have one in their homes. Moreover, a house had one phone, and when you called someone you had to shout into the mouthpiece. During a long-distance call, latency made communication difficult. Either both parties spoke at the same time or waited for the other, while an expensive meter ticked off seconds. Usually, people spent more time shouting "Hello! Hello!" than having a meaningful conversation. Now, users can talk on a phone while walking, running, driving, or flying in an airplane. Signal reception is so clear that you can whisper to a person on the other side of the globe. More important, not only is your phone a voice communication device, but it is also your connection to a computer network, a camera, a calendar and address book, an entertainment center, and a video communication device.

WHY *MULTI*MEDIA COMPUTING?

To understand computing technology's evolution to its current state, as well as to project its future evolution, consider the applications that have been and will be driving the technology's development.

The first computer applications performed numerical computations using data in scientific applications, hence the name *computer*. Business was the next major driving application with so-called data processing as the driving operation. It brought alphanumeric processing and databases in focus for development. Major networking advances resulted in enterprise computing based on the traditional distributed processing approaches that eventually culminated in the Internet.

Personal computers were a major influence on computing. PCs ended reliance on a powerful central computer and brought several applications, including word processing, spreadsheets, and electronic mail, into the consumer space. Combining personal computing and Internet connectivity led to one of the most amazing communication revolutions that human civilization has seen so far: the World Wide Web. The progress continued, and laptop computers replaced most PCs. Laptops are now being replaced by even more personal and sentient computing devices – tablets and mobile phones. These mobile devices can be used for computing, communication, and much more. Moreover, they can use audio and visual mechanisms equally effectively as traditional alphanumeric computing.

They are being better equipped with more diverse sensing mechanisms than humans have, for example, GPS receivers to sense geo-location. These tools are true multimedia computing and communication devices.

Emerging computing and communication applications have clear differences from earlier applications. This allows us to imagine the future of multimedia applications and provides a framework for new ideas. The following is a list of properties of emerging applications as compared to applications developed just in the past decade:

- Spatiotemporal and live data streams are the norm rather than the exception.
- A holistic picture of an event or situation is more important than silos of isolated data.
- Users want insights and information that are independent of the medium and data source. That is, the medium is just the medium; the message is what's important.
- Users do not want information that is not immediately relevant to their particular interests.
- Exploration (browsing), not querying, is the predominant mode of interaction.

Currently emerging applications are pushing computing to use primarily data from multiple sources. Moreover, these applications clearly demand that computing focus more on information, experiences, and understanding than on the medium or data source.

In considering the evolving and emerging nature of computing applications, two threads must be paid attention to: the evolving nature of information and the expected results from computing. The nature of data fed into a computing system used to be alphanumeric and it used to be managed in a well-defined and well-structured database. Emerging systems use heterogeneous multimodal data that is stored in several locations and is continuously changing and evolving. Cloud computing and Big Data are now as common as computing based on a single database was during the last decade of the twentieth century. In early days, however, computing systems were mostly used to obtain information such as *how many flights are operated by United between New York and Los Angeles*. Such information is still expected from modern computing systems, but now one is asking these systems to provide information such as *which parts of the world are seeing rapid growth in air passenger traffic*. Notice that, in the first question, one needs direct information as provided by standard relational databases. To answer the second question requires analysis of a large volume of data over time, and the best way to provide an answer may not be textual but perceptual, such as by using a visualization approach. Now let's consider another example. Suppose one wants to know where the hurricane shelters are in Florida. Such questions could be easily answered by a search engine, and such a search is now a routine operation. However, suppose that during a hurricane, a person stranded in Miami Beach wants to know where he should go. Such a query will require combining information from several sources that give the latest information and the person's location. Some of these sources may be sensor measurements, some may be videos, and some may be map-based information sources. These examples illustrate that, depending on the data types and their sources and the need of the user, different computing techniques need to be applied. In cases where insights are more relevant than raw data, one needs to consider relationships among several information sources, in most cases spanning spatiotemporal and perceptual data.

However, current information environments often work against the human-machine synergy. Humans are very efficient in conceptual and perceptual analysis but relatively weak in mathematical and logical analysis; computers are exactly the opposite. We call an environment where users directly use their senses to observe data and information of interest related to an event, and naturally interact with the data based on their particular set of interests in the context of that event, an *experiential environment.*

Experiential environments have several important characteristics:

*They are direct.*An experiential environment provides a holistic picture of an event without using unfamiliar metaphors and commands. People like to use familiar metaphors and expect that their actions will provide familiar experiences in computing environments also. A familiar example of this is now common in touch-based tablets, where swiping a photo toward the left brings a new photo, or pushing on an icon representing an application launches an application. More physical examples are utilized in game systems like Microsoft Kinect. In experiential environments, users easily and rapidly interpret the data presented and then interact with the dataset to get a modified dataset.

They provide the same query and presentation spaces. Most current information systems use different query and presentation spaces. Popular search engines, for example, provide a box for entering keywords, and the system responds with a list of perhaps thousands of entries spanning hundreds of pages. A user has no idea how the entries on the first page relate to those on the thirteenth, how many times the same entry appears, or even how the *entries on the same page relate to each other*. Contrast this to a spreadsheet. A user articulates a query by changing certain data that is displayed in the context of other data items. This action results in a new sheet showing new relationships. Here, query and presentation spaces are the same. These systems are called What-You-See-Is-What-You-Get (WYSIWYG).

*They consider both the user state and context.*Systems should know the user's state and context and present information that is relevant to the user in that state and context. People operate best when they are in known contexts. If the context changes abruptly in the interaction environment, it results in confusion. Information systems, including databases, should be scalable and efficient. These considerations led to the design of *stateless* systems, such as relational databases. However, this statelessness is why most Internet search engines are so dissatisfying. They don't remember the users' state. *They promote perceptual analysis and exploration.* Text-based systems provide abstract information in visual form. Experiential systems let users analyze, explore, and interact with their environment using all of their senses, and thus are more compelling and easier to understand. Currently, video games provide very good experiential environments. Often, these games effectively use audio, video, and tactile media to create compelling interactive environments.

Now, going back, and reformulating what the technical requirements of experiential systems are, we find that they have to integrate, process, and output data from different sensory modalities. In other words, experiential systems are technically implemented as multimedia systems.

MULTIMEDIA: A MORE FORMAL DEFINITION

One obvious question that comes to mind at this stage is: Are there some fundamental issues in multimedia computing and communication systems that will provide this integrative, experiential perspective? For exploring this, let us consider the problem a bit more precisely.

Consider a system equipped with multiple sensors working in a physical environment. The system continuously receives information about the environment from multiple sensors and uses this information to achieve its goals.

Assume that $S_1, \ldots S_n$ are synchronized data streams from sensors. These data streams have K types of data in the form of image sequence, audio stream, motion detector, and so on. Further, let $M_1, \ldots, M_n$ be metadata, including annotations, for each stream. This metadata might include the sensor's location and type, viewpoint, angles, camera calibration parameters, or any other similar parameters relevant to the data stream. In most cases, feature detectors must be applied to each data stream to obtain features that are relevant in a given application. Let us represent feature stream F_{ij}, where F_{ij} is the jth feature stream from S_i.

Multimedia computing and communication techniques combine the dataset S_i and its feature stream F_{ij} using the metadata M_i to extract information about the environment required to solve a given problem. In this process, the system must often combine partial, sometimes uncertain, information from multiple sources to get more complete and reliable information about the environment.

A defining difference in multimedia from monomedia fields like computer vision or audio processing is that in multimedia, partial information from multiple media sources is correlated and combined to get complete information about the environment. A common experience that most people have is deciding about a thunder and an explosion – appearance of a bright light followed by a strong sound used to detect it. Without correlating the sound with the noise, one cannot conclude that there is an explosion or a thunder.

As we will see, context added by both the senses and prior experience plays a key role in human multimedia analysis. In multimedia computing, the context can come from disparate sources, for example, from data collection parameters, from other sensory data, or from device constraints.

RECOMMENDED READING

Johannes Gutenberg's moveable printing press is one of the most important inventions in the history of civilization. Though printing existed in many parts of the world before Gutenberg, this invention made it practical to produce books easily and cheaply. This simple invention resulted in democratizing creation, production, and distribution of knowledge. Marshall MuLuhan clearly identified the synergy between the medium and the message in his popular book *Understanding Media*. From a more formal and technical perspective, James Gleich's *The Information* provides a very insightful and rigorous perspective on how different media provide alternate and complementary views of the information useful in the experiential computing environments that Ramesh Jain defined and discussed. With the advances in technology during the first decade of the twenty-first century, these environments are finding an increasing role in different applications.

Further Reading

James Burke. *The Day the Universe Changed*. Boston, MA and Toronto: Little, Brown and Company. 1985.

James Gleich. *The Information: A History, a Theory, a Flood*. New York: Pantheon Books. 2011.

Ramesh Jain. "Experiential Computing." In *Communications of Association of Computing Machinery*, July 2003.

Marshall McLuhan. *Understanding Media: The Extensions of Man*, 1st edition. New York: McGraw Hill; reissued by MIT Press, 1994.

EXERCISES

1. Think about techniques developed in history that influenced communication and enabled time and space invariance. Identify at least three techniques not mentioned in this chapter that played a role in the evolution of communication technology.

2. Choose a multimedia application of your choice and design a more experiential environment for interacting with it.

3. Search several definitions of the word "multimedia" in literature and discuss how they combine information coming from different media.

4. Many movies are made based on famous books. Select one of your favorite such books that was produced as a movie. Find five people who read the book and saw the movie. Ask them which one they liked better, the book or the movie. Ask them why. What do you think different media contributed to the presentation of the same story that different people find more or less compelling?

5. Why did the telegraph use Morse code that represents letters of the alphabet using variable length codes? Do you think this idea could be used in other systems? Can this be used at the world level rather than the letter level?

3 | Elements of Multimedia Computing

As discussed in the previous chapter, multimedia is closely related to how humans experience the world. In this chapter, we first introduce the role of different sensory signals in human perception for understanding and functioning in various environments and for communicating and sharing experiences. A very important lesson for multimedia technologists is that each sense provides only partial information about the world. One sense alone, even the very powerful sense of vision, is not enough to understand the world. Data and information from different sensors must be combined with other senses and prior knowledge to understand the world – and even then we only obtain a partial model of the world. Therefore, different sensory modalities should be combined with other knowledge sources to interpret the situation. *Multimedia computing and communication is fundamentally about combining information from multiple sources in the context of the problem being solved.* This is what distinguishes multimedia from several other disciplines, including computer vision and audio processing, where the focus is on analyzing one medium to extract as much information as possible from it.

In multimedia systems, different types of data streams simultaneously exist, and the system must process them not as separate streams, but as one correlated set of streams that represent information and knowledge of interest for solving a problem. The challenge for a multimedia system is to discover correlations that exist in this set of multimedia data and combine partial information from disparate sources to build the holistic information in a given context.

EXPERIENCE AND INFORMATION

We experience our physical environment through our natural senses of sight, hearing, touch, taste, and smell.[1] Every human child starts building models of different objects and events in the world through a learning process from a very early part of life using all senses. Once these models are in place, our senses let us experience and function in the physical

---

[1] Note that this is a traditional classification of human senses. In later chapters, we will see that humans have more senses, for example, proprioception. We will also discuss that for multimedia computing systems, many other (nonhuman) sensory sources are available and could be used.

and social worlds and continue to refine, enhance, and even develop new models. These models are fundamental first, to recognition of objects and events in our world and second, to decision making and prediction based on the models. The model of an object or event helps us in abstracting all sensory information into a simple symbol. The process of assigning a symbol to represent an object or event and then building more complex objects and events using these is at the heart of a field called *semantics*. Semantics is an important area of study in linguistics and is related to the study of the meaning of words, phrases, sentences, and other larger units of text. Semantics is a rigorously studied field (see further reading links at the end of this chapter). In our discussions in this book, we will not address the detailed theory of semantics, but we will consider the basic aspects as needed. For our purpose, we will just consider semantics to be the study of meaning associated with symbols. These symbols could be simple atomic symbols or could be composite symbols built by combining multiple atomic and/or composite symbols. Because our concern is with multimedia signals, these symbols could represent units in different components such as audio and visual data (e.g., an area of a certain texture or an acoustic event), or could represent entities as combinations of different media (such as an audiovisual object), thus resulting in symbols in multimedia.

Webster's dictionary defines *experience* as the "direct observation of or participation in events as a basis of knowledge." We experience the world we live in. The basis of all our interactions is our experience of the world. We learn about the world and accumulate and aggregate our experiences in the form of knowledge. Scientists among us *experi*ment to test their knowledge and to gain new knowledge. Scientific processes rely on experiments to study a hypothesis under different conditions to evaluate its validity. Experimental aspects of a science are fundamental to its progress. Humans make their final evaluations of experiments by using their sensory processes.

As explained in the previous chapter, *communication* is the process of sharing experiences with others. The history of civilization follows the development of our understanding of experiences and how to share them with our fellow humans even in other parts of the world immediately, as well as with those who will follow in future generations. It is interesting to see how many influential innovations and inventions in human history are related to communication and sharing of experiences with people who may be spatially and temporally separated. Again, this process started with the development of languages and has led to the innovations resulting in the World Wide Web.

Information is an efficient but abstract communication of experience. We gain knowledge through the set of experiences that make up our lives and communicate information about those experiences. Because we don't communicate the experiences themselves, we lose a vital element of the act of experiencing in the translation to information. Many of us cannot know, for example, what it is like to hit the game's winning run, to surf the perfect wave, or to fight a war. We can read about the events, of course, and we can view pictures and videos. In the end, however, we are not present in these, so our experience and knowledge of these events is incomplete.

In the communication process, one of the most important elements is to develop a dictionary. A *dictionary* is an exhaustive collection of a selection of the words of a language. It contains information about their meanings, pronunciations, etymologies, and inflected forms, in either the same or another language. Thus, a dictionary is a shared and agreed upon collection of symbols (words) and what these symbols mean. Each language is based on a dictionary containing these symbols and rules, the grammar of the language, to use them. Without a dictionary, communication may not happen. Just imagine a situation in which a person speaking English is talking to a person speaking Mandarin. Each person is using a dictionary, but these are two different dictionaries. Communication requires a shared dictionary. Dictionaries are commonly used in the context of languages and use words as the basic symbols as carrier of meaning. In computer science, dictionaries are extended to use lists of codes, terms, and keys for use by computer programs. Many of the compression algorithms presented in later chapters put dictionaries into practice.

In multimedia, the basic carriers of meaning or symbols are not just traditional words as used in speech and text, but units, similar to alphabet used in text and phonemes used in speech, in a particular medium. A basic perceptual dictionary unit is often referred to as a *percept*. Let's consider visual information. Consider a very simple common task: given an image of an object, name this object and list all objects that look like it and are related to it. Try to extend this to all detailed functions that you commonly see in a dictionary. Visual dictionaries are being developed for different applications and for different kinds of visual information, ranging from shapes of curves to complex objects (see research articles). In these dictionaries, usually visual shapes or objects are stored and all their details are given in multiple languages. These dictionaries will likely play an important role in the understanding of visual information and in applications of emerging technology that will increasingly utilize cameras as information devices.

OBJECTS AND EVENTS

In understanding data of any type, one tries to find which aspect of the world the data represents. As discussed previously, perceptual processes depend on prior knowledge about the world we live in to analyze the signals. An important issue is how to represent the world.

Many researchers believe that the world can be represented using objects. This view argues that the world could be considered as a collection of objects. Many thinkers have challenged this view during the past several centuries (see further reading at the end of this chapter). According to their views, events play an equally important role. Events represent changes in relationships among objects. And these changes are fundamental to understanding the current state of the world. According to emerging views, to model a dynamic world, both objects and events must be used. In a sense, objects are good at capturing static components of the world, while events complement that by capturing dynamic situations.

In computer science, object-oriented thinking has been used in many fields and their applications. Object-oriented approaches have revolutionized many areas of computer science because of the high-level abstractions it offers for design, programming, and even some interactions.

Multimedia brings new challenges to computer science, however. Multimedia, particularly audio and video, are fundamentally dynamic in nature. They capture signals that represent some attributes of the world as a function of time. In fact, in many applications, even those sensors that capture static characteristics of the world, such as temperature at a point in space and time, are used to detect changes in those characteristics as functions of time. A sensor is typically placed in an environment where some event needs to be detected and the sensor measures some physical attribute that helps in detecting the event.

Many fields in computing have used the concept of event in designing systems. Different fields have used this concept very differently, however. With the increasing use of multimedia in computing, a unified approach for event-based thinking is evolving. Many information systems are being designed to deal with event information management.

Note that for modeling the real world using powerful computational approaches, it is essential to use at least objects and events. Objects and events complement each other. Objects in computing capture attributes and functions of physical objects, and other related concepts and events represent relationships and changes among those relationships in space and time. Very soon a balanced approach using both objects and events to model the real world using multimedia data is likely to become common. Later, other percepts will add to that model.

PERCEPTION

Perception is the process of understanding sensory signals to recover useful information. Human perceptual processes have been analyzed for a long time with the goal of understanding them. With the arrival of computing, the field attracted more attention from psychologists and researchers in artificial intelligence and related areas with the goal of developing machines for automatic perception. However, understanding perceptual processes remains a difficult problem despite being actively researched in many disciplines including psychology, neuro-physics, and computer science, particularly computer vision. The understanding of sensory information is an important step in many multimedia systems. We will study important perceptual processes in audio and visual processing in following chapters. Here we present some general aspects of perceptual processes.

A perception system takes sensory signals as input and generates the information that is relevant in its application context as output. This process is based on two important sources: signals and relevant knowledge sources. Figure 3.1 shows the role of existing knowledge in perception. The output of the system is clearly the combination of the input sensory signal as well as the knowledge available to the system. Without any knowledge, the system cannot produce any information, and without the signal, the system can only hallucinate. Perception sometimes is considered as a controlled hallucination process where based on the signal, the system starts simulating and creates multiple hypotheses, then uses the signal to find the best supported hypotheses and recovers information from signal.

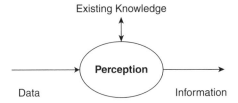

Existing Knowledge

Perception

Data

Information

Figure 3.1. Perception is the process that recovers meaningful information from sensory data using existing knowledge.

Figure 3.2. (A) A Dalmatian dog sniffing around. (B) Unstable perception: two faces or vase?

The role of knowledge, in the form of models of objects and events, is not immediately obvious. Some examples may shine a little light on it, however. We always use the term *recognition* for finding objects in signals, such as images. This term implies that we try to *re cognize* objects – meaning we know about the object or, in other words, have models of objects. Without models, there is no recognition. The models could be in many different forms ranging from very concrete and detailed models to very abstract models. To show the importance of models, we show two very commonly seen pictures in Figure 3.2. In Figure 3.2a, there is a Dalmatian dog sniffing around. If you don't know how a Dalmatian dog looks, you will see only random blobs in this picture, but if you know a Dalmatian dog, you will clearly see it. Figure 3.2b shows a picture that has two interpretations: you can see either two human faces or a vase in it. This shows that your perception system comes up with two hypotheses and admits both as viable, but only from a slightly different gaze point.

PERCEPTUAL CYCLE

In all our activities, we use our senses, brain, and memory to understand our environment, to operate in this environment, to communicate about the environment, and finally to build and update our knowledge repositories for efficient and effective use of what we learn. How we use these senses and how we convert this sensory data to information and knowledge has been a source of intrigue to thinkers for almost all known history. Here we present some ideas to provide historical context and perspectives on the evolution of this understanding.

Writing in a book more than two thousand year ago, UmaSwami hypothesized:

- Understanding of the world is indirectly derived using our senses.
- The fidelity of the model of the world depends on how well a person understands the world.
- People achieve different levels of understanding in terms of their own knowledge structures.
- Nirvana is the highest stage of understanding.

These observations show deep insights about perception. Thinkers even during that time clearly recognized that data from all sensors must be assimilated using existing knowledge to form an understanding of the environment. They also recognized that sensors help us understand the world at different levels of understanding. One evolves to the highest level of understanding by refining their knowledge structures. Modern philosophers propose and discuss similar ideas and models in the theory of objective reality.

To formulate the problem from a computational perspective, we consider the perceptual cycle Ulrich Neisser introduced in 1976. It attempts to model how humans perceive the world. According to this model, a perceiver builds a model of the world by acquiring specific signals and information to accomplish a task in a natural environment. The perceiver continuously builds and refines a schema that is based on the signals he received so far. This schema represents the world as the perceiver sees it at that instant. The perceiver then decides to get more information to refine the schema for accomplishing the task that he has in mind. This sets up the perceptual cycle depicted in Figure 3.3. The basic idea behind the perceptual cycle is that an agent is continuously interacting with the environment using its sensory mechanisms to build the model of the environment that will be useful in its task. At any given time instant, it has a model of the environment, called a *schema*, that is constructed using all the data and information received until that point. The system then decides what more is required to complete the task and how that information could be acquired. Based on this, the agent collects more information using appropriate sensors.

The perceptual cycle model has conceptual similarity to recursive filtering techniques commonly used to estimate the state of a linear dynamic system using observers (sensors) that may provide noisy measurements. In these systems, the state of the system is represented mathematically as a vector. The state vector represents the values of the parameters that are used to characterize the linear dynamic system. In system theory, these vectors represent the system so that the correct amount of control inputs could be applied to the system to bring it into the desired state. In the perceptual cycle, the schema represents the essential parameters that are required to solve the given task. Based on the current schema as compared to the final, or desirable, schema, the agent must decide its action. Later chapters will introduce filters that take the schema into account consciously as well as unconsciously. As mentioned, however, the perceptual cycle is dealing with perception that is not a linear dynamic system. This cannot be easily

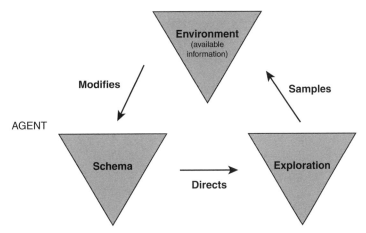

Figure 3.3. Neisser's perceptual cycle: The perceiver gets signals from the environment, interprets them using the current schema, uses the results to modify the schema, uses the schema to decide to get more information, and continues the cycle until the task is done.

modeled using the current tools of the system theory. As progress in technology takes place, more formal tools will presumably be developed to represent and construct the schema using multimedia data.

CHALLENGES IN MULTIMEDIA SYSTEMS

The problem of multimedia computing was formalized in the previous chapter as a problem of information combination from multiple modes of data streams. Assuming this data environment comprising different data streams acquired from diverse sensors, the most fundamental problem that multimedia computing systems must address is extracting the relevant information for solving a given problem using data from these disparate sources. We address many challenging problems in this book:

- How do we represent this data in the most compact form for communication and storage?
- How do we present this volume of data to a user in her computing environment to communicate intended information?
- What system issues must be solved to deal with these disparate types of data and how the system handles them?
- How do we combine these data streams to obtain the information that is essential for solving the problem at hand?

Before we address more specific concepts and techniques related to solving these problems in the rest of this book, the remainder of this chapter discusses two major concepts that are inherent to almost any technique or approach in the field.

SEMANTIC GAP

Computing systems represent data as bits and bytes and build from these more sophisticated representations such as lists, images, audio, and video. All these representations are fundamentally a collection of bits that programmers use to define abstractions to build their applications. The users of these systems, however, are people who define their applications thinking of abstractions that start with objects and events. There is a fundamental gap between the abstractions defined in computing systems and those used by the users of these systems. This situation is shown in Figure 3.4. This gap is defined as stated in Definition 3.1.

Definition 3.1:
The semantic gap is the difference between the information that a machine can extract from the (perceptual) data and the interpretation that a user in a given situation has for the same data.

In current computers, we must build abstractions starting with bits, the most fundamental representation unit of data, and defining concepts that may be needed in specific applications. It is easy to build these concepts by defining various structures and naming and using them as a programmer may want to. We are all familiar with concepts such as images, video, and audio signals as they are represented in computers. Human beings, ultimate users of computing systems, typically do not think in these structures, however. Humans usually think of objects and events and build complex concepts based on complex, often ill-defined and uncertain, relationships among them. As shown in Figure 3.4, a gap exists between the abstractions such as images and video as defined in computers and objects and events as used by people in their minds. This gap is called the semantic gap.

The main reason for the semantic gap, which often even exists between two persons, is that the physical world contains objects and events and people build the models of these objects and events in their mind based on the data that they receive from their sensors. People learn to abstract the data received from their sensors while combining this data naturally from all sources including all sensory organs, context, and memory. Chapter 8 will explain some details of that. In computing, however, we define things based on what can be computed, while as humans we learn to abstract what is needed to survive.

In all cases where human beings are an integral part of a computing system, the semantic gap must be bridged. Therefore, many concepts and techniques developed in multimedia computing are related to bridging the semantic gap. Starting from signal analysis approaches used in audio processing and computer vision to indexing for multimedia information retrieval, many concepts and techniques in multimedia address the problem of bridging the semantic gap. In many mature fields, this is bridged either by developing concepts in the field that bring data and humans conceptually close or by developing interfaces that rely on human intelligence to bridge the gap.

Here is an example: consider common Internet search engines that appear to work so well that we use them every day. A close look at a search system's behavior shows that when searching for keywords that can be matched as character strings, it is easy to get

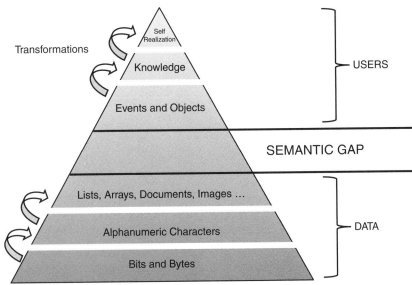

Figure 3.4. Semantic Gap. There is a big gap in how computers represent data like images in bits and bytes and how people think about images as collections of objects or events.

good results. When searching for concepts, such as the success of a peace initiative, that require some interpretation of either data or your intentions, current search systems perform poorly. Most research in improving the relevance of results in search engines aims to bridge the semantic gap. It is concerned with how to interpret data and how to detect a user's intentions based on contextual information.

CONTEXT AND CONTENT

"Content" and "context" are two very commonly used terms in multimedia processing and understanding. There is no rigorous formal definition of content or context, though practitioners and researchers commonly use them. It is important to understand what they mean and how they are related to develop efficient and effective multimedia systems.

Consider Figure 3.5. This is a photo containing 4,224 x 3,168 picture elements (pixels), and each pixel is a color pixel. This photo contains more than 13 million points, each with three color values associated with it. In the most basic form, the content of the file or, as commonly used, photo are these 13 million pixel colors in the spatial configuration as represented by the location of these pixels.

Metadata literally means "data about data." Given data that represent an audio, photo, or video; the metadata for them will describe different characteristics of this data. Some obvious metadata is name, size, date of creation, and type of file. In addition to these, one can include any other information useful for understanding, storing, transmitting, presenting, or any other operation on the file containing the data. Metadata itself is data of some particular type; it is metadata in this particular context because it is used to qualify or help some other data.

Figure 3.5. This photo was taken at Zhujiajiao, Shanghai, China.

Because understanding techniques for text, audio, images, and other sensory data have not matured enough to correctly understand elements in data, metadata has gained in popularity, particularly with the growth of the Web. XML was designed as a mechanism to transport and store data. It accomplishes that by defining a language to describe what data is. Tags used in XML are data about data. Thus, XML is a language to associate metadata with the data explicitly so it could be read by any program. This helps in not only transporting and storing, but analyzing and understanding data.

Let's consider a picture file – say the photo shown in Figure 3.5. This photo was taken at Time (11:31 AM on September 13), Location (Zhujiajiao, Shanghai: Latitude 31 deg 6' 36.34" N, Longitude 121 deg 2' 59.22" E), and using a Nikon Coolpix P6000 camera. For this particular photo, no flash was used, and the focal length (6.7 mm), ISO (64), and aperture (f/4.7) values of the camera are known. All this (and much more) information is captured by the camera and is stored in the picture file along with the pixel data using a popular exchangeable image file format (Exif) standard (see Web links).

In multimedia computing, the use of metadata is increasing rapidly. Many approaches based on XML and tags are becoming commonplace even in audio, images, and video. Researchers expect techniques to evolve enough to eventually represent metadata as intimately as in text. Use of Exif with all stored digital images is a clear example of this trend in this field.

The reason for the rapid increase in use is that metadata represents the context in which the data in the photo was acquired. Context in this sense is the interrelated conditions in which some data (the content) is acquired. As seen earlier, some context parameters are stored by the camera using Exif standards for the photo. Almost all digital camera manufacturers use the Exif standard to store this kind of data with all digital photos.

Other context parameters may help in understanding data. For example, in the context of the picture shown earlier, Exif tells the model of the camera, but it will be very helpful if the owner of the camera is known and profile and calendar information about the owner is also available. In many cases, based on this information it may be possible to understand what the objects are and, more important, who the person in the picture is.

Multimedia research and techniques developed were concerned with only the content of the data in early days. The importance of context is becoming increasingly clear. Recently (see Singavi), researchers are emphasizing that content and context should be combined and should be viewed as all information that must be used for understanding multimedia.

RECOMMENDED READING

Semantics has been a very well-studied discipline in linguistics and is now becoming an important area in computer science. Two aspects of semantics are relevant to computer science. *Descriptive aspect* deals with how to represent semantics to capture aspects of a model. The other aspects are related to detection of the best-fitting model for the given data, or the *recognitive aspect*. This aspect is very important for dealing with multimedia data. We recommend Peregrin's book as a good source and as an introduction to semantics. Another fun book to get a lightweight idea of visual semantics is the book on visual dictionaries. Scherp and Jain discuss a semantic ecosystem from the perspective of multimedia.

Many authors have published books about communication among people using languages and other types of signals. We recommend Gleich's book, again mentioned here, as a good source. Singhavi gives a good exposition to ancient theories that describe how the interpretation of data depends on the knowledge level of the observer. This is described further in the philosophical writings of Karl Popper, where he talks about three worlds we use in understanding the world we live in. This is very closely related to discussions in Tatwarthsutra discussed by Singhavi. For computer scientists and students of multimedia, these philosophical works are made accessible by Irwin Rock and Ulrich Neisser. Neisser's theories are particularly relevant to interpreting multimedia data in real-time context. Communication and control theory people address an engineering version of similar problems for implementing real-time control systems. In those areas, these are commonly called "estimation theory." Kalman filters a popular version of estimation theory used in multimedia-related topics. See Caitlin's book for an introduction to this area.

Smeulder and colleagues popularized the concept of the semantic gap in their article "Image Databases at the End of the Early Years." This topic has received significant attention since the publication of their work.

The idea of representing the world using objects and events has been a topic of exploration in literature for a long time. A very good introduction to this topic is Quinton's article, "Objects and Events." Westerman and Jain discuss the concept of events as used in many different aspects of computer science with a particular emphasis on how events need to be represented in multimedia.

Finally, we suggest that researchers and practitioners in multimedia computing become familiar with Exif standards (see the Web link) to understand what kind of metadata could be captured, making extraction of semantics from modern multimedia data easier.

Further Reading

D. E. Catlin. *Estimation, Control, and the Discrete Kalman Filter*. Springer Verlag. 1988.

James Gleich. *The Information: A History, a Theory, a Flood*. New York: Pantheon Books. 2011.

Hermann Kuhn. *The Key to the Center of the Universe*. Crosswind Publishing. 2001.

Jonathan Metcalf. *Five Language Visual Dictionary*. 2003.

U. Neisser. *Cognition and Reality: Principles and Implications of Cognitive Psychology*. W. H. Freeman. 1976.

Jaroslav Peregrin. *Meaning: The Dynamic Turn. Current Research in the Semantics/Pragmatics Interface*. London: Elsevier. 2003.

Karl Popper. "Three Worlds." The Tanner Lecture on Human Values Delivered by Karl Popper at The University of Michigan on April 7, 1978.

A. Quinton. "Objects and Events." *Mind* 197–214, 1979.

Irvin Rock. *The Logic of Perception*. MIT Press. 1985.

A. Scherp and R. Jain. "An Eco System for Semantics." In *IEEE Multimedia*, June 2009.

L. M. Singavi. *That Which Is: Tattvartha Sutra (Sacred Literature)*. AltaMira Press. 1998.

Arnold Smeulders, Marcel Worring, Simone Santini, Amarnath Gupta, and Ramesh Jain. "Image Databases at the End of the Early Years." *IEEE Transactions on Pattern Analysis and Machine Intelligence* 23 (1), January 2001.

G. Utz Westermann and Ramesh Jain," Towards a Common Event Model for Multimedia Applications." In *IEEE Multimedia*, January 2007.

Web Links

http://www.exif.org/.

EXERCISES

1. Why does the semantic gap become a serious problem in perceptual systems? How would you approach minimizing this gap using contextual metadata?
2. A digital camera collects a lot of metadata related to camera parameters, including its location, and stores that with the intensity vales at every pixel. How can the metadata be used? Can this metadata help in reducing the semantic gap?
3. What is Exif? Why was Exif introduced? Where can Exif be useful? Where can Exif be harmful?
4. How is text related to audio? Why did text become a dominant medium for communication and sharing of knowledge?

5. Which is easier to analyze, speech or text? Discuss.

6. What is the role of knowledge in perception systems? List at least three knowledge sources that could be used in understanding images.

7. What is a model as used in perception systems? Can you develop a recognition system without using a model?

8. How is the perceptual cycle related to estimation theory? Where is the estimation theory used? Can those systems be considered machine perception systems?

9. Multiple sensors are usually used to capture attributes of the real world. Because the sensors have different coverage in space and have different temporal characteristics, how can one combine the data obtained from these sensors?

10. What is a feature in a sensor data stream? What role does it play in analysis of data and correlating different data sources?

4 Introduction to Sensors

Information about the environment is always obtained through sensors. To understand the handling of perceptual information, we must first start with an understanding of the types and properties of sensors and the nature of data they produce.

TYPES OF SENSORS

In general, a *sensor* is a device that measures a physical quantity and converts it into a signal that a human or a machine can use. Whether the sensor is human-made or from nature does not matter. Sensors for sound and light have been the most important for multimedia computing during the past decades because audio and video are best for communicating information for the tasks humans typically perform with or without a computer. That is, most people prefer to communicate through sound, and light serves illustrative purposes, supplementing the need for language-based description of a state of the world. New or different tasks might use different sensors, however. For example, in real-world dating (as opposed to current implementations of online dating), communication occurs on many other levels, such as scent, touch, and taste (e.g., when kissing). Artificial sensors are therefore invented as you read this chapter. Let's start with a rough taxonomy of current sensors interesting to multimedia computing.

We consider three basic types of sensors: sensors that imitate human sensors, sensors that do not imitate human sensors but measure aspects of life, and sensors that measure physical facts about the environment.

Human Sensors

The largest organ on the human body, the skin, is devoted to a very important sensation: touch. As a result, touch is seeing increased use in multimedia computing. Haptic technologies use tactile sensors to translate pressure into signals. Currently, the most common type of tactile sensor is the force feedback joystick, which is used in applications such as computer game controllers, servo mechanisms for aircraft, and remote surgery. Haptic devices receive information from the user through pressure-sensitive sensors, such as piezo crystals, which emit electrical power proportional to the force applied to them. So-called *actuators* transmit the feedback to induce a vibration or another physical motion to communicate to the human hands and arms. Other sensors, such as haptic gloves, allow normal usage of the hand but capture the muscular state of the fingers and other parts of the hand. Often, a remote robotic hand then reproduces the state of the operator's hand on the other end. A major issue with haptic sensors is tuning the feedback or sensor to make the user experience intuitive and natural, so the user does not have to learn how to operate the system.

The biggest portion of the brain, however, is devoted to another sensation: sight. Sight sensors are usually called *eyes*, or in the technical domain, *cameras*. They are described in detail in Chapter 6. In modern digital cameras, a physical reaction occurs in an electrical photovoltaic element, typically a charge-coupled device (CCD) sensor chip. Each sensor creates one picture element (also known as a *pixel*). The number of pixels is usually given as the maximum granularity of a picture, which in the digital world is called *resolution*. Even the highest-resolution cameras are no match for the view angle and resolution of the human eye.

Hearing is a very important sensor that enables several everyday tasks in humans. Audio sensors are usually called *ears* or *microphones*, respectively, and are described in Chapter 5. Like cameras, microphones are very important for multimedia computing. Because sound is a pressure wave traveling through a medium (such as air or water), microphones are very similar to haptic sensors. Often, haptic signals and acoustic signals can be analyzed with similar methods and visualized in the same space.

The very important sensation of smell is technically not completely understood. However, so far the knowledge is that artificial noses need to be able to detect an array of molecules in the air in order to find patterns of smell similar to biological noses. The same goes for the following.

Human taste sensors can be distinguished into bitterness, saltiness, sourness, sweetness, umami (savory), piquance (hotness), and metallic because different regions of the tongue react to them. However, beyond that the chemistry and physics of taste are not well understood, and therefore no artificial tongues have been produced that are used in day-to-day multimedia systems.

A multimedia system that can incorporate vision, hearing, touch, smell, and taste would be close to complete but not quite: along with these, many animals have sensors for temperature, gravity, magnetic fields, humidity, and other properties of their environment. Birds, for example, are believed to have sensors for gravity so that they can navigate to find their habitats during summer and winter; sharks have sensors for magnetism so they can find prey; snakes and other reptiles see infrared light and therefore have a temperature sensor as well as better night vision.

Many nerve systems and chemical sensors also sense internal aspects of the body such as stretch, motion, and position of appendages (proprioception). The latter is very useful as it measures the relative position of neighboring parts of the body and strength of effort being employed in a movement. A major problem in robotics is to be able to do that artificially. Some internal sensors are directly coupled to body functions, such as pain and hunger.

Sensors about Life

The medical field has created an abundance of sensors that are coupled to measuring functions of living organs. These are used by doctors to diagnose diseases or other body malfunctions. What's interesting to multimedia computing is that many of these sensors have become inexpensive and mobile, therefore it's not inconceivable that they'll be used as part of human communication soon. For example, these sensors enable medicine applications to become remote for so-called tele-medicine and allow for health care applications to supervise certain health statistics automatically to prevent malfunctions. In the following, we describe a short list of some of the most important sensors.

Measuring weight electronically has become cheap and easy. Modern scales, however, measure more than sheer bodyweight. They usually also estimate the body fat based on the electric resistance of the body. These two measures, together with basic anatomic data such as gender, height, and age, allow us to roughly estimate a whole set of other body parameters, such as bone weight, muscle mass, and body water content.

Along with weight, measuring temperature electronically has become cheap, easy, and fast. Estimating the body temperature at regular intervals, together with other factors, such as heart rate (which can also be sensed electronically) and motion/acceleration of extremities, allows for a mobile estimation of burned calories. As a result, many mobile exercise helpers and weight loss applications have become popular on the market. Often, these are combined with computer games and/or tutorial videos that react to the measured body parameters – making them everyday multimedia companions.

While this book does not cover these sensors intensively, they will likely become very important for multimedia computing in the future as they continue to become cheaper and more mobile.

Environmental Sensors

Some environmental sensors have undergone the same process as described for the health sensors: they have become cheaper and more mobile, and their output has become digital. The most prominent examples are the compass and the accelerometer. Both of these types of sensors are now available in most smartphones. Additionally, accelerometers play a large role in the gaming industry as parts of video game controllers. Measuring acceleration in shoes, for example, allows walkers to estimate the speed and the distance walked. Coupled with a GPS receiver (global positioning system) which, for our purposes could be seen as a position sensors, makes for a quite accurate estimation of one's speed and location in a given environment. Location sensing has therefore become quite important in many applications, especially mobile Internet applications. The main driving force behind these services is the enabling of a very personalized experience. Some services, for example, automatically locate discount coupons for stores in the user's current geographical area. Also, a growing number of sites now provide public APIs for structured access to their content using geo-location functionality. The reason for this is that exact location and time together are a physically guaranteed unique identifier.

Speaking of time, measuring it has also become easier than ever. Time signals propagated in the Internet and mobile networks originating from atomic clocks are so precise that one no longer has to worry about measuring time accuracy, and one almost forgets that this is the most important environmental sensor of all.

Other environmental sensors can sense physical as well as chemical phenomena, such as radiation, force, flow, and seismic activity. The remaining chapters will mainly focus on the properties of the two major sensations, hearing and vision, as they are utilized most widely in multimedia computing. However, before that we discuss the properties of sensors and introduce an important step that usually follows right after the sensor in the processing chain: digitization.

PROPERTIES OF SENSORS

An ideal sensor is sensitive to the measured property, insensitive to any other property, and does not influence the measured property. Of course, no perfect sensor exists because the laws of physics state that energy is conserved and sensors need a transfer of energy to function.

Fortunately, even imperfect sensors are useful. Moreover, it's these imperfections that multimedia computing exploits for compression, corrects when reproducing signals, and analyzes for content. For example, sometimes, by reducing the resolution of an image, we can save a lot of space without changing the appearance of the image because the eye's maximum resolution might be smaller than the original resolution of the image. This is an example of how to leverage the imperfection of a sensor for multimedia computing. They shape the nature of the perceptual information that multimedia computing processes. Therefore, it is very important to know typical sensor deviations, so we summarize them as follows before they are explained in more detail along with concrete sensors in later chapters.

Every sensor has a limited dynamic range of its operation, that is, the possible intensities of the input signal lie within a certain interval. Going above that interval *saturates* the sensor, that is, whereas the ideal measurement response would suggest a further increase in output, the sensor outputs a maximum value and/or breaks (compare, for example, human ears exposed to too-loud noises). The range's lower bound is defined by the minimum amount of input that can be clearly distinguished from no input. If the output is not zero when the input is zero, the sensor is said to have an *offset* or *bias*. In practice, the sensitivity might differ from the measurement function specified.

Ideally, a sensor will respond linearly to the measured entity; that is, a linear increase in input signal should result in a linear increase of the output of the sensor. A deviation from this is often referred to as *nonlinear behavior*. Most sensors are tuned to behave linearly inside an *operational range*. The nonlinearity is called *dynamic* when the sensor behaves differently based on time or other influencing factors that vary independently

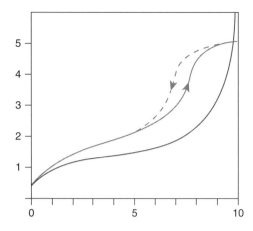

Figure 4.1. A general example for the hysteresis concept. The bottom curve is the sensor input, and the upper curve is the output. As the arrows show, the curve behaves differently when the measured entity decreases compared to when it increases.

from the measured entity. A changing sensitivity given a constant signal is a *drift*. Most sensors have long-term drift due to aging. A random deviation from the measurement function is called *noise*.

The term *hysteresis* refers to any deviation over time: when the measured entity reverses direction (for example, gets higher instead of lower) but the sensor's response has a finite lag, it might create one offset in one direction and a different offset in the other. Figure 4.1 illustrates the concept. A sensor's *resolution* is the smallest change it can detect in the quantity that it is measuring. Of course, resolution might also behave nonlinearly.

DIGITIZATION

To connect a sensor to a digital computer, the output of the sensor signal needs to be digitized. The electric output by a sensor, and possibly amplified and/or integrated with other signals, is usually a continuous electrical signal, with the voltage directly proportional to the sound pressure. Digitizing is to convert signal into a discrete set of its samples, as in Figure 4.2. Instead of representing the signal by an electrical current proportional to its sound pressure, the signal is represented by on-off patterns representing sample values of the analog signal at certain fixed points. The on-off patterns are much less susceptible to distortions than analog signals. Copying in particular is usually lossless. Conceptually, digitization happens in both the time and frequency dimension, illustrated in Figure 4.2. In a *sampling* step, the analog signal is captured at regular time intervals (the *sampling rate*), obtaining the signal's value at each interval. Each reading is called a *sample*. In *quantization*, samples are rounded to a fixed set of numbers (such as integers).

By generating the signal represented by each sample, we could transform a series of quantized samples back into an analog output that approximates the original analog representation. The sampling rate and the number of bits used to represent the sample values determine how close the reconstruction would be to the analog signal.

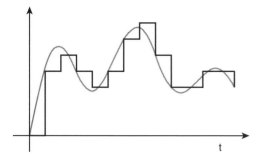

Figure 4.2. Digital representation of an analog signal. Both amplitude and time axis are discretized.

The error the quantization introduces is the *quantization noise*. It affects how accurately the amplitude can be represented. If the samples have very few bits, the signal will only be represented coarsely, which will both affect the signal variance and introduce reconstruction artifacts. Typical for audio and video, eight, sixteen, twenty-four, and thirty-two bits per sample are used.

The error the sampling rate introduces is the *discretization error*. This error determines the maximum frequency that can be represented in the signal. This upper frequency limit is determined by the *Nyquist frequency*,[1] which is half the sampling frequency fs of a discrete signal processing system. In other words, if a function $x(t)$ contains no frequencies higher than B hertz, $x(t)$ is completely determined by giving its ordinates at a series of points spaced $1/(2B)$ seconds apart.

To illustrate the necessity of $fs > 2B$, consider the sinusoid:

$$x(t) = \cos(2\pi Bt + \theta) \equiv \cos(2\pi Bt)\cos(\theta) - \sin(2\pi Bt)\sin(\theta)$$

With $fs = 2B$ or equivalently $T = 1/(2B)$, the samples are given by

$$x(nT) = \cos(\pi n)\cos(\theta) - \underbrace{\sin(\pi n)}_{0}\sin(\theta) = \cos(\pi n)\cos(\theta)$$

These samples cannot be distinguished from the samples of

$$y(t) = \cos(2\pi Bt)\cos(\theta)$$

But, for any θ such that $\sin(\theta) \neq 0$, $x(t)$ and $y(t)$ have different amplitudes and a different phase, as Figure 4.3 illustrates.

---

[1]   Named after Swedish-American engineer Harry Nyquist, or the Nyquist-Shannon sampling theorem.

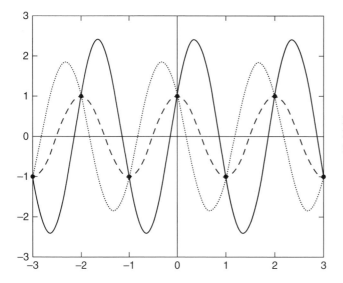

Figure 4.3. Three possible analog signals for the same sampling points.

RECOMMENDED READING

This short chapter on sensors presents only an overview of the most important issues when working with sensoric data other than acoustic and visual. Serious work with sensoric signals, however, can easily fill a book for each particular sensor. The further reading section therefore contains a sample of research articles relevant to the field. Riul and colleagues and Persaud and Dodd present an artificial taste sensor and work on an artificial nose, respectively. The articles from Allen and Nyquist are original articles of high impact to the field that are worth looking at. GPS systems are further described in Misra and Enge. Finally, a more general introduction to the field is provided by Wilson and Fraden. The book by Carryer, Ohline, and Kenny is not really a sensor book, but might be interesting to readers building their own sensor-based devices.

Further Reading

J. F. Allen. "Maintaining Knowledge about Temporal Intervals." *Comm. of the ACM* 26 (11): 832–43 (November 1983).

J. Edward Carryer, Matthew Ohline, and Thomas Kenny. *Introduction to Mechatronic Design.* Prentice Hall, 1st edition. 2010.

Jacob Fraden: *Handbook of Modern Sensors: Physics, Designs, and Applications.* Springer, 4th edition. 2010.

Pratap Misra and Per Enge. *Global Positioning System: Signals, Measurements, and Performance.* 2nd edition. Ganga-Jamuna Press. 2006.

Krishna Persaud and George Dodd. "Analysis of Discrimination Mechanisms in the Mammalian Olfactory System Using a Model Nose." *Nature* 299: 352–55 (September 23, 1982).

A. Riul, Jr., R. R. Malmegrim, F. J. Fonseca, and L. H. C. Mattos. "An Artificial Taste Sensor Based on Conducting Polymers." *Biosensors and Bioelectronics* 18 (11): 1365–9 (October 2003).

Jon S. Wilson: *Sensor Technology Handbook*. Newnes. 2004

EXERCISES

1. Explain how an external observer would perceive sensor hysteresis.
2. Traditional wisdom gives humans five senses: vision, hearing, touch, smell, and taste. Explain why this number is wrong and discuss why it is not easy to define what a sense is.
3. *Habituation* describes an effect in which repeated exposure to a stimulus leads to lower response. Provide examples of human sensors that show habituation.
4. Discuss and experiment with ideas to reconstruct frequencies beyond the Nyquist limit. What are the trade-offs?
5. Explain how the Nyquist limit sometimes becomes visible in the image and video domain. What are the typical artifacts?
6. Explain why haptic sensors in virtual reality require physical robustness beyond what is often technically achievable.

5 | Sound

As discussed in the previous chapter, hearing and vision are the two most important sensor inputs that humans have. Many parallels exist between visual signal processing and acoustic signal processing, but sound has unique properties – often complementary to those of visual signals. In fact, this is why nature gave animals both visual and acoustic sensors: to gather complementary and correlated information about the happenings in an environment. Many species use sound to detect danger, navigate, locate prey, and communicate. Virtually all physical phenomena – fire, rain, wind, surf, earthquake, and so on – produce unique sounds. Species of all kinds living on land, in the air, or in the sea have developed organs to produce specific sounds. In humans, these have evolved to produce singing and speech.

In this chapter, we introduce the basic properties of sound, sound production, and sound perception. More details of audio and audio processing are covered later in this book.

THE PHYSICS OF SOUNDS

The *American Heritage Dictionary of the English Language*, fourth edition, defines *sound* as "a traveling wave which is an oscillation of pressure transmitted through a solid, liquid, or gas, composed of frequencies within the range of hearing and of a level sufficiently strong to be heard, or the sensation stimulated in organs of hearing by such vibrations." This compressed formulation is a perfect start for discussing the properties of sound. Sound is generated by mechanical oscillation, which makes it very similar to haptic phenomena, which are often pressure based as well. Unlike them or light, however, sound must travel through a medium. In a vacuum, there is no sound, so, for example, one can't hear exploding spaceships. The traveling speed of sound varies according to the medium in which it is traveling. In dry air at 20°C, the speed of sound is Mach 1 or 343 meters per second. In fresh water at the same temperature, the speed of sound is much faster at approximately 1,482 meters per second.

Because most sounds are vibrations, their waves are usually sinusoidal in nature, that is, composed of sine waves. For a sound to be heard, the oscillation's frequency and amplitude must fall within a certain range. Human hearing is limited to frequencies between about 12 and 22,000 Hz (22 kHz). The upper limit generally decreases as humans age.

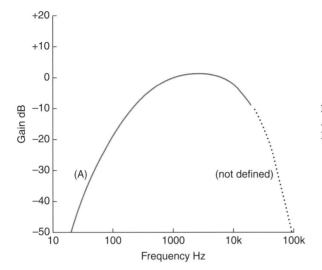

Figure 5.1. Sound pressure A-weighting scheme according to IEC 61672:2003.

Because sound is a pressure wave, one can measure the wave's amplitude by measuring the sound pressure. *Sound pressure* is defined as the difference between the average local pressure of the medium outside of the sound wave that is traveling through it (at a given point and a given time) and its pressure within the sound wave. The square of this difference is usually averaged over time, and then the square root of the average is taken to obtain a root mean square (RMS) value.

The sound pressure perceived by the human ear is nonlinear (see also Chapter 12, where this property is exploited for compression), and the range of amplitudes is rather wide; therefore, sound pressure is often measured on a logarithmic scale using decibels. The sound pressure level (SPL), or L_p, is defined as in Equation 5.1:

$$L_p = 10 \log_{10}\left(\frac{p^2}{p_{ref^2}}\right) = 20 \log_{10}\left(\frac{p}{p_{ref}}\right) \text{ dB} \qquad (5.1)$$

where p is the RMS sound pressure and p_{ref} is a reference sound pressure. A typical reference sound pressure for silence is 20 µPa (micro-pascal) in air and 1 µPa in water. Most sound-recording equipment is calibrated to omit 0-amplitude at these levels.

The human ear, however, does not react equally to all frequencies. That is, the same sound pressure at a different frequency will be perceived as a different volume level; therefore, sound-pressure measurements are often frequency weighted to more closely match perception. The A-weighting scheme, defined by the International Electrotechnical Commission (IEC) and illustrated in Figure 5.1, is the most common.

Sound-pressure levels weighted by this scheme are usually labeled as dBA or dB(A). The terms dB and dBA, like the percent symbol (%), define ratios rather than physical measurement units. A value of 10 dB can refer to completely different sound-pressure levels, depending on the reference.

OBSERVED PROPERTIES OF SOUND

In practice, sounds do not travel exclusively in a homogenous medium from a source to exhaustion. The environment is full of objects that sound can travel through or be reflected from. Sound-pressure waves can collide with each other. The resulting effects of these conditions play an important role in the design of multimedia systems because they make automatic processing and recognition of sounds much harder. The three most important sound effects are echo, reverberation, and interference.

An *echo* is a reflection of sound, perceived by the listener some time after the original. Typical examples are the echoes produced by the bottom of a water well or by mountain enclosures. Because most materials easily reflect sounds, echoes are present in every environment; however, the human ear cannot distinguish between the echo and the original sound if the delay is less than about 1/10 of a second. Thus the reflecting object must be more than 16.2 meters from a sound source traveling at Mach 1 for a person at the source to hear an echo. Physics tells us, however, that traveling requires energy. Of course this is also true for sound waves (otherwise we would be swamped with all sounds and vibrations happening in the universe); therefore, for a sound wave to travel that far back and forth it must have sufficient energy. Normal conversation, for example, usually occurs below this energy threshold and no echo is perceived. A machine-based system, however, trying to recognize sound might still have an issue with sounds being recorded from different rooms.

A *reverberation* is created when a sound is produced in an enclosed space, causing numerous echoes to build up and then slowly decay as the environment absorbs the sound. This is most noticeable to the human ear when the sound source stops but the reflections continue, decreasing in amplitude, until they are no longer audible. Reverberation receives special consideration in the architectural design of large chambers, which need specific reverberation times to achieve optimum performance for their intended activity. Unless a room is specially designed to not cause reverberation, it is always present. Reverberation is also present during the production of speech in the vocal tract. Reverberation is characterized by the *reverberation time*, that is, the length of the sound decay. Multimedia content analysis techniques often suffer from not accounting for reverberation, even when it is inaudible.

Interference is the superposition of two or more waves that results in a new wave pattern. It usually refers to the interaction of waves that are correlated or coherent with each other, either because they have the same source or because they have the same or nearly the same frequency. Sound interference causes different effects, which are described in wave propagation equations in physics.

Multimedia-system designers should be aware of interference, which they can use constructively or destructively. Consider two waves that are in phase, with amplitudes A_1 and A_2. Their troughs and peaks line up, and the resultant wave will have amplitude $A = A_1 + A_2$. This is known as *constructive interference*. If the two waves are 180° out of phase, one wave's crests will coincide with the other wave's troughs, so they will tend to cancel each other out. The resultant amplitude is $A = |A_1 - A_2|$. If $A_1 = A_2$, the resultant amplitude will be zero. This is known as *destructive interference*. Audio engineers and signal processing experts often use destructive interference to eliminate unwanted sounds – for example, in noise-canceling earphones. Note this is not the same as masking effects, which is caused by the perceptual properties of the human brain (discussed in Chapter 13).

RECORDING AND REPRODUCTION OF SOUND

Humans have tried to accurately record sound for a long time. The first notable device that could record sound mechanically (but could not play it back) was the phonautograph, developed in 1857 by Parisian inventor Édouard-Léon Scott de Martinville. This machine produced *phonautograms*, the earliest known recordings of the human voice. Thomas A. Edison invented the mechanical phonograph cylinder in 1877. The recordings were initially stored on the outside surface of a strip of tinfoil wrapped around a rotating cylinder. To play back the recordings, a needle ran along the cylinder, applying less pressure than in the recording process to convert the mechanical engravings into sound waves that would then be mechanically amplified. Not surprisingly, modern sound recording still obeys the same principle. Nowadays, however, sound waves are converted into electrical waves by a microphone and recorded to a digital medium – that is, sound waves are converted into binary numbers before they are imprinted on the medium. The media themselves, such as CD-ROM or DAT, are a bit more sophisticated than Edison's cylinders. Currently, generic media, such as hard disks and flash memory, are replacing these specialized media. The next sections explain the governing principles of modern sound processing.

MICROPHONES

A *microphone* is an acoustic sensor that converts sound into an electrical signal. The general principle is that a membrane is exposed to sound pressure which then varies its electrical resistance according to the movement. Most current microphones use electromagnetic induction (dynamic microphone), by letting the membrane swing a magnetic field produced by a coil; capacitance change (condenser microphone), by letting the membrane be part of a capacitor that varies capacity with movement, where piezo crystals emit electricity when put under pressure (piezoelectric microphones). The different microphone types have different electrical properties. These and other characteristics of the microphone, some of which are described later in this chapter, ultimately determine the properties of the recorded sound space.

A microphone's most important characteristic is its *directionality*, which indicates the sensitivity to pressure waves arriving at different angles. Directionality is usually represented by a polar pattern visualizing the locations that produce the same signal level output in the microphone if a constant sound-pressure level is generated. Figure 5.2 shows idealized example patterns. The patterns are considered idealized because, in the real world, polar patterns are a function of frequency.

Headset and *lavalier microphones* are designed for hands-free operation. These are small microphones worn directly on the body. They are typically used attached to clothing.

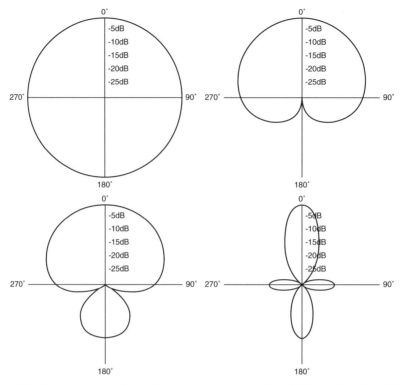

Figure 5.2. Four common polar patterns of microphones: (top left) omnidirectional, (top right) cardiod, (bottom left) supercardiod, and (bottom right) shotgun. The diagrams are created by recording a constant sound (frequency, intensity) from different directions and plotting the microphone response in each direction. Note that the resulting graphs are usually frequency dependent, therefore an averaged result is often shown.

These directed microphones allow mobile use for voice recording. They are in everyday use for videoconferencing, personal recording, theatrical performances, and dictation applications.

Very similar to a satellite dish, *parabolic microphones* use a reflector to collect and focus sound waves onto a microphone receiver, usually from many meters away. Their use is equivalent to the use of a high-zoom camera for vision, for activities such as animal-in-nature recording and eavesdropping.

Noise-canceling microphones have highly directional characteristics intended for noisy environments where direct attachment to the body is not desirable. For example, a singer might use this type of microphone on a loud concert stage. Often, noise-canceling microphones obtain two signals: one from the source, and one from the environment to be subtracted from the source signal by destructive interference.

Arrays of *omnidirectional microphones* are best for picking up as much sound from the environment as possible. These are typically used for auditory scene analysis, where objects can be located by analyzing the time delay of arrival between microphones (due to the speed of sound). In addition, combining the signals from a larger set of microphones can enhance the signal quality. This technique is often used in speech recognition, when head- or body-mounted microphones are not desirable.

The electric current output by a microphone, and possibly amplified and/or integrated (mixed) with other signals by further equipment, is a continuous electrical signal, with the voltage directly proportional to the sound pressure. In practice, sound recording has a linear area for certain sound-pressure levels and frequency ranges and nonlinear areas for sound pressures and/or captured frequencies that are too low or too high. If the sound-pressure level is too low, the signal will mostly just be zero; if the level is too high, the signal will reach an internal clipping point (which in the worst case is a short circuit) and will be severely distorted. Even if it does not reach the clipping point, the nonlinear behavior of sound-processing devices will lead to distortion when the captured signal is outside the nonlinear scope. In this case, the signal is referred to as *overdriven*. When the signal falls outside the recording device's linear frequency range, harmonic distortion is introduced. For example, a sine curve might be converted into a much less regularly shaped signal.

A microphone's output is usually amplified using an analog amplifier before it is digitized. Some microphones already directly output a digital signal, as standardized by the so-called AES 42 standard.

Even if standardized, all sound-processing devices have slightly different linear ranges. Sound cables, especially when very long, can also inhibit certain frequencies and, because they often work as "involuntary antennas," might introduce electric distortion from the outside, the most current type being a "buzz" from the 50 Hz/60 Hz electrical systems. Recording media, such as old vinyl records or audio cassettes, also introduce their own nonlinearities, and the effects stack up with each copy made; therefore, in the past two decades, sound processing has shifted from analog to digital. At the time of this writing, many microphones, mixers, and preamplifiers are still analog, but storage and processing are digital. With standards such as AES 42 growing increasingly popular, digitization will soon come much earlier in the processing chain.

Because of the Nyquist limit (see Chapter 4) and because the maximum frequency perceptible to the human auditory system is about 22 kHz, compact discs sample at 44 kHz. Human speech, which usually peaks between 6 and 8 kHz, is considered completely represented by a 16-kHz sampling frequency. Professional audio-recording equipment frequently uses sampling frequencies of about 44 kHz, such as 48 kHz and 96 kHz. If the analog equipment supports it, these devices can capture frequencies that are imperceptible to the human ear while allowing for better reproduction of overtones. Further processing, such as digital filtering and machine learning, might use the higher frequencies too, so saving them is useful even if the human ear cannot perceive them.

REPRODUCTION OF SOUND

Up to this point, we have assumed the existence of a sound signal. This assumption is generally a safe one because sound-pressure levels can be measured virtually anywhere on earth; however, reproducing sound from storage requires special devices. The most common sound-reproduction device is the loudspeaker.

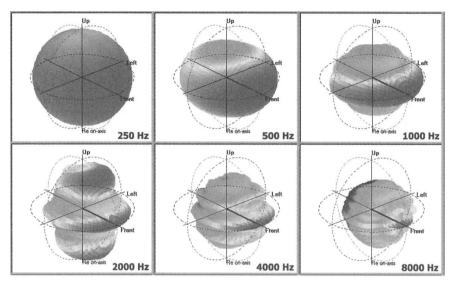

Figure 5.3. Polar patterns of a typical home speaker system consisting of four drivers at different frequencies. (Source: Wikimedia Commons). (See Plate I for color version.)

A loudspeaker (or speaker) is the exact reverse of a microphone. A speaker is an electroacoustic transducer that converts an electrical signal into sound. The speaker pulses or vibrates according to the variations of an electrical signal and causes sound waves to propagate through a medium such as air or water. Like microphones, speakers have directionality – that is, their frequency (re)production properties vary in space. Figure 5.3 shows the directionality of a typical home audio system speaker.

Speakers are designed with different directionalities for different applications (for example, car speakers have a different polar pattern than do supermarket speakers used for making announcements). Other factors that determine a speaker's properties are

- the rated power, which determines the maximum input a speaker can take before it is destroyed;
- the maximum sound-pressure level (SPL), which defines how much sound pressure the speaker can emit;
- the impedance, which determines the electrical compatibility with different amplifiers;
- the crossover frequencies, which define the nominal frequency boundaries of the signal division by the drivers; and
- the frequency range, which determines the speaker system's linear frequency response range.

The enclosure type determines some of the loudspeaker's perceptual properties. Another important factor for sound-reproduction quality is the relationship between the number of channels used (for example, two, four, or six), how they have been encoded (for example, stereo or surround), and how the speakers are placed in the room when reproducing sound.

Speakers and microphones are the most variable elements in terms of perceived sound quality. Except for lossy compression, they are responsible for most of the distortion and audible differences in sound systems. Our practical advice is to use high-quality headphones when experimenting with sound algorithms.

PRODUCTION OF SOUND

Sound-creation tools are very sophisticated and create signals with unique and interesting properties on the signal level. Multimedia computing widely exploits these properties on many levels when compressing, editing, and analyzing sounds. In this short chapter, we summarize the most salient properties of signals coming out of music and speech production. Whereas entire books have been written on single musical instruments, this chapter conveys only a top-down view relevant to processing and understanding multimedia computing.

Speech

The production of random sound is relatively easy, but modulating sound in a way suitable for communication requires sophisticated apparatuses. Although humans are not the only species to produce sophisticated sounds, they seem to have developed the most sophisticated machinery for expressive communication.

Speech has become the most common communication medium among humans. The frequency range of normal human speech is between 80 Hz and 5 kHz. The pitch of the human voice is between 120 and 160 Hz for adult males and between 220 and 330 Hz for women and children. Vowels can reach frequencies up to about 5 kHz. Sibilants emit the highest frequencies, which can easily reach the nonaudible spectrum (above 20 kHz). The frequency dynamics of speech are relatively high compared with those of many other sound sources, such as some musical instruments. In general, the volume of the human voice is limited to the sound energy the human body can produce. At 60 cm from the mouth, the human voice can typically reach a sound volume of about 60 dBA. A stronger voice can raise the volume by about 6 dB. Yelling measures about 76 dBA for males and 68 dBA for females.

The articulatory phonetics field, a branch of linguistics, investigates how the tongue, lips, jaw, and other speech organs produce sounds. As already explained, sound consists of pressure waves traveling through a medium. In the case of human speech, that medium is air; therefore, human speech is directly connected to the body's respiratory system. Almost all speech organs have additional functions. In addition, of course, different speech organs have more than one function in speech production, and, to make matters even more complex, different combinations of organs can produce the same sounds. Figure 5.4 shows a schematic of the human speech production apparatus.

Speech sounds are usually classified as

- stop consonants (with blocked airflow, such as the English pronunciations of "p," "t," or "k"),

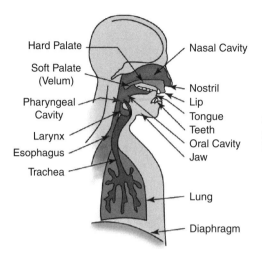

Figure 5.4. A schematic of the human speech production apparatus.(Source: National Cancer Institute)

- fricative consonants (with partially blocked and therefore strongly turbulent airflow, such as the English "f" or "v"),
- approximants (with only slight turbulence, such as the English "w" and "r"), and
- vowels (with full, unimpeded airflow, such as the English "a," "e," "i," and "o").

Other classes exist, and variation appears among languages; in Mandarin, for example, tonality determines meaning. Vowels are usually classified into *monophtongs*, having a single vowel quality, and *diphtongs*, which manifest a clear change in quality from start to end as in the words "bite," "bate," or "boat."

Consonants and vowels are the building blocks of speech. Linguists refer to these building blocks as *phonemes*. American English has forty-one phonemes, although the number varies according to the speaker's dialect and the classification system the linguist uses. A phoneme's concrete pronunciation depends on the previous and the following uttered speech sounds. It also depends on the type of speech (for example, whispering versus screaming) and the speaker's emotional state, as well as the anatomy of the throat, the age of the speaker, the native language and dialect, and social and environmental surroundings. Diseases of the lungs or the vocal cords and articulatory problems, such as stuttering, lisping, and cleft palate, affect the sound and clarity of speech. In other words, the actual frequency pattern of a specific uttered consonant or vowel has a large variance.

Environmental effects and the brain's processing of input from other modalities, such as sight or touch, can greatly affect speech. This *Lombard effect* describes an involuntary tendency to increase volume, change pitch, or adjust duration and sound of syllables in response to external noise. This compensation effect increases the auditory signal-to-noise ratio of the speaker's spoken words. This is one reason why automatic speech recognition algorithms trained in a quiet environment are difficult to transform to noisy environments. For example, an algorithm trained in a developer's cubicle will rarely work in a car.

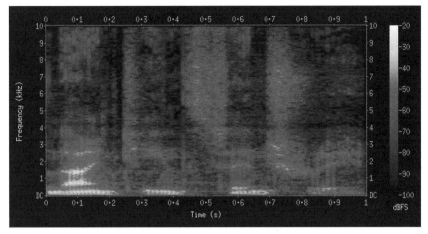

Figure 5.5. A spectrogram of a male voice saying: "nineteenth century." The yellow bands of energy are the formants. (Source: Wikimedia Commons). (See Plate II for color version.)

The *spectrogram* (see Figure 5.5) is a standard tool for visualizing and further analyzing sound patterns. A *spectrogram* is an image that shows how a signal's spectral density varies with time – that is, it shows the distribution of the energies in different frequency bands in time.

Each phoneme is distinguished by its own unique pattern in the spectrogram. For voiced phonemes, the signature involves large concentrations of energy, the *formants*. Reading a speech spectrogram mainly involves recognizing patterns that are independent of particular frequencies and speakers and identifying the various phonemes with a high degree of reliability. Unvoiced speech does not reflect in the spectrogram as formants. Still, plosives are usually recognized as strong bursts of energy across all frequency bands occurring after a short silence. Aspirates and fricatives are recognized as "large clouds" of smooth energy.

Properties of Human-Created Sounds

From a technical perspective, normal, conversational speech differs from general acoustics in the following ways.

Limited bandwidth: the spectrum and clearness (harmonicity) of the human voice varies with age, gender, and with the language spoken. While the audible spectrum of sounds is between 16 Hz and 22 kHz, speech as generated by humans usually does not go below 80 Hz and does not exceed 5 kHz. Differences from this general rule might exist when examining individuals. However, it is generally assumed that the human ear disregards speech sounds below 80 Hz in adult males and below 100 Hz in women and children. The pitch of the human voice is between 120 and 160 Hz for adult males and between 220 and 330 Hz for women and children. Vowels are most important for the intelligibility of speech; they can reach frequencies up to 5 kHz. The highest frequencies are emitted by sibilants, such as "s" or "f." The frequencies can easily reach into the nonaudible spectrum (above 20 kHz).

Consequently, to capture the whole frequency range of language, a 16-kHz sampling rate is currently the gold standard, which according to the Nyquist theorem, guarantees the reproducibility of 8 kHz. Telephone systems usually use 8 kHz, which allows the reproduction of a signal up to 4 kHz. This still enables the capture of most of the vowels, but consonants and sibilants are only understandable in context. This is why spelling on the phone usually has to be performed in whole words: "Alpha," "Beta," "Charlie," rather than "a," "b," "c."

Limited volume: the dynamic of speech is relatively high compared to that of many other sound sources, such as some musical instruments; however, in general, the volume of the human voice is limited to the sound energy the human body can produce. Motorbikes or gunshots can produce a much higher energy level, for example. At a 60-cm distance from the mouth, the typical sound volume of the human voice is about 60 dBA. A stronger voice can raise the volume by about 6 dB. The sound volume is reduced by about 4 dB every time the distance to the microphone is doubled or increased by 4 dB when the distance is halved. In general, 16 bits per sample are used to represent the dynamics of speech completely. However, so-called plosives like "p" or "t" can easily cause clipping, even in a well-defined capturing environment.

Limited variance in harmonicity: in contrast to generic audio, speech usually has certain characteristics governed by the underlying language. This is similar to instruments: a violin, for example, almost exclusively generates harmonic sounds, while a drum almost exclusively generates inharmonic sounds. Languages usually dictate a certain ratio between vowels and consonants, which translates into a constant ratio of voiced and unvoiced sounds. So, when the language is known, these characteristics can, for example, be exploited in a predictive coder (see Chapter 14). In general, the properties of the governing language will also have an impact on the expected dynamics and frequency range of the uttered speech.

It is important to remember at this point that the human vocal tract can create a much greater variety of sounds than would generally be classified as speech. Apart from noise imitations (have you ever tried to meow back to a cat?), the most important one is singing. If you ever try to sing into a cell phone, you will notice that the quality isn't really as good compared to regular speech. This is because the methods used in cell phones assume normal, conversational speech, as will be explained in Chapter 14. Also, the classification "normal" and "conversational" is important because human speech can differ significantly in other situations, such as in emotional states of anger, happiness, or enragement. Whispering is a still different form of speech humans produce that has very distinct properties, as is yelling. The properties of the human voice also change with health states. Alzheimer's disease, drug influence, or simply a stuffy nose will change different characteristics of speech. Also, as the anatomy of the vocal tract changes, so does the produced speech. Speech signals can therefore be used to not only identify speakers, but also to determine the age or the height of a speaker.

Music

Researchers have discovered archaeological evidence of musical instruments dating as far back as thirty-seven thousand years ago. The building and use of musical instruments vary with history and culture as do the sounds that these instruments produce and the musicians playing them. For multimedia computing, we are interested in determining instruments' general properties so we can leverage them for compressing audio, detecting instruments, and manipulating or artificially synthesizing recordings.

The *fundamental frequency*, abbreviated as f_0 or F_0 (speak: f-zero), is the inverse of a period length of a periodic signal. Pitch represents a sound's perceived fundamental frequency. Although the fundamental frequency can be precisely measured, it might differ from the perceived pitch because of overtones. An overtone is either a harmonic or partial (nonharmonic) resonance. In most musical instruments, the frequencies of these tones are close to the harmonics.

Timbre describes the quality of sound that distinguishes different types of sound production, such as different musical instruments. The frequency spectrum and time envelope are two physical characteristics of sound that mediate the perception of timbre.

Spectrum is the sum of the distinct frequencies emitted by an instrument playing a particular note, with the strongest frequency being the fundamental frequency. When an instrument plays a tuning note (for example A = 440 Hz), the emerging sound is a combination of frequency components, including 440 Hz, 880 Hz, 1,320 Hz, and 1,760 Hz (harmonics). The relative amplitudes of these different spectral components are responsible for each instrument's characteristic sound.

The model typically used to describe a timbre's time envelope divides sound development into four stages: *attack* (the time from when the sound is activated to its reaching full amplitude), *decay* (the time the sound needs to drop from maximum amplitude to sustain level), *sustain* (the volume level the sound is at until the note is released), and *release* (the time needed for the sound to fade when the note ends). This is also known as the *ADSR envelope*. Psychoacoustics uses the phrases *tone quality* and *tone color* as synonyms for *timbre*.

The three main categories of musical instruments in the Western world are string, wind, and percussion. A string instrument, such as a violin or a guitar, produces sound by vibrating strings. The strings' vibrations have the form of standing waves that produce a single fundamental frequency (pitch) and all harmonics of that fundamental frequency simultaneously. These frequencies depend on the string's tension, mass, and length. The harmonics make the sound timbre fuller and richer than the fundamental alone. The particular mix of harmonics present depends on the method of excitation of the string, such as bowing or strumming, as does the timbre. Resonances in the body of the instrument itself also significantly affect the sound timbre.

A wind instrument contains some type of resonator, usually a tube, in which a column of air is set into vibration by the musician blowing into the end of the resonator. The length of the tube determines the vibration's pitch. The length is usually varied artificially by manual modifications of the effective length of the vibrating column of air – for example, by covering or uncovering holes in the tube. The sound wave travels down the tube, reflects at one end, and comes back. It then reflects at the other end and starts over again. For a note in the flute's lowest register, for example, the round trip constitutes one cycle of the vibration. The longer the tube, the longer the time taken for the round trip, and so the lower the frequency.

A percussion instrument produces sound by being hit, shaken, rubbed, scraped, or by any other action that sets it into vibration directly. The acoustics of percussion instruments are the most complex because most percussion instruments vibrate in rather complex ways. In general, at low to medium amplitudes, their vibrations can be conveniently described by the terms introduced in this chapter. At large amplitude, however, they might show distinctly nonlinear or chaotic behavior. Percussion instruments have the highest variance in frequency and amplitude range and are therefore the most difficult to process.

Many musical pieces contain a mixture of instruments, including human voices. Once mixed, separating the individual instruments would require an adequate model of each instrument's behavior in its environment and with the recording equipment used. For this reason, music is not only recorded and digitized, but also saved in a note-like format, called MIDI, that defines a protocol to control electronic instruments. Electronic instruments have long tried to mimic traditional ones through a process called music synthesis, which we briefly describe next.

Synthesis of Sound

The artificial generation of speech and music is called *synthesis*. The first music synthesizers date back to 1876. Then, as today, the main goal was not necessarily to correctly imitate a physical musical instrument. Often, the goal was to create new sounds of artistic value. The difficulty and complexity of the exact simulation of a real instrument depends of course on that instrument's properties. It's easier to simulate a flute than a piano or an organ. It's not unusual for algorithms to be invented for a particular subtype of instrument. In general, though, modern music synthesis is performed by physical modeling of the instrument as well as incorporating original samples of the instrument – the *wavetables*.

Research has recently converged to apply these synthesis techniques to speech. Synthesized speech is often created by concatenating pieces of recorded speech from a database, so-called *concatenative synthesis*. Systems currently differ in the size of the stored speech units. A system that stores phones or tuples of phones (*diphones*) provides the largest range of possible synthesized output, but might lack clarity and naturalness in the produced voice. Trading off this output range for usage in specific applications, the storage of entire words or even sentences allows for higher-quality output but the lowest range of possible outputs. The database is usually combined with a model of the vocal tract (such as LPC, see Chapter 14) and other human voice characteristics to create a completely synthetic voice output. This concept of *adaptive concatenative sound synthesis* is the same as for both speech and music synthesis.

Obviously, sound is a large topic. It spans many fields of study that no one person can master. However, for the purposes of getting the fundamental information about sounds needed for multimedia computing, we have created an initial reading list. This book will cover more topics on sound in subsequent chapters. First, a very pragmatic programmer's view on sound, discussing many sound formats, is presented by Tim Kientzle. Everst and Pohlmann take a technician's view on sound while Blackstock does the same with physical phenomenon. Then, Ben Gold and colleagues present a signal processing view that includes programmatic processing and machine learning; their book will be referenced in future chapters as well. Bickford and Floyd discuss speech creation. We have also included several original research publication and standards in the literature, which are highly recommended to get an expert's view on many of the topics touched on in this chapter.

Further Reading

A. C. Bickford and R. Floyd. *Articulatory Phonetics: Tools for Analyzing the World's Languages*. SIL International, 4th edition, July 2006.

D. T. Blackstock. *Fundamentals of Physical Acoustics*. Wiley-Interscience, 1st edition, February 2000.

Ecma International. *Data Interchange on Read-only 120 mm Optical Data Disks (CD-ROM)*. ECMA-130. June 1996.

F. Alton Everst and Ken Pohlmann. *Master Handbook of Acoustics*. McGraw-Hill, 5th edition, June 2009.

B. Gold, N. Morgan, and D. Ellis. *Speech and Audio Signal Processing: Processing and Perception of Speech and Music*. John Wiley & Sons, 2nd edition, 2011.

T. Kientzle. *A Programmer's Guide to Sound*. Addison-Wesley, October 1997.

Research Papers

Junqua, J. C. "The Lombard reflex and its role on human listeners and automatic speech recognizers," *Journal of the Acoustic Society of America*, Jan. 93(1): 510–24, 1993.

Lombard, É. "Le signe de l'élévation de la voix," *Annales des Maladies de L'Oreille et du Larynx*, Vol. XXXVII, No. 2: 101–19, 1911.

Scheifele, P. M., Andrew, S., Cooper, R. A., Darre, M., Musiek, F. E., and Max, L. "St. Lawrence River beluga indication of a Lombard vocal response in the St. Lawrence River beluga," *Journal of the Acoustic Society of America*, 117(3 Pt 1): 1486–92, 2005.

Schötz, S. and Müller, C. A Study of Acoustic Correlates of Speaker Age, Pages 1–9 in *Speaker Classification II: Selected Projects*. Springer-Verlag Berlin, Heidelberg, 2007.

Slabbekoorn, H. and Peet, M. "Birds sing at a higher pitch in urban noise," *Nature*, 424(6946): 267, 2003.

Web Links

Comp.Speech FAQ: http://www.speech.cs.cmu.edu/comp.speech/.

MIDI specifications: http://www.midi.org/.

Neck anatomy: http://training.seer.cancer.gov/head-neck/anatomy/overview.html.

EXERCISES

1. How many dBs are 50%, 1%, 0.01%, and 200%? How many dBs can be stored in 16 bits, 24 bits, and 32 bits?
2. List the factors that would influence echo and reverberation in a lecture hall.

3. You are a researcher on a project that requires you to make frequent sound recordings. Unfortunately, your officemate needs to have a very noisy server farm standing beside him. Given no social rules or limitations, what would be the best thing to do to isolate the noise?

4. Discuss what would be the best directionality for a microphone that is used for field studies where you interview people in noisy environments.

5. Explain the artifacts you would expect from a microphone/loudspeaker that is forced to record/play sound both (a) outside its frequency range and (b) outside its amplitude range.

6. Assume you want to record a classroom seminar with many participants. What environmental noise would you expect?

7. When a microphone receives a signal, it is amplified and passed out of a loudspeaker. The sound from the loudspeaker might be received by the microphone again, amplified further, and then passed out through the loudspeaker again. This effect is known as the *Larsen effect* or, more colloquially, as the *feedback loop*. Describe what happens and what the signal looks like.

8. What differences would you expect to see between male and female speakers in a spectrogram? What would you expect to see between younger and older speakers?

9. What is the typical spectrogram of a flute, a violin, or a drum?

10. Implement an ADSR envelop filter and play around with it. Apply it to different sounds and waveforms, including noise.

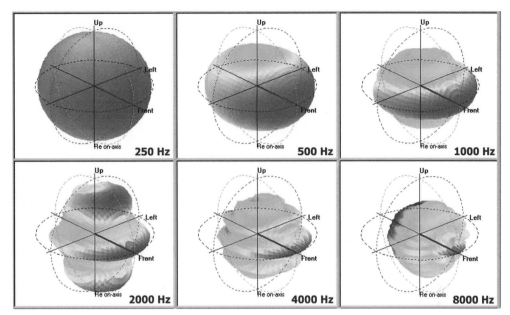

Plate I. Polar patterns of a typical home speaker system consisting of four drivers at different frequencies. (Source: Wikimedia Commons)

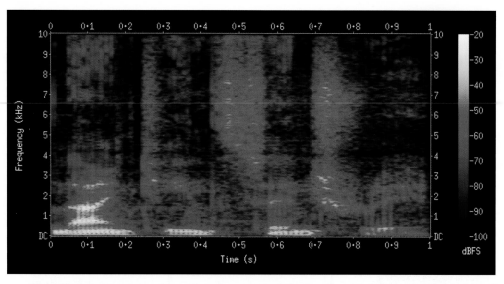

Plate II. A spectrogram of a male voice saying: "nineteenth century." The yellow bands of energy are the formants. (Source: Wikimedia Commons)

Plate III. Anaglyph 3D photograph viewable with red/green glasses. If you are viewing this photo on a computer screen and the 3D effect does not work, adjust your display settings to match the filters in your glasses.

Plate IV. An image and its Y, U, and V decompositions.

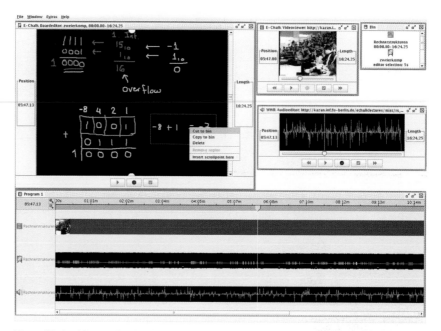

Plate V. A video authoring/editing environment uses a timeline for showing how different components can be organized.

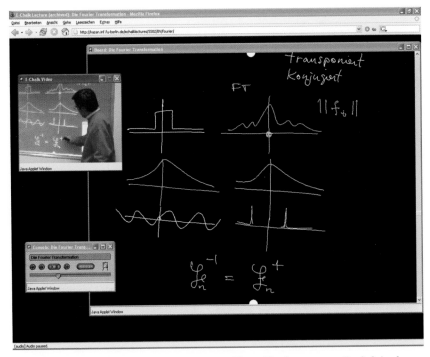

Plate VI. An example of a split attention problem. The lecturer on the left is shown as a video, and the dynamic board content he creates is shown on the right. The additional video window is used to convey gestures and finger pointing. However, presenting the lecturer in a second window causes cognitive overhead usually referred to as split attention because the viewer switches between the content on the board and the lecturer on the left.

Plate VII. Sample JPEG image with increasing amount of quantization (increasing in order top-left, top-right, bottom-left, bottom-right).

Plate VIII. A screenshot showing the selected image, the weights for different features, and results corresponding to this query.

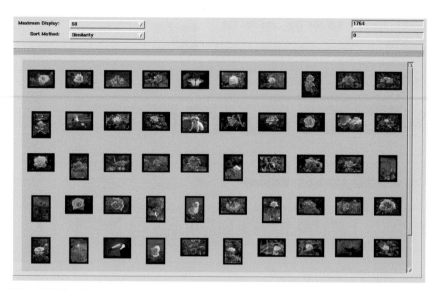

Plate IX. For the query related to a rose, in the top left corner as the first result, the top 50 results are shown here.

6 Light

Light is one of the most basic phenomena in the universe. The first words in the Bible are, "Let there be light!" A large part of the human brain is dedicated to translating the light reflected off of objects and onto our eyes to form an image of our surroundings. As discussed in Chapter 2, many human innovations have evolved around capturing and storing that image, mostly because of its use for communication purposes: first were the Stone Age cave painters; then followed the painters and sculptors of the Middle Ages and the Renaissance; then came photography, film, and digital storage of movies and photographs. Most recently, a computer science discipline evolved around computer-based interpretation of images, called *computer vision*. Recent years have brought rapid progress in the use of photography and movies through the popularity of digital cameras in cell phones. Many people now carry a device for capturing and sharing visual information and use it on a daily basis.

In this chapter, we introduce the basic properties of light and discuss how it is stored and reproduced. We examine basic image processing and introductory computer vision techniques in later chapters.

WHAT IS LIGHT?

Unlike sound, which is clearly defined as a wave with a certain frequency traveling through matter (see Chapter 5), light has both wave and particle properties. It is beyond the scope of this book to discuss the nature of light in depth. We therefore define *light* as the portion of electromagnetic radiation that is visible to the human eye.

Visible light has a wavelength of about 400 to 780 nanometers, which corresponds to a frequency of 405 to 790 Terahertz (THz). The adjacent frequencies of infrared on the lower end and ultraviolet on the higher end are still called light, even though they are not visible to the human eye. Note that infrared light is usually captured by digital cameras unless filtered out. The traveling speed of light in a vacuum is one of the fundamental constants of nature, as it is the fastest speed observable at 299,792,458 meters per second. In addition to frequency or wavelength and speed, light's primary measurable properties are propagation direction, phase, polarization, and intensity.

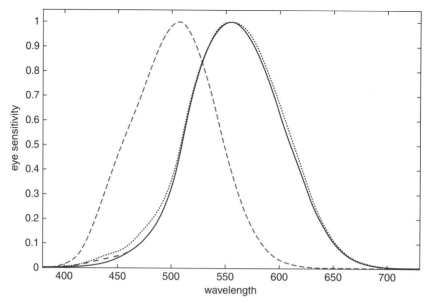

Figure 6.1. This graph shows different luminosity functions describing the sensitivity of the human eye to light of different wavelengths. Several luminosity functions are currently in use (see references) as measuring luminosity is still a matter of research. The dotted line is the most currently accepted luminosity function from 2005.

The *phase* is the fraction of a wave cycle that has elapsed relative to an arbitrary point. One can use filters to manipulate the phase to change the appearance of light.

Polarization describes the light waves' orientation. Sound waves in a gas or liquid do not have polarization because vibration and propagation move in the same direction. If the orientation of the electric fields the light emitters produce are not correlated, the light is said to be *unpolarized*. However, if there is at least partial correlation between the emitters, the light is *partially polarized*. You can then describe the light in terms of the degree of polarization. One can build filters that only allow light of a certain degree and angle of polarization, an effect that is often used in 3D vision. A pair of 3D glasses will often have filters for the left and the right eye that allow different polarized light to go through to each eye so the two eyes see images with slightly different disparity. More on this will be discussed later.

Light intensity is measured in three units: candela, lumen, and lux. The *candela* (cd) measures *luminous intensity*, which is defined as power emitted by a light source in a particular direction, weighted by the luminosity function – a standardized model of the sensitivity of the human eye to different wavelengths. Figure 6.1 illustrates this function. The unit is derived from the light emitted by a common candle (hence its name). A typical candle emits light with a luminous intensity of roughly one candela. The physical definition is as follows: the candela is the luminous intensity, in a given direction, of a source that emits monochromatic radiation of frequency 540×10^{12} hertz and has a radiant intensity in that direction of $\frac{1}{683}$ watt per steradian. A 100-watt incandescent light bulb emits about 120 cd.

The *lumen* (lm) is the unit of luminous flux, that is, the total light an object emits. Because a full sphere has a solid angle of 4·π steradians, a light source that uniformly radiates one candela in all directions has a total luminous flux of 1 cd·4π sr = 4π ≈ 12.57 lumens. The light output of video projectors is typically measured in lumens. The American National Standards Institute (ANSI) standardized a procedure for measuring the light output of video projectors, which is why many projectors are currently sold as having a certain amount of "ANSI lumens" even though ANSI did not redefine lumen as a physical unit.

Lux (lx) is the physical unit of illuminance and luminous emittance measuring luminous power per area. The unit is equivalent to watts per m² (power per area) but with the power at each wavelength weighted by the luminosity function (see Figure 6.1). So 1 lx = 1 lm/m². A full moon overhead at tropical latitudes emits about 1 lx of light. Office lighting usually ranges from 320 to 500 lx, and TV studio lighting is at 1,000 lx. Inside the visible frequency range, humans can see as little as one photon in the dark, yet a person's eyes can be open in a desert at noon with the sun exerting up to 130,000 lx. This is an incredible adjustment that current human-made light sensors rarely can match!

OBSERVED PROPERTIES OF LIGHT

Like sound, light exhibits properties while traveling through space. In addition, light rarely travels exclusively in a homogenous medium from a source to exhaustion. For example, lenses are typically used in recording. Moreover, the environment is full of objects that can absorb, dampen, or reflect light. Especially outdoors, other light sources might appear and collide with the light waves in question. Again, the resulting effects of these conditions must be considered when designing multimedia systems. For practical purposes, however, environmental conditions have a lesser impact on sound waves than on light waves.

Reflection of light is simply the bouncing of light waves from an object back toward the light's source or other directions. Energy is often absorbed from the light (and converted into heat or other forms) when the light reflects off of an object, so the reflected light might have slightly different properties because it might have lost intensity, shifted in frequency, polarization, and so on. Solid objects, such as a concrete wall, usually absorb light – light waves cannot travel through these objects. On the other extreme, when light can travel through an object seemingly unchanged, the object is called *transparent*. Detecting transparent objects is probably one of the most challenging tasks in vision, including computer vision.

The most important effect observed when light passes through a transparent object is *refraction*. Refraction is the "bending" of light rays during the transition from one optically transparent material to another. The reason for the effect is that the light's wavelength changes with the frequency remaining constant. Therefore, if a light ray does not cross the boundary in an orthogonal angle, the change in wavelength results in a change in the

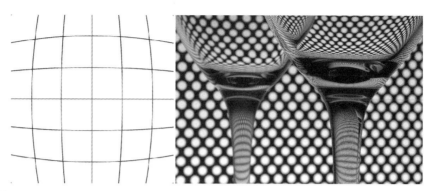

Figure 6.2. Left: Typical lens distortion pattern. Right: A picture from Wikimedia Commons showing the distortion created by wine glasses (picture by Atoma).

beam's direction. Refraction can be observed in everyday examples, such as when trying to grab a fish in an aquarium or observing a "bending" straw in a glass of water.

The study of light and its interaction with matter is called *optics*. Because this book focuses on multimedia computing, we will discuss light and optics only as much as is required to understand their role in multimedia communication.

A common phenomenon sometimes neglected but also sometimes reluctantly addressed by multimedia researchers is *lens distortion*. In a lens, a straight light beam hits a transparent object from varying angles, so the refraction also varies. The image that is projected through the lens is therefore distorted. Figure 6.2 shows some typical distortions.

Correcting lens distortion can be difficult. Distortion can sometimes be corrected through calibration – that is, by projecting a well-defined object onto the lens (such as a grid, as shown in Figure 6.2) and calculating a correction function between the actual image and the distorted image. Often, however, you will only have the projected image, making distortion hard to correct.

RECORDING LIGHT

Cameras store and reproduce light as images and video. The term "camera" comes from the Latin *camera obscura* ("dark chamber"), an early mechanism that could project light but could not store images (see Figure 6.3). The device consists of a box (which can be the size of a room) with a hole in one side. Light from an external scene passes through the hole and strikes a surface inside, where it is reproduced, upside down, but with both color and perspective preserved. In a modern camera, the image is projected onto a light-sensitive memory. At first this memory was light-sensitive chemical plates, later it became chemical film, and now it is photosensitive electronics that can record images in a digital format.

The image formation process consists of two parts:

- The geometry of image formation, which determines where in the image plane the projection of a point in the scene will be located.

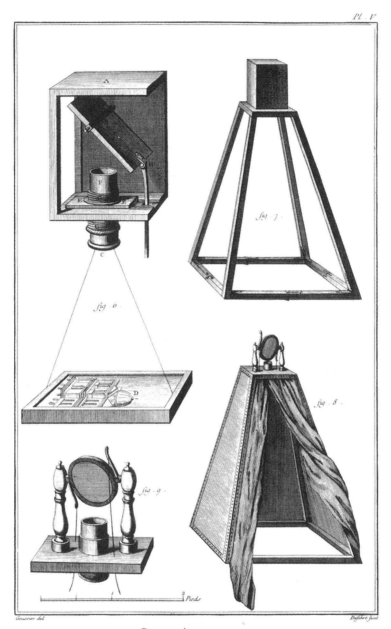

Figure 6.3. Historical drawings of a camera obscura often used for paintings.

- The physics of light, which determines the brightness of a point in the image plane as a function of scene illumination and surface properties.

The geometry of image formation uses the basic model for the projection of points in the scene onto the image plane as diagrammed in Figure 6.4. In this model, the imaging

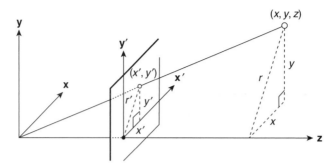

Figure 6.4. The point on the image plane that corresponds to a particular point in the scene is found by following the line that passes through the scene point and the center of projection of the coordinate system.

system's center of projection coincides with the origin of the three-dimensional coordinate system. The coordinate system for points in the scene is the three-dimensional space spanned by the unit vectors **x**, **y**, and **z** that form the axes.

A point in the scene has coordinates (x, y, z) and its projection in the camera image appears at location (x', y'). The x coordinate is the horizontal position of the point in space as seen from the camera, the y coordinate is the vertical position of the point in space as seen from the camera, and the z coordinate is the distance from the camera to the point in space along a line parallel to the z axis. The *line of sight* of a point in the scene is the line that passes through the point of interest and the center of projection. The line drawn in Figure 6.4 is a line of sight.

The image plane is parallel to the x and y axes of the coordinate system at a distance / from the center of projection, as shown in Figure 6.4. This figure helps us understand how a camera converts a three-dimensional world to a two-dimensional image by essentially a many-to-one mapping. This means that without knowledge about the domain and the context, an image cannot be unambiguously interpreted. This is the fundamental reason behind the complexity in visual processing.

Today, most photos are recorded electronically. Digital cameras follow the original camera obscura principle, but a modern camera consists of a visual sensor that converts light into an electrical signal. There is a maximum granularity, which in digital cameras is defined by the number of photoelectric sensors. Each sensor creates one *pic*ture *el*ement (also known as a *pixel*). The number of pixels is called *resolution*.

Typical photo cameras have a resolution of several megapixels (millions of pixels). Resolutions of the resulting image are usually specified as X x Y axis resolution – for example, 1,024 × 768 or 1,280 × 1,024. Although today's digital cameras would have the memory to store images by representing each pixel directly as a sensor value, the earliest digital cameras didn't. Therefore, images are still usually compressed by applying spectral compression (see Chapter 13). The so-called JPEG format, for example, uses this type of compression. Uncompressed images (or raw images) are rare but sometimes needed for content analysis (see Chapter 17) and for editing high-quality images.

Video cameras have recorded light electrically for a longer time. TV cameras evolved as analog devices, storing the electrical changes on the CCD sensors on magnetic tapes and transmitting them through the air using analog radio waves. Video cameras also record sound at the same time. For many years, cinematic cameras used chemical film (usually 35mm film) because TV cameras only delivered images with very small resolutions not suitable for the "big screen." Typical TV resolutions were PAL (Phase Alternating Line), SECAM (Sequential Color with Memory, with 720×576 analog picture elements), and NTSC (National Television System Committee, with 640×486 analog picture elements). These formats' color encodings differ, as we discuss later in this chapter.

The introduction of digital video cameras not only made the photographic and the videographic worlds converge, it also allowed videos to be recorded at much higher resolutions, especially because image compression methods could be modified to support moving pictures. Modern cameras store videos in a compressed format, such as MPEG (see Chapter 13). The resolution of digital photo and video cameras has increased constantly. As we write this book, photo cameras with up to thirty-two megapixels and video cameras with up to sixteen megapixels are on the market.

Although photographic and cinematographic recordings can only be performed as a projection onto a surface, the resulting images do not have to be flat (that is, 2D). Of course, actual reflection in space is 3D and humans can perceive the distances between objects in space three dimensionally. The desire to capture scenes with depth is relatively old; the first commercial 3D photo cameras date back to 1947. The stereo camera is the predominant technology for capturing 3D images. A stereo camera has two (or more) lenses and a separate photographic sensor (of film) for each lens. This allows the camera to simulate human two-eyed vision, which is the basis for depth perception. The distance between the lenses in a stereo camera (the *intra-axial distance*) is usually made the same as the distance between human eyes (the *intra-ocular distance*), which is about 6.4 centimeters. However, a greater inter-camera distance can produce pictures where the three dimensionality is perceived as more extreme. This technique works with both images and movies, as long as images are kept separate and only one eye is exposed to each image. Therefore, for watching a 3D movie, viewers usually wear polarizing or red/cyan filter glasses (the *anaglyph technique*). These glasses separate the two images by superimposing them through two filters, one red and one cyan, or two polarizing filters. Glasses with colored/polarizing filters in each eye separate the appropriate images by canceling the filter color/polarization out and rendering the complementary color/polarization black. Although other technologies exist to create 3D projection, including autostereoscopic methods that do not require glasses, these two techniques are currently predominant. Figure 6.5 shows an example of a 3D photography.

Figure 6.5. Anaglyph 3D photograph viewable with red/green glasses. If you are viewing this photo on a computer screen and the 3D effect does not work, adjust your display settings to match the filters in your glasses. (See Plate III for color version.)

Most important, these techniques aim at human perception and require the human brain to "decode" the stereoscopic image. Computing the depth encoded in a stereoscopic image is still an open research area. Therefore, different devices that try to estimate depth information in a way that it is directly available to a computer are currently under development.

REPRODUCING LIGHT

Two main methods exist for reproducing a specific light pattern:

Subtractive methods rely on intensity variations of the reflection of ambient light and do not work when no light is present. Paper, for example, reflects patterns differently once it has been modified by ink or toner.

Additive methods work with active light sources that are mixed together. The most common example is the display in a TV or monitor, as explained next.

As mentioned earlier, the first electronic storage and transmission of light was through TV equipment. As a result, the TV was the first technology for reproducing (moving) images electrically. Early TVs adopted CRT technology, which was invented by German Telefunken in 1934. A CRT is a vacuum tube with a source of electrons projected onto a fluorescent screen. The fluorescent material on the screen reflects light when hit by the electron beam. The beam is controlled by an electromagnetic field that accelerates and/or deflects the beam to control its impact on the fluorescent surface, thereby controlling

Figure 6.6. Two interlaced video frames showing a fast motion.

the amount of reflection and forming a grayscale image. Color TV, which was not widely available until the 1970s, uses a CRT with three phosphors, each emitting red, green, or blue light. Most perceivable colors can be created using different strengths of these three colors. Modern graphic cards and displays still use RGB, even though the eye's perception of light uses different base frequencies.

It is important to note that while analog TV content is still available in large amounts, digital video compression and content analysis algorithms often perform suboptimally with old analog video. Figure 6.6 shows an example of typical artifacts resulting from analog TV interlacing: the so-called *interline Twitter*. Modern digital video encoders usually include a feature for de-interlacing image frames. Because the lost information cannot be precisely restored, however, de-interlacing algorithms use heuristics to guess the content of the lost lines. A common method is to duplicate lines or to interpolate between two lines.

Modern TVs and computer monitors do not use CRT. Instead, they use technologies that allow higher resolution in update time and image granularity, save energy, and are less bulky than CRT displays, thereby allowing larger screen size, which also prompted demand for higher resolution, helping to popularize the HDTV standard. Full HDTV is currently at a resolution of 1,920 × 1,280 pixels and 120-Hz refresh rate.

The major challenge in reproducing 3D photos and video is creating *autostereoscopic* displays – that is, displays that do not require special viewing devices, such as glasses. Nintendo's portable game console 3DS is implementing an autostereoscopic display using the *parallax barrier* method. The parallax barrier is placed in front of the LCD. It consists of a layer of material with a series of precision-angle slits, guiding each eye to see different set of pixels based on each eye's angular direction of focus. However, because the viewer must be positioned in a well-defined spot to experience the 3D effect, the technology is used mostly for small displays, such as portable gaming systems.

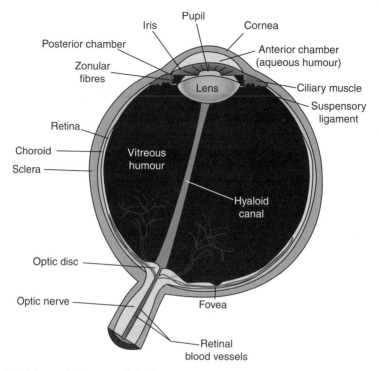

Figure 6.7. Schematic diagram of the human eye. The rods and cones are found on the retina.

PERCEPTION OF LIGHT

Multimedia computing cannot be understood without at least a basic comprehension of how human vision works. The more we learn about the mechanics of human vision, the more we can make computer systems and algorithms adapt to it and thereby increase their (perceived) performance.

Figure 6.7 shows a schematic image of a vertebrate eye. It is a quite complex system that collects light from the environment, regulates its intensity through a diaphragm (similar to a shutter in a photo camera), focuses on certain points through an adjustable assembly of lenses to form an image (similar to a zoom in a photo camera), converts this image into a set of electrical signals (similar to a digital camera), and finally transmits these signals to the so-called visual cortex of the brain. So, in many aspects, an eye is a complex camera obscura. We cannot explain all of the processes involved in human vision because it would fill several books and, most important, human vision is not completely understood. However, multimedia computing has exploited several important properties of human vision.

One of the most important properties of the human eye is that it blurs together images shown quickly enough so they are perceived as one, enabling video. This property is present in all animals; however, different eyes have different frequency thresholds. The threshold for a human eye is about 20–25 Hz to perceive objects as a movie rather than (flickering) still images. Most video technologies have frame rates of 25–30 images per second (as a note: compare this to the lowest frequency acoustic stimulation, perceived as tone rather than period beats).

Like most human sensory organs, eyes perceive light intensity logarithmically – that is, they obey the Weber-Fechner law.

To perceive colors, the retina contains two types of light-sensitive photoreceptors: rods and cones. The rods are responsible for monochrome perception, allowing the eyes to distinguish between black and white. Rods are very sensitive, especially in low-light conditions. This is why darker scenes become increasingly colorless. The cones are responsible for color vision. They require brighter light than the rods. Most humans have three types of cones, each of them maximally sensitive to different wavelengths of light. The color perceived is the combined effect of the three sensors. Overall there are more rods than cones, so color perception is less accurate than black-and-white contrast perception. This affects the variety of perceived colors in contrast to gray tones as well as the accuracy of spatial color distinction in contrast to black and white. In other words, reducing the spatial resolution of the color representation while maintaining the black-and-white resolution has little perceptible effect. As we will see later, this property of the eye has been used heavily in compression techniques. JPEG image compression, for example, uses the variance in color insensitivity in several ways, as discussed in Chapter 13.

Other properties of human vision that can be leveraged in multimedia computing are based not on the eye's anatomical properties, but on the brain's functional properties. These can be complex and are typically studied in optical illusions. Some, if not most, of these properties are learned. For example, if you draw a dark border on the lower right edge of a window, it will appear to be in front of the others because people have learned to interpret the dark edge as shadow. Evidence suggests that even binocular depth perception is learned (see references).

COLOR SPACES

As we discussed earlier, colors can be captured and reproduced by varying the intensities of fixed colors. Children learn this concept from watercolor painting in elementary school: you can use red, blue, and yellow in varying amounts to make all other colors. CRT displays used red, green, and blue; the human eye uses yet another set of filters based on pigmenting. Mathematically speaking, we can describe all colors using a linear combination of base colors. In other words, the base colors form a 3D color space. Color spaces are an important concept because different sensors and light reproducers can only work with a different set of fixed colors. Most printers use the CMYK (cyan, magenta, yellow, black) color space because it is most convenient for ink producers. The "K" stands for black, which could be created by mixing yellow, magenta, and cyan; however, this would be costly. So even though K is mathematically not needed, economic reasons prevail. Most important, color spaces are often used to analyze an image or video computationally. We present three important color spaces here and other color spaces in later chapters.

For computer scientists, the RGB color space is probably the canonical color space. Most displays, graphics cards, and raw image formats support this space. As a result, most

Figure 6.8. An image and its Y, U, and V decompositions. (See Plate IV for color version.)

programming tools, especially those for graphical user interfaces, work in this space by default. The RGB space is often augmented by a fourth component, often called *alpha*, that controls the transparency of a pixel. It is important to know that the RGB color space is furthest away from human perception because contrast is not modeled explicitly. So the perceptual importance of a color component and the similarity of two colors cannot be judged easily.

For image compression, the YUV color space (and technical variants) has therefore been predominant. The YUV model defines a color space based on one intensity (Y) and two color (UV) components. Both the PAL and SECAM standards use the YUV color model, therefore being backward compatible to previous black-and-white TV systems that only used the intensity information. A variant of YUV is used for JPEG compression because it makes it easier to scale color and black-and-white channels independently. Conversion between RGB and YUV (and back) can be performed by a simple linear transformation:

$$\begin{bmatrix} Y' \\ U \\ V \end{bmatrix} = \begin{bmatrix} 0.299 & 0.587 & 0.114 \\ -0.14713 & -0.28886 & 0.436 \\ 0.615 & -0.51499 & -0.10001 \end{bmatrix} \begin{bmatrix} R \\ G \\ B \end{bmatrix}$$

Representation

$$\begin{bmatrix} R \\ G \\ B \end{bmatrix} = \begin{bmatrix} 1 & 0 & 1.13983 \\ 1 & -0.39465 & -0.58060 \\ 1 & 2.03211 & 0 \end{bmatrix} \begin{bmatrix} Y' \\ U \\ V \end{bmatrix}$$

The Y component is denoted with a prime symbol Y′ to indicate gamma adjustment of the Y component. A close look at the formula reveals the weighting of the different components, which corresponds to experimental evidence for human color perception. Figure 6.8 shows the result of this decomposition for an example image.

As you probably suspect, a linear transformation from a color space that was invented for CRT displays cannot describe human color perception exactly enough to measure color differences. Unfortunately, although extremely important, the measurement of perceived color differences is extremely difficult because perception of color differences varies not only with lighting, but also with the colors surrounding the color difference.[1] Obviously, the

---

[1] Also, a significant number of optical illusions create "fake" colors – that is, colors that are not there but perceived to be.

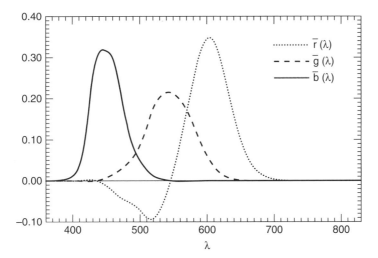

Figure 6.9. CIE XYZ space color matching function. The curves show the amount of primary color mix needed to match the same monochromatic color generated by light at wavelength lambda.

objective color difference would be zero but the perceived color difference is greater than zero. Nevertheless, one color space – CIELAB – has been created to model perceived color differences using an abundance of human-subject experiments. It has recently gained attention in the computer vision and image retrieval communities. CIELAB is designed to be perceptually uniform – ideally, the Euclidean distance between two colors reveals its perceptual difference.

The CIELAB space is based on the opponent colors theory of color vision. The theory assumes that two colors cannot be perceived as both green and red or blue and yellow at the same time. As a result, single values can be used to describe the red/green and the yellow/blue attributes. When a color is expressed in CIELAB, L defines lightness, A denotes the red/green value, and B the yellow/blue value. Different standard illumination conditions are defined using a reference white. The most commonly used reference white is the so-called D65 reference white. CIELAB's perceptual color metric is still not optimal, and the aforementioned assumption can lead to problems. But in practice, the Euclidean distance between two colors in this space better approximates a perceptually uniform measure for color differences than in any other color space, such as YUV or RGB. The color space uses an intermediate space, the CIE XYZ space. The XYZ space was designed to eliminate metamers – that is, different colors that are perceived as the same color. Figure 6.9 shows the color matching function used by the XYZ space.

The following formula converts RGB to CIE XYZ space:

$$
\begin{bmatrix} X \\ Y \\ Z \end{bmatrix} = \frac{1}{0.17697} \begin{bmatrix} 0.49 & 0.31 & 0.20 \\ 0.17697 & 0.81240 & 0.01063 \\ 0.00 & 0.01 & 0.99 \end{bmatrix} \begin{bmatrix} R \\ G \\ B \end{bmatrix}
$$

Conversion from CIEXYZ to CIELAB is performed by the following formula:

$$L^* = 116 f\left(Y/Y_n\right) - 16$$
$$a^* = 500\left[f\left(X/X_n\right) - f\left(Y/Y_n\right)\right]$$
$$b^* = 200\left[f\left(Y/Y_n\right) - f\left(Z/Z_n\right)\right]$$

where

$$f(t) = \begin{cases} t^{1/3} & \text{if } t > \left(\dfrac{6}{29}\right)^3 \\ \dfrac{1}{3}\left(\dfrac{29}{6}\right)^2 t + \dfrac{4}{29} & \text{otherwise} \end{cases}$$

This chapter only gives a quick introduction to light as relevant for multimedia computing. Further properties of light, human perception, and the devices that record and reproduce light will be discussed when important in connection to concrete algorithms.

LIGHT PRODUCTION

It is remarkable that vision is so important, yet there is as of yet no real benefit in studying the nature of light creation tools for multimedia computing. We believe that in future holographic light sources and other light synthesizing, objects may be used as the mainstream multimedia output devices. They were already envisioned in the original *Star Trek* series (the "holodeck"). Except for light bulbs and LEDs, at the moment, light is mainly reproduced rather then produced. About the only thing that we could say about light creation is that different light sources cover different spectra, with laser the most spectrally narrow and different light sources, such as planets or chemical reactions on earth, covering different color ranges. On a different level, light creation and shaping tools include the ball pen and paper, the chalkboard, and, of course, the more sophisticated computer-aided tools like vector graphics editors and 3D animation rendering. These will be discussed in Chapter 7.

RECOMMENDED READING

There is a sheer unlimited amount of literature about light and vision. For the purpose of this book, we suggest starting with the Web links as they present optical illusions and visual effects that show how complex vision really is and that we definitely do not yet understand the full extent of how it works. This is also supported by a quick look into the book by Wyzecki and Stiles. Guild's article offers a little more explanation. To get an idea about the technical intricacies of video and television, we recommend taking a peek at the actual standards outlined here. If you are not actually working with one of them, glimpsing over the standards to get an idea of the concepts involved is enough and reading them in detail is discouraged. We recommend the research articles outlined here as reading material, especially the ones dealing with 3D as they outline the basic ideas of several 3D technologies.

Further Reading

CIE. *Commission Internationale de l'Éclairage Proceedings, 1931.* Cambridge: Cambridge University Press. 1932.

J. Guild. "The Colorimetric Properties of the Spectrum." *Philosophical Transactions of the Royal Society of London*, A230, 149–87, 1931.

ITU-R BT.470-6, Conventional Television Systems.

ITU-R Recommendation BT.709, High-definition Television.

National Television System Committee. [Report and Reports of Panel No. 11, 11-A, 12–19, with some supplementary references cited in the reports, and the petition for adoption of transmission standards for color television before the Federal Communications Commission, n.p., 1953], 17 v. illus., diagrs., tables. 28 cm. LC Control No.:54021386, 1951–3.

W. S. Stiles and J. M. Burch. Interim report to the Commission Internationale de l'Éclairage Zurich, 1955, on the National Physical Laboratory's investigation of colour-matching. *Optica Acta*, 2: 168–81, 1955.

G. Wyzecki and W. S. Stiles. *Color Science: Concepts and Methods, Quantitative Data and Formulae.* Wiley-Interscience, 2nd edition, 1982.

Research Papers

Bernardini, F. and Holly E. Rushmeier. "The 3D model acquisition pipeline," *Comput. Graph. Forum*, 21 (2): 149–72, 2002.

Crane, R. J. *The Politics of International Standards: France and the Color TV War.* Ablex Publishing Corporation, 1979.

Curless, B. "From range scans to 3D models," ACM SIGGRAPH *Computer Graphics*, 33 (4): 38–41, November 2000.

Gonzalez, F. and R. Perez. "Neural mechanisms underlying stereoscopic vision," *Prog Neurobiol*, 55 (3): 191–224, 1998.

Qian, N. "Binocular disparity and the perception of depth," *Neuron*, 18: 359-68, 1997.

Santrac, N., G. Friedland, and R. Rojas. "High resolution segmentation with a time-of-flight 3D-camera using the example of a lecture scene." Technical Report B-06-09, Freie Universitaet Berlin, Institut fuer Informatik, Berlin, Germany. 2006.

Song Zhang, S. and H. Peisen. "High-resolution, real-time 3-D shape measurement" (PDF). *Optical Engineering*: 123601. http://www.math.harvard.edu/~songzhang/papers/Realtime_OE.pdf, 2006.

"A time-of-flight depth sensor – system description, issues and solutions," *Proceedings of IEEE Conference on Computer Vision and Pattern Recognition*. Washington, DC.

Zitnick, C. L. and T. Kanade. "A cooperative algorithm for stereo matching and occlusion detection," *IEEE Transactions on Pattern Analysis and Machine Intelligence*, 22 (7): 675-84, 2000.

Web Links

Atlas of Visual Phenomena: http://lite.bu.edu/vision/applets/lite/lite/lite.html.
Silencing: http://visionlab.harvard.edu/silencing/.

EXERCISES

1. List the factors that contribute to an object reflecting more light than another one.

2. When a powerful light source and a less powerful light source are placed adjacent to each other, the less powerful light source might appear to not even emit light (for example, a small LED in the midday sun). Explain.

3. Write a program that can correct lens deformations using a calibration process – that is, the photographed shape is known and a function is fitted to correct the photograph to the actual shape.

4. How much space is needed to store a raw image in NTSC and full HDTV format?

5. Take a pencil and hold it in front of your eyes. Close one eye, observe, open it again, then close the other eye and observe again. Repeat the experiment with the pencil at different distances in front of your eyes. What can you observe?

6. Describe a procedure to calibrate a 3D display with anaglyph technology and with parallax barrier technology.

7. How many bits are needed to store a pixel in CIELAB space?

8. Explain which part of visual perception is most often utilized by magicians doing magic tricks.

9. What is the equivalent of sound synthesis in the visual domain? What is the main issue when doing this?

7   Multimedia Documents

As we have seen in the previous chapters, a variety of sensors can measure and record data in various modalities. However, how does a stream of sensory data become *multimedia*? We have discussed the *multi* part before. In this chapter, we will take a first look at a very important concept that combines sensory data into a palatable and presentable format, making it a *medium*. We are talking about the concept of a document.

The concept of a document has been used over centuries as a device or mechanism to communicate information. Because the technology to store and distribute information has been evolving and changing, the nature and concept of a document has been evolving to take advantage of the new media technology. At one time, one considered a document in the form of physical embodiment, such as a book, that mostly contained text as the source of information. This popular notion of a book as a document has gone through changes over the past few decades and has now transformed the notion of document into a (virtual) container of information and experiences using sensory data in multiple forms. In this modern reincarnation of the document, it is not limited to one medium, but can use different media as needed to communicate the information most effectively to a recipient. This means, however, that textual and sensory output needs to be combined in various ways to communicate different aspects and perspectives of information related to an event or an object. This chapter deals with the properties of applications and systems that do exactly that.

In this chapter, we discuss the different types of multimedia documents, and we present concepts and techniques behind many established as well as emerging systems for creating them. Creation of multimedia documents has been a very active area, and people already use many popular commercial products on a day-to-day basis. Our emphasis, however, is on a conceptual view of the technology rather than details of a particular product.

WHAT IS A DOCUMENT?

The most commonly used document is a book. Gutenberg's invention of the moveable printing press popularized the book by facilitating creation and distribution of books. Even today, when somebody talks about a document, most people think about a book. However, to the generation of people growing up with the Internet and the WWW, a book will evoke

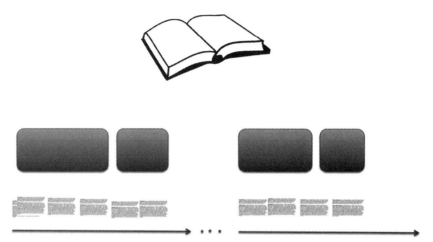

Figure 7.1. Organization of a book. Each page really takes an interval of the text stream and converts it into visual representation that has to be spatial – a page. Then pages are assembled into chapters, which in turn are assembled into a book.

a different image. They will consider a book a collection of text and images presented by an author to make it coherent and complete, but frozen in a particular time. Because a book was printed on paper with substantial effort and cost involved, it could not be easily modified or updated. Each subsequent edition was once again carefully thought about and prepared to make it complete and to keep it current for the foreseeable future. A book was divided into multiple chapters. Each chapter addressed a particular topic, again trying to be complete on that topic. In most cases, a book's organization could be represented as a tree structure, as shown in Figure 7.1. This tree structure was mapped into pages. One may consider pages as necessary structure imposed by physical requirements. On one hand, the text and images in a book have to be readable and hence of some minimum size. On the other hand, the whole book should be such that a normal person should be able to handle it. This can be easily accomplished by designing a book as a series of attached pages so that one can flip them in the sequence in which the material in the book is presented.

An important thing to note in a book is that the text is limited to pages. As we considered earlier, text is a symbolic representation of speech. And speech is a temporal signal. Thus one may keep in mind that a book is created by considering a timeline corresponding to the text describing the topic and dividing it into appropriate intervals, which are converted into pages. Each page is a folded version of the timeline.

The concept of representation of temporal information visually on a page became the dominant, if not the only, mode of creating documents because of the available technology. Authors and printers used different techniques, such as bold face, larger fonts, and different colors, to highlight important parts of the text. They used different spatial layouts to emphasize different aspects of the text.

Arrival of audio and video technology changed the book metaphor for documents. Audio and video allow rendering of time-varying audio and video signals in their natural audio and video form. The limitation of having to artificially represent time as visual pages no longer constrains the types of documents that can be rendered. Now a document can contain time-varying signals in time-varying form.

Another major transformation in documents is their linear nature. Paper-based physical representation forced linear structure on books. A book could be theoretically read in any order, but authors prepare a book assuming that it will be read linearly, from beginning to end. Some people read books in somewhat random order, but most books, particularly fiction, are read in the linear order. Arrival of hyperlinks in electronic documents and the introduction of hyperlinked pages on the Web changed this notion. As we will see, now a document can be read in an order that a reader finds appropriate rather than what the author intended. More important, now a document is no longer a compact and closed physical artifact, but a dynamically and organically growing result of collaborative authoring that presents multimedia in all its forms – and we have seen only the very beginning of the replacement of the book.

EVOLVING NATURE OF DOCUMENTS

Most documents may be considered a composition of many *content segments* (CS). A CS is a component that has been either authored or captured and can be considered an independent unit of media that could be combined with other segments. It is like an atomic segment that could be combined with other units to build increasingly complex documents. A CS could be a text document, a photo, a video segment, an audio segment, or any other similar data that represents a particular media. Given several relevant CS for producing a document, one may combine them in many different ways. Different combinations may result in different documents. To understand different ways to combine these, let us consider ten different segments shown in Figure 7.2. In Figure 7.3, we show three possible combinations in which a document may use these segments. The first composition approach used in Figure 7.3a combines them in a fixed linear document that is rendered, using conventions of English text, in left to right sequence in time. In Figure 7.3b, the author composes these documents as sub-documents that could then be used as new CS that are rendered linearly. It is possible to combine different components in many different ways. In Figure 7.3c, we show linking of documents so a user can go from one composite document to another if she so wishes by breaking the strict sequence that is followed in Figures 7.3a and 7.3b.

One may consider evolution of documents along three important dimensions:

Type of Media: Until recently, documents were mostly text and were commonly available in printed form on paper. Occasional photos or figures were included to enhance understanding of concepts or details that were considered too complex for text.

During the past few years, because of the emergence of new media technology, the nature of documents has gone through a complete metamorphosis. Text is and will remain an important component of documents, but now documents use different media as the author deems suitable for communicating information and experiences in the best possible manner. The author can combine different media in space and time to communicate his ideas in the most compelling manner. Moreover, the same CS can be used as many

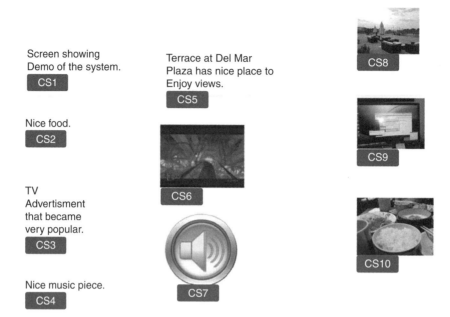

Figure 7.2. Ten different media segments. Each of them is an independent unit and is considered a atomic unit.

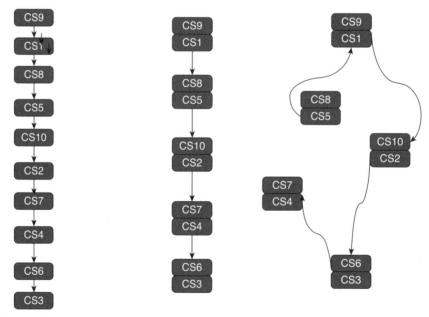

Figure 7.3. Three different combinations of the segments of Figure 7.2. In Figure 7.3a, the traditional linear segment is presented; Figure 7.3b shows some atomic documents combined to form composite elements and then used in the document; and Figure 7.3c shows how a user may navigate from one unit to the other as she may wish.

times in a document or in as many documents as the author deems necessary. This is possible because a CS is in electronic form and hence can be copied and used effortlessly or linked for rendering it without copying it. This ability has resulted in revolutionary changes in creating new documents and has provided new, powerful approaches for expressing ideas.

Nonlinear Flow: Because of the nature of physical documents, text was designed to flow linearly. This was strongly influenced by the temporal nature of narrative structures natural to text-based storytelling. With the advent of electronic media and the ability to create links, the limitation of linearity can be easily overcome. People accustomed to linear structures find nonlinearity confusing and unnatural at first. However, the fact that one can compose independent CS and then can link these to form multiple linear structures using different links is making this approach very popular. This provides a very flexible method of authoring documents that may be customized for different types of audiences.

Dynamic Documents: Older documents required significant efforts to create and then were distributed using static medium such as paper. This resulted in a significant latency between an event and sharing information and experiences of the event. During early days, the latency was really long. Newspapers were invented for reducing this latency between an event and its report. Television brought live events, but resource limitations kept this limited to only important events. The Web brought blogs, micro-blogs, and now real-time automatic updates for sharing live event information and experiences. There is an increasing trend to compile a document related to an event as it is unfolding, facilitated through so-called Wikis, for example.

In addition to such event reports dynamically unfolding, they can also be designed to suit information relevance and personal needs. This is resulting in creation of personalized dynamic documents.

STAGES IN DOCUMENT CREATION

Every document is created using a three-step process. These three stages do have some overlaps, but are distinct enough to consider them separately.

Data acquisition and organization: When a person decides to create a document, he or she starts thinking about the information, experiences, and message that the document will communicate to its user. This involves thinking about the relevant events and related information the document must convey. In some cases, this information is already available to the user, while in other cases, this must be acquired. In most cases, the information available is significantly more than what can be used in the document because of the size limitations of the document. The size limitations of the document are due to the attention span of the user more than the physical requirements, which in earlier times were more dominant.

A major change technology has brought during the past few years has been the increasing inclusion of metadata during acquisition to aid in organizing and using the data. Metadata is available for text files, as well as photos, videos, and all other data that is created or collected. In most cases, metadata is stored with the data in the same file. What is

Table 7.1. Content segments of different media and metadata commonly associated with those: a. text document, b. photo, c. audio, and d. video

File Type	Common metadata associated with the file
Text Document	Name, Author, Length, Date Created, Date Last Modified, Type, ...
Photo	Name, Capture Time, Compression Scheme, Exif, ...
Audio	Sampling Rate, Number of Channels, Encoding, ...
Video	Name, Creation Time, Compression, Length, Type, ...

stored in metadata is dependent on the media and application domain. Some metadata elements that have become de facto standard across different media are size, name, date, and place of author or device acquiring the data, and coding method to convert the media to bits. We discussed Exif for photos in Chapter 3. One may want to look at the metadata related to text files or other data on any system to get a good feel for how metadata looks. In Table 7.1, we show some content segments and elements of metadata associated with those.

Selection: An author[1] of a document usually collects two orders of magnitudes more material in preparation than appears in the final version. All this material must be organized so that it is available to support the author in selection of all pertinent material. Many metadata management tools have been developed to help potential authors to organize and select such material.

The author selects the material from the content segments in the database considering the message he or she wants to convey. The factors considered in selection of the segment are: relevance of the segment to the message, length of the segment, media of the segment, and how this segment could be combined with other segments.

This step is usually an iterative process. Once initial material is selected, the author must consider which material should be included in the final document. The author must consider the type of media available to convey the same information and experience and which one will be the best in the given context. Another important factor considered in the iterative process is the length of the document as well as the effectiveness of the information and media used to convey that. The output of the process is a set of segments to be included in the final document.

Editing: Editing is the process of taking an existing document and modifying it for its use in a given context, or simply refining it. Editing is media dependent. Many powerful tools have been developed for editing documents of specific media type. Here we briefly discuss operations used in common professional tools.

Text Editing: Many tools have been developed for editing text documents. Commonly used operations involved in editing a text document are:

---

[1]   We will use the term *author* for the person who prepares a document. In some cases, like for video, the term *producer* is more common, but we will use *author* consistently for all types of documents.

- insert;
- delete;
- format to change the layout; and
- emphasize using different styles, sizes, and colors.

The first two operations are obvious for changing the text. Formatting is used to provide structure to the text and includes breaking the text into sections or paragraphs, adding footnotes or references, and creating special textboxes and similar things to provide clear visual separation on a page. The final operation of emphasizing is to clearly display relative importance of certain text segments by using bold, italics, underline, larger font, different font styles, or different colors. Human beings use different intonations and inflections in oral communication. Because text is often a static representation of oral communication, these emphasis tools are used to capture some of the characteristics of oral communication.

Photo Editing: A photo is a flat, static representation of visual information. Most photos are captured using a photographic device, but authors can use other mechanisms such as computer graphics or human painting for the creation of photos. Some of the common operations used in photo editing are:

- selection of important objects;
- addition of objects;
- deletion of objects;
- enhancement or restoration of visual characteristics;
- changing visual characteristics in parts of a photo; and
- applying filters to a complete image.

In photographs, the most important aspect is to clearly mark pixels in an image that may represent a particular object. This operation is significantly more difficult than it appears. Many tools such as magic wand and cropping are provided to facilitate this operation. Enhancement and restoration are normally used to compensate for artifacts introduced because of imperfections during the photo capture operation. Visual characteristics are changed in parts of a photo to make its appearance more appealing. Finally, addition and deletion of objects are used to fundamentally change the content of a photo. A photo represents the state of the real world captured at a particular time. By inserting or deleting an object, an editor is changing the state of the world as depicted by the photo.[2]

Audio Editing: While many older audio editing tools try to simulate a tape recorder, modern editing operations on audio are usually based on a visual representation of the amplitude space (going from left to right in time). Audio can be:

- cut out;
- copied;

---

[2] Before photo editing tools became common, some editing was done in the dark room. Before digital tools arrived, a photo was considered strong evidence of what the state of the real world was at the time the photo was taken. Digital photo editing tools allowed manipulation of photos and made photos as evidence of the real world less credible.

- pasted; and
- filtered.

The problem with most visual representations of audio recordings is that they are not intuitive; for example, the user must listen in very often as the amplitude space representation does not indicate the final acoustic experience accurately enough. Several tracks are usually visualized above each other. Speech editors therefore often show a spectrogram (see Chapter 5) of the speech signal, allowing a more intuitive representation for experts. MIDI editors allow the editing of notes, which makes it easier for musicians. They work with MIDI editors like a text processing tool.

Video Editing: Video is different from the aforementioned media in that it combines all of them and adds new dimensions. It has spatial dimension and characteristics of photos, but represents a rapidly varying sequence of photos, thus bringing in temporal dimensions. It is also a combination of not only a photo sequence, but of audio that is either captured with the video or added to the photo sequence. Moreover, one could either overlay text in some parts of video or use text exclusively as video segments. Video editing tools usually contain:

- photo editing tools;
- adding a video segment at a particular time, say T_i;
- deleting a video segment from time T_1 to T_2;
- adding a text box at specified location from time T_s to T_e;
- adding an audio channel from time T_i;
- adding an image box at a specified location from time T_s to T_e;
- adding another video, usually of a much smaller size, at a specified location from time T_s to T_e; and
- adding a specific transition between segment S_k and S_{k+1}.

As the reader might have observed, video editing tools utilize results of editing of all other media and must provide spatial and temporal composition operations to coherently combine different media. In Figure 7.4, we show a video authoring/editing environment that contains photos, video, and audio components that are combined using timelines.

Emerging Multimedia Editing Tools: In a way, multimedia editing tools are extensions and collections of individual medium editing tools. Because in most current multimedia systems a screen is also used for rendering, spatial layout is manipulated similar to text and photos. Audio and video bring in temporal elements. This means that tools must be provided to manage time. Multimedia editing tools are similar to video editing tools. The major difference between multimedia and video editing tools, however, is that video editing tools consider the photo sequence the driving medium and other media play a supporting role. In multimedia, video is considered at the same level as any other media. In fact, a good multimedia authoring environment considers all media equally important, and one must use a specific medium to convey or emphasize important information or an experience that is most relevant. A multimedia authoring environment must consider elements discussed in the following section.

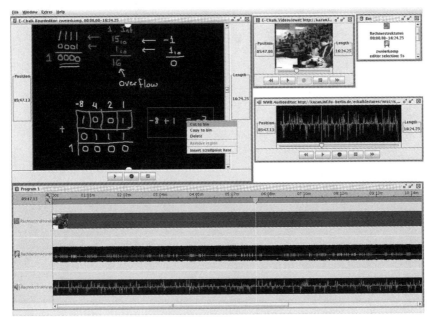

Figure 7.4. A video authoring/editing environment uses a timeline for showing how different components can be organized. (See Plate V for color version.)

BASIC ELEMENTS OF A MULTIMEDIA AUTHORING ENVIRONMENT

Because a multimedia document utilizes all media to make a document that combines appropriate media to communicate the message in the most compelling manner, it must provide facilities to author each individual medium and to combine them effectively and efficiently. Moreover, a multimedia authoring environment must consider mechanisms for user interactivity. Based on the emerging changes in the nature of documents, one must consider different factors in designing multimedia authoring environments. Two very important fundamental aspects are related to spatial and temporal composition of different media assets. As we see later, one must pay careful attention to layout as well as to synchronization issues.

Characteristics of Media Assets: Different media assets have different spatial, temporal, and other informational attributes that play important roles in the combined documents in terms of designing their layout and synchronization. In many cases, these characteristics are stored as metadata along with the data corresponding to the media. In some dynamically created content, this metadata as well as the data becomes available only at the rendering time. An authoring environment should account for this.

Spatial Layout: Most multimedia documents in current systems are rendered on a screen. The screen has fixed spatial dimensions, such as 640 x 480 pixels or 1,920 x 1,200 pixels. An author decides which media item should be displayed in which area of the screen

Figure 7.5. A spatial layout showing three different windows. Each window's location and size must be specified. Windows A1 and A2 are within A; and C1 and C2 are within C.

Video1	P1	Video2	P2	Video3

Audio1	Audio2

Figure 7.6. The timeline representation of each content item is shown on the timeline. For each item the start time and the duration must be specified.

and what its resolution should be. In some cases, an item must be scaled up or down to fit the selected window size. Thus, with each media item, there is an associated spatial window where it should appear. In Figure 7.5, we show the screen and multiple windows. Each window size must be specified using a rectangle either in absolute locations or in terms of a corner and its size. For each window, one must also specify the type of content and the source from where the content must be displayed.

Temporal Layout: Because multimedia content can be displayed as video on the screen, an authoring environment should specify different content that will be used to constitute this video. The earliest authoring tools in this area appeared in video editing systems. Multimedia authoring systems extend them to include more sources of data and to provide more flexibility and control in using and combining the data. An example of temporal layout is shown in Figure 7.6. This layout essentially provides tools to specify the time interval for the appearance, transitions, and disappearance of each content item on the screen. The location of the content on the screen could also be specified.

Synchronization: A multimedia document comprises different media contents of different types that must be rendered in space and time to give a coherent and unified experience. It is important to make sure that spatial and temporal relationships among different items are clearly specified by the author and are carried out by the system. Because synchronization is an important topic, we will discuss this in Chapter 8. Most multimedia authoring environments provide basic tools to specify which media elements should be synchronized.

Publishing Formats: Multimedia documents are rendered on many different sized screens, ranging from large TV screens to computer screens of many different sizes and resolutions, and now on many – some say too many – sizes of mobile phone screens. A good authoring environment may allow adjustment in spatial layout as well as temporal rendering considering the screen characteristics used to render the document. It is also important to consider the bandwidth available to render the content and adapt the rendering process based on the availability of the bandwidth. If the authoring paradigm results in a fixed format, then the final document can be rendered correctly only for the specific screen and bandwidth assumed available while authoring the document. Most current systems assume that the same content may be displayed under different rendering contexts. In all these cases, the document is stored in an intermediate format that is finalized only at the time of rendering when all the parameters are known.

REPRESENTATION OF A MULTIMEDIA DOCUMENT

As may be obvious from the previous discussion, the structure of a multimedia document is relatively complex. A text-only document has a fairly linear structure consisting of chapters, sections, and subsections. With modern hyperlinking capabilities, nonlinearity has been introduced in otherwise linear text documents. Now a user may play a role in defining the rendering of these documents, as discussed earlier in this chapter. Because of flexibility in the organizing and use of multiple types of media, the nature of multimedia documents becomes relatively more complex. Many different models have been used to represent multimedia documents. In this section, we discuss two of these models that cover many requirements of multimedia authoring environments and that have gained popularity.

Structure-based Representation: Common structure-based representation uses a tree structure in which the root is a complete document and the leaf nodes are individual media elements or a pointer to those. Intermediate nodes are "sub-documents" comprised of combinations of individual media elements. For each intermediate node, the composition rules and spatial and temporal layouts may be explicitly specified. Figure 7.7 shows structure of a multimedia document that contains multiple text, photos, audio, and video segments. One content element could be used multiple times if desired.

Time-based Representation: Time-based representations evolved from video editing. In these representations, one considers that a multimedia document is organized around a timeline. Different media elements are represented as different tracks synchronized with the master timeline. Each track specifies which content element will appear during which time interval. One may also specify the relative spatial position of each media element. This representation makes the relative appearance and disappearance of different media elements explicit and easy to represent and understand.

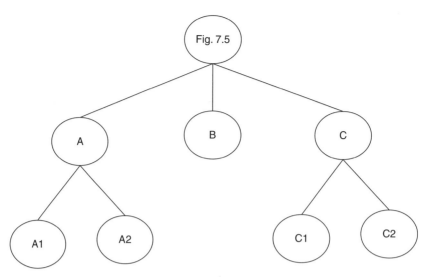

Figure 7.7. The tree structure shown represents a complete multimedia document that uses several media components. This structure represents the window shown in Figure 7.5.

CURRENT AUTHORING ENVIRONMENTS

Many multimedia authoring environments have been developed during the past two decades. One of the biggest drivers for developing these environments has been the Web. Many other systems were also defined for general multimedia authoring environments, such as MPEG4 and SMIL. Rapid convergence is taking place in devices, communication, and computing. It appears that the Web environment may become the unifying environment. In the following, we briefly discuss key concepts and trends among emerging authoring environments.

HyperText Markup Language (HTML) was defined as the first publishing language of the Web and has remained the main language for preparing documents so they can be published on different platforms. Like any other markup language, HTML uses tags to specify how an element on a page should be published. The language syntax defines how to specify tags for different actions to be performed. These tags are in pairs like <T1> and </T1>, where the first tag declares the beginning of T1 and the second tag is the *end tag* that closes it. Most of the information in text, tables, and images is between the tags. A browser uses the tags to interpret the intent of the author in displaying the content of the page or the document. In the early days of the Web, most of the documents contained only text. Tags in those days usually specified presentation-related operations on text. HTML1.0 was a key component of the launch of the Web and was predominantly concerned with presentation of the text on a page.

As the nature of documents changed, subsequent versions of HTML provided specifications for inclusion of multimedia content. These specifications had richer tags for layout of media items. Another challenge browsers faced in the presentation of multimedia content was use of proprietary technology for playing video. HTML5 finally has introduced specific features to author multimedia content as easily as text. In particular, it now has four specific constructs: <video>, <audio>, Canavas, and SVG. These features make inclusion of multimedia content in a document much easier.

RECOMMENDED READING

Clay Shirky presents an excellent history of development of different media and their impact on society in *Cognitive Surplus*. James Gleick's book, *Information: A History, a Theory, a Flood*, is an excellent source that examines the changing nature of information and how it has affected our society. These and many similar sources convey a compelling message – information and knowledge are captured using multiple media and are communicated best by combining these media in appropriate proportions. Modern multimedia allows us to select and combine media to convey the message in compelling way.

In the evolution of multimedia authoring, major activity started during the 1980s. By that time sensors, storage, and computing had evolved enough to make basic authoring of photos, audio, and video possible. In the history of photo editing, Photoshop was a major force in converting photos from a visual record to an authoring environment. Photos, often called images, used to be a record that could be processed to enhance them and to recover information. By providing simple tools to edit them, Thomas Knoll's Photoshop, developed when he was a doctoral student supervised by Ramesh Jain at the University of Michigan, changed the way photos were viewed. From a record, a photo became a creative environment for expressing visual thoughts. The impact of Photoshop on multimedia authoring is not only in photos, but also in video production. However, as a side effect, Photoshop destroyed what used to be considered irrefutable evidence – a photo of an event – and has now resulted in the creation of multimedia forensics as a field.

An important multimedia authoring project that contributed many ideas and resulted in development of a complete multimedia environment was Synchronized Multimedia Integration Language (SMIL). This environment developed over several years and was one of the first authoring environment to consider all aspects of multimedia authoring and to make it compatible with emerging concepts and tools from the Web community.

MPEG4 was the first effort to consider video as composition of objects and events both for compression as well as for providing an interactive, dynamic visual environment. For the first time, in MPEG4, video is not considered a signal captured by a camera, but a perspective of the real world where one could consider different objects, at different locations, under different conditions and synthesize how a scene will look to a camera.

As computing power increased, efforts started in creating multiple perspective and immersive video during the last decade of the twentieth century, but because of technology limitations remained in the conceptual stages. With advances in technology, these techniques will evolve rapidly and will result in powerful immersive telepresence systems.

Finally, one is seeing the emergence of new media as a new communication mechanism for knowledge. Unlike the medium of text that started with Gutenberg's moveable printing press and has remained dominant, emerging social media systems rely on a combination of multiple media to communicate and share experiences.

Another major emerging trend is to capture and use metadata effectively. Exif became very popular as digital cameras replaced traditional camera. As phones become primary media capture devices, the role of metadata is likely to dramatically increase. For example, it is now possible to attach significantly more information, or metadata, to a photo captured using a smartphone.

Further Reading

Stefano Battista, Franco Casalino, and Claudio Lande. "MPEG-4: A multimedia standard for the third millennium, Part 1," *IEEE Multimedia*, October 1999: 74–83.

Dick Bulterman and Lloyd Rutledge. *Interactive Multimedia for the Web, Mobile Devices and Daisy Talking Books*. Springer. 2008.

James Gleick. *The Information: A History, a Theory, a Flood*. Pantheon Books. 2010.

Takeo Kanade, P. J. Narayanan, and Peter Rander: "Virtualized reality: Being mobile in a visual scene," *Object Representation in Computer Vision*, 1996: 273–85.

Arun Katkere, Saied Moezzi, Don Y. Kuramura, Patrick H. Kelly, and Ramesh Jain. "Towards video-based immersive environments," *Multimedia Syst.*, 5 (2): 69–85, 1997.

Ramesh Raskar, Greg Welch, Matt Cutts, Adam Lake, Lev Stesin, and Henry Fuchs. "The office of the future: A unified approach to image-based modeling and spatially immersive displays," *SIGGRAPH*, 1998: 179–88.

Clay Shirky. *Cognitive Surplus: Creativity and Generosity in a Connected Age*. Penguin Books. 2010.

SMIL 3.0.

EXERCISES

1. What is Exif? Who invented it? What was the initial goal of capturing and storing Exif data? How can you use it in automatic interpretation of photos? Can you use it for organization and search of photos? Why?

2. Suppose you capture a photo or a video using a smartphone. List all information about the photo that you could attach to the photo using time, location, sensors in the phone, and the Web. Assume that you take a photo on a trip to New York and want to send it to a friend in the form of a story around the photo. What information is available to you that you can automatically convey to the recipient?

3. Printed books usually followed a tree structure for organizing their content. Why was this structure so popular? What kind of difficulties will make graph structure very difficult, if not impossible, to organize a book?

4. Can you consider a book as a presentation in time?

5. A document using only text is one dimensional. Explain.

6. A multimedia document is at least three dimensional, containing two spatial dimensions and one time dimension. Can it have higher dimensions? Give examples.

7. Why is a basic media segment also called an atomic media element? How can it be used to form a media document?

8. Given N atomic segments, how many different media documents could be generated from these segments?

9. What is a dynamic document? Give an example of at least one dynamic document that you would consider very useful in an education-related application.

10. What are the stages in multimedia document creation? Which one will most limit the quality of the final document? Explain.

11. Compare editing operations used in text, photo, audio, and video. Explain the role of timeline in each of these.

12. Timelines have received a good amount of attention during the past few years. What role can they play in multimedia computing and communication?

13. What role does spatial layout play in multimedia documents? Compare the role of spatial layout in text documents.

14. Can space be three-dimensional in spatial layouts considered in multimedia documents? Give examples.

15. What are immersive environments? What is immersive video? How do you compare immersive video to immersive environments?

16. What is Multiple Perspective Interactive Video? When does this become immersive video?

8 Multimodal Integration and Synchronization

A multimedia system, including a human, understands the domain of discussion by correlating and combining partial information from multiple media to get complete information. In most situations, without correlating the information from multiple data streams, one cannot extract information about the real world. Even in those systems where multimedia is for humans' direct consumption, all correlated information must be presented, or rendered, for humans to extract information that they need from the multimedia data. It is well known that humans combine information from multiple sensors and apply extensive knowledge from various sources to form the models of the real world in which they live. Humans also use different media, assuming the familiarity and knowledge of a recipient, in communicating their experiences and knowledge of the world. Most human experiences are multimedia and are easily captured, stored, and communicated using multimedia.

We already discussed the nature of sensory data and the emerging nature of documents that are increasingly inherently multimedia. Here we discuss the nature of individual sensor streams with a goal to convert them to a multimedia stream. We also start the discussion on how a computing system should view multimedia to develop systems that are not just a simple combination of multimedia, but are inherently multimedia such that they are much more than the sum of their component media elements.

MULTIMODAL INTEGRATION

In a computer, a multimedia stream usually comprises n sensor streams, $S_1, \ldots, S_n$ from different sources of K types of data in the form of image sequence, audio stream, photos, motion detector, and other types including text. Each data stream has $M_1, \ldots, M_n$, as its metadata that may include location and type of the sensor, viewpoint, angles, camera calibration parameters, or other similar parameters relevant to the data stream. This metadata is used in computing features in each stream for understanding individual streams as well as the holistic combination of multiple streams. Metadata is also very relevant in the presentation of streams to convey experiences appropriately. Different data streams and their metadata are used to decide the role of specific streams in different operations that include selection and assignment of weights to data streams, placement and synchronization of different data streams to form documents, communication of multimedia streams in practical networks, and the decision by an operating system to schedule appropriate use of resources. Data and metadata streams are also correlated and combine such that sometimes a stream becomes the context stream for other data and is used in interpretation and understanding of the multimedia streams. These issues will be discussed throughout the remainder of this book.

In contrast to current computer systems, the human brain can integrate different sensory modalities, such as sight, sound, and touch, into a coherent and unified perceptual experience. Several experiments, of which some are described later, show that by considering input from multiple sensors, humans can solve perceptual problems more robustly and quickly. This *multimodal integration*, or *multisensory integration*, is not yet completely understood, but it is fundamental to the success of multimedia systems. Multimedia computing strives to imitate the properties of multimodal integration regardless of the incomplete understanding of the mechanisms in the brain. For example, multimedia content analysis (as described in Chapter 17) combines audio and video in an attempt to gain accuracy, robustness, and sometimes speed. Here, we describe well-known observable phenomena that might clarify the process and highlight the design considerations for multimedia systems.

McGurk Effect

Two converging sensory stimuli can produce a perception that differs not only in magnitude from the sum of the two individual stimuli, but also in quality. The classic study, which introduced the *McGurk effect*, dubbed a person's acoustic phoneme production with a video of that person speaking a different phoneme. The result was that the user perceived neither the visual nor the acoustic pronunciation but instead heard a third phoneme. McGurk and MacDonald explained in their 1976 article that phonemes such as ba, da, ka, ta, ga, and pa can be divided into two groups:

Phonemes that can be visually confused (da, ga, ka, ta), and
Phonemes that can be acoustically confused (ba and pa).

The combination of the visual and acoustically confused phonemes results in the perception of a different phoneme. For example, when an uttering of ba is dubbed on a video showing the uttering of ga, which is processed visually through lip reading, the visual modality sees ga or da, and the auditory modality hears ba or da, which combine to form the perception of da.

Ventriloquism

Ventriloquism is another important effect. It describes the situation in which acoustic tracking of a sound's origin shifts toward the visual modality. In conditions where the visual cue is unambiguous, the perception of the visual location overrides the acoustic location. Artists throughout the world use this effect. Ventriloquists manipulate how they produce sound so it appears that the voice is coming from elsewhere, usually a puppet.

This is used in many multimedia systems, for example, in ordinary television sets, as the loudspeakers are usually not located exactly where the actors move their mouths on the visual screens.

Body Transfer Illusion

An almost "magic" effect is called *body transfer illusion*. Botvinick and Cohen performed the original so-called rubber hand experiment in 1998. Human participants sat in front of a screen showing a dummy hand being stroked with a brush while they felt a series of synchronized and identical brushstrokes applied to their own hands, hidden from their view. The result was that if the dummy hand was similar to the participant's hand in appearance, position, and location, the human subject was likely to feel that the touches on his or her hand came from the dummy hand. Furthermore, several participants reported that they felt the dummy hand to be their own hand. Virtual reality applications try to exploit this effect and try to induce the perception of owning and controlling someone else's body (usually an avatar) by applying visual, haptic, and sometimes proprioceptual stimulation synchronously (sensors are described in more detail in Chapter 4).

Uncertainty Reduction

The brain exploits multimodal integration in different ways. The two most important are the decrease of sensory uncertainty and the decrease of reaction time. Experiments have shown that uncertainty in sensory domains leads to an increased dependence of multisensory integration. If a person sees something moving in a tree and isn't sure whether it is a bird or a squirrel, the natural reaction is to listen. If the object emits a chirp and the brain localizes the sound to be coming from the tree, the person takes this as proof that the creature is a bird. Hence, acoustic information augments the lack of visual information. The so-called Hershenson experiments also showed that responses to multiple simultaneous sensory stimuli can be performed faster than responses to the same stimuli presented in isolation. Participants were presented a light and tone simultaneously and separately, and were asked to respond as rapidly as possible by pressing a button. Reaction time differed with varying levels of synchrony between the tone and the light. This result is, however, hard to generalize as multiple synchronous stimuli might also cause the opposite effect, as we discuss in the next section.

Split Attention

Split attention, the opposite effect of multimodal integration, manifests when the same media (for example, visual and visual) is used for different types of information at the same time. This is usually a problem in multimedia systems, rather than functionality.

To understand and use the materials provided, one must split attention between them. Split attention should not be confused with distraction, although the two problems are related. Distraction is caused by the lack of ability to pay attention to a particular object due to lack of interest in the object or the greater intensity, novelty, or attractiveness of

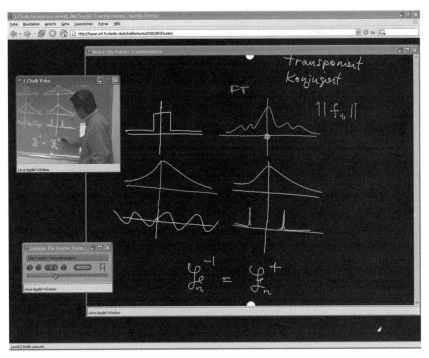

Figure 8.1. An example of a split attention problem. The lecturer on the left is shown as a video, and the dynamic board content he creates is shown on the right. The additional video window is used to convey gestures and finger pointing. However, presenting the lecturer in a second window causes cognitive overhead usually referred to as split attention because the viewer switches between the content on the board and the lecturer on the left. (See Plate VI for color version.)

something other than the object. However, split attention is caused by the lack of integration of the object to be paid attention to.

Figure 8.1 shows an example multimedia system known to have caused a split attention problem. The E-Chalk lecture recording system showed dynamic board content in addition to a video of the lecturer. In a typical E-Chalk lecture, two areas of the screen compete for the viewer's attention: the video window showing the instructor and the board or slides window. Several researchers tracked students' eye movements as they watched a lecture recording containing slides and an instructor video in a setup similar to that shown in Figure 8.1. Measurements showed that a student often spends about 70 percent of the time watching the instructor video and only about 20 percent of the time watching the slides. For the remaining 10 percent of the time, the eye focus was lost to activities unrelated to lecture content. When the lecture replay consists of only slides and audio, students spend about 60 percent of the time looking at the slides because they have no other place to focus their attention in the lecture recording. The remaining 40 percent, however, was lost because of distraction.

It is still an open question whether attention can be split to attend to two or more sources of information simultaneously. Psychologists and neuroscientists have discussed this topic for decades. Most researchers, however, now accept that attention can be split at the cost of cognitive overhead. It is this cognitive overhead that is to be avoided when designing multimedia systems. See the references at the end of this chapter for more information.

So far, we have described sensory phenomena on a high level and discussed important properties of the human system. We will now begin to dig deeper into what it means to process sensory information using computers. While reading the next chapters you might find it useful to go back to these introductory chapters from time to time to remind yourself of the fundamentals. However, you will do so at the cost of split attention.

SENSOR INTEGRATION IN MULTIMEDIA COMPUTING

Combining sensory inputs optimally in computer systems is an active area of research. In fact, it is probably the most central theme of research in multimedia computing, especially because in comparison to the effects observable in human beings (explained earlier), which must stem from rather elaborate computing methods in the brain, multimedia computing methods are very basic.

The subfield of multimedia computing that deals with an important step in sensor integration is called synchronization. The remainder of this chapter therefore deals with synchronization. Another field that deals with sensor integration in machine learning is multimodal fusion, which is explained in Chapter 17.

INTRODUCTION TO SYNCHRONIZATION

Synchronization is not a new problem. Whenever coordination among two or more sources is required to complete a task, synchronization is required. In many cases, this means establishing, specifying, and then performing this coordination precisely in space and time. Two common examples of these are team sports and an orchestra. In soccer or football, two or more players must be in a particular spatial configuration and must perform their roles perfectly for a desirable outcome. In music, space is not that important, but multiple players must produce particular sounds at specific instants for effect. In fact, *orchestrate* in the *Merriam-Webster Dictionary* is defined as "Arrange or direct the elements of (a situation) to produce a desired effect." A music conductor uses specifications in a music book to coordinate the timing by individual players. As we will see in this chapter, *synchronization* is to specify timing and location of each multimedia stream to create a holistic impact.

A common first step in extracting information from multiple streams as well as presenting information for final consumption from multiple streams is to make sure that they represent the same event, although from different perspectives and maybe using different modality. Because in most cases, the data from different sensors is collected independently and transmitted and stored using different channels, care needs to be taken that all the data is synchronized. The process of synchronization usually refers to processes that are required to make sure that events in a multimedia system operate in the same unison as they do in the real world. The relationships that exist in the real world among different media components should be captured and maintained for information extraction as well as proper rendering for human experience. As we will see, the most important relationship that needs to be maintained is time, but spatial and content relationships also need to be maintained in many applications. In this chapter, we will discuss these synchronizations' affect and different techniques that are used to ascertain that such relationships are maintained.

In the following, we first discuss content synchronization, then spatial synchronization. After these two concepts, we discuss temporal synchronization in more depth. Note that temporal synchronization is the main synchronization approach. Much of the efforts spent in multimedia synchronization are on temporal synchronization because time plays a very important role in rendering time-dependent media. As we will see, increasingly people present even time-independent media such as text or photos in a video environment, where time plays a key role.

CONTENT SYNCHRONIZATION

In many applications, different types of data sets are semantically or functionally related to each other and make sense only if they appear together in terms of space or time or both. The important relationship is the content relationship, and it should be rendered such that it makes sense. A common example could be the appearance of a figure, or in some cases a text box or even a slide, close to the concept that it is related to. Embedding of figures close to their citation is common. Increasingly, people are developing approaches to embed slide presentations along with a scientific paper. In all these techniques, the emphasis is that one must present contents that are related to each other somehow close to each other.

It is very common that researchers present their work in a research article as well as a slide presentation that they may have made at a professional meeting. Usually, these two constitute a dual view of the same work, often quite different from each other. Slides represent the work at a high level, and the research paper presents detailed arguments. Because these two modes of presentations constitute a dual view, further utility can be gained if the two media are synchronized. In such a synchronized, fine-grained alignment between slides and document, passages could be constructed and presented, allowing a user to view the slides and the document simultaneously.

This joint presentation of slides and a document can be prepared by finding a suitable fine-grained synchronization between them. Such a synchronization may be formulated as a problem of aligning slides to a corresponding paragraph span in the document. This problem was formalized in the Slideseer system as document-to-presentation alignment:

> Given a slide presentation S consisting of slides s1 to sn and a document D consisting of text paragraphs d1 to dm, an alignment is a function f(s) = (x, y), mapping each slide to a contiguous set of document paragraphs, starting at dx and ending at dy where x < = y, or to nil.

The results of such an alignment are shown in Figure 8.2.

Of course, this is only an example of content synchronization. One could consider many situations, and the number of situations is increasing rapidly with the availability

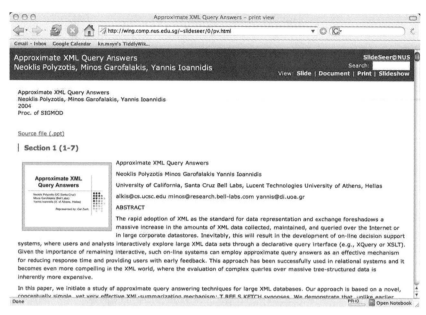

Figure 8.2. Alignment of slides and a research publication can be done analyzing contents of both and synchronizing them as reported in the Slideseer system.

and discovery methods now found on the Web. In most situations, the first step is to discover the content, then align it and finally present it.

TEMPORAL SYNCHRONIZATION

Because many multimedia components are captured as time-varying signals and are also displayed in time, the majority of the synchronization techniques have addressed issues in temporal synchronization. In this section, for brevity, we will drop "temporal" unless needed in the context.

Synchronization techniques specify relationships that must be maintained among different media elements that must be interpreted or rendered together. In some cases, all media elements are time dependent, while in other cases, such as making a video, some elements may not be time dependent, but must be rendered at a specific time. A time-dependent object is a stream in which each element has a specified time associated with it, while in a time-independent medium there may not be a stream (such as a photo or a text box) or the time relations may not be as critical, as in a slide deck. A time-dependent object is presented or rendered as a media stream because a temporal relation exists between consecutive units of the stream. The time-independent object is the traditional medium such as text or images and could be rendered independent of time, except when it becomes part of a time-dependent media stream. Temporal dependencies among multiple media objects specify temporal relationships among objects that must be maintained for correct interpretation or understanding. A common example is the lip synchronization used in making movies. The image sequence stream showing a video must have a very

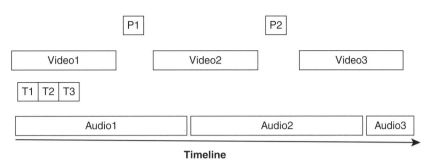

Figure 8.3. The duration of each media element, audio, video, text (T), and photo (P), are shown on the timeline.

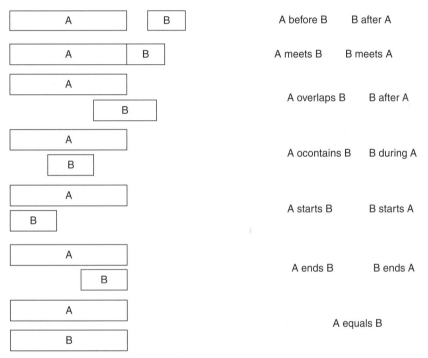

Figure 8.4. Thirteen temporal relations between two intervals A and B are shown here. Six of these are inverse of each other and hence there are only seven relationships shown in this figure.

precise temporal relationship with the audio stream representing speech for understanding what a person is saying. If the correct relationship is not maintained, then a viewer may find the experience either poor or utterly confusing.

In many applications, temporal synchronization includes relations between time-dependent and time-independent objects. A slide show usually includes temporal synchronization of an audio stream, either music or narration or both, which is time dependent, and individual slides, which are time-independent media objects. In Figure 8.3, we show a timeline and many different media objects that may be used to create a presentation or rendering of media as a function of time. For each media object, its time duration is shown as a box on a timeline. It is possible that at a given time multiple media objects may be rendered or at some times, no media object may be rendered. The temporal relationships among time durations (commonly called time intervals) of different media objects may be specified using relationships first specified by Allen. Allen considered two processes and defined thirteen possible temporal relationships among them (see Figure 8.4). These relationships have been used in specification of temporal relationship in many applications.

SYNCHRONIZATION LEVELS IN A SYSTEM

Synchronization has to be implemented at multiple levels in a system. We can consider three common levels of synchronization.

Level 1: At the lowest level, support must be provided to display each stream smoothly. Operating systems and lower communication layers are responsible for ascertaining a smooth single stream by bundling and making sure about the display requirements. They ensure minimal jitter at the presentation time of the stream.

Level 2: The next level is commonly called the *RUN-TIME* support for synchronization of multimedia streams (schedulers) and is implemented on top of level 1. This level makes sure that skews between various streams are bounded to acceptable limits dictated by applications.

Level 3: The top level deals with the run-time support for synchronization between time-dependent and time-independent media. This level is also responsible for handling of user interaction. The main responsibility of this level is to make sure that the skews between time-dependent and time-independent media are within acceptable limits.

SPECIFICATION OF SYNCHRONIZATION

There are many ways to specify synchronization requirements among different media objects. In this section, we discuss different specification approaches that may be used in applications depending on the type of media used and application requirements.

Implicit specification: In many applications, temporal relations among different media components are determined implicitly during their capture. The goal of a presentation of these objects is to present media in the same way as they were originally captured. The relationships among media objects are considered specified implicitly at the capture time. A common example of this is the capture of a video that consists of two media components: audio stream and image frame stream. These two streams are captured by the system using the same timeline. Thus we may consider that the synchronization requirements are specified implicitly.

Explicit specification: Temporal relation may be specified explicitly in the case of presentations that are composed of independently captured time-dependent objects such as audio or video, time-independent objects such as photo, and manually created objects such as text boxes and slides. Similarly, in applications like a slide show, a presentation designer selects appropriate slides, selects audio objects, and defines relationships between the audio presentation stream and slides for presentation. In such cases, the designer must explicitly define and specify the relationships among different media objects.

Intra-object Specification: An animation video comprises all manually created image frames that are presented at an appropriate frame rate to create a video. In all such cases, though there is only one media stream, the objects in each frame in the sequence must be drawn to create specific visual effects. This requires that considering the motion characteristics to be conveyed, relationships and positions of different objects in each frame must be specified precisely. Thus, one needs to consider synchronization of the objects, their attributes, and their positions in each frame as a function of time in the presentation stream.

DEADLINES

For synchronizing two streams, applications may specify whether their requirements for starting or ending media are rigid or flexible. In cases of rigid requirements, the system must make sure that the deadlines are considered hard and must meet specification. Soft or flexible requirements mean that there is some tolerance specified within which the relationship must be maintained. For example, in case of speech-related audio and corresponding video showing a person's face, it is important that audio and video are played within a specified interval.

SPATIAL SYNCHRONIZATION

Spatial placement of different components of a document have played an important role. As we saw in multimedia authoring, relative placement of a photo and its caption is important and must be clearly specified. If a caption and its corresponding figure do not appear together, then it may result in significant confusion. In fact, in many cases, the semantics of the document or a simple figure may completely depend on the relative placement of its component. In Figure 8.5, we show many components in a random order. By placing them appropriately with respect to each other in a spatial configuration, we get Figure 8.6, which depicts a stick figure representing a person. Without spatial relationships among different components, we will not be able to render the message that we want to communicate. In fact, one can easily see that by a different spatial arrangement of components, one will get a different object.

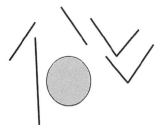

Figure 8.5. Several components displayed in a random order.

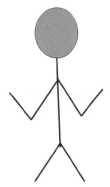

Figure 8.6. The same components as in Figure 8.5 displayed in a specific order.

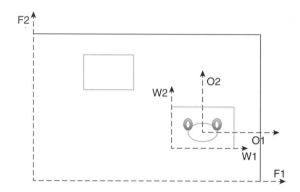

Figure 8.7. Use of multiple coordinate systems to specify positions among objects that must be maintained among them. The dashed lines represent three different coordinate systems F, W, and O, for Frame, Window, and Object, respectively.

Rendering of different components of media is usually on a screen that is two dimensional. In some cases, one may want rendering to take place in three dimensions, but in this chapter we will limit our discussion to two-dimensional screens. On this screen, one must specify the location of each media component as well as the locations of subcomponents in each specific media.

A first step toward specifications is to define the space used for the presentation of a media object on an output device at a certain point of time in a multimedia presentation. For this, *layout frames* are defined on an output device, usually a screen, and each content is assigned inside this frame. Positioning of the layout frame is usually the size of the screen used by the application. Within this frame, windows corresponding to different media (photos, video, or even audio symbols) to be displayed could be defined. In many systems, the layout frame corresponds to the complete screen, and the positions of the other windows are then defined relative to the layout frame.

In defining relative layouts and even objects within each media window, it is useful to define more than one coordinate system. For example, in Figure 8.7, we have defined three coordinate systems. We have a coordinate system, F, defined for the layout frame. Each media window is defined inside this window so the objects within each window could be defined with respect to the coordinate system, W, defined for it. Finally, components of an object in a window could be defined in coordinate system, O, defined for a specific object in the window. By using multiple coordinate systems and defining relationships among them, it is easier to define relationships that must be maintained with respect to different components.

RECOMMENDED READING

The area of multimodal integration in the brain is still being explored on a very basic level. Psychologists and brain researchers are working together to understand the mechanisms that evolved in biology. In the references, we therefore cited many individual research papers on the topic, including those describing the original experiments mentioned briefly in our chapter. We recommend reading McGurk and Hershenson. Calvert, Spence, and Stein have summarized many of the multimodal experiments in a handbook. The most elaborate experiments relating to multimedia computing are probably the ones regarding split attention. Split attention has been a major issue in many early multimedia systems and remains a design flaw of many current systems. Baars was probably the first to create a framework of consciousness to explain this and other effects.

Synchronization was a popular research topic in the early days of multimedia computing. It is very well covered in the textbook on multimedia by Steinmetz and Nahrstedt. Different aspects of synchronization and their implementation are described in this book. Anybody interested in the topic may want to start with this as the entry resource.

A very good example of content synchronization is in the article on the Slidesheer system by Min Yen Kan.

Further Reading

J. F. Allen. "Maintaining knowledge about temporal intervals," *Comm. of the ACM*, 26 (11): 832–43, November 1983.

B. J. Baars. *A Cognitive Theory of Consciousness*. Cambridge: Cambridge University Press. 1988.

P. Bichot Narcisse, Kyle R. Cave, and Harold Pashler. "Visual selection mediated by location: Feature-based selection of non-contiguous locations," *Perception & Psychophysics*, 61 (3): 403–23, 1999.

M. Botvinick and J. D. Cohen. "Rubber hand 'feels' what eyes see," *Nature*, 391: 756, 1998.

Gemma Calvert, Charles Spence, and Barry E. Stein. *The Handbook of Multisensory Processes*. MIT Press, 2004.

P. Chandler and J. Sweller. "The split attention effect as a factor in the design of instruction," *British Journal of Education Psychology*, 62: 233–46, 1992.

C. A. Grimes, E. C. Dickey, and M. V. Pishko. *Encyclopedia of Sensors* (10-Volume Set). American Scientific Publishers. 2006.

S. Hahn and A. F. Kramer. "Further evidence for the division of attention among non-contiguous locations," *Visual Cognition*, 5 (1–2): 217–56, 1998.

M. Hershenson. "Reaction time as a measure of intersensory facilitation," *J Exp Psychol*, 63: 289–93, 1962.

Min-Yen Kan. "SlideSeer: A digital library of aligned document and presentation pairs." In Proceedings of the Joint Conference on Digital Libraries (JCDL '07). Vancouver, Canada, June 2007.

H. McGurk and J. MacDonald. "Hearing lips and seeing voices," *Nature*, 264 (5588): 746–8, 1976.

R. Mertens, G. Friedland, and M. Krueger. "To see or not to see: Layout constraints, the split attention problem and their implications for the design of Web lecture interfaces." In Proceedings of the AACE E-Learn – World Conference on E-Learning in Corporate, Government, Healthcare, and Higher Education, Honolulu, Hawaii, 2006.

Ralf Steinmetz and Klara Nahrstedt. *Multimedia Systems* (X.media.publishing). December 2, 2010.

J. Sweller, P. Chandler, P. Tierney, and G. Cooper. "Cognitive load as a factor in the structuring of technical material," *Journal of Experimental Psychology: General*, 119: 176–92, 1990.

EXERCISES

1. Explain why the McGurk effect is generally not a problem for dubbing TV shows and movies into a different language.

2. Find at least one more example of the split attention issue in daily life. Propose a solution.

3. Why is synchronization an important consideration in multimedia systems? What will happen if the system does not provide the right synchronization?

4. What is content synchronization? Give at least two examples of content synchronization.

5. Temporal synchronization is the most commonly discussed form of synchronization. At how many levels should multimedia computing systems deal with synchronization? How are these levels related?

6. When would you specify synchronization requirement implicitly and when would you specify it explicitly?

7. Suppose that you obtain photographs of an event, say a goal in a world cup soccer match, captured by many people attending the event. You are given the exact time instant and the location of the camera. Design a system similar to Photosynth for this event by considering timing and location for exploring this event. Discuss the nature of the synchronization requirement in this application.

8. What factors should one consider in spatial synchronization?

9. What are the different types of coordinate systems that one may need to use in spatial synchronization? Discuss why these are required. Can you manage without these?

9 | Multimedia Systems

A multimedia computing system is designed to facilitate natural communication among people, that is, communication on the basis of perceptually encoded data. Such a system may be used synchronously or asynchronously for remote communication, using remote presence, or for facilitating better communication in the same environment. These interactions could also allow users to communicate with people across different time periods or to share knowledge gleaned over a long period. Video conferencing, video on demand, augmented reality, immersive video, or immersive telepresence systems represent different stages of technology enhancing natural communication environments. The basic goal of a multimedia system is to communicate information and experiences to other humans. Because humans sense the world using their five senses and communicate their experiences using these senses and their lingual abstractions of the world, a multimedia system should use the same senses and abstractions in communications.

Multimedia systems combine communication and computing systems. In multimedia systems, the notions of computing systems and communication systems basically become so intertwined that any efforts to distinguish them as computing and communications result in a difficult and meaningless exercise. In this chapter, we discuss basic components of a multimedia system. Where appropriate, differences from a traditional computing system will be pointed out explicitly along with the associated challenges.

COMPONENTS OF A MULTIMEDIA SYSTEM

Computing systems have evolved with advances in technology and the changing requirements of users. At a very high level, such systems can still be considered the same and be used to understand major evolutionary changes in different aspects of computing as multimedia started playing roles and started enforcing new requirements. The traditional computing architecture is shown in Figure 9.1. It consists of four basic components: processing unit, storage, input, and output. In this section, we consider the changes in this basic architecture to accommodate multimedia systems. A fundamental requirement of many multimedia systems is that audio and video must be rendered continuously, maintaining specified time constraints as required by an application.

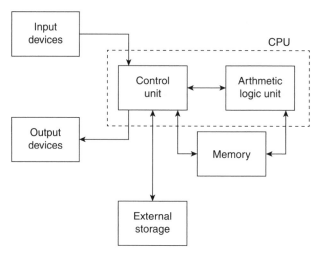

Figure 9.1. The basic components of a traditional computing system are: Processing unit, Storage, Input, and Output. The system must coordinate activities among all these components.

In a traditional computing system, most input is an independent data stream that may have inherent temporal relationships within its data elements. Such data can be considered as one stream independent of any other data sources/streams. Even in cases when data is coming from many sources, the system considers them independent sources and can process, send, and receive them using different networks. This is because the semantics of each stream are independent of those of other streams. Using this data characteristic as a fundamental assumption. traditional systems as well as many current systems deal with data streams that are independent of each other and hence can be processed, transmitted in networks in packets, and assembled at the receiver independent of other streams. In multimedia systems, as shown in Figure 9.2, data streams have semantics that are intertwined, and efforts to consider them independently result in loss of semantics and information. This intertwining of data streams and joint semantics is what makes multimedia systems different and needs to be considered in most components of multimedia systems. Some aspects and approaches for this intertwining and maintaining semantics of multimedia streams are discussed in the previous chapter on synchronization.

Processing Unit

The brain of computers are their processing units. The fundamental processing units in digital computers remain the same, though they have become many orders of magnitude faster, smaller, and cheaper. A mobile phone today packs more processing power than the computers that occupied large, air-conditioned rooms. Another major difference is that processing can be distributed using powerful networks so many, sometimes millions, processors located geographically at different places may function in concert as one processor.

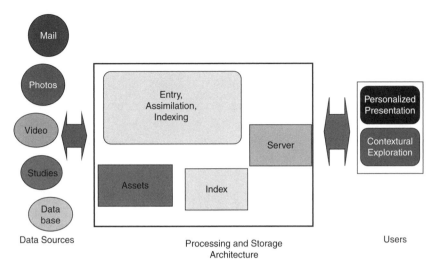

Figure 9.2. A multimedia computing system has the same architecture as the traditional computing system, with the major difference that all the components have now become very sophisticated because of the use of multiple sensory data as well as the need to manage and organize this data. Most modern systems now have architecture that is similar to the one shown in this figure.

Storage

During the past six decades of digital computing, many different types of storage mechanisms have evolved and continue to change. Many levels of storage systems have been designed based on their relationships to the processing units. These are commonly called main (or primary) memory, secondary memory, and tertiary memory. Like processing units, storage units at every level have seen enormous growth in their capacity and speed with equally dramatic reductions in their cost. Memories now have their own processing units to make them more effective in communicating with the processing unit as well as with input output devices. However, the fundamental nature and role of memory remains the same: store binary data. All multimedia data is ultimately converted to binary data along with its associated metadata that is also binary.

Input/Output Devices

All multimedia input devices are sensors that capture physical measurements in an environment and convert it to a signal that is then converted to its digital form and handled in the system appropriately. This will be discussed in depth in the subsequent part of this book. In addition to the sensor inputs, metadata is often used to conserve the spatial and temporal relationships among various signals, as already discussed in Chapter 2. Each signal type is then finally rendered in its type using a physical device. Thus, audio signals captured using a microphone must be rendered using a speaker and visual signals captured using a camera must be rendered using a display device. The characteristics of the output device on which a signal is rendered should meet characteristics of the input device for reproducing the signal in the same way. We discussed some characteristics of these in other chapters. Details of these should be found from the manuals from the devices and are not discussed here.

Networking

Traditional computing used input from local devices and the output was also provided to local devices. With the popularity of PCs, the World Wide Web, and cloud computing, communication became a major component of computing, and that expanded the role of networks in computing. Once communication grew popular and multimedia devices started becoming affordable, the nature of computing went through a major transformation. The first decade of this century saw major growth in audiovisual information, experiential knowledge, and audiovisual communication and entertainment. Multimedia information is naturally produced at one place and is edited, stored, and disseminated at other geographic locations. Increasingly, live communications rely, however, on large volumes of data transferred as high-fidelity and high-definition data across the world. To feed this trend, most mobile phones are now multimedia communication devices and more than 75 percent of the population of the world owns one. All these facts suggest that in the near future, we are likely to see increasing use of multimedia communications in all aspects of human activities. This is a very important consideration in multimedia systems.

In current multimedia systems, input devices convert the analog signals commonly created in the physical world to digital signals and then these digital signals are appropriately processed and stored. Similarly, all digital signals must be converted to analog signals for rendering them in consumable form. This is shown in Figure 9.3. Because most data is processed and stored as digital signals, all multimedia communication is mediated by computing systems. In the figure, we show only two different nodes for input and output of the multimedia data streams. One must consider several such nodes and consider how these nodes are placed and how they are related in space and time to understand how multimedia systems may be designed.

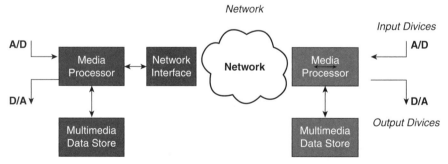

Figure 9.3. Multimedia communication systems capture and render signals in analog form, but process and store it in digital format. This makes computing systems an essential component of communication systems.

DIFFERENT CONFIGURATIONS OF MULTIMEDIA NODES

Multimedia content is created and consumed in many different forms. The way content is created and then distributed determines the architecture and technology required. In this chapter, we discuss some modes that have been commonly used for some time and others that are evolving rapidly and are likely to be common in the near future. Before discussing different modes of multimedia consumption, we briefly discuss the notions of *Quality of Service* (QoS) and *Quality of Experience* (QoE) that are used in quantitatively characterizing parameters for measuring performance of the overall system as well as using these parameters for controlling resources in the system.

QOS AND QOE

Quality of Service is commonly used to define and control performance of applications distributed over several computing resources. For applications that consume many resources (including processing, storage, bandwidth, and I/O devices), techniques to ensure end-to-end service quality by managing resource utilization are essential. As we will see, resource management and protocol implementation need to consider the effect of decisions on the overall performance of the system as perceived by the user. QoS allows specification of the expected performance of the system by combining effects at different layers of the system. QoS specifications must consider a multitude of properties including performance characteristics, availability, responsiveness, dependability, security, and adaptability of individual layers and components.

In developing approaches to specify QoS, one considers descriptions of quantitative QoS parameters (jitter, delay, and bandwidth) and qualitative QoS parameters, such as processor scheduling policy and error recovery mechanisms. QoS specifications must be declarative in nature. They should specify what is required without specifying how the requirement should be carried out. Finally, these declarative specifications should be accompanied by a process to map the specification to underlying system mechanisms and policies.

Quality of Experience (QoE) is related to but different from QoS. QoE is a subjective measure of a user's experiences with a media element as delivered by the system. Unlike QoS, which focuses on the performance of the system and is measured in objective terms such as delays, use of bandwidth, and jitter, Quality of Experience systems try to quantify what customers will directly perceive as a quality parameter. QoE usually measures and characterizes the performance in subjective terms. Thus, most QoE measures require human evaluations. On the other hand, in QoS, measurable system parameters are used to characterize the system performance.

DIFFERENT MODES OF MEDIA DELIVERY

Different applications of multimedia require different modes of media delivery approaches. In the following, we first discuss common media delivery modes and then discuss the implications of these modes for system design.

Stored Video

In this mode, a video stream has been acquired, edited, and stored on a server. This video is now ready for distribution. The video data contains two major streams, one containing an image sequence and the other containing an audio stream. Both these may be already compressed and stored, with proper synchronization information. Depending on the location of the user, the copyright and other business issues, and the technical specifications of the server and client, the video may be made available in one of the possible two modes.

Download and Play

In this mode, the whole video is first downloaded on the client so it is stored there. Then the user can play it. In this mode, the client requires enough storage, and the video is downloaded once and then can be played many times.

Streaming Multimedia

Streaming multimedia usually means real-time transmission of stored video such that it is rendered at the client maintaining synchronization among different components. In some cases, even live video from multiple locations could be combined into streaming multimedia components.

In streaming mode, the content to the client need not be fully downloaded before it starts rendering. While later parts of media components are being downloaded, the streaming player starts playing the media. In effect, the system maintains a buffer of the content by estimating network conditions so the application can display media to users while guaranteeing quality of experience.

Figure 9.4 shows components of a streaming video system. In the following, we discuss the components of streaming media systems, considering the most common example of video streaming.

Application Layer QoS Control: In networks, packet loss and congestion affect the timing and quality of streams received. Application layer QoS control is responsible for maximizing video quality even when packet loss takes place. Network congestion may result in bursty loss and excessive delays. Congestion control techniques attempt to minimize the effect of congestion by matching the transmission rate of the media stream to the projected available bandwidth. These techniques usually try to control the rate based on source, receiver, or both.

Continuous Media Distribution Services: Audio, video, and other media streams are continuous media because they represent a sequence of media values that are time ordered and make sense only in that order for the media as well as in relation to other media. Moreover, with respect to other media, synchronization is required to preserve the semantics as well as the quality of the experience. Because this media is transmitted over the Internet, using IP protocol, the sequence of received data may not be the same as transmitted. From the early days of the Internet, researchers have developed many techniques to address this problem. Some approaches used are discussed later in this chapter.

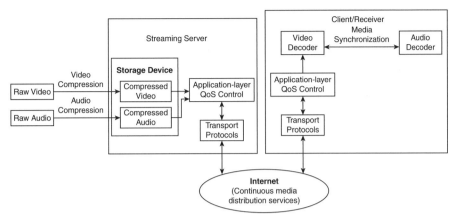

Figure 9.4. A streaming media system uses a streaming server to manage data that must be sent to clients. The clients should use appropriate mechanisms to interpret the protocol and render the streaming data in proper synchronized order.

In many applications, the rate at which the video server sends the data does not need to be the same as the one received at the client. *Network filtering* techniques maximize video quality by estimating network congestion and adapting the rate of video streams according to the network status. These filters may be placed in the network so they do not load the server. Server and clients may have separate channels for control signals and for data to the filter.

In many applications, media distribution may use *IP Multicast*. In normal applications, content or data is delivered to only one client. In IP Multicast, the content is delivered simultaneously to multiple clients by building such a service on top of the Internet protocol. This allows application providers to build their multicast services to send their content simultaneously to multiple consumers on top of the regular Internet.

For improving scalability of media delivery, *content replication* techniques have been developed and used. Two common approaches for content replication are caching and mirroring. These are used for reducing the load on the streaming servers, reducing bandwidth requirements, improving latency for clients, and for increasing availability to more clients. Mirroring techniques estimate requests for the content from different locations and place a copy of the original content at multiple locations in the network. Multiple users are then directed to the copy that is relatively locally stored. This reduces bandwidth requirement and latency for all users. Caching of the content is more local to individual clients. For a client, use of specific content is predicted and cached for delivery reducing latency.

Streaming Servers: In many applications, the data from a server to client is transmitted with the assumption that it will not be stored on the client. In such applications, streaming servers must process multimedia data under timing constraints to meet presentation requirements at the clients. They must also meet requests for stop, pause/resume, fast forward, and fast backward operations. Retrieving different media components and presenting them while guaranteeing synchronization requirements is also their responsibility. Streaming servers use three main components to make this happen: Communicator,

Operating System, and Storage System. As shown in Figure 9.4, the communicator involves the application layer and transport protocols. A client communicates with a server and receives multimedia contents continuously while meeting synchronization requirements. The operating system requirements in multimedia systems are significantly different compared to general computers. The operating system for such streaming services must satisfy real-time requirements for streaming applications. Similarly, the storage system has to consider the continuous nature of media components and support storage and retrieval to meet those requirements.

Like an operating system in a general computing system, a real-time operating system is responsible for controlling and coordinating all resources in the computing environment by considering all requests and managing and scheduling all resources including processors, main memory, storage, and input/output devices. The major new requirement is to manage additional requirements resulting from the large volumes of continuous data that also have synchronization and timing requirements. The added requirements in real-time operating systems in multimedia computing are addressed by considering process management for addressing the timing requirements of streaming media, resource management for meeting timing requirements, and file management to address storage management.

Storage management for multimedia data becomes challenging because of the large volume of continuous data, high throughput, strict synchronization requirements, and fault tolerance. One of the most challenging issues has been related to high throughput requirements for the data while maintaining synchronization among different streams. Three commonly explored approaches have been: data stripping, disk-based storage, and hierarchical storage. Data stripping techniques are used to allow multiple users to access the same video content at high throughput. A video is split into many segments and these segments are scattered on multiple disks, which can be accessed in parallel. This scheme allows multiple users to access different segments in parallel, enabling high throughput. In this scheme, multiple disk arrays are used to manage large volume of video data. These disk arrays can become very large and expensive. Cost considerations result in the hierarchical storage architecture. Thus, one uses three levels of storage: memory, primary storage commonly in the form of disks and disk arrays, and tertiary memory in the form of tape library. For larger-scale deployment of content services, storage area networks comprising high-speed data pipes and multiple storage centers are implemented.

Media Synchronization: The semantics as well as the quality of experience of multimedia depend on ascertaining proper synchronization among different streams. Synchronization becomes challenging because of the nature of current networks and protocols designed for traditional data streams.

Protocols for Streaming Media: Communication between clients and streaming servers is specified at three different levels: network layer, transport, and session control. For addressing and basic services in the network, IP used commonly in Internet services is also used by multimedia services. Transport protocols, such as user datagram protocol (UDP) and transmission control protocol (TCP) are used at the lower layer for basic transport of data. Real time transport protocol (RTP) and real time control protocol (RTCP) are implemented on top of those basic data protocols and used to manage multimedia communication. During a session between a client and a stream server, all messages and control communications use session control protocols. Real time streaming protocol (RTSP) is used for establishing and controlling sessions. This protocol is responsible for specifying and performing familiar VCR-like operations. Session initiation protocol (SIP) is used for creating, modifying, or terminating communications using multiple media streams. The compressed media data streams are assigned sequence numbers as well as associated synchronization information. These packetized streams are then passed to UDP/TCP layers, which in turn pass this to the IP layer for transporting to the Internet. The control signals using RTCP and RTSP packets are multiplexed and move to the IP layer for transport over the Internet.

LIVE VIDEO

Video is the most common form of streaming media. A video usually combines at least two continuous media: audio and image sequences. In many applications, text streams may also be associated. Recently, tactile and other media are also being combined in special applications of video. In this section, some established modes of video are discussed along with some emerging forms of video. It is important to see how different types of streams are prepared and consumed to design architectures for these systems. It is expected that this area will remain very active, and with advances in technology, many new modes and applications will emerge. However, in this section we will discuss only those modes that have been active for some time.

One Camera Video

A significant fraction of video applications uses video captured using only one video camera. Such video usually has single image and audio streams and both those streams are captured using closely located camera and microphone. During the editing process, other streams may be added, but in this case, synchronization issues are the easiest and video can be easily transmitted using common video transfer or streaming techniques.

Multiple Camera Videos/Produced as Single

Most sports and entertainment videos are captured using multiple cameras and then edited and produced into a single video stream. If the video streams are edited just by selecting cameras and their associated audio stream in a particular segment, then synchronization issues remain easy. If one selects an image stream from one camera and an audio stream from another camera or an independent microphone, then in the editing phase one must consider the relative location of the image and audio source to synchronize them to make them natural. In this case, the editor has to take care of synchronization issues during the editing phase. Once the video is produced, it becomes a single video stream stored on the server and transported always as a single stream.

Multiple Perspectives Interactive (MPI) Video

The traditional model of television and video is based on a single video stream transmitted to a viewer. A viewer has the option to watch and to use standard VCR controls in recorded video, but little else. In many applications, such as in sports, several cameras are used to capture an event. A human producer decides which video stream should be transmitted to users at any given time in the event. Thus, the producer acts like a multiplexer deciding the stream that is transmitted while blocking all other streams. This model ignores the fact that different people may be interested in different perspectives of the event and hence may consider a different sequencing of events more desirable. Multiple Perspective Interactive Video, or MPI Video, can provide true interactivity to viewers. A viewer could view an event from multiple perspectives, even based on the content of the events. MPI video may overcome several limitations of the conventional video and provide interactivity essential in applications ranging from scientific inventions to entertainment. In the conventional video, viewers are passive; all they can do is control the flow of video by pressing buttons such as play, pause, fast forward, or fast reverse. These controls essentially provide you only one choice for a particular segment of video: you can see it or skip it. In the case of TV broadcast, viewers have essentially no control. Even in those sports and other events where multiple cameras are used, a viewer has no choice except the obvious one of keeping the channel or using the remote control and channel surfing.

An MPI video system integrates a variety of visual computing operations along with three-dimensional modeling and visualization techniques to provide automatic analysis and interactive access to data coming from multiple cameras concurrently monitoring an environment. The system creates a three-dimensional model of dynamic objects, for example, people and vehicles, within this environment, and provides tracking and data management of these objects. Using this information, the system supports user queries regarding the content of the three-dimensional scene. Such a system is shown in Figure 9.5.

In MPI video systems, the system knows the location of various cameras and the locations of objects of interest at every time instant. Such a system could then create a dynamic sequence of video based on a user's request. Because there could be many users and each

Multiple Perspective Interactive Video

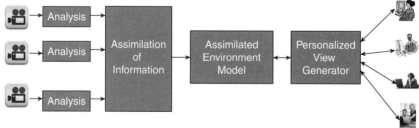

Figure 9.5. In an immersive video system, including a Multiple Perspective Interactive Video, multiple video sources are individually analyzed to extract object information. This information is assimilated at every time instant into an environment model containing all relevant 3D information objects. This model can then be used to generate personalized views for each user.

may have a different request, the system must prepare as many different video sequences as different queries.

Immersive Video

Immersive video is a further enhanced version of MPI video. In immersive video, one uses visual analysis and reconstruction techniques to create a complete three-dimensional model of the environment observed by the cameras. This model contains all dynamic objects and also has their models in the system. Because the system has a complete three-dimensional model of the environment, it can recreate the scene from any perspective that a user wants. This may allow a user to imagine that he is standing on a football field where players are in action and is observing all actions as in a virtual reality system. In fact, these systems could be called real reality systems because they create the model of a real world to allow a user to experience this world in its complete visual reality.

The high-level software architecture of an immersive video system contains the following components:

1. A video data analyzer detects objects from each individual input video.

2. An environment model builder combines a priori knowledge of the scene with information obtained by the video data analyzers to form a comprehensive model of the dynamic environment.

3. A visualizer generates a realistic, virtual video sequence as interactively requested by the user.

EMERGING SYSTEMS

Multimedia systems are going through rapid evolution. Just two decades ago, most computing used only alphanumeric data. All computing systems were designed to deal with limited data types and their creators did not consider continuous media in their design. Today, the main computing and communication client is a smartphone. Smartphones have more media power, in terms of number of sensors, than human beings. Using these devices and social networks, communications are becoming multimedia contextual experience sharing rather than abstract textual description of experiences. It is difficult to imagine how we will share our experiences with people and how we will record and advance knowledge in the future. What is clear is that the evolution of this trend is going to continue for some time. In this section, we presented fundamental nature of multimedia systems. To understand details, one must approach vast literature in this area.

RECOMMENDED READING

A significant number of research efforts in computing systems design after 1990 has addressed issues related to multimedia. Many issues in designing input/output, networks, and storage management are dominated by the requirement of multimedia. Video pushed technologists to deal with storage, communication, and presentation issues and continues to dominate in its demand on technology. Lately, combination of text, images, audio, and video became dominant. With the emergence of mobile devices as clients, these research issues have remained dominant and are likely to push both development and use of technology. In this book, we did not make any effort to bring to the center all the systems issues. Our goal was to show the fundamental issues that are the result of multimedia computing and communications. We also wanted to indicate the directions of technology as it is emerging at the time of publication of this book. We will update this with time.

The article by Wu and colleagues is a very rich resource for concepts as well as related sources for streaming media. We strongly recommend this article for anybody interested in this area. Any modern book on networks and systems discusses different issues and protocols related to streaming media in current network systems. We recommend that researchers and practitioners interested in knowing more details about these topics start with the book by Steinmetz and Nahestedt.

One of the most promising emerging area in multimedia systems is immersive environments. This is clearly the next step of multimedia systems that capture real environments and then present them remotely in immersive and interactive ways. These systems are in the early stages, but are likely to emerge as powerful multimedia systems that will play a key role in many aspects of human life. One should not confuse these systems with virtual reality systems or augmented reality systems. In virtual reality systems, the environment rendered for a user does not come from a real environment. In augmented reality, a photo or some other media is augmented with information from the real world. Immersive systems capture real environments using multiple sensors and then render this remotely for providing telepresence.

Further Reading

J. F. Allen. "Maintaining knowledge about temporal intervals," *Comm. of the ACM*, 26 (11): 832–43, November 1983.

Jingwen Jin and Klara Nahrstedt. "QoS specification languages for distributed multimedia applications: A survey and taxonomy," *IEEE Multimedia*, July 2004.

Min-Yen Kan. "SlideSeer: A digital library of aligned document and presentation pairs," in Proceedings of the Joint Conference on Digital Libraries (JCDL '07). Vancouver, Canada, June 2007.

T. Kanade, P. Rander, and P. J. Narayanan. "Virtualized reality: Constructing virtual worlds from real scenes," *IEEE Multimedia*, January 1997.

A. Katkere, S. Moezzi, D. Kuramura, P. Kelly, and R. Jain. "Towards video-based immersive environments," *ACM-Springer Multimedia Systems Journal, Special Issue on Multimedia and Multisensory Virtual Worlds*, Spring 1996.

S. Moezzi, A. Katkere, D. Kuramura, and R. Jain. "An emerging medium, interactive three-dimensional digital video," *IEEE Multimedia*, June 1996.

Ralf Steinmetz and Klara Nahrstedt. *Multimedia Systems* (X.media.publishing). December 2, 2010.

Greg Thompson and Yih-Farn Robin Chen. "IPTV reinventing television in the Internet age," *IEEE Internet Computing*, May 2009.

Dapeng Wu, Yiwei Thomas Hou, Wenwu Zhu, Ya-Qin Zhang, and Jon M. Peha. "Streaming video over the Internet: Approaches and directions," *IEEE Transactions on Circuits and Systems for Video Technology*, 11 (3), March 2001.

Zhenyu Yang, Wanmin Wu, K. Nahrstedt, G. Kurillo, and R. Bajcsy. "Enabling multi-party 3D tele-immersive environments with ViewCast," *ACM Transactions on Multimedia Computing, Communications, and Applications* (TOMCCAP), 6, 2010.

EXERCISES

1. What are the fundamental differences in a multimedia computing system from a traditional system dealing with only alphanumeric data? Explain your answer considering the fact that ultimately each multimedia data stream is a numeric data stream.

2. In a multimedia system, inputs and outputs are not alphanumeric data. What other factors or I/O are important in system design? Explain your answer.

3. Is it important to consider individual media streams in terms of their temporal nature and their viewpoints in processing and communicating them through the system? Why?

4. What specific considerations of storage must one consider when dealing with multimedia data?

5. Why does one require complex storage architectures to deal with multimedia data? Explain considering an application.

6. What role does compression play in multimedia systems? Does it introduce any additional operations in I/O systems?

7. What special considerations are required in networks to deal with multimedia data, particularly video streams? Is standard packet-based Internet protocol satisfactory for multimedia streams? Why?

8. What is Quality of Service (QOS)? How is it used in network design?

9. Can we use QOS specifications for the design of multimedia systems? How?

10. What is Quality of Experience (QoE)? How is it different from QoS?

11. What is streaming media? How is it different from stored media?

12. What special considerations are required in playing streaming media?

13. What is a video server? Compare a video server to a Web server.

14. What is Multiple Perspective Interactive (MPI) video?

15. What is immersive video? Compare an MPI video system to an immersive video system. When will you use an immersive system and when will you use an MPI system?

10 The Human Factor

So far, we have mostly described ideal and typical environments. In this chapter, we will discuss some issues that designers need to consider when building multimedia systems. We call this chapter "The Human Factor" because the content of this chapter deals with effects that can be observed when multimedia systems are exposed to human beings. Of course, ultimately, all computer systems are made to be used by us human beings.

PRINCIPLES OF USER INTERFACE DESIGN

Most of today's applications, especially ones that support multimedia in any way, use a graphical user interface (GUI), that is, an interface that is controlled through clicks, touch and/or gestures and that allows for the display of arbitrary image and video data. Therefore, knowing how to design GUI-based applications in a user-friendly manner is an important skill for everybody working in multimedia computing. Unfortunately, with the many factors that go into the behavior of a program and the perceptual requirements of the user, there is no unique path or definite set of guidelines to follow. Here is an example: Is it better to have the menu bar inside the window of an application, or is it better to have one menu bar that is always at the same place and changes with the application?[1] As we assume the reader knows, this is one fundamental difference between Apple and Microsoft's operating systems – and it is hard to say one or the other is right or wrong. However, some standards have evolved over many years, using research results and feedback from many users. These standards can be seen in many places today in desktop environments, smartphones, DVD players, and other devices.

This chapter presents rules that will help build multimedia applications that provide a good experience to the user. The examples are mostly based on the GUI standards at the time of writing this book. Ideally, many issues will not arise anymore when the typical point and click GUI has been replaced by applications with immersive sensor experience. In the meantime, how can we make our multimedia application friendly to its human user?

There is no easy answer to this question. Therefore, we opt to focus on a few important aspects of human-computer interaction (HCI) that we think provide enough introduction

---

[1]   This particular example has been studied quite thoroughly; see the references for details.

Figure 10.1. The developers of an application thinking inside out is one of the most frequent causes of bad user interface design. This real-world example of a confusing dialog box presented itself to the authors during the creation of this chapter. The content is probably only useful for the programers who know the application from the inside. What would provide a better experience? In this case the solution would be to not show any dialog at all as the fault is purely technical with no consequence to the user.

for the reader to be able to start thinking about the major issues and to continue studying the field. We start with general rules of user interface development and then continue with an introduction to human-based evaluation. We want to point out, though, that user interface design is not an exact science. Therefore, many solutions might exist apart from the ones pointed out here. Furthermore, some rules stated here might be wrong in a different context. Many of the examples shown here could not be derived from general principles, but are based on anecdotal evidence and experiences.

Thinking outside in: There is one important principle that we believe is universally true for any machine or application interface: never assume that the user knows what is happening inside the program. This is called "thinking inside out." The interface should assume no knowledge of any kind of the insides of the program. While this seems obvious, it is more than easy to accidentally require much more knowledge about a program than a user has because the creator of the program has intimate expert knowledge. Most user interface glitches are the result of a violation of this rule. When we introduce ourselves to people, we start with stating our name and then go on to a small selection of facts that are relevant in the context of the conversation. A program should follow the same guideline: it should present itself inside the user interface conventions of the particular device and then only expose those details the user requires and expects. If the program "introduces" itself with difficult technical details, the user, especially a first-time user, will probably reduce his or her interaction to finding a way to end the program and think about a different solution to his or her problem. The dialog box in Figure 10.1, from a modern, heavily used application, shows a bad real-world example of a developer thinking inside out. The dialog box is completely useless to the user as there are no actual consequences when using the system. It would have been better to put this message into a debugging console so that developers who understand the message can react accordingly.

Task orientation: In multimedia applications, designers tend to present users with as many outputs (that is, different media) as possible. This is often confusing to the users, who would find the system easier to use if there were fewer choices. Choosing wisely is the key here. Most important, one has to focus on what the task is and what the user is capable of once the technology fulfills all requirements. Larry Wall, the creator of the PERL programming language, is often quoted saying: "Common things should be easy, advanced

Figure 10.2. Left: An "OK" button in a normal dialog box usually suggests everything went fine. In this case a process failed, however, so the user should be presented with a warning message. Right: Our suggestion on how the dialog box with a warning message should look.

things should be at least possible." Especially for multimedia applications, this means having the function in mind first and then the presentation.

A common example that demonstrates this is: just because you have several hundred fonts to choose from doesn't mean a document should use all of them. In fact, typical publications only use one to three fonts because most readers would not find it appealing to look at a mess of fonts. Figure 10.2 shows a more subtle example of this problem: a user is presented with a dialog box when a problem occurs. Technology-wise, it is easiest to think of any warning message as a dialog box. Task-wise, this could result in disappointment and frustration for the user as an "OK" button in a dialog box usually suggests everything went fine. In this case, a process failed, however, so the user should receive a warning message.

In general, when designing the user interface to your application you should ask yourself the following questions:

1) What are the (mental and physical) capabilities of the user, for example, what are the technical terms the user understands?
2) What tasks is the program helping the user to achieve and what information has to be presented and asked from the user for doing so?
3) What are the upper and lower limits for resource requirements needed to accomplish the tasks, for example, how much disk space is required and how much memory has to be allocated? A typical error made here is to restrict array lengths arbitrarily and to expose the limitation to the user. Many of the year-2000 bugs fell into this category, as developers underestimated how long their application would be used. In the multimedia community, screen resolutions and sampling rates have often been part of this problem.
4) How can the application make the most important tasks easy and quick and the less frequent tasks at least possible? In other words, find the right compromise between the ease of use and the complexity of the program.

The most common issue for multimedia computing in this regard is probably a device that everybody has at home in abundance: the remote control. Remote controls are inherently technology oriented, especially multi-device remote controls used to command TVs, DVRs, and home theater systems alike. While some of the buttons, such as volume control, program up and down, and play and pause show standardized symbols, most other buttons look different on every type of remote control, and most users will agree that the

Figure 10.3. The electronic chalkboard system E-Chalk is an example of a multimedia system that would not work with the desktop metaphor.

function of some buttons remains a mystery forever. A task-oriented remote control would only show buttons that are interesting to the user at a given point (e.g., when the DVR is used to playback a recording, the program buttons could be grayed out). Also, buttons that are rarely used should be hidden in an advanced setting. Of course, this is harder to realize with a physical remote control, but it is possible in a display-based remote, for example, on a cell phone (see exercises).

False creativity: Suppose you meet with your friends to play soccer. You have been doing this together for a long time, but this time you decide to change the rules without telling them. Small children know that such a behavior will most likely lead to confusion, frustration, and conflict. The same applies to user interface design. When the device or operating system manufacturer sets a standard for certain GUI elements to behave a certain way, your program should not change the behavior. You must understand the rules for a certain GUI element (such as a modal dialog box) and not use the element in a different way. Like the soccer example, doing so will lead to confusion and frustration for the user and also potentially to conflict with other applications that share GUI elements. Some device manufacturers also enforce GUI standards and will likely cause you to redo your interface during quality assurance. While this rule is true for any application, multimedia applications are the most prone to tempt you to abuse predefined UI components. The reason for this is that conventional operating system interfaces are originally created for text and mouse input and output while multimedia applications might deal with various inputs and require content-based selection and editing operations. Figure 10.3 shows an example of a system that uses a chalkboard metaphor instead of a desktop metaphor. As of the writing of this book, most of these are not yet standardized. As a result, many requirements of the desktop metaphor had to be ignored when designing the system and replaced by rules that make more sense. The recommendation here is to stay as close as possible to the interface standard and only take as much freedom as is required. Finding the right and

Figure 10.4. Fostering the learning process the wrong way: Even an experienced user will have to think twice to know which button to press. This is a case where the functionality should not be available to the user in this way. In our opinion, there are two ways to fix this: Not allow changes by non-meeting organizers or allow changes by non-organizers but automatically notify the organizers of the changes.

intuitive solution might require user interface studies, as explained later in this chapter. Another firm rule here is that the user should never have to perform unnatural or unintuitive actions. For example, having to drag the trashcan to the file rather than the file into the trashcan or having to perform special mouse click patterns to perform certain actions.

Fostering learning: One of your goals as an application developer should be to bind the user to your program for a long time. This is best achieved when the user incorporates your application into daily life and thinks of it when a new problem comes up. A user's first use of any program is likely to be something simple, but each task should increase the user's understanding of the program so that the user gradually learns to use the application to solve more sophisticated problems. In this way it is very likely that the application will become an important tool in a user's life.

To foster the learning process, your application interface should follow one concrete philosophy. For example, many operating systems follow the desktop metaphor, therefore using terms like "folder," "file," and/or "trash bin." Sticking to the metaphor or philosophy is very important; inconsistencies or contradictions should be avoided. Most important, the environment should be made riskless along the philosophy. For example: like in real life, things put in the trash bin can also be taken out of it when they haven't been in the bin for too long. Undo and redo functionality makes using computers for typewriting even less risky than using a physical typewriter. Riskless environments promote learning because making a mistake is not penalized heavily, encouraging exploration. Another example is intelligent default values: they help exploration because the user can see what happens before understanding what the values mean. Figure 10.4 shows another bad real-world example: even an experienced user would have to think twice about whether to say "Yes" or "Cancel."

Another property of a program that promotes learning is transparency. Of course, the user does not always have to know what is going on – this would contradict the first paradigm of not thinking inside out. However, the user should always know what is expected of him and what he can expect from the computer. So if a certain action triggers an LED to light up, it should always do that. Programs should also not start tasks on their own without educating the user about it. Numerous system tools, such as virus scanners, have violated that rule in the past, by starting background or update processes with the result that the user becomes frustrated because the computer is slower or unresponsive without the user causing any action. A typical multimedia example here is fast forwarding or rewinding a video using a typical Internet player interface: often it is not clear how long the process will take because it depends on the encoding of the video and the bandwidth of the connection between video server and player client. So many users don't even want to touch the controls once a video has started playing. This issue is called *responsiveness*.

Responsiveness refers to the ability of a program to complete a task within a given time. The paradigm of transparency requires educating a user about tasks that will take longer than expected. For example, when the computer is not responsive because of a compute or an I/O-intensive operation, a busy cursor should be displayed, otherwise the user will think something is wrong. If the operation takes longer than a while, the operation should be cancelable and a progress indicator should indicate the estimated time until completion of the operation.

Responsiveness has been studied, especially in connection with multimedia computing. The general rule is that when a program cannot respond to user interaction for more than one to three seconds (depending on the general responsiveness of the device), the user should see an indicator for this being normal, for example, an hourglass cursor. Other rules of thumb include the following: if an operation occupies the machine for more than ten seconds, the application should show a progress bar. Operations of twenty seconds or longer or for which the duration is hard to determine should show a progress indicator and should also be easily cancelable. Operations that take several minutes, for example, the conversion of videos from one format to another, should inform the user of this and prompt confirmation.

Sometimes it can be tricky to assess the time duration of an operation because the computation time to perform a task varies from computer to computer, depends on the data being processed, and may change with available bandwidth. One solution to the problem is to perform a small subset of the task (e.g., convert only a couple seconds of a video) and then estimate how long the completion of the entire task will take. It is usually acceptable to slightly overestimate. Another solution might be to perform the task in the background (e.g., on a secondary CPU core) and have the computer not be unresponsive to user interaction. Rather than disabling all the interaction, only interaction that depends on the task being completed is disabled. For example, further operation on a video being converted might be prevented, but loading a second video might still be enabled. So the user may choose to perform a different task instead of waiting. Of course, it must be transparent to the user what the computer is occupied with and what interaction is still possible. A third solution that works particularly well with many multimedia applications is to visualize the progress in addition to showing a progress bar. For example, when transforming a video, the program could show the frame currently being processed. While this does not cut down on processing time – in fact, it will most likely increase processing time – it might cut down on perceived processing time as the user is engaged in the visualization of the content. As explained earlier, user interface design is not about objective numbers; it is about subjective satisfaction.

Test your program with real users: the most important rule is to always test your application with real users. The aforementioned principles and rules are neither comprehensive nor do they guarantee success of an application. Furthermore, let's assume you think your program presents itself in a learning-promoting way and hides exactly the right amount of details. How can you be sure? After all, you might be thinking inside out.

The rest of this chapter will introduce the basics of human-based evaluation.

Evaluation of Software through Human Subjects

Dix formulated a simple equation for the measurement of the usability of a program:

$$Usability = Effectiveness + Efficiency + Satisfaction$$

Of course, quantifying the parameters of the equation is not only complicated, but subjective. Different parameters might have different importance in different applications. In a computer game, for example, satisfaction probably equals effectiveness. Depending on the game, efficiency might or might not matter. So how does one measure the usability of an application?

Again, there is no silver bullet to measure the usability of an application. An often used method in the industry is to equate user satisfaction with profit. For example, one of two Web page designs is shown to new visitors at random and then the company appearance is further optimized in the direction of the page that results in most sales. The method is called "split test." The main drawback of the method is that sales numbers might correlate with many other factors and decreasing sales numbers might not be caused by bad Web page design. Two more verifiable methods are the video surveillance tests and questionnaires. Of the two, video surveillance tests are probably the most effective.

Video Surveillance Test

For a video surveillance test, candidates are chosen that represent the typical users of a particular application. It is best to select persons to represent a variety in gender, age, and ethical, social, and educational background. The candidates are then given a set of tasks to solve with the application. Sometimes it can be effective to also set a time limit. With the consent of the participants, video equipment records audio and video of the users' behavior together with the screen of the running application. It is best to not at all interfere with the test participants and to isolate the test subjects so that they cannot interfere with each other before, during, and after the test. Keep in mind that, often, the experiments as well as the subjects do not know what kinds of issues they are looking for. Of course the tasks should be chosen wisely and probably in order of increasing difficulty. The tasks should be formulated generally enough so that a user does not only have to follow instructions, but has to figure out the steps to achieve the task on his or her own. It may sometimes make sense to ask for tasks that are not achievable. In any ways, to avoid frustration, clear instructions must be given what to do in the case that a user does not find a solution, for example, that he is allowed to skip a task. One of the most important suggestions with any kind of user study is that the higher the number of participants ("higher n") the better.

More participants will not only allow for a significant result, but also help to find errors both in the application and in the test setup. Unfortunately, too many user studies are still often performed using "*n=20* students from my department" because a video surveillance test with a high number of users is expensive and time consuming.

For example, a well-known beverage manufacturer created a new vending machine and used a video surveillance test to find out about users' reactions to interacting with the machine. After watching all the videos and discussing among management and developers, they found that everything seemed to be in order, except the user experience could be improved by an option to not only pay with coins, but also with bills. So this was added to the machine.

Questionnaires

To reach a greater audience, for example, over the Internet, questionnaires can be used. It is usually best to try a video surveillance test using a small set of participants first, address the issues raised as a result of the test in the application, and then create a questionnaire that targets the improvements in the application along with other issues raised in the video surveillance test. Questionnaires can only get feedback on potential problems that the maker of the questionnaire is already aware of. While adding free form space to a questionnaire is possible, one should not expect the most extensive feedback from it – after all, testers are not software developers!

Continuing the beverage manufacturer example: to quickly prove that allowing users to pay with bills was successful, another user study was performed. This time, many more people were asked to participate and the only thing they had to do was fill out a questionnaire rating their experience using the machine on a scale from one to ten. As a control, the old vending machine was tested with the same questionnaire. Now, most questionnaires for the new machine had a worse score than the control test using the old machine. Development and management were devastated: How could adding a feature that people wanted to a vending machine that was already quite good make the experience so much worse? The solution is this: when the vending machine only accepted coins, participants had been told in advance to bring coins. So the vending went smoothly and comments in the videos were mostly about details. Now that the vending machine also accepted bills, the participants were not told anything about payment modalities. As a result, most participants ended up not having coins and tried the bill slot. This would have been no issue, except the bill slot happened to not have worked very well because the bills could only be inserted in one particular way that the developers had already trained themselves to do. As a result, the machine did not work at all for many subjects because the bill was rejected several times, resulting in many participants just giving up. So while the rest of the vending machine stayed the same, adding a feature made the user experience of the vending machine much worse and finding out about it was hard from the survey questions as developers expected the responses to them to be mostly positive.

Good design and thorough reviewing of questionnaires is very important. A large number of well-filled-out questionnaires will lead to significant results that are reportable in scientific publications and to an improvement of the application.

Significance

Especially when surveys are performed for scientific publications the question often arises whether the outcome of the responses to a question on a questionnaire is statistically significant, that is, when performed for a second, third, and further time, would the questionnaire lead to the same results? In other words: Is the outcome of this questionnaire random or a valid result? Fortunately, statistics can help here. Significance testing allows the survey analyst to assess evidence in favor of some claim about the participants from which the sample has been drawn. We included references that give examples of how these techniques work.

In the end, though, mathematical significance testing is not a guarantee for actual results. Consider the following real-world example: to test a new audio codec, the developers compressed several audio files using the different codecs and let users on the Internet listen to the codecs and rate them according to their perceived quality. To their big surprise, the codec with the highest bandwidth got the worse results, which was obviously better than the worse codec whenever it was presented to individuals outside the test. The test was definitely repeatable and statistically significant. What had happened? The developers had used different audio recordings. However, the one using the highest-bandwidth codec was a speech recording from a nonnative speaker who some of the participants had a hard time understanding. This led the test subjects to give the codec a bad score because they had only been asked to rate "the perceived quality." So the mistake here was to not eliminate all factors. A short interview after the test might have helped eliminate this oversight in the first place.

Again, this example shows, there is no silver bullet, and human-computer interaction is a hard soft topic (hard in the sense of difficult and soft in the sense of not strictly logical). The reader is encouraged to delve into the literature for more information but, most important, to go ahead and try it out!

PRIVACY

Another issue that needs to be discussed as part of the human factor is privacy. While often related to GUI design, there are some unique issues regarding privacy and multimedia data. In contrast to written text, multimedia captures a snapshot of the reality without filtering. Even in staged scenarios, such as movies, people find bloopers that were not intended to be shown and were not part of any script. Spontaneous recordings such as vacation photographs of home videos show even more information that was not the focus of the attention of the creator. This must be taken into account when publishing photographs, audio, and video recordings on the Internet or elsewhere.

The widespread use of social Internet sites to disseminate multimedia materials is especially problematic. A photo of a person could be posted without the person knowing about it; the person in question might even have opted to not participate in the social networking site and is now forced to do so. In many countries, publishing a photograph of the face of a third person requires the permission of that person. Copyrighted objects, such as a painting in the background, require permission of the author or current copyright holder.

Figure 10.5. An example of geo-tagging allowing for easier search and retrieval of images. The photo shows a partial screenshot of flickr.com.

Both human intelligence and multimedia retrieval may be used on multimedia data to extract some of the unintended information. For example, face recognition or speaker identification (as described later in this book) may be used to find the identity of a person, even if the Web site has no other indication for a person's identity. This could de-anonymize Web site postings and accounts. Furthermore, multimedia retrieval, even though not perfectly accurate, makes it unsafe to say that data would be anonymous on the site: only one match of a face or voice between the anonymized site and a public site where the user's identity is known is enough to expose the user.

Metadata and annotation are also issues here. For example, tagging somebody publicly in a picture makes searching for that person's identity much easier as textual search has higher accuracy than multimedia search. Often, cameras and multimedia editing tools embed metadata in videos and images, the most common being the Exif header in JPEG images (as described in Chapter 3). Exif data can contain geo-tags, that is, longitude and latitude coordinates of the place where the photo was taken. Figure 10.5 shows an example. This is enabled through different localization systems, such as GPS and cell tower information, as well as wireless network SSID maps. Geo-tags in combination with time allow easy tracking of a person. Also, implicitly exposing places, such as home addresses, can be dangerous. Usually, when taking a photograph, the creator is not thinking about this metadata, and so will broadcast this valuable information in an otherwise anonymous post.

Because a potential attacker might gather information from different Web sites and infer from the collective, it becomes even harder to track what information is out there about an individual or entity. So conserving privacy becomes a difficult task.

Time is another variable in the equation. What people might find adequate to post and publish now might later be an issue for their reputation. The need for privacy shifts with age, social status, occupation, and other factors. On the other hand, the Internet potentially saves material forever and in many copies. Once data has been published, it might be downloaded by various search engines for caching and individuals might re-post it.

As multimedia researchers, we have special responsibility in this regard as we are the original enablers of most of the technology. Many people are unaware that multimedia retrieval technologies exist, and even many experts often fail to assess the capabilities of today's multimedia retrieval technologies and the potential inference possibilities. Even though current retrieval methods are not perfectly accurate, with billions of pictures and millions of videos available, even a seemingly small fraction of true positive results can enable de-anonymization, find potential victims for crimes, or reveal other secrets.

Countermeasures

The first thing to do is to check whether a particular post is really necessary. What is the target group of the post, and is it possible to make the post only available to that group? This is an example where appropriate GUI design is very useful. Privacy settings should be easily understandable to everybody and there should be a way of simulating "what if" scenarios to be able to tune privacy settings without actually changing them.

The most important privacy-conserving countermeasure, then, is to make sure the information that is published is only what is supposed to be published. Photos, for example, should not contain faces of people that were not involved, or at least these faces and other identifying characteristics should be blurred. Likewise, multimedia data should be checked for hidden metadata. If metadata is to be included, the level of detail should be controllable. Camera serial numbers might not be needed and geo-tags might be included with a reduced accuracy that is enough to organize the data but not enough to pinpoint individual addresses. Inserting noise into the signal that might or might not be audible might help to make it more difficult to apply acoustic matching. Applying compression often helps to reduce camera artifacts. Many of these measures can be automized and be part of the upload process. Appropriate visualization, for example, of metadata, can be part of the user interface.

These are only a few examples of privacy issues and countermeasures. Spotting the issues and inventing new methods to prevent them is an active area of research; we suggest the reader check out the literature.

SECURITY

Another part of the human factor is evilness and negligence. In computer systems, this is usually discussed as part of the field of computer security. Multimedia data often contribute to computer security issues. Malware can be embedded in various forms into videos and presentations. This is mostly enabled through the fact that some multimedia data formats are Turing complete, that is, their representation is powerful enough to allow the execution of arbitrary programs. Prominent examples of these formats are Postscript and Flash, the first being a printer language, the second being an interactive video and animation format. PDF, which has mostly replaced postscript, is intentionally not a Turing complete programming language.

Security breaches exploiting buffer overruns in multimedia formats have also been reported. Often, decoders and viewers of multimedia data are tailored to and tested only with regular images and videos. However, the nature of compression formats makes it possible to artificially create a video or image file that expands into a super large file upon decompression. The memory used to hold that overlarge data chunk could overwrite code, leading to crashes, or could be used to insert malicious code into the decoder/viewer. Several such viruses have been reported. These viruses are especially powerful because they spread when a person views an image or video embedded in a Web page or e-mail, thereby not even consciously executing a program.

Reportedly, programs using microphones and cameras have been built into laptops without notifying the user. This spy behavior inadvertently leads to trust issues as the user should be always informed about the fact that he or she is being recorded. More so, it should be clear what is being done with the recording and how to stop the recording at any time. A video feedback helps improve a user's trust in what's being recorded and or transmitted. Needless to say, in many countries recording a person without their knowledge is against the law.

SAFETY

Probably the most commonly discussed human factor of multimedia is that of the effect of multimedia content on people. Technically, humans could be interpreted as sensors perceiving the data encoded and then interpreting it. This can lead to emotional reactions ranging from entertainment and excitement to sadness and even trauma because multimedia data allows us to perceive people, objects, events, actions, and places that we would not otherwise know about. Perceiving things that are way out of their usual world can especially cause harm in children. Therefore, magazines, movies, and computer games are usually rated for a certain age group. While this is true for books as well, it's not as strongly enforced in most places – another indication of the power of direct encoding for perception. News broadcasts usually do not show scenes that are too cruel to not expose the audience to material that they may have never experienced and that potentially would lead to trauma and other negative psychologic effects. Some material, such as pornographic videos, is directly targeted to evoke certain emotions and even anatomic reactions.

The creation and distribution of certain multimedia material is forbidden in almost all countries. While different countries have different rules and reasons to prohibit handling different types of multimedia data, the cause usually is the same: society fears the power of multimedia data to directly manipulate people and is still researching long-term effects. An issue related to this is best described as "seeing is believing." A photo or video seems to more truthfully represent the world than text. As a consequence, a forged photo, audio recording, or video is more easily believed than text.

Multimedia data can also cause physical harm. The easiest example is audio that is too loud or pitched at a certain high frequency. Ear damage is caused by listening to ear phones too loudly. While this seems almost obvious, it is very important that any multimedia system has the ability to be shut down quickly, for example, with a pause button. When presenting sound, a user-friendly method of regulating the volume should be provided. People should not be exposed to loud pop sounds and/or be surprised by a sudden increase in volume. Pitch also plays a role. Certain tones can be perceived as uncomfortable when the audience is exposed to them for too long.

Visual data can also do harm. Spending too much time concentrating on low-contrast content, for example, reading yellow font on white background, will usually be reported as uncomfortable and is often considered a cause for headaches. Stroboscopic light, for example, induced by flashing monitors, can cause epileptic seizures. Many computer games warn about this issue. For the same reason, the Web Content Accessibility Guidelines (WCAG) Version 2.0, produced in 2008, specifies that content should not flash more than three times in any one-second period.

Three-dimensional video and augmented reality applications are sometimes the cause for sea sickness symptoms. The reason for this is that our visual perception does not exactly match our proprioception and other sensors and the reaction varies from person to person: from no reaction to dizziness and nausea. The effects of 3D displays on young children are currently discussed; because visual perception may not have fully developed yet, consuming artificial 3D data may cause perceptual issues due to the brain adapting to wrong realities.

Consuming multimedia data can also cause unwanted and potentially life-threatening distractions, especially when operating machinery or driving a car. While it is generally acknowledged that listening to music on moderate levels while driving is not harmful, listing to music using earphones is prohibited in many countries as the music would mask acoustic events from the outside and therefore reduce the ability of the driver to react to them. Watching a movie while driving would make it nearly impossible to drive a car, as the split attention effect (see Chapter 8) would slow down reactions to traffic to a very dangerous level even at low speeds. Operating a cell phone or a navigation system while driving has a similar negative effect.

It is possible to manipulate a human being in a very subtle way and potentially cause deep emotions (whether planned or not). Therefore, it is very important for multimedia researchers to design systems in a way that obeys the laws of different countries when handling multimedia data globally and make sure to prevent any harm to users.

RECOMMENDED READING

The recommended reading for this chapter is divided along the sections of this chapter. For a general overview of how to design things, we recommend reading D. Norman's book before diving deeper into a lively and comic discussion on user interface designed by J. Johnson. J. Nielsen and J. Raskin present a more comprehensive discussion on user interface design for interactive systems. Dix and colleagues and Sharp, Rogers, and Preece present a more scientific discussion into human computer interaction topics. They also discuss how to perform user studies. M. Jones and G. Marsden finally present mobile computer interfaces. The effects of multimedia on society are discussed in Durham and Kellner, Gauntlett, and Anderson and Bushman from various perspectives. Children are especially discussed in Mussen and Rutherford as well as in Jones. Note the different time periods during which these publications were written. Safety issues are described by Bureau, Hirsch, and Vigevano, as well as in the WCAG guidelines. The research paper by So and Lo provides further examples. Some security issues are described in the referenced CERT publication and also in Harold. Friedland and Sommer present a privacy issue with geolocation data that turned into a security problem.

Further Reading

C. A. Anderson and B. J. Bushman. "Media violence and the American public: Scientific facts versus media misinformation," *American Psychologist*, 2001.

M. Bureau, E. Hirsch, and F. Vigevano. "Epilepsy and videogames," *Epilepsia* 45 Suppl 1: 24–6. PMID 14706041, 2004.

Alan Dix, Janet Finlay, Gregory Abowd, and Russell Beale. *Human-Computer Interaction*. Prentice Hall, 3rd edition, 2003.

M. Durham and D. Kellner. *Media and Cultural Studies*. UK: Blackwell Publishing.

Jib Fowles. *The Case for Television Violence*. Thousand Oaks, CA: Sage. 1999.

G. Friedland and R. Sommer. "Cybercasing the joint: On the privacy implications of geotagging," accepted for Usenix HotSec 2010 at the Usenix Security Conference, Washington, DC, August 2010.

David Gauntlett. *Moving Experiences – Second Edition: Media Effects and Beyond*. London: John Libbey. 2005.

Elliotte Rusty Harold. "Tip: Configure SAX parsers for secure processing," *IBM Developer Works*, May 27, 2005.

Jeff Johnson. *GUI Bloopers: Don'ts and Do's for Software Developers and Web Designers (Interactive Technologies)*. Morgan Kaufman, 1st edition, March 31, 2000.

Gerard Jones. *Killing Monsters: Why Children Need Fantasy, Super Heroes and Make-Believe Violence*. New York: Basic Books. 2002.

Matt Jones and Gary Marsden. *Mobile Interaction Design*. John Wiley and Sons Ltd. 2006.

P. Mussen and E. Rutherford. "Effects of aggressive cartoons on children's aggressive play," *Journal of Abnormal and Social Psychology*, 62: 461–4. PubMed, 1961.

Jakob Nielsen. *Usability Engineering*. Boston: Academic Press. 1993.

Donald A. Norman. *The Psychology of Everyday Things*. New York: Basic Books. 1988.

W. Prinz. "A common coding approach to perception and action." In O. Neumann and W. Prinz (Eds.) *Relations between Perception and Action*. Berlin: Springer. 1990.

Jef Raskin. *The Humane Interface: New Directions for Designing Interactive Systems*. Boston: Addison-Wesley. 2000.

Helen Sharp, Yvonne Rogers, and Jenny Preece. *Interaction Design: Beyond Human-Computer Interaction*. John Wiley & Sons Ltd., 2nd edition, 2007.

R. H. Y. So and W. T. Lo. "Cybersickness: An experimental study to isolate the effects of rotational scene oscillations." Proceedings of IEEE Virtual Reality '99 Conference, March 13–17, 1999, Houston, Texas. Published by IEEE Computer Society, 237–41, 1999.

Web Links

CERT: Email bombing and Spamming: http://www.cert.org/tech_tips/email_bombing_spamming.html.

GUI Bloopers 2.0: Common User Interface Design Don'ts and Dos. http://www.gui-bloopers.com/.

Web Content Accessibility Guidelines (WCAG) 2.0 – W3C Recommendation December 11, 2008: http://www.w3.org/TR/2008/REC-WCAG20-20081211/.

EXERCISES

1. List examples of thinking inside out that do not pertain to UI development.
2. What are the major advantages and disadvantages of command-line interfaces?
3. Give one example where the desktop metaphor fails and explain why.
4. Create a program to measure the time it takes to find a random specific point on the screen and click on it with the mouse. Then create a program that asks the user to press a certain key on a random point on the screen and measure the response time. Compare the two and discuss.
5. Design a task-oriented remote control that can control a TV and a DVR.
6. Explain the notion "Responsiveness = Perceived Performance" and give more examples of techniques that increase perceived performance.
7. Find three GUI bloopers on the Internet that fall under the category "don't be creative when you are not supposed to."
8. Choose an office program (e.g., OpenOffice writer) and create three tasks that a user should solve using the program. Choose three test subjects from your friends and family and watch them while they are performing the task. If you can, you should use a camera to make sure not to interact with them.
9. Repeat 7 but this time create a questionnaire. What is different?
10. Find examples in the media where multimedia data is attributed to a crime. Discuss the coverage with your fellow students.
11. Enter your name into a search engine. Count the number of occurrences where a) the content is about you and b) the content is about you but not published by yourself. Find the oldest post about you.
12. List potential multimedia retrieval technologies (from this book and elsewhere) that could be used to invade privacy. Discuss possible countermeasures.

13. Describe an inference chain over several Web sites that would compromise privacy. Discuss a second one that includes multimedia data.

14. Find your personal privacy sweet spot by discussing what would still be okay to be published about you and what would not.

15. Discuss the buffer overrun mentioned in the chapter in detail by taking one of the entropy compression algorithms from Chapter 11 and creating a file that would expand into a very large file.

11 Fundamentals of Compression

A major difference between multimedia data and most other data is its size. Images and audio files take much more space than text, for example. Video data is currently the single largest network bandwidth and hard disk space consumer. Compression was, therefore, among the first issues researchers in the emerging multimedia field sought to address. In fact, multimedia's history is closely connected to different compression algorithms because they served as enabling technologies for many applications. Even today, multimedia signal processing would not be possible without compression methods. A Blu-ray disc can currently store 50 Gbytes, but a ninety-minute movie in 1,080p HDTV format takes about 800 Gbytes (without audio). So how does it fit on the disc? The answer to many such problems is compression.

This chapter discusses the underlying mathematical principles of compression algorithms, from the basics to advanced techniques. However, all the techniques outlined in this chapter belong to the family of lossless compression techniques; that is, the original data can be reconstructed bit by bit. Lossless compression techniques are applicable to all kinds of data, including non-multimedia data. However, these techniques are not always effective with all types of data. Therefore, subsequent chapters will introduce lossy compression techniques that are usually tailored to a specific type of data, for example, image or sound files.

RUN-LENGTH CODING

Before discussing what compression is and how you can develop algorithms to represent different types of content with the least amount of space possible, let's start with a simple and intuitive example. In addition to introducing the concept of compression, this example demonstrates a practical method that computer scientists often use to compress data with large areas of the same values.

Suppose we have a black-and-white image. The black pixels are encoded with 1 and the white pixels are encoded with 0. It looks like this:

0000000000000000
0000011111100000

```
0000100000110000
0000100011010000
0000100110010000
0000111000010000
0000011111100000
0000000000000000
```

As is, the bitmap representation would take 16 x 8 = 128 zeros and ones. Let's assume we want to cut the number of zeros and ones.

Observe that many zeros and ones appear in a row. We could represent these characters only by the number of consecutive zeros and ones starting with the zeros. The result would be:

$$21\ 6\ 9\ 1\ 5\ 2\ 8\ 1\ 3\ 2\ 1\ 1\ 8\ 1\ 2\ 2\ 2\ 1\ 8\ 6\ 21$$

The highest number represented is twenty-one. So we could represent each of the numbers in the row with five bits: 101010011001001 and so on. We need twenty-one numbers in this encoding, so we can represent the digit in one hundred five bits, saving twenty-three bits. Of course, we would have to represent a bitmap containing more than two colors – say, sixteen – slightly differently. Consider the following one-line example:

$$RRRRRGGGBBBBBRRRRGB$$

Using a variant of the concept of representation, we would get:

$$5R3G5B4R1G1B$$

This method – called *run-length encoding*, or RLE – is used in many image formats, such as Windows BMP and TIFF, and, in a slightly modified version, on CD-ROMs because it is especially effective in representing data with large areas of the same values. Several unanswered questions remain, however. For example:

- Is RLE the best way to compress the example cited earlier?
- Would applying RLE to the file again further compress the bitmap?
- What is the minimum amount of space needed to represent this image?

Answering these questions requires a more in-depth discussion of the topic. In fact, it leads to an entire theory in mathematics, the so-called information theory. The following sections introduce the most important concepts in information theory.

INFORMATION CONTENT AND ENTROPY

To determine how far we can compress a certain piece of data, we first need a measurement for information. The smallest amount of information is the bit. A *bit* is a symbol that can be 0 or 1. Every string in the world can be reduced to bits, so we could say that one measure for information is the minimum number of bits needed to represent a string. But how can we calculate this number?

Table 11.1. The probability that a bit (with the symbol 0 or 1) will appear in a particular place on a string (b = the bit, i = the bit's place on a string, and P = probability)

i	1	2	3	4	....	32	33	...	62	63	64
P(bi = 0)	63/64	62/63	61/62	60/61		32/33	31/32		2/3	1/2	0
P(bi = 1)	1/64	1/63	1/62	1/61		1/33	1/32		1/3	1/2	1

Assume we have a sixty-four-bit-long string consisting of sixty-three zeros and one one. The one can be at any place in the string. We denote this place with an i, so i is a number between zero and sixty-three. Next, assume we read the string from the left to the right, symbol by symbol, until we find the one. We can then ask: At each character, what is the probability P that the next character will be a one or a zero, given that we have not yet found the one? Table 11.1 shows the probability P for each bit, from one to sixty-four.

As the table demonstrates, the probability P depends only on the index until the one is found. Of course, the probability after reading sixty-three zeros is one and the probability after reading the one is zero. In other words, the zeros after a one are completely predictable and carry no information. We can also reverse this argument: the higher an event's probability, the less information it carries. This means the *information content* is inversely proportional to the probability of a symbol's occurrence. What's left is to count how many characters we actually need to represent the content. In the binary system, this is the number of digits needed. We therefore define the information content $h(x)$ as:

$$h(x) = \log_2 \frac{1}{p(x)} \tag{11.1}$$

The choice of a logarithmic base corresponds to the choice of a unit for measuring information. If we use base 2, the resulting units are bits (as in this example). If we use another alphabet (for example, the decimal system), we must adjust the base accordingly.

So let's measure the information content for each symbol for the given example by inserting the values from Table 11.1 into the formula in Equation 11.1. Table 11.2 shows the results.

The sum of the information content of bits 1 to n is six when the n-th bit is a one. For example, $h(00010\ldots0) = 0.0227 + 0.023 + 0.0235 + 5.9307 + 0 + \ldots + 0 = 6$.

So, in general, the formula is:

$$\sum_{n=1}^{i} h(b_n) = \left(\sum_{m=66-i}^{64} \log_2 \frac{m}{m-1} + \log_2 \frac{1}{1/(65-1)} \right) = \log_2 \left(\left(\prod_{m=66-i}^{64} \frac{m}{m-1} \right) * (65-i) \right) = 6 \tag{11.2}$$

The summation of the information content for each symbol reveals the string's total information content. In other words, we need a minimum of six bits to represent the string as described. To do this, all we need to save is the index i (a number between zero and sixty-three), which can be represented by a six-digit binary number.

Table 11.2. The information content of each symbol calculated from the probabilities in Table 11.1

i	1	2	3	4	....	32	33	...	62	63	64
	0.0227	0.023	0.0235	0.0238		0.444	0.458		0.585	1	0
	6	5.977	5.954	5.9307		5	5.0666		1.585	1	0

There is a caveat, however. To measure the string's information content, we use probabilities, which requires knowledge about the data structure. In other words, if we don't know how many ones appear in the string and the string's total length, we can't calculate the information content. Again, this is intuitive. For a string to contain any information, someone or something must process and interpret the string. That is, a string must be put into a context to make sense.

Information content gives us a method to measure the number of bits required to encode a certain message. In practice, however, the message might not be known in advance. Instead, you might have a language and arbitrary messages encoded in that language. Formally, we can define a *language* as a set of symbols or words. Each word or symbol has an associated probability. The probability can usually be determined by the frequency with which a symbol or word appears in the language. In English, for example, the word "the" appears more often than the word "serendipity." As a result, the probability of an article ("the") appearing in a message is much higher than that of the word derived from the old Persian name for Sri Lanka ("serendipity's" origin).

So what is the expected length of a message given a set of symbols and their probabilities? This measure – *entropy* – is defined as follows:

$$H(X) = \sum_i P(x_i) * h(x_i) \tag{11.3}$$

Entropy is the expected information content – not coincidentally similar to probability theory's expectation value. Entropy is an important measure used across scientific disciplines. Shannon's source coding theorem gives the information theoretic background for entropy. The theorem shows that entropy defines a lower bound for the number of bits that a system can use to encode a message in that alphabet without losing information. Entropy's value is maximized when the alphabet is uniformly distributed – that is, each character has the same probability. This is also often referred to as *chaos*: given a subset of a string, there is no possibility of a prediction about the next symbols because all symbols have equal probability. Random noise has this property and is therefore incompressible.

Entropy is a fundamental measure with analogies in thermodynamics, quantum mechanics, and other fields. In general, it can be described as a measure of chaos: the more chaotic a system, the higher its entropy. In information theory, this means that the more chaotic a string is, the more bits we need to encode it.

COMPRESSION ALGORITHMS

Information content and entropy let us measure a message's expected minimum length. However, given a string, how do you construct a code for that string that uses the minimal number of bits? Unfortunately, no single answer to this problem exists. There are many ways to construct the string and none of them achieves perfect results in all cases. Therefore, the best compression method depends on the data you are processing. The following sections present the most important compression algorithms.

Huffman Coding

Before we dig into the details of how to create good compression algorithms, let's quickly review the features we would expect from a good encoding:

- The code must be unambiguously decodable – that is, one coded message corresponds to exactly one decoded message.
- The code should be easily decodable – that is, you should be able to find symbol endings and the end of the message easily. Ideally, you should be able to decode it online (that is, as the symbols come in) without having to know the entire coded message.
- The code should be compact.

In 1952, David A. Huffman invented a coding algorithm that produces a code fulfilling these requirements. *Huffman coding* is in frequent practical use and part of many standard formats. The algorithm's design is elegant, easy to implement, and efficient. Also, because of the vast mathematical work scholars have done on tree structures, the algorithm is well understood.

The algorithm constructs a binary tree in which the symbols are the leaves. The path from the root to a leaf reveals the code for the symbol. When turning right on a node, a 1 is added to the code; when turning left, a 0 is added. The idea is to have long paths for symbols that occur infrequently and short paths for symbols that occur frequently.

Figure 11.1 illustrates the construction of a Huffman tree. In the beginning, the leaf nodes containing the frequencies of the symbol they represent are unconnected. The algorithm creates a new node whose children are the two nodes with the smallest probabilities, such that the new node's probability equals the sum of the children's probability. The new node is treated as a regular symbol node. The procedure is repeated until only one node remains – the root of the Huffman tree.

The simplest construction algorithm uses a priority queue in which the node with the lowest probability receives highest priority. The following pseudo-code illustrates the process:

```
// Input: A list W of n frequencies for the symbols
// Output: A binary tree T with weights taken from W
Huffman(W, n):
    Create list F with single-element trees formed from elements of W
```

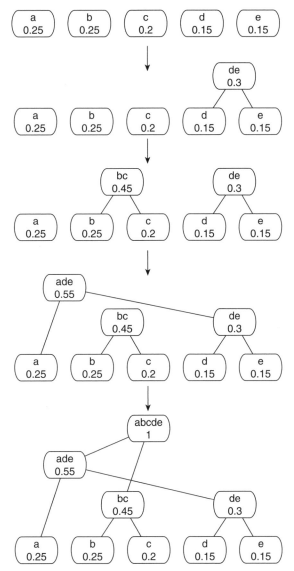

Figure 11.1. Construction of a Huffman tree.

```
WHILE (F has more than one element)
    Find T1, T2 in F with minimum root values
    Create new tree T by creating a new node with root value T1+T2
    Make T1 and T2 children of T
    Add T to F
Huffman := tree stored in F
```

You can now use the tree to encode and decode any message containing symbols of the leaf nodes, as Figure 11.2 shows.

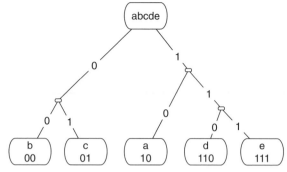

Figure 11.2. Codes generated by the Huffman tree.

To encode a message, the algorithm traverses the tree completely and saves the paths into a lookup table. So, in our example, the encoding for the word "cab" is 011000. The following pseudo-code describes the procedure:

```
// Input: A Huffman tree F and a string S containing only symbols in F
// Output: A bit-sequence B
Encode_Huffman(F, S)
   Traverse F completely and create a hash table H containing tuples (c,p)
   // c = character, p = path from root to of F to character
   B := []
   FOREACH (symbol s in S)
      Add path H(s) to bit sequence B.
Encode_Huffman := B
```

To decode a message, the algorithm interprets the code as encoding a path from the root to a leaf node, where 0 means going right, and 1 means going left (or vice versa), as described in the following pseudo-code sequence:

```
// Input: A Huffman tree F and a bit sequence B
// Output: An uncompressed string S
Decode_Huffman(F, B)
   Traverse F completely and create a hash table H containing tuples (p, c)
   // c = character, p = path from root to of F to character
   S := " "
   node n = root node of F
   FOREACH (bit b in B)
      if (b==0) n := left children of n
      if (b==1) n := right children of n
      if (n has no children)
         Add character represented by n to S
         n := root node of F
Decode_Huffman := S
```

Static Huffman compressors use a fixed tree for all incoming data; dynamic Huffman compressors serialize the tree, so that each file can be decoded using a different tree. The code this algorithm generates is optimal in the sense that each symbol has the shortest possible representation for the given probability. However, the Huffman algorithm assumes that symbol frequencies are independent of each other. In reality, a "q," for example, is usually followed by a "u." In addition, the Huffman algorithm cannot create codes with a fraction of bits per symbol.

Lempel-Ziv Algorithms

The LZ family of algorithms (derived from its creators' – Abraham Lempel and Jacob Ziv – last names) is divided into two groups: successors of the LZ77 algorithm and successors of the LZ78 algorithm. Lempel and Ziv developed the base algorithms in 1977 and 1978, respectively. The algorithms use completely different approaches, despite their similar names. Most variations of the LZ algorithms can be identified by the third letter – for example, LZH or LZW. In contrast to Huffman coding, which is based on symbol probabilities, the algorithms account for repeated symbol combinations (words) in a document. The algorithm is best suited for limited alphabets, such as large archives containing text and/or source code. Two very popular image formats, GIF and PNG, use one variant of each of the algorithms when only a limited amount of color is used. The LZ compression algorithms are therefore the single most often used compression algorithms of all time. Once one has understood both LZ77 and LZ78, the derivate algorithms are conceptually similar. This section will therefore describe the two fundamental algorithms: LZ77 and LZ78.

LZ77 achieves compression by replacing portions of the data with references to matching data that have already passed through the encoder and decoder. This algorithm works with a fixed number of symbols – the *look-ahead buffer* (LAB) – to be coded. Additionally, the algorithm looks at a fixed number of symbols from the past – the *search buffer* (SB). To encode the symbols in the LAB, the algorithm searches the SB backward for the best match. The encoding (often called a *token*) is encoded by a tuple (L, D) defining the length and the distance from the current token to a past token. A token basically says, "each of the next L symbols is equal to the D symbols behind it in the uncompressed stream." In actual implementations, the distance D is often referred to as *offset*. The current chunk of processed symbols – that is, SB+LA – is often called a *sliding window*. Typical sizes for the sliding window are several kilobytes (2 kB, 4 kB, 32 kB, and so on).

Consider the example shown in Table 11.3. It encodes the string "cabbdcbaacbd-ddabda" using LZ77. The currently processed symbol is underlined.

The LAB is also used as the SB, as position 13 demonstrates. The original LZ77 algorithm uses a fixed-size SB, so it can use constant-bit-length tokens. The encoding is the final token. For our example, the encoding is 0,0c 0,0a 0,0b 1,1d 5,1b 6,1a 4,2d 1,2a 5,2a.

The following is the pseudo-code for an LZ77 encoder:

```
// Input: A lookaheadbuffer LAB a substring of a message...
// Output: An LZ77 encoding C
Encode_LZ77(LAB)
```

Table 11.3. Encoding of the string "cabbdcbaacbdddabda" using the LZ77 compression algorithm

		Sliding window			
Position	Code to be processed	Look-ahead buffer (next three symbols)	Search buffer (previous seven symbols)	Already encoded	Token
	cabbdcbaacbdddabda				
1	bdcbaacbdddabda	cab			(0,0,c)
2	dcbaacbdddabda	abb	c		(0,0,a)
3	cbaacbdddabda	bbd	ca		(0,0,b)
4	baacbdddabda	bdc	ca<u>b</u>		(1,1,d)
6	acbdddabda	cba	<u>c</u>abbd		(5,1,b)
8	bdddabda	aac	c<u>a</u>bbdcb		(6,1,a)
10	ddabda	cbd	bbd<u>cba</u>a	ca	(4,2,d)
13	bda	<u>d</u>da	cbaac<u>bd</u>	cabbd	(1,2,a)
16		bda	ac<u>b</u>ddda	cabbdcba	(5,2,a)
19			dddabda	cabbdcbaacb	

```
C := ""
WHILE (LAB not empty)
    p := position of the longest match in the window for the LAB
    l := length of the longest match
    Add the tuple (p, l) to C
    Add the first character in LAB to C
    Shift LAB by l
Encode_LZ77 := C
```

To decompress the code, the algorithm reads the constant-sized tokens. The distance and length always refer to already decoded values. Choose a string and try this algorithm for yourself. You may use the following pseudo-code as a guide:

```
// Input: A string C containing LZ77 code
// Output: A string S containing the decoded code
Decode_LZ77(C)
    S := ""

    FOREACH (token in S)
        Read token and obtain the triple (p, l, c)
        // p = position, l = length, c = character
```

Table 11.4. Compressing the string "abacbabac-cbabbaca" using the LZ78 algorithm

Step	Input	Token	New Dictionary Entry/Index
1	a	0,a	a,1
2	b	0,b	b,2
3	ac	1,c	ac,3
4	ba	2,a	ba,4
5	bac	4,c	bac,5
6	c	0,c	c,6
7	bab	4,b	bab,7
8	Baca	5,a	Baca,8

> Add to C the l characters from position length(C)-p
> Add to C the character c
> Decode_LZ77 := S

As explained earlier, many variations of the LZ77 algorithm exist. LZR, for example, has an unrestricted search buffer and therefore variable bit-length tokens. In LZH, a commonly used variant, the token values are compressed using a Huffman encoding. The currently most popular LZ77-based compression method is called DEFLATE, which is part of the very common Unix compression program "gzip."

DEFLATE combines LZ77 with Huffman coding, placing literals, lengths, and a symbol to indicate the end of the current block of data together in one alphabet. It places distances into a separate alphabet. The Portable Network Graphics (PNG, see also Chapter 12) image format also uses a variation of DEFLATE. PNG combines DEFLATE with a filter to predict each pixel's value based on previous pixels' colors and subtracts the prediction from the actual value. The encoder and the decoder use the same prediction table. This way, only the prediction differences are transmitted. An image line filtered this way is usually more compressible than the raw image line because DEFLATE does not understand that an image is a 2D entity. It sees the image data as a stream of bytes, whereas the prediction accounts for neighboring pixels in all dimensions. We discuss this algorithm in more detail in Chapter 12.

Whereas the LZ77 algorithm works on past data, the LZ78 algorithm attempts to work on future data. It achieves this by maintaining a dictionary. The algorithm forward scans the input buffer and matches it against the dictionary. The algorithm scans the input buffer for the longest match of the buffer with a dictionary entry until it can no longer find a match. At this point, it outputs the location of the word in the dictionary (if one is available), the match length, and the character that caused a match failure. It then adds the resulting word to the initially empty dictionary. Table 11.4 shows an example in which the word "abacbabaccbabbaca" is compressed using LZ78.

Like in LZ77, the tokens are the actual coding. Therefore, the code for our example is "0a0b1c2a4c0c4b5a."

```
// Input: A string S
// Output: A string C containing the LZ78 code
Encode_LZ78(S)
  Start with empty dictionary D
  C := ""
  prefix := "" // stores the prefixes
  FOREACH (character c in S)
    IF (prefix + c is in D)
      prefix := prefix + c
    IF (prefix + c is not in D)
    Add the string prefix + c to D
    Add the index of prefix in D to C
      Add c to C
    prefix := c
Encode_LZ78 := C
```

Decompression of LZ78 tokens is similar to compression. The algorithm extends the dictionary by one entry when it decodes a token using the dictionary index and the explicitly saved symbol.

```
// Input: An LZ78 encoded string C
// Output: A string S containing the original message
Decode_LZ78(C)
  Start with empty dictionary D
  old index := index value of the first token in C
  S := ""
  FOREACH (token t in C)
    index := index value of t
    IF (D has entry with index)
    Add the string at index to S
      c := first character of the string at index
    Concatenate entry at old index and c and add to D
    IF (D has no entry with index)
    c := first character of the string at old index
    Concatenate entry at old index and c and add to D
      Concatenate entry old index with c and add to S
    Old index := index
Decode_LZ78 := S
```

Both compression and decompression benefit from an easy-to-manage dictionary. Usually, you would use a tree in which each node has a certain number of children that equals the number of valid input symbols. In the original LZ78 algorithm, the dictionary's size is unrestricted. Therefore, the index values must be saved with a variable number of bits. The dictionary index length is rarely explicitly defined; the algorithm uses the dictionary's size to determine the index's bit length. In other words, the algorithm allocates enough bits so that the largest index can be stored. For example, for a twenty-four-bit dictionary, all we need is $[\log_2 24]$ = five bits per index.

LZ78 has many variants too: LZC uses a maximum size for the dictionary. If it reaches the maximum number of entries, the algorithm continues with the current dictionary under the hope that the output file does not become too long. If it determines that the output length has passed a threshold, it recompresses the data by creating an additional dictionary. The Unix compress tool uses LZC. However, the LZC is patented, so users must pay a license fee. LZW, a common LZ78 variant, does not store the following symbol explicitly but as the first symbol of the following token. The dictionary starts with all possible input symbols as first entries. This leads to a more compact code and lets users define the input symbols (which can vary in bit length). The popular Graphics Interchange Format (GIF) uses the LZW variant. Although initially popular, enthusiasm for LZ78 dampened, mostly because parts of it were patent protected in the United States. The patent for the LZW algorithm was strictly enforced and led to the creation of the patent-free PNG image format.

As mentioned earlier, the RLE algorithm is most useful when characters repeat often, and Huffman compression is most useful when you can build a nonuniformly distributed probability model of the underlying data. The LZ algorithms are especially useful with text-like data – that is, data where strings of limited but variable lengths repeat themselves. Typical compression ratios are (original:compressed) 2:1 to 5:1 or more for text files. In contrast to RLE and Huffman, LZ algorithms need a certain input file size to amortize. Compressing a file with just a few bits, such as our example from the beginning of the chapter, won't yield a very good compression result. The Unix program "tar," for example, therefore concatenates all files into one large archive and then invokes "gzip" on the entire archive.

Arithmetic Coding

Arithmetic encoding approaches seek to overcome Huffman encoding's limitations – namely, that messages can only be encoded using an integer number of bits per symbol. JPEG image compression and other standards use arithmetic coding.

Arithmetic coding maps every symbol to a real number in the open interval between 0 and 1, formally $[0,1) \subset R$. Because this interval contains nondenumerable infinite elements, every message can be mapped to one number in this interval. A special termination symbol denotes the end of a message. Without this symbol, you would not know when to stop the decoding process. To encode a message, arithmetic coding approaches partition the start interval $[0,1)$ into subintervals sized proportionally to the individual symbols' probabilities. The algorithm is as follows.

Choose the symbol with the highest probability and split the interval according to its probability. Using the remainder of the interval, repeat the process until you reach the symbol with the lowest probability. Table 11.5 illustrates the process for the string "bac#"

Table 11.5. Steps involved in encoding the string "bac#" using arithmetic coding

x_i	A	B	c	#
$P(x_i)$	0.5	0.2	0.2	0.1
Step 1: read "b"				
Partition (decimal)	[0,0.5)	[0.5,0.7)	[0.7,0.9)	[0.9,1)
Partition (binary)	$[0,0.1)_2$	$[0.1,0.\overline{10110})_2$	$[0.\overline{10110},0.\overline{11100})_2$	$[0.\overline{11100},1)_2$
Step 2: read "a"				
Partition (decimal)	0.5,0.6)	[0.6,0.64)	0.64,0.68)	[0.68,0.7)
Partition (binary)	$[0.1,0.\overline{1001})_2$	$0.\overline{1001},$ $0.1010001\ldots)_2$	$[0.1010001\ldots,$ $0,1010111\ldots)_2$	$[0.\overline{1010111}\ldots,0,$ $10110)_2$
Step 3: read "c"				
Partition (decimal)	[0.5,0.55)	[0.55,0.57)	[0.57,0.59) $\begin{bmatrix}0.100100011\ldots, \\ 0.100101110\ldots\end{bmatrix}_2$	[0.59,0.6)
Step 4: read #				
Partition (decimal)	[0.57,0.58)	[0.58,0.584)	[0.584,0.588)	[0.588,0.59) $=$ $\begin{bmatrix}0.100101101\ldots, \\ 0.100101110\ldots\end{bmatrix}_2$

("#" denoting the end symbol) with the probabilities given in the first row. The table also shows how the actual binary code is created by converting the decimal representation to binary.

The message "bac#" is encoded as a number in the interval [0.588,0.59) or [0.100101101 ..., 0.100101110 ...) binary. More exactly formulated, this interval contains all messages starting with "bac." The decoder, however, stops because it reads the terminal symbol "#." Because the start interval is open and does not contain the one, there is no need to transmit the numbers before the point. So the code for "bac#" is 10010111. The following pseudo-code snippet illustrates the idea:

```
// Input: A string S containing a message, ending with a stop symbol
// Output: An arithmetically encoded string C,
// a table P mapping probability ranges to symbols
Encode_Arith(S)
    FOREACH (character c in S)
      Get the frequency and assume as probability p[c]
    Create a table P that assigns characters to probability
```

```
      ranges in [0,1), each range with a size proportional to p[c]
   lower_bound := 0
   upper_bound := 1
   FOREACH (character c in S)
       current_range := upper_bound-lower_bound
       upper_bound := lower_bound+(current_range*upper_bound[c])
       lower_bound := lower_bound+(current_range*lower bound[c])
   C=upper_bound+lower_bound/2.0
Encode_Arith := (C, P)
```

To decode the message, the algorithm needs the input alphabet and the intermediate partitions. Given an encoded message, the algorithm then chooses the subinterval containing the code in each intermediate partition until the algorithm finds the termination symbol. The table with intermediate partitions is rarely transmitted; instead, it is typically generated identically by the coder and decoder. The following lines of pseudo-code illustrate the decoding:

```
// Input: An arithmetically encoded string C,
// a table P mapping probability ranges to symbols
// Output: A string S containing the original message
Decode_Arith(C, P)
   encoded_value := C
   WHILE (we have not seen the terminal symbol)
       s := symbol in P where encoded_value is within its range
       //remove effects of s from encoded_value
       current_range = upper_bound of c - lower bound of c
       encoded_value = (encoded_value-lower_bound of c)/current_range
     Add s to S
Decode_Arith := S
```

Accurate representation of the interval boundaries creates a major problem in implementing arithmetic codes. Standard processors use single- (32 bit) or double-precision (64 bit) floating-point numbers, but this representation is, of course, not precise enough. Different arithmetic encoders use various tricks to overcome this problem. Rather than try to simulate arbitrary precision (which is a possibility but very slow), most arithmetic coders operate at a fixed limit of precision. The coders round the calculated fractions to their nearest equivalents at that precision. A *renormalization* process keeps the finite precision from limiting the total number of symbols that can be encoded. Whenever the range decreases to the point at which the interval's start and end values share certain beginning digits, the coder sends those digits to the output, thus saving the digits in the CPU, where the interval boundaries shift left by the number of saved digits. This lets the algorithm add an infinite number of new digits on the right, even when the CPU can handle only a fixed number of digits.

Different multimedia data formats use variants of arithmetic coding. Although every arithmetic encoding implementation achieves a different compression ratio, most compression ratios vary insignificantly (typically within 1 percent). However, the CPU time varies greatly – easily an order of magnitude depending on the input. This runtime unpredictability is a major usability concern.

WEAKNESS OF ENTROPY-BASED COMPRESSION METHODS FOR MULTIMEDIA DATA

All of the compression techniques we've described so far try to reconstruct the data in full, without losing any information, so are called *lossless* compression methods. Another name for these techniques, because they can be described by information theory, is *entropy encoders*. When entropy compression routines were developed, most of the data in computing systems were programs or text data. This does not mean that these compression methods cannot be used for images, sounds, or videos. However, the compression obtained when using LZ77 or other variants is usually a factor of two or less. Many reasons exist for the lower compression rates, including:

- Entropy is usually higher for multimedia signals than for text data and differs across files, even if the multimedia data contains no noise (think of the alphabet needed to store an English text versus the alphabet needed to store an amplitude-modified clean sine signal).
- Because sampled signals contain noise, it is almost impossible to find repeating patterns, such as is done in LZx algorithms.
- Multimedia data is usually multidimensional. To leverage redundancies between neighboring pixels or frames requires knowing the data's basic structure. For example, you must know the image's resolution to know what the neighboring pixels are.
- Many algorithms – for example, arithmetic coding – could work well with some multimedia content; however, their asymptotic runtime behavior makes using them for multimedia practically prohibitive.

The next chapters discuss methods for overcoming these challenges.

RECOMMENDED READING

Entropy compression is a strictly mathematical topic and is therefore widely presented in the further reading. Sayood and Salomon present comprehensive, though quite technical, coverage. For an in-depth discussion of many of the more advanced mathematical topics, we recommend McKay. We also recommend the original research articles on the algorithms presented in this chapter by Shannon, Huffman, Ziv and Lempel, Welsh, and Witten.

Further Reading

D. A. Huffman. "A method for the construction of minimum-redundancy codes," *Proceedings of IRE*, 40 (10): 1098–1101, 1952.

David MacKay. *Information Theory, Inference and Learning Algorithms*. Cambridge: Cambridge University Press. 2006.

David Salomon. *Data Compression – The Complete Reference*. New York: Springer, 2nd edition, 2000.

Khalid Sayood. *Introduction to Data Compression*. New York: Morgan Kaufmann, 2nd edition, 2000.

E. Shannon. "A mathematical theory of communication," *Bell System Technical Journal*, 27, (July, October, 1948): 379–23, 623–56.

T. A. Welsh. "A technique for high-performance data compression," *Computer*, 17 (6): 8–19, 1984.

I. H. Witten, R. M. Neal, and J. G. Cleary. "Arithmetic coding for data compression," *Communications of the ACM*, 30 (6): 520–40, 1987.

J. Ziv and A. Lempel. "A universal algorithm for sequential data compression," *IEEE Transactions on Information Theory*, 23 (3): 337–43, 1977.

J. Ziv and A. Lempel. "Compression of individual sequences via variable-rate coding," *IEEE Transactions on Information Theory*, 24 (5): 530–6, 1978.

Web Links

Compression Frequently Asked Questions: http://www.faqs.org/faqs/compression-faq/.

EXERCISES

1. Give one example of content for which run-length encoding (RLE) would work very well and one for which it would work pretty badly.
2. Specify three implementations of RLE that handle short run lengths differently. Discuss their advantages and disadvantages.
3. What is the information content of a coin toss?
4. Show that it is impossible to construct a compression algorithm that takes an arbitrary input string and always produces a shorter output string without losing any information.
5. Show that applying one compression method repeatedly does not yield significantly better results than applying it only once.
6. Create a tool that measures a file's entropy. Use the tool to calculate the entropy of three different text files containing English text, source code, a binary program, an uncompressed image file (for example, TIFF), and an uncompressed audio file.
7. Many file archival utilities provided in today's operating systems first concatenate a set of files and then apply compression techniques on the entire archive rather than on each file individually. Why is this method typically advantageous?
8. Discuss the efficiency of Morse code.
9. Construct the Huffman tree for the word "Mississippi."
10. Write a dynamic-tree Huffman encoder/decoder in a programming language of your choice. Don't forget to encode the tree.
11. What is the minimum number of bits needed to represent an arbitrary Huffman tree?

12. Would it make sense to combine Huffman encoding with RLE encoding? If yes, give an example where this would be useful.

13. Compress the word "Mississippi" using LZ77 and LZ78 as described in this chapter.

14. Discuss the usefulness of using an LZX algorithm to compress a video file (images only).

15. How would you compress an audio file using LZ77? Define a filter that would allow for better compression.

16. Compress the word "Mississippi" using arithmetic coding.

17. Give an example of a symbol distribution in which arithmetic coding could result in a shorter output string than Huffman coding

18. Implement a simple arithmetic coder using the Unix tool "bc."

19. Explain how arithmetic coding accounts for repeating words.

20. Which of the methods – RLE, Huffman, arithmetic coding, or LZW – would you use for the following files: a text file, an image file containing a screenshot, a photograph containing a portrait, a midi file, a sampled audio file containing rock music, a sampled audio file containing a generated sinus waveform, a movie (images only), and a cartoon animation (images only).

12 Lossy Compression

Entropy-based compression as presented in the previous chapter is an important foundation of many data formats for multimedia. However, as already pointed out, it often does not achieve the compression rates required for the transmission or storage of multimedia data in many applications. Because compression beyond entropy is not possible without losing information, that is exactly what we have to do: lose information.

Fortunately, unlike texts or computer programs, where a single lost bit can render the rest of the data useless, a flipped pixel or a missing sample in an audio file is hardly noticeable. Lossy compression leverages the fact that multimedia data can be gracefully degraded in quality by increasingly losing more information. This results in a very useful quality/cost trade-off: one might not lose any perceivable information and the cost (transmission time, memory space, etc.) is high; with a little bit of information loss, the cost decreases, and this can be continued to a point where almost no information is left and the perceptual quality is very bad. Lossless compression usually can compress multimedia by a factor of about 1.3: to 2:1. Lossy compression can go up to ratios of several hundreds to one (in the case of video compression). This is leveraged on any DVD or Blu-ray, in digital TV, or in Web sites that present consumer-produced videos. Without lossy compression, media consumption as observed today would not exist.

MATHEMATICAL FOUNDATION: VECTOR QUANTIZATION

Consider the following problem: We have an image that we want to store on a certain disc, but no matter how hard we try to compress it, it won't fit. In fact, we know that it won't fit because information theory tells us that it cannot be compressed to the size of the space that we have without losing any information. What choice do we have? Well, we could either not put the image on that disc or we could try to put as much of the image on the disc as we can fit, losing some of the information.

There are multiple variants of how this could be performed: one could crop the image margins or extract the parts of the image that are relevant to, let's say a customer. Of course, it would require an expert to judge the relevance of each pixel.

A variant that can be performed automatically in a computer, without knowing anything about the data we are looking at, is called *vector quantization*. *Quantization* is a general mathematical term and means discretizing a value range using different step sizes. Any given function f can be transformed into a quantized version q by using a transformation g. Often, a real-valued function f is converted to an integer-valued representation. For example:

$$Q(x) = g\left(\lfloor f(x) \rfloor\right)$$

Vector quantization involves vectors; that is, instead of a single-valued function, tuples, triples, or n-dimensional vectors are quantized. In other words, vectors $[x_1, x_2, \ldots, x_k]$ are to be mapped to values $[y_1, y_2, \ldots, yn]$ with n<<k. Think of these vectors as being anything, for example, 8 x 8 pixel blocks in an image, red/green/blue triplets in a video, or sixteen subsequent samples in an audio file.

So what is the best way to do it? The answer is: there is none, but there are many to choose from! Which algorithm to use depends on the type and content of the data and the application. In the following we will present some common approaches.

Linear Quantization

The easiest way to map n vectors to k vectors with k < n is linear quantization. All of the n numbers are distributed evenly into k buckets. This is done by simple arithmetic rounding, for example.

The problem with this method is that assuming an even distribution does not often yield very good results because the distribution of the n numbers is not even. For example, consider an image where colors are to be reduced. Very often there may be a large amount of one color but not such a large amount of a second color.

K-means

The K-means algorithm is well known in statistics and machine learning as a clustering algorithm. This is an algorithm to partition n objects into k clusters, where k < n. The algorithm is based on the so-called expectation maximization principle. The idea of the algorithm is to minimize the intra-cluster variance that is the squared distance between each member of a cluster to the mean value of each member of the cluster. Formally, the function V

$$V = \sum_{i=1}^{k} \sum_{x_j \in S_i} (x_j - \mu_i)^2$$

where there are k clusters S_i, i = 1, 2, …, k, and μi is the centroid or mean point of all the points $x_j \in S_i$ is to be minimized. If the x_j are of higher dimension than one, a different subtraction function has to be chosen, for example Euclidean distance.

The pseudo-code description of the code looks like this:

```
// Input: a set of data points X, an integer number k
// Output: a set of k data points representing the set μ
k_means(X, k)
    Choose k initial means μᵢ from X at random
    WHILE (means μi are not updated significantly anymore)
    // maximization:
        FOREACH (sample xⱼ: from X)
            assign membership of each element to a mean (closest mean)
    // expectation:
        FOREACH (mean μᵢ)
            calculate a new μᵢ by averaging xⱼ that were assigned members
    k_means := {μᵢ}
```

Variants of the algorithm exist where the means are not initialized at random, but based on some assumptions or properties of the data. In practice, it is often hard to decide when the stopping criterion "not updated significantly anymore" is true. Therefore, different criteria are used; often a fixed amount of iteration is preferred (loop n times). K-means is a very popular algorithm for all kinds of quantization tasks and is used in many fields as a "first guess" approach, that is, try this one before you try anything more complicated. However, K-means has three major limitations: the computational complexity increases dramatically with large amounts of data and, obviously, one has to know the amount of clusters k in advance. For example, the algorithm is well suited for reducing 16,777,216 colors in an image to 65,536 colors. But what if we don't know how many colors are really needed in the image to represent it well? For example, if the image content is really just black and white but it is still represented by the aforementioned 65,536 colors, we will use more colors than needed and waste memory, network bandwidths, or storage space. However, if we reduce a rainbow image to two colors, we might not be very happy with the appearance of the image in the end.

X-means

An algorithm that tries to overcome the problem of having to know the number of clusters k in advance by guessing it is the X-means algorithm. X-means extends K-means in several ways, including making the means computation more efficient by effectively caching computation results from previous iterations. The following section will discuss only the heuristics for automatically guessing k. The algorithm starts with a k_{min}, which defines the lower bound of the range where k is to be searched, and a k_{max}, which defines the upper bound.

```
// Input: a set of data points X,
// kmin and kmax denoting lower and upper boundaries for k
// Output: a set of k data points representing the set μ
```

```
x_means(X)
    k := k_min
    Run k_means(X,k) until it converges
    Score the quality of the clustering
    IF (k>k_max) stop and report the best scoring clustering during the search
x_means := {μ_i}best
```

The main question with this algorithm is: How do we score the quality of the clustering? Of course, we cannot do it optimally. If we could do it optimally, we could greatly reduce the number of steps in this algorithm in the first place. Also, the optimal clustering depends on the underlying data we are processing and might be different for different types of image, video, and audio data.

However, the authors of the X-means algorithm, Pelleg and Moore, proposed the following heuristics based on general statistic assumptions. To score the quality of a clustering, each mean is split into two children: the children are moved a distance proportional to the size of the region in opposite directions. Next, in each parent region, a local K-means with k=2 is run for each pair of children. Local means that the children are affected only by the points in the parents' regions and not by any other parts of the data. Once this two-means run has converged, a test is performed on all pairs of children. Informally, the test asks: "Is there statistical evidence that the two children are modeling a real structure here, or would the original parent model the distribution equally well?"

Many metrics have been defined in statistics to answer this question. None of them works perfectly, because the solution to this problem depends on the structure of the data one is dealing with and on the task one wants to ultimately accomplish. Some metrices are described in Chapter 17.

PERCEPTUAL QUANTIZATION

The mathematical methods described earlier are very useful for many tasks, especially if one wants to quantize data that one has no knowledge about other than general statistics. The main limitation of all of the methods described previously in this chapter and of most other methods is that they tend to converge to local minima. Also, there is no way to tell whether they converged to a local minimum. Therefore, when applied to a concrete piece of data, the results can vary greatly, for example from one photo to another.

Fortunately, with acoustic and visual data we often have more background knowledge than just the theorems of mathematical statistics. As explained in Chapters 5 and 6, we have a great deal of knowledge of how human perception works. Until the arrival of the digital age, the paradigm was that audio and video content should be reproduced as accurately as possible whenever copied. This means that when comparing the original and the copy, the difference should be as small as possible. The idea behind perceptual quantization is that even though it is highly desirable to reproduce content as accurately as possible, the term "accurate" is not defined as a simple mathematical distance (such as an L-norm distance or a root-mean-square error), but using some perceptual model. In other words, two signals are accurately reproduced if they sound the same or they look the same, even if they have many differences when compared bitwise. To achieve this, one needs a model of the perceptual sensors. The following sections describe the most important ideas of perceptual coding.

Sound Amplitude Quantization: A-law and μ-law

The simplest and yet most widely used perceptual quantization techniques for audio data include the A-law and μ-law algorithms. This area is also referred to as *companding algorithms*, which is the older term inherited from analog signal processing. The idea is to exploit the Weber-Fechner law, which attempts to describe the relationship between the physical magnitudes of stimuli and the perceived intensity of the stimuli. As explained in Chapter 6, the Weber-Fechner law assumes that just noticeable differences are additive. As a consequence, sound intensity is perceived logarithmically. In other words, a sound must be twice as intense to be perceived as a constant factor more intense in the human ear. The idea behind the A-law and μ-law algorithms is to exactly exploit this fact: rather than quantizing the intensity of the sounds, that is, the sample values, linearly, they are quantized logarithmically, thereby mapping slightly different intensities to the same value and losing small sound intensity changes. Figure 12.1 shows the idea.

The companding formula for encoding a sample x normalized to the interval [-1,1] in μ-law is:

$$F(x) = \text{sgn}(x) \frac{\ln(1 + \mu|x|)}{\ln(1 + \mu)} \qquad -1 \leq x \leq 1$$

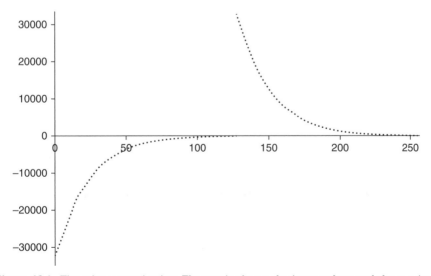

Figure 12.1. The μ-law quantization. The y-axis shows the input values and the x-axis shows the encoded values. One can see the logarithmic scale and the much denser concentration of values for low-amplitude input signals where the ear is more sensitive.

where μ is usually 255 for eight bits and sgn(x) is the sign function. Uncompressing requires the inversion of the formula, which is:

$$F^{-1}(y) = \text{sgn}(y)(1/\mu)\left[(1+\mu)^{|y|} - 1\right] \quad -1 \leq y \leq 1$$

The companding formula for A-law is:

$$F(x) = \text{sgn}(x) \begin{cases} \dfrac{A|x|}{1+\ln(A)}, & |x| < \dfrac{1}{A} \\ \dfrac{1+\ln(A|x|)}{1+\ln(A)}, & \dfrac{1}{A} \leq |x| \leq 1, \end{cases}$$

where A is the compression parameter. In Europe, A = 87.7; the value 87.6 is also used.
   Decompression works as follows:

$$F^{-1}(y) = \text{sgn}(y) \begin{cases} \dfrac{|y|(1+\ln(A))}{A}, & |y| < \dfrac{1}{1+\ln(A)} \\ \dfrac{\exp(|y|(1+\ln(A))-1)}{A}, & \dfrac{1}{1+\ln(A)} \leq |y| < 1. \end{cases}$$

Conceptually, both algorithms are the same. The μ-law algorithm provides a slightly better compression than A-law at the cost of worse proportional distortion for low-amplitude signals. Both of them are used worldwide in digital telephony, usually for compressing a sixteen-bit signal into a twelve-bit signal. Because A-law is slightly better quality, telephony companies prefer A-law for an international connection if at least one country uses it. The μ-law algorithm has become a quasi standard for low-bandwidth voice recordings, as it is the default encoding of Sun's audio file format (file extension ".au"). This format is also the default format of Linux's /dev/audio device and is supported by most common audio APIs. It has been standardized as ITU-T Recommendation G.711. Both algorithms are practically implemented by one lookup table for encoding and one lookup table for decoding.

Visual Quantization

Like researchers have observed with the ear, different quantities sensed by the eye scale logarithmically with intensity. One example is brightness, which the ancient Greeks discovered: stellar magnitude, which measures the light intensity of stars in the sky and which Hipparchus invented about 150 BC, has a logarithmic scale. So by using a logarithmic scale for brightness, something like μ-law for audio could be effectively used for image data as well. A. B. Clark of AT&T first patented a system that accomplishes this in 1928. Many different patents exist in this domain, and image data can be quantized in many ways. Therefore, no one algorithm standard exists for brightness quantization. We leave the creation of a grayscale image compression algorithm using a brightness compander as an exercise to the reader.

The old NTSC TV standard, as well as the JPEG compression algorithm, uses quantization in the different color channels. However, this is a different quantization; it involves spatial information.

Motion Quantization

Video itself is the best example of quantization at work. A video is a sequence of images replayed in a rapid succession. Just as any other sampling, a video is a quantized version of the reality it represents. The human eye can fuse the images into moving scenes if the images are presented with about one-thirtieth of a second between them. In other words, we need a frame rate of about 30 Hz to create the illusion of a moving scene. This, however, is just a rule of thumb. The actual frame rate depends on the physical state of an individual and on the content that is shown. The coexistence of a lip-synchronous audio track generally allows for lower frame rates because the human brain is good at filling missing information across modalities. Therefore, when wanting to compress a video, it is often adequate to quantize the reality even further and play back a video at about fifteen frames per second, a technique scholars in the field very often used for Web demonstrations and other bandwidth-critical applications.

DIFFERENTIAL CODING

Quantization methods are relatively simple to implement and offer a decent lossy compression scheme. However, they will usually not work beyond a compression ratio of 2:1 with acceptable perceptual reproduction quality. Differential coding is a scheme that may or may not build on quantization. It leverages global knowledge about the properties of the signal to encode. It is widely used for audio, image, and video compression, and scales very well from lossless to entirely lossy. The general scheme is presented in Figure 12.2.

The main component of a differential encoder is the predictor. The predictor takes as input the n samples of the signal to predict the next m samples. The predicted samples

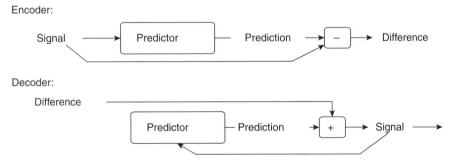

Figure 12.2. Schematic of a differential encoder: The signal is used as the input for a prediction model. The predictions are then subtracted from the original signal. The difference is transmitted. Decoding uses the previously decoded signals to feed the predictor which must, of course, be identical in both encoder and decoder.

are then compared to the original input. The difference is considered to be the encoding. If the prediction was perfect, only zeros would have to be transmitted to the decoder. Of course, nothing is ever perfect, but good decoders will produce very small differences that do not need many bits. Different strategies are used to model predictors and the next section will present some of them. To decode the signal, previously decoded samples are used to feed an identical predictor. The prediction is then added to the encoding to reproduce the signal. To bootstrap the process, the first few samples can be predicted with zero so that the actual signal is transmitted for initialization. This scheme by itself is lossless. However, some predictors have a build in quantization and sometimes the output difference is thresholded. To avoid errors growing too large over time, some algorithms alternate between lossy and lossless encoding; for example, every couple of frames, an un-encoded sample has to be part of the stream. For better compression, difference encoding is often combined with entropy encoding.

Differential Coding in Audio: ADPCM

As a first example of a differential encoder, we look at adaptive differential pulse code modulation (ADPCM). ADPCM is standardized in ITU-T G.726. It is a widespread audio format used mainly for speech encoding. The idea behind the difference encoding of audio is that sound other than noise follows a rather predictable wave pattern; that is, the differences between consecutive samples will usually be much smaller than the samples themselves. Still, in some cases, sample values might drop from very high amplitude to very low amplitude. To maintain a constant-rate difference bit stream, one must furthermore predict whether these differences are large for the next couple of sample values. This, together with a quantization of the difference values, is the idea of ADPCM.

The ADPCM algorithm is used to map a series of twelve-bit μ-law (or A-law) PCM samples into a series of four-bit ADPCM samples. Given the original sample values as input, ADPCM predicts both the next sample and the step size. A large step size means that the audio sample differences are large; a small step size means the differences are small. The Interactive Multimedia Association (IMA) standard defines ADPCM as shown in Figure 12.3. The IMA ADPCM code consists of four bits: one bit for the sign and three bits for the difference.

Using a prediction model, an adaptive predictor guesses if future samples values might be large. If so, the algorithm increases the bits available for the difference encoding by adjusting the initial quantization. If the step sizes might be smaller, the quantization is adjusted to a smaller bit length per sample. For every sample, two values have to be calculated: the difference to the previous (inverse quantized) signal sample and a value that determines the current step size. The process is bootstrapped by the first values all set to zero and the original sample being passed through.

Decoding works almost the same way: the compressed signal enters the decoder. The encoded value is the difference to the previously predicted value. This difference is added to the previous output value and constitutes the new output value. At the same time, the new step size is calculated, which is needed to calculate the next prediction. Because the decoder and the encoder are very similar and yet ADPCM, we will only provide the pseudo-

Encoder:

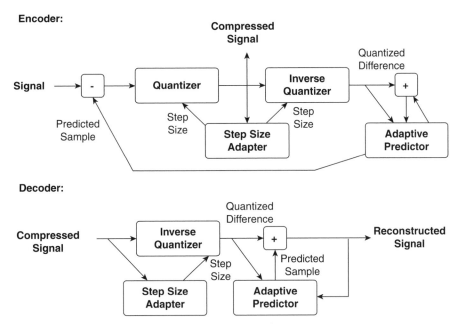

Decoder:

Figure 12.3. ADPCM encoder and decoder. A differential coder for audio signal that takes into account both the first and the second derivative of the signal. As with any predictive coding algorithms, the decoder block is embedded in the encoder.

code for a decoder here. For the concrete values of tables, header information, and magic numbers, please refer to the standard itself.

```
// Input: a sequence of ADPCM-coded samples C
// Output: a sequence of raw audio samples S
adpcm_decode(C)
    Read header information from C
    First sample of S := first sample in C
    step_size_index := initial index provided in header
    step size := step size table[step_size_index]
    old sample := first sample in C
    FOREACH (sample c in C)
      delta := step size encoded in c
      s := old sample + delta
    Add s to S
    step_size_index := indexTable[s]
    step size := step size table[step_size_index]
    old sample := s
  decode_adpcm := S
```

ADPCM achieves a decent compression rate (about 4:1) and is very useable for speech signals. Music and other noise is not compressed very well using this methodology as the quality can suffer greatly. The resulting quality is not unbearable, though, so it could be used as a poor man's music compressor.

Differential Coding in Images: PNG

The PNG image format uses a differential encoding step before an LZ-derivate entropy encoder is used. The algorithm predicts the color of each pixel based on the colors of previous neighboring pixels and subtracts the predicted color of the pixel from the actual color. An image line compressed in this way is often more compressible than the raw image line would be, especially if it is similar to the line above, because the differences from prediction will generally be clustered around zero, rather than spread over all possible image values. This is particularly important in relating separate rows because the later applied entropy compression (DEFLATE; see Chapter 11), has no understanding that an image is a 2D entity, and of course interprets the image data as a stream of bits. The predictor uses the pattern depicted in Figure 12.4 to sift through the image.

The predictor has five states that predict the value of each byte (of the original image data) based on the corresponding pixel to the left (a), above (b), above and to the left (c), or some combination thereof, and encodes the difference between the predicted value and the actual value. The states are shown in Table 12.1:

The Paeth filter computes a simple linear function of the three neighboring pixels (a, b, c), then chooses as a predictor the neighboring pixel closest to the computed value as defined by the following pseudo-code:

```
// Input: color values a, b, and c as illustrated in Figure 12.3
// a = left, b = above, c = upper left
// Output: a paeth prediction for a, b, and c
paeth_predict(a,b,c)
    p := a+b-c
    pa := abs(p-a)
    pb := abs(p-b)
    pc := abs(p-c)
    IF (pa<=pb AND pa<=pc) p := a
    ELSE IF (pb <= pc) p := b
    ELSE p := c
paeth_predict := p
```

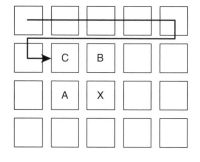

Figure 12.4. The PNG image is scanned line by line. The color value of pixel x is the one to be predicted and one of five different predictor states can be used that depend on the color values of a, b, and c.

Table 12.1. Predictor states used for differential encoding in the PNG image format

State	Name	Predicted Value
0	None	Zero (so that the raw value passes through unaltered)
1	Sub	Value of a (to the left)
2	Up	Value of b (above)
3	Average	Mean of bytes a and b, rounded down
4	Paeth	a, b, or c, whichever is closest to p = a + b − c

Compression of a pixel value x dependent on its neighbors a, b, and c works by calculating

$$compressed(x) = x - paeth\_predict(a,b,c)$$

and decompression works by reversing the formula to

$$uncompressed(x) = compressed(x) + paeth\_predict(a,b,c).$$

The particular states are chosen adaptively on a line-by-line basis based on a heuristic developed by Lee Daniel Crocker, who tested the methods on many images during the creation of the format. If interlacing is used, each stage of the interlacing is filtered separately. It makes the compression generally less effective, however.

Differential Coding in Video: Motion Compensation in MPEG-1

Differential encoding is also used for videos. Every video that is shipped on video CD, DVD, Blu-ray disc, or through digital cable, satellite, or antenna television is compressed using an algorithm that contains a differential encoder. The idea is that at twenty-five or more frames per second, the differences between two or even more consecutive video frames are minor. Any object in the camera view that does not change its appearance or position during 0.04 seconds will not have changed between two frames. Also, physical objects tend to not randomly change position. In other words, an object that is visible on the left and is known to have changed its position rightward over the previous couple of frames will probably either stop in the next frame or continue to do so. This is the idea behind motion compensation: rather than just encoding video frames as stand-alone images, the difference between them is modeled by a differential encoder. This technique is used in different variations in all versions of MPEG video and in many other video codecs. In the following, we will describe one version of the MPEG-1 motion compensation.

The MPEG-1 algorithm works on a block-by-block basis. In the next chapter, we will outline the advantages of this approach. For now, it is important to know that an 8 x 8 pixel block is called a *macro block*. To decrease the amount of spatial redundancy in a video, only macro blocks that change inside a certain amount of consecutive frames are updated.

This is known as *conditional replenishment*. However, conditional replenishment is not very effective by itself. Movement of large objects and/or the camera may result in large portions of macro blocks needing to be updated, even though only the position, not the appearance, of the previously encoded objects has changed. Through motion prediction, the encoder can compensate for this movement and remove a large amount of redundant information. The encoder compares the current frame with adjacent parts of the video from the previous frame up to an encoder-specific predefined radius limit from the area of the current macro block. If a match is found, only the direction and distance (i.e., the vector of the motion) from the previous video area to the current macro block need to be encoded.

Of course, a predicted macro block rarely matches the current frame perfectly. The difference between the predicted matching area and the real macro block is therefore the lossy part of the process. The larger the error, the more data must be additionally encoded in the frame.

The distance between two areas in a frame is measured in number of pixels but is often referred to as *pels*. MPEG-1 video uses a motion vector precision of one half of a pixel or *half-pel*. The finer the precision, the more accurate the match is likely to be, and the more efficient the compression. Higher precision, however, also requires higher runtime of the encoder and a larger encoding bitrate because potentially more motion vectors have to be stored. In the end, because neighboring macro blocks are very likely to have similar motion vectors, only the difference between the motion vectors has to be encoded for each macro block. The pseudo-code for a very simple, exhaustive motion estimator is:

```
// Input: REF = reference frame, CUR = current frame
// Output: K a set of indices to the 8 x 8 blocks in REF most
// closely the matching the block in CUR
motion_Estimate(REF, CUR)
    FOREACH (block MB in CUR)
        FOREACH (i := 0,1,...,64) //8 x 8 block
        pcur[i] := pixel in MB
        pref[i] := pixel in REFMB
        FOREACH (block k in REF)
            distortion[k] := SUM(distortion(pcur[i],pref[k,i])
    Add minimum value for distortion[k] to K
motion_Estimate := K
```

Ideally, the distortion function reflects human perception. Unfortunately, this is still a matter of research, therefore Euclidean distance or other similarly simple metrics are often used.

To bootstrap the process, the first frame does not depend on any other frame. It is just a JPEG image (so-called I-Frame). The frames after the I-Frames are called P-frames (predictive frames). MPEG also defines B-frames. These frames take into account the previous and the next frame for motion prediction and can therefore achieve a higher compression ratio. However, it is necessary for the player to first decode the next frame sequentially after

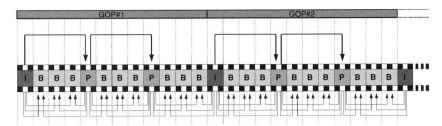

Figure 12.5. Video compression typically organizes frames into B, P, and I frames for motion compensation. Several of them form a group of pictures (GOP).

the B-frame, before the B-frame can be decoded. Therefore B-frames are computationally more complex in both encoding and decoding.

Because motion compensation is lossy and each frame depends on the previous one, the error propagates easily and grows with every frame. Therefore, and also for the ability to play a video from a random time position, I-frames are inserted every couple of frames. The I-frame and all frames that ultimately depend on it are called *group of pictures* (GOP). A typical GOP size is about twenty frames. Figure 12.5 illustrates this concept.

Except ADPCM, differential encoding is rarely used alone. Both MPEG and PNG rely on additional compression steps. The next chapter explores the ideas behind them and other, more advanced, techniques.

RECOMMENDED READING

Knowledge about lossy compression is mostly found in original research papers and standards. Therefore, our references are either of the two, with the exception of Pohlmann's textbook on digital audio. We recommend starting with the research article before going to the ITU.T, ISO, and RFC standards because the standards do not provide a very good overview, but often already assume conceptual knowledge of a certain compression scheme. For a lighter introduction to the topic, we provided links to some demonstration and explanation Web sites, which we recommend as an introduction after reading our chapters.

Further Reading

Franklin S. Cooper and Ignatius Mattingly. "Computer-controlled PCM system for investigation of dichotic speech perception," *Journal of the Acoustical Society of America*, 46: 115, 1969.

P. Cummiskey, N. S. Jayant, and J. L. Flanagan. "Adaptive quantization in differential PCM coding of speech," *Bell Syst. Tech. J.*, 52: 1105–18, September 1973.

Didier Le Gall. "MPEG: A video compression standard for multimedia applications," *Communications of the ACM*, 43 (4): 46–56, April 1991.

J. B. MacQueen. "Some methods for classification and analysis of multivariate observations." *Proceedings of 5th Berkeley Symposium on Mathematical Statistics and Probability*. Berkeley: University of California Press, 1:281–97, 1967.

Ralph Miller and Bob Badgley. U.S. Patent 3,912,868 filed in 1943: N-ary Pulse Code Modulation.

A. W. Paeth. "Image file compression made easy." In *Graphics Gems II*, James Arvo, editor. San Diego, CA: Academic Press. 1991.

Dan Pelleg and Andrew Moore. "X-means: Extending K-means with efficient estimation of the number of clusters." *Proceedings of the Seventeenth International Conference on Machine Learning*, pp. 727–34. San Francisco, CA. 2000.

Ken C. Pohlmann. *Principles of Digital Audio*. Carmel, IN: Sams/Prentice-Hall Computer Publishing, 2nd edition, 1985.

Web Links

PNG home: http://www.libpng.org/pub/png/.

Quantization links in data compression info: http://datacompression.info/Quantization. shtml.

Quantization threads in comp.dsp: http://www.dsprelated.com/comp.dsp/keyword/ Quantization.php.

STANDARDS

ADPCM: ITU.T Recommendation G.726.

MPEG-1 Video: ISO/IEC-11172–2.

PNG: RFC 2083.

μ-law: ITU.T Recommendation G.711.

EXERCISES

1. Implement linear quantization and K-means and use the implemented quantization algorithms to reduce the colors of several color images to 2, 4, 8, 16, 64, and 256 colors. Which algorithm performs "best"?

2. Try linear quantization on an audio file with different granularity. What artifacts can you hear?

3. Find or implement a μ-law compression and decompression table. Modify the algorithm such that it compresses down to four bits.

4. As described in the text, create a logarithmic compander for light intensity and try it on grayscale images.

5. Try to apply μ-law compression as a color quantization algorithm for an image.

6. Apply an entropy encoder of your choice to a set of companded audio files and compare the compression of applying the same entropy encoding to the uncompanded files. How do you explain the results?

7. Create a simple predictive coder and decoder for a sampled audio file based only on the difference between two sample values. This algorithm is often referred to as *differential pulse code modulation* (DPCM).

8. Change your DPCM encoder so that instead of trying to minimize the amount of bits for each sample, it maximizes the amounts of bits (probably even taking more bits than the original). Make sure it is still a differential compression scheme (although a maximally bad one).

9. Design a differential encoder/decoder for ASCII text files containing natural language. Try to model your predictor so it takes into account the properties of the natural language the original text is encoded in (e.g., the frequency of the individual characters following other characters).

10. Discuss the properties of sound files when ADPCM compression will work well and when it won't. Describe both compression efficiency and perceptual accuracy.

11. Would the application of a smoothing algorithm improve the quality of the output of the ADPCM encoder?

12. Implement the PNG difference encoder as described in the text and apply it to test images. Describe how you choose the heuristics to find the state of the predictor.

13. Add another predictor state to your PNG algorithm – when would you choose it and why do you think it is good?

14. Extract several consecutive frames from a video and save them as JPEG.

15. Calculate the difference image and discuss why certain pixels are shown in the difference image.

16. Using several frames from the video, implement a routine to calculate the motion vectors for 8 x 8 blocks.

13 Advanced Perceptual Compression

The lossy compression techniques presented so far have tried to exploit the fundamental mathematical properties of information (lossless coding), to model and approximate the properties of the signal directly (differential coding), and to model the creation of the signal (source coding, such as in speech compression). We also presented simple perceptual methods, such as the μ-law encoder.

The methods presented in this chapter use transformations modeled after how human sensory perception works, using a much greater sophistication level. These perceptual coders are so effective that they are used in virtually every device today that handles images or sound, from photo cameras to mobile phones to DVD players to mobile digital music players.

Before we introduce them, we recapitulate two fundamental signal transformations that are an important prerequisite for all the algorithms presented in this chapter, as well as for many of the analysis algorithms presented later. When explaining perceptual compression, two transformations are very important: the Discrete Fourier Transform (DFT) and the Discrete Cosine Transform (DCT), which are described in the following sections. Other transforms, such as the Discrete Wavelet Transforms (DWT), which are a generalization on the transforms mentioned, are also used in multimedia signal processing, and the references cited at the end of this chapter are well worth looking up.

DISCRETE FOURIER TRANSFORM (DFT)

A given signal can be converted between the time and frequency domains with a number of mathematical operations.[1] The theory of the Fourier transform goes back to 1822, when Jean-Baptiste-Joseph Fourier found that any function can be described as a sum of sine and cosine functions. Periodic functions need a finite set of sine and cosine functions and aperiodic functions an infinite number of sine and cosine functions. The original Fourier transform assumes continuous functions rather than discrete sequences and an open interval domain. Therefore, in practice, the discretized version of the Fourier transform

---

[1]   If the concept of frequency space and the math underlying it is not familiar to you, we recommend consulting the literature referenced at the end of this chapter.

results in artifacts at the borders of the sequence, which have to be gotten over by windowing strategies. Both the Discrete Fourier Transform and the Discrete Cosine Transform are in theory reversible without signal loss, but in practice, numerical constraints make the transforms often slightly lossy. However, unless noted otherwise, we will assume the transforms to be lossless.

The input to the DFT is a sequence of N real or complex numbers $x_0, \ldots, x_{N-1}$, which is transformed into a sequence of N complex numbers $X_0, \ldots, X_{N-1}$ by the DFT according to the following equation:

$$X_k = \sum_{n=0}^{N-1} x_n e^{-\frac{2\pi i}{N} kn} \quad k = 0, \ldots, N-1 \tag{13.1}$$

where $e^{\frac{2\pi i}{N}}$ is a primitive N'th root of one. The inverse transform is given by:

$$x_n = \frac{1}{N} \sum_{k=0}^{N-1} X_k e^{\frac{2\pi i}{N} kn} \quad n = 0, \ldots, N-1. \tag{13.2}$$

A direct algorithmic translation of these two equations requires $O(N^2)$ operations. However, it is possible to execute the same computation with only $O(N \log N)$ complexity by factorizing the equation and reusing an intermediate result by applying dynamic programming. The resulting algorithms are called the Fast Fourier Transform (FFT) and the Fast Cosine Transform (FCT). These algorithms are the ones most often implemented into actual codecs. In addition, the DFT and DCT computations are parallelizable, which results in speed gains on manycore architectures.

The following pseudo-code can transform a given signal into frequency domain using the Discrete Fourier Transform. The algorithm is called the Cooley-Tukey Algorithm and it is the most common algorithm for the Fast Fourier Transform.

```
// Input: A number N of samples X. N must be an integer power of two.
//        s the stride
// Output: The Discrete Fourier Transform of X in the array Y.
FFT(X, N, s)
   IF (N==1) THEN
      Y[0]:=X{0] // Trivial size-1 case: Sample = DC coefficient
   ELSE
      Y[0,...,N/2]:=FFT(X,N/2,2*s) // DFT of (X[0],X[2s},X[4s}, ...)
      Y[N/2,...,N-1]:=FFT(X[s,...,N-1],N/2,2*s)
            // DFT of (X[s],X[s+2s],X[s+4s], ...)
   FOR k:=0 TO N/2 // Combine the two halves into one
      t:=Y[k]
      Y[k]:=t+exp(-2*pi*k/N)*Y[k=N/2]
      Y[k+N/2]:=t-exp(-2*pi*k/N)*Y[k=N/2]
FFT := Y
```

Cooley-Tukey Algorithm for FFT

The elements of the converted signal are called *coefficients*. The first coefficient corresponds to $sin(\pi/2)$, which is one. Therefore, it is called the *DC coefficient* (from the electrical engineering interpretation DC = direct current); the rest of the coefficients are called *AC coefficients* (AC = alternating current).

DISCRETE COSINE TRANSFORM (DCT)

The discrete cosine transform (DCT) expresses a finite sequence of data points as a sum of cosine functions, rather than as sine functions in the DFT, at different frequencies. The most important difference between DCT and DFT for practical applications is that the DCT uses only real numbers. The DCT is equivalent (up to an overall scale factor of two) to a DFT of 4N real inputs of even symmetry where the even-indexed elements are zero. This property allows applying the transformation without increasing the number of elements in the sequence. Some variants of the DCT differ slightly in property, but the most common one is given in the following equation. The N real numbers $x_0, \ldots, x_{N-1}$ are transformed into the N real numbers $X_0, \ldots, X_{N-1}$ according to:

$$X_k = \sum_{n=0}^{N-1} x_n \cos\left[\frac{\pi}{N}\left(n+\frac{1}{2}\right)k\right] \quad k=0,\ldots,N-1. \tag{13.3}$$

The inverse DCT (IDCT) is then given by multiplying the DCT with

$$X_k = \frac{1}{2}x_0 + \sum_{n=1}^{N-1} x_n \cos\left[\frac{\pi}{N}n\left(k+\frac{1}{2}\right)\right] \quad k=0,\ldots,N-1. \tag{13.4}$$

Figure 13.1 shows a visualization of the DCT coefficients given an input signal. Again, the DC coefficient determines the overall gain of the signal, while the AC coefficients represent the energies of the signal in different frequency bands.

To compute the DCT, DFT, inverse DCT, and inverse DFT on multidimensional data, that is, matrixes or N-dimensional data, all one needs to do is compose the DCTs and DFTs computed along each dimension. A two-dimensional DCT, for example, is therefore given as:

$$X_{k_1,k_2} = \sum_{n_1=0}^{N_1-1}\sum_{n_2=0}^{N_2-1} x_{n_1,n_2} \cos\left[\frac{\pi}{N_1}\left(n_1+\frac{1}{2}\right)k_1\right] \cos\left[\frac{\pi}{N_2}\left(n_2+\frac{1}{2}\right)k_2\right]. \tag{13.5}$$

The following two pseudo-code snippets compute a two-dimensional DCT.

```
// Input: A number N
// Output: An NxN DCT matrix H.
dct_matrix(N)
  FOR i:=0 TO N
    FOR j:=0 TO N
      H[i][j]:=sqrt(2/N)*cos(pi*i*(2*j+1)/(2*N))
```

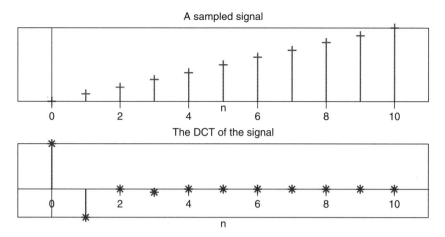

Figure 13.1. Example DCT transform of a small sequence of samples.

```
FOR j:=0 TO N
    H[0][j]=H[0][j]/sqrt(2)
dct_matrix := H

// Input: N, an NxN matrix of samples M, a DCT matrix H
// Output: The DCT coefficients of M, called C.
DCT(N,M,H)
    // Transform columns
    FOR k:=0 TO N
        FOR l:=0 TO N
            sum:=0
            FOR m=0 TO N
                sum:=sum+H[k][m]*M[m][j]
            C[k][l]:=sum
    // Transform rows
    FOR k:=0 TO N
        FOR l:=0 TO N
            sum:=0
            FOR m=0 TO N
                sum:=sum+H[l][m]*M[k][m]
            C[k][l]:=sum
dct_matrix := c
```

This code is not very efficient because it does not reuse intermediate results. However, it shows the strategy of precomputing the matrix, which has advantages when experimenting with different variations of the function.

Figure 13.2 shows a combination of horizontal and vertical frequencies for an $N=8$ two-dimensional DCT. Each step from left to right and top to bottom is an increase in frequency

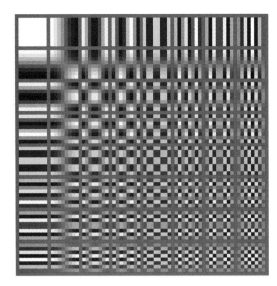

Figure 13.2. DCT frequencies for 8x8 matrixes in X- and Y- increasing order.

by 0.5 cycle; for example, moving right one from the top left square yields a half-cycle increase in the horizontal frequency. The picture provides an initial intuition for why the DCT is useable for image compression: a given 8 x 8 square in Figure 13.2 is imaginable to be a part in a black-and-white image. In other words, any given 8 x 8 pixel square in an image can be reduced (lossy) to one of the 8 x 8 blocks in Figure 13.2. This is exploited in a very common image compression algorithm, commonly referred to as JPEG, which is explained in the next section.

THE CONVOLUTION THEOREM

Convolution is an operation on two functions *f* and *g* that produces a third function. This third function is typically viewed as a modified version of one of the original functions. For example, a function such as an image, a video, a set of measurement samples, or an audio track may be modified by a second function, usually called a *filter*. A fundamental correspondence exists between the time space and the frequency space: *the convolution theorem*. It states that a convolution filter in one domain (e.g., time) equals point-wise multiplication in the other domain (e.g., frequency). In multimedia computing, this is the most important fact about convolutions. Also, it means when discussing compression, processing, and analysis techniques, we can switch between frequency-domain and time-domain operation as we please. Here is an explanation of how this works.

Let *f* and *g* denote two functions and *f* * *g* their convolution. (Note that * denotes convolution, not multiplication, in this context.) Let *F* denote the Fourier transform, so $F\{f\}$ and $F\{g\}$ are the Fourier transforms of *f* and *g*, respectively. Then

$$F\{f*g\} = F\{f\} \cdot F\{g\} \tag{13.6}$$

where the dot denotes point-wise multiplication. The other direction is also true:

$$F\{f \bullet g\} = F\{f\} * F\{g\} \tag{13.7}$$

By applying the inverse Fourier transform, one can write:

$$f * g = F^{-1}\{F\{f\} \cdot F\{g\}\}. \tag{13.8}$$

The theorem allows us to design convolution filters in either time or frequency space, whichever is more convenient for the concrete problem. This is done in practice, usually for efficiency reasons. Therefore, some of the frequently used filters presented in this chapter have their "home" in frequency space and others seem to be mostly applied in time space.

JPEG

JPEG is the single most common image format used by digital cameras and other photographic image capture devices. JPEG stands for Joint Photographic Experts Group, the name of the committee that created the standard. The group was organized in 1986, issuing a standard in 1992, which was approved in 1994 as ISO 10918–1. The file format is named JPEG File Interchange Format (JFIF), but the acronym *jpeg* or *jpg* is used more commonly both as a file extension and a name of the file format. Apart from JFIF, there is also another standard, called Exchangeable Image Format (Exif), which on top of the image content also standardizes the storage of specific metadata, such as geo-location and camera manufacturer. The following section presents an overview of the image compression part of the algorithm. The encoding uses several steps, of which the most important is a quantization in frequency space, generated by the Discrete Cosine Transform.

The following pseudo-code outlines the algorithm:

```
// Input: A color image I in twenty-four-bit RGB format
// Output: A JFIF-compressed image J.
JPEG(I)
    transform color space from RGB to Y, Cr, Cb
    split I into 8 x 8 blocks for each Y, Cr, Cb
    scale down the resolution of the Cr and Cb blocks to 4 x 4 blocks
    Apply DY:=DCT(Y), DU:=DCT(Cr), DV:=DCT(Cb).
    Quantize DY, DU, and DV according to a user setting
    Linearize DY, DU, and DV into a stream S
    Apply static Huffman(S)
    J := Header information + S
JPEG := J
```

In the following, we will now describe each step and why it is applied.

Tiling

The first step is to split the image into 8 x 8 pixel blocks. The splitting was originally performed to make the computation of the DCT more tractable. On today's computers, this is no longer an issue, and a larger block size, such as 16 x 16, is sometimes applied. Furthermore, the splitting allows for very efficient and easy parallelization on multi-core architectures.

Chroma Quantization

Pixels are then converted to the Y, Cb, Cr color space (color spaces are described in Chapter 6). This allows the application of a technique called *chroma quantization*. The idea is that because the human visual system is less sensitive to the position of color than to brightness, bandwidth can be saved by storing more detail about the brightness of a pixel than of the color. At normal viewing distances, no perceptible loss is incurred by sampling the color detail at a lower rate. The signal is divided into a luma (brightness) component Y and two chroma (color difference) components Cr, Cb (see Chapter 6). The subsampling scheme is commonly expressed as a ratio R:A:B (e.g., 4:2:2) that describes the number of luminance and chrominance samples in a conceptual region that is R pixels wide and two pixels high. R is the width of the region (e.g., four pixels), A is the number of chrominance samples (Cr,Cb) in the first row of R pixels, and B is the number of chrominance samples (Cr,Cb) in the second row of R pixels. The old analog TV standard NTSC, for example, used a fixed 4:1:1 chroma quantization scheme.

Frequency Space Quantization

The human eye can perceive small differences in brightness over a relatively large area. However, human visual perception does not easily distinguish high-frequency brightness variations. In other words, details in a texture may be blurred without reduction in perceived image quality. JPEG utilizes this fact by reducing the amount of information in the high-frequency components. Therefore, each block is converted into frequency space by applying a DCT. Then each coefficient in the block is divided by a constant for that component, rounding to the nearest integer. The division constants are specified in a so-called quantization matrix, which is varied depending on a user-definable quality factor. A typical quantization matrix looks like this:

$$
\begin{bmatrix}
16 & 11 & 10 & 16 & 24 & 40 & 51 & 61 \\
12 & 12 & 14 & 19 & 26 & 58 & 60 & 55 \\
14 & 13 & 16 & 24 & 40 & 57 & 69 & 56 \\
14 & 17 & 22 & 29 & 51 & 87 & 80 & 62 \\
18 & 22 & 37 & 56 & 68 & 109 & 103 & 77 \\
24 & 35 & 55 & 64 & 81 & 104 & 113 & 92 \\
49 & 64 & 78 & 87 & 103 & 121 & 120 & 101 \\
72 & 92 & 95 & 98 & 112 & 100 & 103 & 99
\end{bmatrix}
\tag{13.9}
$$

Figure 13.3. Sample JPEG image with increasing amount of quantization (increasing in order top-left, top-right, bottom-left, bottom-right). (See Plate VII for color version.)

Note that, apart from the DC coefficient in the upper left corner, the lower frequencies have smaller quantization and the higher frequencies have higher quantization. When the user wants higher quality, the quantization values can be lowered; when higher compression is a goal, the quantization coefficients can be increased in value. Figure 13.3 shows an image with different strengths of quantization applied.

As a result of applying quantization to the DCT blocks, many of the higher-frequency components are typically rounded to zero, and many of the rest become small positive or negative numbers, which take fewer bits to store.

Linearization and Lossless Encoding

After quantization, many of the higher-frequency components of a block are zero or close to zero. Therefore, the final step is to use run-length encoding, followed by a Huffman compressor (see Chapter 11). To apply run-length encoding, the blocks are linearized using a scheme that allows the same frequencies to be in sequences, which makes many zeros and the potentially same values in X- and Y- direction appear in sequence. Figure 13.4 shows the linearization scheme.

Depending on the image and chosen quantization, compression rates of 1:2–20 and higher compared to an uncompressed image are possible. Decompression works by reversing the process, for example, multiplying with the quantization matrix, using the inverse DCT, and so on. Figure 13.5 shows a comparison of compression and decompressions.

Newer versions of the JPEG standard, for example JPEG2000, use different transforms, such as Wavelet transforms (see references), instead of the DCT to reduce artifacts after quantization in higher compression modes. Also, some implements allow the use of

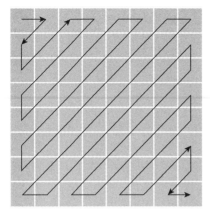

Figure 13.4. Linearization scheme for an 8x8 JPEG block.

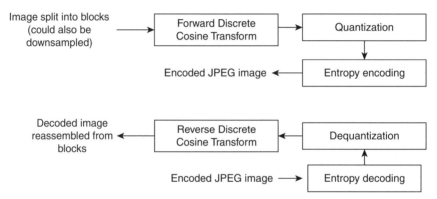

Figure 13.5. Overview of the JPEG compression/decompression algorithm.

arithmetic coding instead of Huffman coding. Many video codes have adopted the JPEG encoding methods, but sometimes vary the block size and the linearization scheme.

PSYCHOACOUSTICS

Similar to the exploitation of brightness versus chroma perception and high-frequency blurring in JPEG, audio signals can be compressed based on human auditory perception. We already described audio codecs that utilize perceptual properties of the human ear, such as the μ-law compression examined in Chapter 11 that utilizes the nonlinear perception of amplitude. Like JPEG, audio codecs can leverage perceptual properties to determine which parts of the signal can be quantized more aggressively or even removed without changing a human's perception of the result. Unfortunately, the human ear is more sensitive to signal alterations than the human eye. So applying the JPEG scheme of transforming the signal into the frequency domain and then linearly scaling the coefficients would work for compression, but would result in significant audible artifacts.

To achieve acceptable quality and compression at the same time, one has to take into account a wider range of perceptual properties of the human auditory system. As a result, the development of modern audio compression methods is mostly one of measuring and estimating how people perceive various sounds, a field known as *psychoacoustics*. The resulting lossy compression schemes, however, routinely lead to audio files that are about 10 percent the size of high-quality masters with very little discernible loss in quality. Formats based on psychoacoustics include Ogg Vorbis, Dolby AAC, Microsoft WMA, MPEG-1 Layer II (used for digital audio broadcasting in several countries), and Sony ATRAC. In the following, we will provide an overview of the functionality of one version of the most prominent representative of perceptual audio codecs: MPEG-2 Audio Layer 3, or MP3.

We start with the presentation of the most important psychoacoustic phenomena that audio codecs utilize.

Frequency/Loudness Resolution

As explained in Chapter 5, the human ear perceives sounds in the range of about 16 Hz to 20 kHz. The smallest pitch differences a human can perceive depends on the absolute pitch values, but is reported based on clinical experiments to be about 3.6 Hz within the frequency range of 1,000–2,000 Hz. However, smaller pitch differences may be perceived through the interference of two pitches, an effect known as *beating*: the phase variance caused by two interfering frequencies might be heard as a low-frequency difference pitch.

The intensity range of audible sounds is enormous, but also depends on the frequency. Roughly speaking, the lower the frequency, the louder a sound is perceived. This is expressed in different scales that have been proposed in the literature derived from psychoacoustic experiments, such as the Mel scale and the Bark scale. The Bark scale was proposed by Eberhard Zwicker in 1961 and is named after Heinrich Barkhausen, who proposed the first subjective measurements of loudness. It seems to be more popular in music processing, while the Mel scale is used more often in speech processing. The Bark scale is also used for equal loudness assumptions in audio codecs. It is approximated by the following equation:

$$Bark = 13\arctan(0.00076 \cdot f) + 3.5 \cdot \arctan\left(\left(\frac{f}{7500}\right)^2\right) \qquad (13.10)$$

In this equation, f is the frequency of the tone in Hz. Sounds of equal Barks are estimated to have equal loudness. Figure 13.5 shows a plot of the Bark scale.

Very important for compression are the lower limits of audibility. This so-called absolute threshold of hearing (ATH) curve is derived by exposing humans to testing tones of various frequencies. Typically, the ear shows its lowest ATH between 1 kHz and 5 kHz (the range of speech), though this threshold also changes with age, with older ears showing

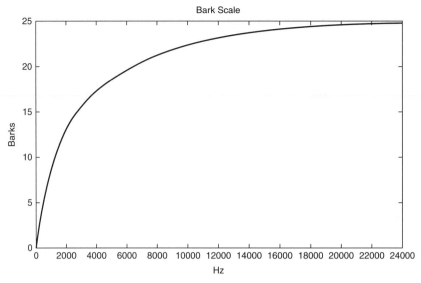

Figure 13.6. An example of an equal loudness scale curve: The Bark scale.

decreased sensitivity above 2 kHz. ATH is usually approximated by the following formula (from Terhardt 1979):

$$T_q(f) = 3.64 \left(\frac{f}{1000} \right)^{-0.8} - 6.5 e^{-0.6(f/1000-3.3)^2} + 10^{-3} \left(\frac{f}{1000} \right)^4 \tag{13.11}$$

Figure 13.6 shows the resulting curve.

Masking

While the two properties studied earlier were on measurements of isolated sounds, *masking* describes a property of the ear that concerns the interaction of different sounds: an otherwise clearly audible sound can be masked by another sound and thus become imperceptible.

This phenomenon can be experienced very easily, for example, in a situation where two people have a conversation at a bus stop. Suddenly a truck drives by and its noise interrupts the conversation: the voices have become imperceptible in the presence of the truck noise. A weaker sound is called *masked* if the presence of a stronger sound makes it inaudible. This phenomenon occurs because the loud sound distorts the ATH, making the quieter sounds (partially) fall below the threshold.

Masking can occur simultaneously (as in the bus stop example) and sequentially. A quieter sound emitted very soon after the decay of a stronger sound is masked by the louder sound. Also, a quieter sound just before a louder sound may be masked by the stronger sound. These two effects are called *forward* and *backward temporal masking*, respectively. Figure 13.7 illustrates the phenomenon of masking. An important property

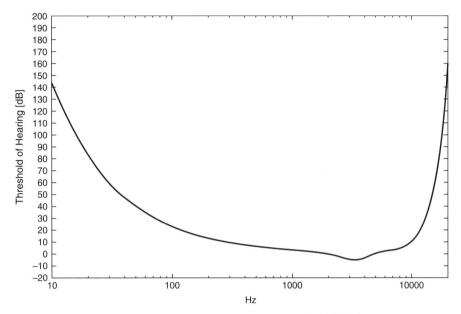

Figure 13.7. An estimate of the average lower hearing threshold (ATH).

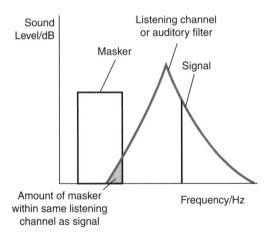

Figure 13.8. Illustration of Masking: A signal is masks large parts of the frequency space, rendering sounds in it (partially) imperceptible (adapted from Moore 1998).

that determines how a particular sound can mask another one is its tonality. For example, a sinusoidal masker requires a higher intensity to mask a noise-like "maskee" than a loud noise-like masker does to mask a sinusoid. Quantization can be seen as introducing noise and thereby masking good sounds with bad sounds. Psychoacoustic models used for compression take this into account by quantizing pure tones less than noisy ones. This is mostly accomplished by binning the frequency bands appropriately and quantizing frequency bins with higher energy less than those with lower energy.

In addition to frequency and temporal masking of sounds, sounds are also masked spatially. This means a sound perceived in one ear might prevent perception of sounds arriving at the other ear. This phenomenon is exploited to reduce perceptual redundancies across channels when stereo coding.

MP3

There are many implementations of MP3 encoders, and they differ in quality, compression rate, and many technical details. The ISO standards (see references) only describes the methods needed to decode a stream, which are much simpler, as will be explained later. Encoders usually reduce perceptual redundancy by first identifying sounds that are perceptually irrelevant, such as high frequencies and sound levels below ATH. Unfortunately, the reduction of imperceptible portions of sounds in audio files usually only accounts for a small percentage of the bits needed to represent the signal. Therefore, like in JPEG, the more effective method is to quantize the signal.

As mentioned earlier, a simple linear quantization with linear frequency bins, such as frequently applied in image and video compression, would not yield high enough quality as the ear is more sensitive to artifacts than the eye. The method used for audio is called *noise shaping*. Reducing the number of bits used to code an audio signal increases the amount of noise in the signal. The idea of noise shaping is to hide the noise generated by the quantization in areas of the audio stream that is least perceived, based on masking tables, ATH, and the Bark scale. Noise shaping can also be understood as distributing a predefined number of bits to the different frequency bands according to their perceptual priority given a psychoacoustic model. For example, higher frequencies of the signal might be coded with fewer bits as it is harder to perceive small differences in these regions. If reducing perceptual redundancy does not achieve sufficient compression for a particular application, it may require further lossy compression. Depending on the audio source, this still may produce acceptable perceptible quality. Let's look at the concrete implementation of an MP3 encoder, the open source compressor LAME.

Algorithm

Similar to the tiling in JPEG, the first operation on the audio signal is splitting it into packets, so-called granules (sometimes also called *frames* or *chunks*). LAME uses a granule size of 576 samples. These are then transformed into frequency space. This is usually done using a modified version of the DCT, called MDCT (see references). Once in frequency space, the coefficients are split into thirty-two different equal-sized frequency bands (each of them roughly 700Hz). For each granule, the algorithm then reserves a certain amount of bits usually predefined by the user. Constant bitrate (CBR) encoders allow only a certain maximum amount of bits per granule; average bitrate encoders (ABR) let the encoder try to achieve an average bitrate over the entire stream and variable bitrate encoders enable maximum audio quality by allowing a variable bitrate on the stream.

The following pseudo-code describes the operation of LAME's so-called outer loop, which is the algorithm that finds the combination of quantization coefficients (here called *scalefactors*) to produce the least amount of audible distortion:

```
// Input: A number of MDCT coefficients C binned in frequency bands.
// Output: A set of scalefactors S.
MP3_outerloop(C)
   S[]=0
   DO
      compute better quantization using S (call inner_loop)
      compute distortion within each scalefactor band
      compare distortion to allowed distortion (from psy-model)
      over := number of bands where distortion > allowed_distortion
      tot_noise :=
      average over all bands of distortion(db) – allowed_distortion(db)
      over_noise :=
         see tot_noise but only bands with distortion > allowed_distortion
      IF this quantization takes the least bits so far, save it in S.
      IF over=0 THEN return S.
         reduce quantization (use more bits) for bands with distortion
   WHILE (over>0) OR NOT (all scalefactors set to their max)
MP3_outerloop := S
```

To find the "better" quantization scalefactors in each iteration, both noise shaping and the bitrate that the user specified are taken into account in the "inner loop." The algorithm performs an exhaustive search over all possible values for the quantization factors, measuring both the resulting bitrate and the resulting perceptible noise as given by the psychoacoustic model and chooses the optimal configuration. This search is what takes most of the runtime of an MP3 encoder.

When a stereo signal is to be encoded, LAME knows two stereo modes: stereo and joint stereo. The stereo mode treats the left and right channels completely independently. Joint stereo means individual audio frames may be encoded in either normal stereo or mid/side stereo.

Mid/side stereo encodes the stereo signal into two channels, the middle channel, which contains the sum of the left and right channels, and the side channel, which contains the channel differences between the middle channel and the left and right channels, according to this scheme:

$$Middle = \frac{L+R}{2} \quad Side = \frac{L-R}{2} \tag{13.12}$$

with L=left channel and R=right channel. For decoding, $L=Middle+Side$, $R=Middle-Side$. More bits are allocated to the middle channel than to the side channels. Audio signals where the stereo channels are not well separated have very little information in the side channel. Therefore, this technique will improve bandwidth. However, there will be little gain for well-separated channels, and any encoding errors in this mode will show up as noise in *both* the left and right channels after decoding. Therefore, LAME chooses to switch between mid/side stereo and regular stereo on a frame-by-frame basis based on the difference in masking thresholds between the right and the left channel; that is, when LAME decides that the perceptual difference between the left and right channel is less than 5dB, it uses joint stereo.

After bit encoding the quantized coefficients, a Huffman encoder is used to compress the final stream. Decompression is computationally less expensive than compression. After Huffman decoding, only an inverse DCT has to be applied, and optionally the mid/side stereo coding has to be converted back. For this reason, MP3 players can be easily realized as mobile devices and built into cell phones. The compression rates of MP3 encoders vary depending on the content, the chosen bitrate, and the quality of the encoder. The rate of 128kbit/s for music that comes from a stereo CD (raw 1.34Mbit/s) is not atypical, thereby achieving a compression of about 1:10.

PERCEPTUAL VIDEO COMPRESSION

The search for efficient video compression techniques dominated multimedia research activity in the early 1980s. The first major milestone was the ITU H.261 encoder, from which JPEG later adopted the idea of quantizing DCT coefficients. Since then, advancements have been made mostly in the field of motion estimation, and with TV and cinema becoming digital, algorithms have been adopted into day-to-day use. Codecs have been mostly standardized by the ITU and ISO and popular standards are:

ISO/IEC 11172 aka MPEG 1 is designed to compress VHS-quality raw digital video and CD-quality audio down to 1.5 Mbit/s (26:1 and 6:1 compression ratios, respectively). It is mostly used in video CDs, older digital cable, and satellite TV.

ISO/IEC 13818 aka MPEG 2 is designed to be higher quality than MPEG1 while being backward compatible. It is used for encoding DVDs and digital TV of all kind (DVB-x).

ITU-T H.264 (formerly ISO/IEC 14496–10) aka MPEG4 is used for high-quality, high-definition video, such as on Blu-ray discs or in the iTunes Store.

Since approximately 2000, the focus for multimedia research on video codecs, as well as MPEG standardization, has been more on metadata and video search, resulting in MPEG-7 and MPEG-21.

Conventional Video Encoding

In essence, video compressors are a combination of audio and image compressors that account for the fact that the images differ only slightly from frame to frame. The popular MPEG 1 and 2 video compression algorithms, for example, are conceptually a combination of JPEG, MP3, and the motion compensation technique, described in the previous chapters.

A typical video encoder works like this:

- Encode the first frame as a JPEG image.
- Find blocks that changed compared to reference frames (reference frames are selected based on I, B, or P frame strategy).

- Encode the changed blocks with JPEG compression; encode the movements of unchanged blocks as motion vectors.
- Encode the corresponding audio independently of the video stream.

Modern Video Encoding

Two major drawbacks of the current video encoding schemes are that they do not take into account correlating information across media sources and that they do not allow for a semantic interpretation of the signal, but rather only work using block-based signal processing. The latter issue is addressed, even though not solved, in the newer MPEG standards, such as MPEG-7 and MPEG-21. While MPEG-1 and MPEG-2 are currently in widespread use, MPEG-7 and MPEG-21 have to be considered research at the time of the writing of this book. We want to mention, however, one more standard that is currently between production and research: MPEG-4. MPEG-4 is often used as a carrier to the more modern audio and video compression algorithms. Moreover, MPEG-4 introduced the so called Binary Format for Scenes (BIFS). BIFS includes support for the vector-based storage of 2D and 3D scenes, as well as some interactivity. BIFS is a binary representation that has to be compiled from a user-editable source format, called Extensible MPEG-4 Textual (XMT). Streaming of MPEG-4 scene content requires the addition of so-called hints that enable partial playback of MPEG-4 files. However, the conversion itself does not work incrementally. In other words, streaming of MPEG-4 files is only possible after a recording has been fully completed. Live streaming is usually done using the Realtime Transport Protocol (RTP), and MPEG-4 supports the streaming of BIFS content using so-called BIFS commands. Because of these complications, although many programs are available that are described as capable of playing back MPEG-4 content, most of them only support movie profiles and cannot play back MPEG-4 scene content.

While perceptual video coding is very effective, knowledge about it is mostly technical and not conceptual beyond what was described in this chapter. The various standards focus on different ways of performing the block search for motion encoding, optimizing to certain pixel resolutions, and guaranteeing certain bitrates. Audio compression, in particular speech compression, however, is not that effective and requires much conceptual knowledge. Also, it is exploiting a production model, rather than only a perception model. We therefore dedicated the next chapter to it.

RECOMMENDED READING

As described in previous chapters, information about lossy compression is mostly found in original research papers and standards. Therefore, again, our references are mostly comprised of documents of these types. As before, we recommend starting with the research articles before going to the IEC standards. We did not include all standards mentioned in the chapter because we think it is better to focus on conceptual knowledge for a first reading. The signal processing background introduced in the start of this chapter can be deepened by taking a reading into Ahmed, Oppenheim, Schafer, and Buck, and Broughton and

Bryan. Daubechies and Addison provide deep mathematical introductions to orthogonal functions. Brandenburg and Stoll are credited for inventing MP3, so the original publication and the included references make for an interesting read. Further details on the topics touched on in this chapter can be found in Terhardt, Princen, Johnson, and Bradley, and Johnston and Ferreira, as well as Harris.

Further Reading

Paul S. Addison. *The Illustrated Wavelet Transform Handbook*. London: Institute of Physics. 2002.

N. Ahmed, T. Natarajan, and K. R. Rao. "Discrete cosine transform." *IEEE Trans. Computers*, 90–3, January 1974.

Brandenburg and Stoll. "ISO-MPEG-1 audio: A generic standard for coding of high-quality digital audio." *J. Audio Eng. Soc.*, 42: 780–92, 1994.

Bosi et al. "ISO/IEC MPEG-2 AAC." *J. Audio Eng. Soc.*, 45: 789–814, 1997.

S. A. Broughton and K. Bryan. *Discrete Fourier Analysis and Wavelets: Applications to Signal and Image Processing*. New Jersey: Wiley. 2008, p. 72.

Ingrid Daubechies. *Ten Lectures on Wavelets*. Society for Industrial and Applied Mathematics, 1992.

Fredric J Harris. "On the use of windows for harmonic analysis with the discrete Fourier transform." *Proceedings of the IEEE*, 66 (1): 51–83. Article on FFT windows that introduced many of the key metrics used to compare windows. January 1978.

Johnston and Ferreira. "Sum-difference stereo transform coding." *Proc. IEEE ICASSP*, 569–71, 1992.

B. C. J. Moore. *Cochlear Hearing Loss*. London: Whurr Publishers Ltd. 1998.

Alan V. Oppenheim, Ronald W. Schafer, and John A. Buck. *Discrete-Time Signal Processing*. Upper Saddle River, NJ: Prentice Hall. 1999. pp. 468–71.

J. P. Princen, A. W. Johnson, and A. B. Bradley. "Subband/transform coding using filter bank designs based on time domain aliasing cancellation." *IEEE Proc. Intl. Conf. on Acoustics, Speech, and Signal Processing* (ICASSP), 12: 2161–4, 1987.

E. Terhardt. "Calculating virtual pitch." *Hearing Res.*, 1: 155–82, 1979.

Web Links

ISO/IEC 11172 aka MPEG 1.
ISO/IEC 13818 aka MPEG 2.
ITU-T H.264 (formerly ISO/IEC 14496–10).
Lame Open-Source MP3 encoder: http://lame.sourceforge.net/ Standards.

EXERCISES

1. Implement the two-dimensional Discrete Cosine Transform and the two-dimensional Inverse Discrete Cosine Transform in a programming language of your choice. Apply your DFT and IDFT implementation to different signals of your choice and visualize them.

2. For a grayscale image, implement a "poor man's JPEG" algorithm by applying your DCT implementation to the image, applying quantization, and then retransforming.

3. Which class of images is most/least prone to ugly JPEG artifacts? First think about it, then try different images in the implementation from exercise 2.

4. What effects would increasing the block size from 8 x 8 to 16 x 16, 32 x 32, or even higher have on the JPEG algorithm?

5. How would you parallelize the JPEG algorithm on a manycore processor?

6. What happens when you encode a JPEG using JPEG repeatedly? Explain.

7. Mix a sound file of your choice with different levels of noise. Explain the effects.

8. Write pseudo-code for the search for an optimal parameter configuration for the quantization of an MP3 granule given different bands, a quality function, and a minimum and maximum target bitrate. Analyze the runtime and discuss possibilities to optimize the runtime with and without trading of accuracy.

14 Speech Compression

While the compression techniques presented so far have assumed generic acoustic or visual content, this chapter presents lossy compression techniques especially designed for a particular type of acoustic data: human speech. Almost every human being on earth talks virtually every day – needless to say, there is a lot of captured digital speech content. Every movie or TV show contains an audio track, most of which usually consists of spoken language. The most important use of captured speech, however, is for communication, such as in cell phones, voice-over IP applications, or as part of video conferencing and meeting recordings. Most of the compression concepts discussed so far will also work on speech. The algorithms presented in this chapter were developed to achieve a higher compression ratio while preserving higher perceptual quality by exploiting speech-specific properties of the audio signal. We discussed human speech in Chapter 5. This chapter will directly dig into the algorithmic part using that knowledge.

PROPERTIES OF A SPEECH CODER

As explained in Chapter 5, the properties of every sound are defined by the properties of the objects that create the sounds, by the environment that the sound waves travel in, and by the characteristics of the receiver and/or capturing device. The object that creates human speech is the vocal tract. Vocal tracts also exist in animals, such as birds or cats. As we all know, the sounds they produce differ substantially from average human speech, so creating a bird-sing compression or cat's meow encoding algorithm would also be substantially different. The following algorithms all try to exploit the characteristics of speech and have very limited applicability to music or other nonspeech. However, all of them are of importance to multimedia computing because millions of people use them in everyday life.

Speech codecs are applied in two main areas: telephony and voice-over IP applications. While the two areas seem to increasingly merge, historically the problems that presented themselves in these two areas required slightly different solutions. Other applications, such as Internet radio or speech compression for archival purposes, introduce other priorities.

In general, the targets for a speech coder are:

- Good compression.
- Minimum impact on speech intelligibility.

- Maximum preservation of speaker characteristics.
- Good handling of background noise (e.g., background noise should be eliminated when speech is present, but transmitted when not).
- Low computational complexity (e.g., cell phones need to be small and should not need large amounts of energy).
- Minimum latency, that is, the delay introduced between transmitter and receiver must be small.
- Transmission error resistance (e.g., packet losses might be concealed).
- Text independence.

Sometimes, language independence is sacrificed for a more efficient codec when a specific target market is aimed at.

LINEAR PREDICTIVE CODING (LPC)

One of the earliest models used for the compression of speech sounds is the so-called Linear Predictive Coding, or LPC. It is widely used in many places from telephony to military applications (low-quality, ultra-low bandwidth) and is part of many, if not most, of today's speech compression algorithms in cell phones. Typical rates of encoded streams vary from eight hundred bits per second to sixteen kbits per second.

As the name implies, LPC is a predictive coder – and it is linear. The underlying assumption of LPC is that a speech signal is produced by a buzzer at the end of a tube, with occasional added hissing and popping sounds (sibilants and plosive sounds). Although apparently crude, this model is a close approximation to the reality of speech production: the vocal tract forms a tube, which is characterized by its resonances because of its shape, and the buzz is produced by the glottis, the space between the vocal folds, and is characterized by its intensity. Some literature calls methods that model signal production for efficient representation *parametric redundancy exploitation methods*. Figure 14.1 shows a diagram of one of the earliest LPC algorithms.

It consists of several steps that are explained as follows. The sampled audio signal is packetized into small segments with a typical length of about 10ms. These atomic segments are usually called *frames*. A preemphasis filter increases the magnitude of the higher-frequency parts with respect to the lower frequencies in order to increase the quality of the following steps. This trick is used often to increase the perceptual signal-to-noise ratio. This enhanced signal is then used for several steps. A voiced/unvoiced detector finds the regions where pitch can be calculated, for example speech regions that contain mostly vowels. The pitch and the power are then also estimated and later encoded into the bit stream. In parallel, an LP analysis is performed on the signal. The LP signal is then used for error prediction as discussed in the previous chapter. The difference between the LP estimation and the actual signal is encoded together with the power and pitch in the actual bit stream. If the frame is voiced, the pitch prediction is estimated from the prediction error signal. The compression achieved usually allows the transmission of an 8-kHz mono using twenty-four hundred bits per second in an understandable quality. The compression works in real time (e.g., can be applied during the transmission of a conversation),

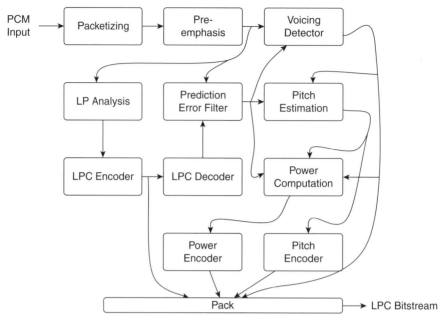

Figure 14.1. The LPC compression algorithm as defined in the NATO standard FS-1015 (LPC10).

even on home-sized computers from the 1970s. Not only is the LPC speech compression a very fundamental algorithm that is used in many different versions in a whole range of speech processing devices, it also allows us to discuss a couple of fundamental speech processing techniques.

Voiced/Unvoiced Detection

How can we determine if a speech frame contains a vowel or not? The methods currently available for doing this are not perfect, but work in about 99 percent of the cases. Usually, a bag of features is used, combining the results from several computations on the signal. The most obvious feature is energy: to have pitch – this means to have periodicity – the signal must cross the zero amplitude line a couple of times. Thus the integral (or the sum of samples) of that signal should be close to zero. An unpitched signal can have any shape and the integral might be heavily biased toward a positive or negative number. To determine the energy E of a frame of length N containing samples s and ending at instant m, the following simple equation is usually used:

$$x_{rms} = \sqrt{\frac{1}{n}(x_1^2 + x_2^2 + \ldots + x_n^2)}$$

Energy is always a positive number, hence the square root. Alternatively, the absolute value of the sample can be used, resulting in the so-called Magnitude-Sum Function:

$$MDF[l,\, m] = \sum_{n=m-N+1}^{m} |S[n] - S[n-1]|$$

As already said, a voiced signal might cross the zero amplitude line more often than a non-pitched signal. Of course, this can also be measured directly, by calculating the Zero-Crossing-Rate SC:

$$SC_{[m]} = \frac{1}{2} \sum_{n=m-N+1}^{m} \left| \text{sgn}(s_{[n]}) - \text{sgn}\, s_{[n-1]} \right|$$

The *sgn()* function returns one or zero, depending on the sign of the operand. A third method is to calculate the prediction gain:

$$PG_{[m]} = 10 \log_{10} \left(\frac{\displaystyle\sum_{n=m-N+1}^{m} s^2[n]}{\displaystyle\sum_{n=m-N+1}^{m} e^2[n]} \right)$$

Note that voiced frames on average achieve three decibels or more in LPC prediction gain than unvoiced frames, mainly because of the fact that periodicity implies higher correlation among samples, and thus is easier to predict. Unvoiced frames are more random and therefore less predictable. For very low-amplitude frames, prediction gain is normally not calculated to avoid numerical problems; in this case, the frame can be assigned as unvoiced by verifying the energy level. Thresholding energy, zero-crossing rate, and prediction gain is not an exact science. Modern systems use machine learning to find good values for estimating these values on a concrete data set. Finding a perfect boundary between a voiced and an unvoiced segment is nearly impossible.

Pitch Estimation

The fundamental frequency (F0) of a periodic signal is the inverse of its period. The subjective "pitch" of a sound usually depends on its fundamental frequency, but also depends on other factors. Given that a frame is voiced, estimating the pitch of the frame is one of the most important and frequently demanded operations in audio processing. In speech processing, the *pitch period* is defined as the time between successive vocal cord openings. Expected values for pitch periods of male persons lie between 4ms and 20ms (frequency between 50Hz and 250Hz) and for women and children between about 2ms to 8ms (frequency between 120Hz and 500Hz). Unfortunately, estimating this time is, like the voiced/unvoiced detection, not an exact science. Unless the signal is artificially generated, pitch period estimation is a complex undertaking because of the lack of perfect periodicity in real-world signals. Unless trained thoroughly, even a singer's voice has no perfect pitch because of interference with formants of the vocal tract (voice impurities). Also, the uncertainty of the starting point of a voiced segment and other real-world problems, such as noise and echo, make perfect pitch estimation hard. For this reason, arbitrarily complex pitch estimation algorithms have been developed and refinements will be presented in research papers to come. In practice, pitch period estimation is implemented as a trade-off between computational complexity and performance. From the many algorithms proposed for this task, only two will be presented here. The first and most frequently used method is the so-called autocorrelation method.

The autocorrelation value reflects the similarity between the frame *s[n]* and the time-shifted version *s[n-l]*. Again, the frame has length *N* containing and is ending at instant *m*. The variable *l* is a positive integer representing a time lag and *n= [m–N+1,m]*. The range of lag is selected so that it covers a wide range of pitch period values. For example, at 8kHz sampling rate, if *l* is between 20 and 147 (2.5ms to 18.3ms), the possible pitch estimation times values range from 54.4Hz to 400Hz. By calculating the autocorrelation values for the entire range of lag, it is possible to find the value of *l* associated with the highest autocorrelation representing the pitch period estimate. In other words, the autocorrelation *R* is maximized when the lag *l* is equal to the pitch period.

The pseudo-code for the algorithm would look like this:

```
// Input: last index in frame m, number of samples N,
// sampling rate sr per second
// Output: The pitch period in seconds.
pitch(m, N, sr)
    peak := 0
    FOR l:=20 TO 150
        autoc:=0
        FOR n:=m-N+1 TO m
        autoc:=autoc+s[n]*s[n-l]
    IF (autoc>peak)
        peak:=autoc
        lag:=l
pitch := lag/sr
```

A second method for pitch estimation is the so-called Magnitude-Difference Function. The idea is that for short segments of voiced speech, it is reasonable to expect that s[n]-s[n-l] is small for l =0,±T,±2T,. ., with T being the signal's period. By computing the MDF for the lag *l* range of interest, we can estimate the period by locating the lag value associated with the minimum magnitude difference.

Note that from the same equation, each additional accumulation of term causes the result to be greater than or equal to the previous sum because each term is positive. Thus, it is not necessary to calculate the sum entirely: if the accumulated result at any instance during the iteration loop is greater than the minimum found so far, calculation stops and resumes with the next lag. Also, no multiplication is involved in this method, which is sometimes interesting for speed and memory usage on small devices. Overall, this method is faster than the regular autocorrelation method. The idea is implemented with the following pseudo-code:

```
// Input: last index in frame m, number of samples N, sampling rate sr per second
// Output: The pitch period in seconds.
pitch2(m, N, sr)
    min := infinity
    FOR l:=20 TO 150
    mdf:=0
      FOR n:=m-N+1 TO m
        mdf:=mdf+ABS(s[n]-s[n-l])
        IF (mdf>=min) BREAK
      IF (mdf<min)
          min:=mdf
          lag:=l
pitch2 := lag/sr
```

Note that these two methods really only estimate pitch. In fact, it is likely that nobody will ever be able to accurately calculate pitch, because pitch, even though depending on the fundamental frequency, is subjective. Even when focusing only on speech, many factors distort pitch. For example, periodic vibration at the glottis may produce speech that is less perfectly periodic because of movements of the vocal tract that filter the glottal source waveform. Then, glottal vibration itself may also show aperiodicities, such as changes in amplitude, rate, or glottal waveform shape. Reverberations inside the vocal tract also distort pitch.

LP Analysis

The underlying model for LPC is this:

$$\tilde{x}(n) = a_1 x(n-1) + a_2 x(n-2) + \ldots + a_M x(n-M) = \sum_{i-1}^{M} a_i x(n-i)$$

where x̃(n) is the prediction of the present sample generated through linear combination of the past M samples x(n) to x(n-i). The a_i are called the linear prediction coefficients. In other words, the predictor tries to predict a sample as a linear combination of the previous outputs. Usually ten to thirty-two linear prediction coefficients are used. The number of coefficients is usually chosen depending on the frequency used, for an 8kHz sampling rate, ten-dimensional LPC analysis is usually good; for 16kHz, twenty is a typical value.

The idea is, then, to minimize the error between the actual and the predicted value:

$$\varepsilon(n) = x(n) - \tilde{x}(n) = x(n) - \sum_{i-1}^{M} a_i x(n-i)$$

This is usually solved by mathematical optimization, such as the Levinson-Durbin recursive method; the scientific literature also discusses other methods (see research references).

For an order N filter, the filter coefficients a_i are found by solving the $N \times N$ linear system $Ra=r$, where

$$R = \begin{bmatrix} R(1) \\ R(2) \\ \vdots \\ R(N) \end{bmatrix} \quad R = \begin{bmatrix} R(0) & R(1) & \cdots & R(N-1) \\ R(1) & R(0) & \cdots & R(N-2) \\ \vdots & \vdots & \ddots & \vdots \\ R(N-1) & R(N-2) & \cdots & R(0) \end{bmatrix}$$

$$r = \begin{bmatrix} R(1) \\ R(2) \\ \vdots \\ R(N) \end{bmatrix}$$

with $R(m)$ being the autocorrelation of the signal $x[n]$, computed as described earlier (and implemented later):

$$R(m) = \sum_{i=0}^{N-1} x[i]x[i-m]$$

and r being the so-called reflection coefficient. The following pseudo-code illustrates a practical implementation of this method first invented by N. Levinson in 1947 and modified by J. Durbin in 1959 (see references).

```
// Compute LPC coefficients from a series of autocorrelation coefficients
// Input: dim order of LPC analysis,
//        ac [0...dim+1]autocorrelation values (see helper function)
// Output: ref[0...dim] reflection coefficients R(N),
//         lpc[0...dim] LPC coefficients,
//         error       residual error
levinson_durbin(dim, ac)
  error := ac[0]
  IF (error == 0)
    set all ref[i]:=0
    levinson_durbin := ([0...0],[0...0],0)
    // return and exit routine
  // main loop
  FOR i:=0 TO dim-1
        // Calculate the reflection coefficient
    r:=-ac[i+1]
    FOR j:=0 TO i
      r:=r-lpc[j]*ac[i-j]
      r:=r/error
      ref[i]:=r
    // Update LPC coefficients and total error
    lpc[i]:=r
```

```
        FOR j:= 0 TO (i/2)-1
           temp := lpc[j]
           lpc[j] := lpc[j]+r*lpc[i-1-j]
           lpc[i-1-j] := lpc[i-1-j]+r*temp
        IF (i%2 == 1)
           lpc[j] := lpc[j]+lpc[j]*r
        error := 1.0-r*r
     levinson_durbin := (ref,lpc,error)
```

The autocorrelation values can be calculated as follows:

```
// Compute the autocorrelation coefficients needed for the LPC
// Input: n number of audio samples,
//       x[0..n-1] audio samples
//       lag a maximum lag range
// Output: ac[0...lag-1] autocorrelation values
lpc_autocorrelation(n, x, lag)
   WHILE (lag>0)
     lag:=lag-1
     FOR i:=lag TO n
       d:=0
       d:=d+x[i]*x[i-lag]
     ac[lag]:=d
lpc_autocorrelation:=ac
```

With the increasing availability of multiple CPU core architectures, an alternative solution to the Levinson-Durbin recursion is in frequent use that is easier to parallelize. The so-called Schuer recursion is related to the Levinson-Durbin method but faster on parallel architectures. On multiple cores, Levinson-Durbin would take time proportional to $O(dim*log(dim))$; Schuer requires time proportional to dim. The following pseudo-code, which again relies on *lpc_autocorrelation*, shows the idea:

```
// Alternative recursion algorithm for parallel architectures
// Input: dim order of LPC analysis,
//       ac [0...dim+1]autocorrelation values (see helper function)
// Output: ref[0...dim] reflection coefficients R(N),
//       error     residual error

schuer(dim,ac)
   error := ac[0]
   IF (error == 0)
     set all ref[i]:=0
     schur := ([0...0],0)
```

```
// Create a so-called generator matrix G with dimensions [2,dim]
FOR i := 0 TO DIM-1
   // Calculate this iteration's reflection coefficient and error.
   G[0][i] := ac[i+1]
   G[1][i] := ac[i+1]
i:=0
WHILE (true)
   r := -G[1][0]/error
   ref[i] := r
   error := error + G[1][0]*r
   i:=i+1
   IF (i>=dim)
      schur := (ref,error)
      // return and exit routine
   // Update the generator matrix.
   // Unlike the Levinson-Durbin summing of reflection coefficients,
   // this loop could be distributed to many processors which
   // each take only constant time.
   FOR m := 0 TO dim-i-1
      G[1][m] := G[1][m+1] + r * G[0][m]
      G[0][m] := G[1][m+1] * r + G[0][m]
schur := (ref,error)
```

The calculation of the related LPC coefficients is left as an exercise.

As mentioned earlier, the building blocks introduced here for explaining the LPC algorithm have been reused many times in other speech compression algorithms. LPC modeling is also used for speech synthesis. For example, the very popular "speak 'n' spell" toy from the 1980s (see Web references) has used LPC for reading words. LPC can also be used as a feature in speech analysis, for example, for speech or speaker recognition. Most important, though, the LPC algorithm was used as a basis for further, more complex algorithms for speech compression, of which some are described in the next sections.

CELP

CELP is an enhancement of the LPC compression providing better-quality speech than LPC-10e, described earlier, without increasing the bit rate too much. Because LPC is a synthesizer, a natural extension is to use a wavetable to increase the quality, trading off the increase of coder and decoder complexity for smaller bitrates. Therefore, many successful methods use a so-called codebook, usually a table of typical residue signals. In a nutshell, the analyzer compares the residue to all the entries in the codebook, chooses the entry that is the closest match, and sends a reference to that entry. The synthesizer receives the reference, retrieves the corresponding residue from the codebook, and uses the "code" to "excite" the resynthesized signal, hence the name Code Excited Linear Prediction (CELP). The principle behind

CELP is also called *analysis by synthesis* because the encoding (analysis) is performed by perceptually optimizing the decoded (synthesis) signal in a closed loop.

CELP search is broken down into several steps. Typically, encoding is performed in the following order:

1. Linear prediction coefficients are computed, converted to Line Spectral Frequencies, and then quantized.
2. An adaptive codebook is searched and its contribution removed.
3. A fixed codebook is searched.

The steps will be explained in the following.

LSF encoding

An essential idea is to transform the linear prediction coefficients into so-called line spectral frequencies (LSF), sometimes also called line spectral pairs (LSP).

The linear prediction polynomial can also be written as:

$$A(z) = 1 - \sum_{k=1}^{p} a_k z^{-k}.$$

which can be decomposed into the following two complex equations:

$$P(z) = A(z) + z^{-(p+1)} A(z^{-1})$$

$$Q(z) = A(z) - z^{-(p+1)} A(z^{-1})$$

where *P(z)* is said to correspond to the vocal tract with the glottis closed and *Q(z)* with the glottis open. The reason for this transformation is to exploit the following mathematical trick.

A(z) has complex roots anywhere within the unit circle (z-transform), but *P(z)* and *Q(z)* have the very useful property of only having roots directly on the unit circle. So to find the roots, one takes a test point $z = exp(jw)$ and evaluates $P(exp(jw))$ and $Q(exp(jw))$ using a grid of points between zero and π. The zeros of *P(z) and Q(z)* also happen to be interspersed, which is why one swaps coefficients as one find roots. Therefore, the process of finding the LSP frequencies is finding the roots of two polynomials of order *p+1*.

And here is why this helps: LPC coefficients do not quantize well because small quantization errors may lead to large spectral distortion. Of course, the higher-order bits in the representation of the coefficients are naturally more sensitive to transmission errors than are lower-order ones. The LPC coefficients also do not interpolate well; that is, one cannot compute them at two distinct times and expect to accurately predict values in between. Therefore, instead of encoding the coefficients, it would be better to encode the zeros of the LPC equation. However, finding these zeros numerically entails a computationally complex two-dimensional search, while the zeros of *P(x)* and *Q(x)* can be found by simple one-dimensional search techniques. Over the years, researchers have found that LSP frequencies quantize well and interpolate better than all other parameters that have been tried in speech applications.

To convert back to LPCs, one evaluates $A(z) = 0.5[P(z) + Q(z)]$ by putting signal samples through it in the order of the LPC times, yielding back the original $A(z)$.

Adaptive Codebook

The entries in the adaptive codebook consist of delayed versions of the excitation to make it possible to efficiently code the portions of the signal that are periodic, such as the voiced parts of speech. In the decoder, the final excitation is produced by summing the contributions from the adaptive codebook and the fixed codebook:

$$e[n] = e_a[n] + e_f[n].$$

where $e_a[n]$ is the adaptive codebook contribution and $e_f[n]$ is the fixed codebook contribution. The filter that shapes the excitation has an all-pole model of the form $1/A(z)$, where $A(z)$ are obtained using linear prediction. An all-pole filter is used because it is a good representation of the human vocal tract and because it is easy to compute.

Fixed Codebook

A good choice for a fixed codebook is normal distributed random vectors. The reason for this is that the LPC filtering and the adaptive codebook remove large parts of the interdependencies between the samples, yielding relatively white-noise-like residual. Usually, the codebook comprises about 1,024 excitation vectors (ten-bit codebook) for a forty-sample subframe with an 8kHz sampling frequency.

The methods for finding the right entry in the adaptive codebook vary from coder to coder. Many coders simply use the Euclidian distance to determine the similarity between code vectors. Speex uses the Euclidian distance shaped with a perceptual weighting function that tries to roughly approximate noise perception in the human ear. Figure 14.2 shows the optimization loop.

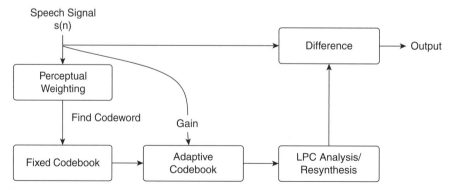

Figure 14.2. The CELP encoder loop performing analysis by synthesis until the perceptually weighted difference is minimal.

Table 14.1. A typical CELP bitstream

Parameters	No. of bits
LSF	34
Adaptive Filter	48
Fixed Codebook Index	36
Gains	20
Synchronization	1
Error Correction	4
Future Use	4
Total	**144**

In the end, the encoder transmits 144 bits of information based on 240 audio samples of speech (30 ms). The bit allocation is shown in Table 14.1.

The CELP algorithm is most prominently described in the NATO standard FS 1016, which provides good-quality, natural-sounding speech at 4,800 bit/s and in ITU-T recommendation G.728 operating at 16 kbit/s. The popular open source speech codec Speex (see Web references) is also based on CELP. Speex is targeted at voice-over IP applications.

GSM

GSM stands for Global System for Mobile communications and is the number one standard for mobile phones in the world. The GSM Association estimates that 80 percent of the global mobile market uses the standard. Its ubiquity, which now spans the world, makes international roaming easily possible and enables subscribers to use their phones in many parts of the world. The main difference between GSM and its predecessors is that both its signaling and speech channels are digital, and thus it is considered a second generation (2G) mobile phone system. This also makes data transmission over the same line very easy, enabling services such as text and multimedia messaging. The GSM standard describes more than just voice compression. It specifies everything necessary to build a global communication infrastructure, such as the structure of the radio network, the frequency ranges, the antennas and cells, subscriber identification mechanisms, security standards, power control, and so on. GSM has used a variety of voice codecs to compress a 3.1kHz sampling rate audio captured by the cell phone into between 6.5 and 13 kbit/s. The original specification only defined a so-called Half Rate (5.6 kbit/s) and Full Rate (13 kbit/s) codec. These used a system based on linear predictive coding. In 1997, the Enhanced Full Rate (EFR) codec working on a 12.2 kbit/s basis was introduced. With the development of UMTS, this codec was modified into the so-called Adaptive Multi-Rate (AMR) codecs. This is a variable-rate codec that is high quality and robust against interference when used on Full Rate channels, and less robust but still relatively high quality when used in good radio conditions on Half Rate channels.

Even though still built almost exclusively from the concepts explained in this chapter, current codecs such as GSM-AMR have grown in complexity beyond a size that can be presented in pseudo-code in this book. We therefore need to guide the reader to the references for further information.

Not only mobile phones use LPC variants; Skype's SVOPC and the later SILK codec use them too. SVOPC and Silk are also tuned to conceal frame drops. This is done by interpolating LSF parameters between two received frames to make up for the missing one.

All speech codecs have in common that they use a model of speech production to save bits. The next chapter will explain perceptual codecs. These use a model of perception. Of course, these codecs can be used for speech compression as well, although, as of today, speech production coders still seem to do better on speech than perceptual coders.

RECOMMENDED READING

Like in previous chapters, information about lossy compression is mostly found in original research papers and standards. We again recommend starting with the research articles before going to any standards because research articles usually describe ideas better on a conceptual level. The list of research papers corresponds directly with the algorithms described in this chapter. We do recommend Web links as well as they are more current and a huge commercial market is driving fast-paced change in this community.

Further Reading

B. S. Atal, "The history of linear prediction." *IEEE Signal Processing Magazine*, 23 (2): 154–61, March 2006.

B. Bessette, R. Salami, R. Lefebvre, M. Jelinek, J. Rotola-Pukkila, J. Vainio, H. Mikkola, and K. Jarvinen. "The adaptive multirate wideband speech codec (AMR-WB)." *IEEE Transactions on Speech and Audio Processing*, 10 (8): 620–36, 2002.

Y. Bistritz and S. Peller. "Immittance spectral pairs (ISP) for speech encoding." *Proceedings of IEEE ICASSP*, 12: 9–12, April 1993.

J. Durbin. "The fitting of time series models." *Rev. Inst. Int. Stat.*, 28: 233–43, 1960.

N. Levinson. "The Wiener RMS error criterion in filter design and prediction." *J. Math. Phys.*, 25: 261–78, 1947.

M. R. Schroeder and B. S. Atal. "Code-excited linear prediction (CELP): High-quality speech at very low bit rates." *Proceedings of the IEEE ICASSP*, 10: 937–40, 1985.

W. F. Trench. "An algorithm for the inversion of finite Toeplitz matrices." *J. Soc. Indust. Appl. Math.*, 12: 515–22, 1964.

P. Vary and R. Martin. *Digital Speech Transmission: Enhancement, Coding and Error Concealment.* West Sussex, UK: Wiley. 2006.

Wang Xianglin and C.-C. Jay Kuo. "An 800 bps VQ-based LPC voice coder." *The Journal of the Acoustical Society of America*, 103 (5): 2778, May 1998.

Web Links

Comp.Speech FAQ: http://www.speech.cs.cmu.edu/comp.speech/.

GMS World: http://www.gsmworld.com.

Speak 'n' spell history page: http://www.speaknspell.co.uk/.

Speex: http://www.speex.org/.

EXERCISES

1. Elaborate which target properties for a speech coder would be most important for: a regular phone, a cell phone, Internet radio, and an Internet teleconferencing application.

2. Describe how speech intelligibility differs from audio quality.

3. Implement a voiced/unvoiced detector. Then try it on different voice recordings and describe the limits of your approach.

4. Implement a pitch estimator. Then try it on different voice and music recordings and describe the limits of the approach.

5. Perform a runtime analysis of the Levins-Durbin and Schuer algorithms on a single CPU. Then describe how the Schuer algorithm performs better on multiple CPUs. Calculate the runtime for it on different CPUs.

6. If one were to use LPC to model music, which types of instruments would be modeled well and which ones would not? Give examples and explain why.

7. Write the (pseudo-)code for calculating the LPC coefficients from the reflection coefficients as output from the Schuer pseudo-code presented in this chapter.

8. Write (pseudo-)code for calculating the LSF coefficients from LPC coefficients.

9. Write (pseudo-)code to implement a CELP encoder.

10. Use a current implementation of a speech encoder (e.g., in your cell phone or using a voice-over IP application) and transmit speech, music, and noise through it. Describe and explain the artifacts observed.

11. Given the models presented in this chapter, discuss what other elements are contained in speech that were not discussed. Describe how these could be handled.

12. Use a speech compression algorithm of your choice and describe how you would handle packet loss.

15 Multimedia Information Retrieval

Consumer-produced videos, images, and text posts are the fastest-growing type of content on the Internet. At the time of the writing of this book, YouTube.com alone claims that seventy-two hours of video are uploaded to its Web site every minute. At this rate, the amount of consumer-produced videos will grow by 37 million hours in one year. Of course, YouTube.com is merely one site among many where videos may be uploaded. Social media posts provide a wealth of information about the world. They consist of entertainment, instructions, personal records, and various aspects of life in general. As a collection, social media posts represent a compendium of information that goes beyond what any individual recording captures. They provide information on trends, evidence of phenomena or events, social context, and societal dynamics. As a result, they are useful for qualitative and quantitative empirical research on a larger scale than has ever been possible. To make this data accessible, we need to automatically analyze the content of the posts and make them findable. Therefore, Multimedia Information Retrieval (MIR) has rapidly emerged as the most important technology needed to answer many questions people face in different aspects of their regular activities. The next chapters will focus on multimedia organization and analysis, mostly from retrieval aspects. We begin by defining multimedia retrieval and the set of challenges and algorithms that dominate the field. In this chapter, we will present basic concepts and techniques related to accessing multimedia data. We will start with the structured data in databases, discuss information retrieval to deal with accessing information in text, and then present techniques developed and being explored in MIR.

The basic problem in MIR systems is connecting different types of appropriate data sources to users with diverse backgrounds and different needs. As shown in Figure 15.1, data exists in many forms, ranging from bits to alphanumeric documents to photos and video. Users of the data in a modern computing environment, however, may come from many different education backgrounds, different cultures, and different socioeconomic status. The challenge is how to connect a user with a data source so the user can use the data he needs to solve his application. A user is never interested in what and where the data is; she is only interested in solving the problem at hand. The major hurdle in connecting users to the data is often referred to as the *semantic gap*. This is explained in more detail in Chapter 19.

Figure 15.1. Multimedia data could be in any form ranging from text to signals like video. People from very diverse background may come to a repository in a MIR system to access the data to satisfy their needs.

Multimedia Information Retrieval (MIR) contains three important components: Multimedia, Information, and Retrieval. Here are some general observations on the meaning of each of these terms in this context.

Multimedia: When thinking of the MIR problem, it is natural to think that increase in number of types of data such as images, text, and audio will result in increased complexity of organization, indexing, and retrieval; however, by adopting the right perspective and using opportunistic information from disparate sources, the availability of correlated and complementary multimedia data simplifies the problems significantly.

Information: MIR is naturally influenced by Information Retrieval (IR), which originates from retrieval dealing with text. In text, most successes are because the information retrieved is directly available in the data. The information of interest in sensory data must be extracted by processing. Whenever IR systems try to retrieve information not directly available in data, they also face challenging problems, especially the semantic gap.

Retrieval: Retrieval is usually interpreted as the operation of accessing information from human or computer memory. *Retrieval, query,* and *search* are used to mean similar things, although there are subtle differences. All of these terms are related to finding appropriate information in some application context from a large volume of data in memory. Depending on the sources of data and the application context, sometimes one is interested in precise answers that are directly available in the data; sometimes in information that is derived from the data; and in other cases in finding related sources that may contain information. These cases have different scope and require different techniques. In most applications, retrieval is one step in the overall solution, and the application context influences the requirements from this step significantly.

DATABASES

Searching for data is an old problem. When computers started becoming popular, and started finding applications in businesses as well as in applications involving large volumes of data, it became important to develop systems to help in organization, storage, management, and retrieval of data (OSMR). After early navigational and network databases, the

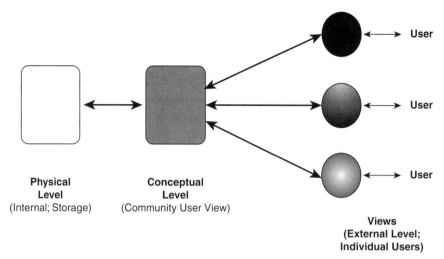

Figure 15.2. Three Database Layers.

relational model introduced by Edgar Codd became popular and became the foundation for most of the commercial database systems. The uniform set-theoretic representation of entities and their attributes allowed efficient OSMR operations on large volumes of data. The basic data structure behind the relational data model is the concept of a table. All information in relational databases is stored in tables in which each row represents an entity and columns represent their attributes. In most traditional database systems, these attributes are human created. In multimedia systems, one may try to extract such information using understanding techniques.

A very important concept commonly used in databases is that there are three distinct levels, shown in Figure 15.2, at which data must be viewed and managed:

1. **Physical:** At this level, the system takes care of storing all data and takes care of accessing, adding, deleting, and updating any particular records that are rows in a table, without other levels having to worry about where it is really stored in a storage device.

2. **Logical:** This level represents how application designers model the data. Thus, at this level, the system knows what are the entities and their attributes that the database will use. Using techniques like entity-relationship models, the logical model is designed and then translated to tabular representations in the database. At this level, the system is only aware of the models of objects (entities) and their characteristics (attributes) used in the system. This level is designed based on the desired functionality that a particular application must have.

3. **View:** A database is used by many different types of users, each of which must have different rights and privileges to access different types of data. Thus, in a university database, an instructor may have access to look at the grades of every student in his class and modify those, but a student can only see his/her grades and will not be able to modify those. Not all functionality of a database is exposed and made

available to every user. Different users see only a subset of data and have different rights with respect to addition, deletion, and updating of the data. Each user thus has just *a view* of the database.

An operation to access information from a database is commonly called a *query*. A query in a relational database is articulated using a sentence in Structured Query Language (SQL).

STRUCTURED, UNSTRUCTURED, AND SEMISTRUCTURED DATA

The nature of data plays a very important role in how it can be organized and retrieved. In computing, one commonly refers to data as *structured* or *unstructured*. Structured data is organized according to a well-defined structure. This structure could be a table with clearly marked rows and columns, a tree, or any other predefined organization. Traditional databases, particularly the popular relational databases, are a very good example of structured data. In general, when one needs to search and organize data, a well-defined structure is used. This is even true when one deals with physical things. Warehouses are organized according to a well-defined structure, and so are stores and libraries.

When data is not organized according to a structure, it is called *unstructured data*. Any sensory data is by default unstructured. Adding structure to this type of content will be discussed in the remainder of this chapter and the following chapters.

There is, however, a third type: *semistructured data* is unstructured data in which some structure is introduced by defining tags or other mechanisms. During the past two decades, one particular semistructured data format has grown popular. Data may be in a structured format such that the sequence of data items is well defined and is known to the system, as in databases. In such a case, the system knows how to interpret data and can store it using indexing techniques for efficient retrieval of the data. For example, one may have a database of photos organized based only on which photos, represented by the name of the file, were taken on which day. At the other extreme is the case where all data appears in a form that is not known to the system and may be of random type or order. For example, one does not even know the types of objects in photos, and current understanding techniques are not ready to find all objects in a photo. Thus each photo itself is an unstructured data. For such unstructured data, the system cannot use any indexing schemes.

Because there was a clear need to access an increasing volume of text data, commonly considered unstructured data, people developed techniques that could help in providing some structure to this new common type of data and introduced a new structure using Extensible Markup Language (XML). XML uses a different approach to structuring data by asking document creators to introduce enough clues, or structure, in the document so that an automatic process can read what the document or a section of it is about. This metadata approach enables advanced systems to know more about the document than today's automatic techniques can. It also has the ability to work gracefully with more automation. Note, however, that most documents on the Web are not in XML even now, so most of the text on the Web is considered unstructured and searched accordingly.

XML introduces structure in otherwise unstructured documents. That is, it structuralizes text. Multimedia data, like other data, must be stored using organization principles that will enable management and retrieval. Moreover, multimedia data should be organized more carefully because of its time-serial nature and its enormous size. Another difficulty is that current metadata for audio, video, images, and other similar sources is more about the data than about its semantic content. The tags in XML introduce semantic partitioning of text. Techniques for introducing the semantic partitioning of video, audio, and images are needed. Multimedia researchers have spent considerable effort on developing automatic techniques for video and audio segmentation and for indexing images based on basic characteristics such as color and texture. These techniques are very useful and will revolutionize how we will organize multimedia data in the future. However, we need to organize multimedia data today. The current automatic techniques for semantic partitioning are even more infantile than those for text. The only solution may be to develop powerful approaches for structuralizing multimedia data, which could prove as revolutionary as the introduction of XML. Many emerging techniques for searching multimedia have started using tags and other user-generated information.

One cannot provide organization and access to large volumes of data without using some structure in the data. In some cases, such as relational databases, the data is created and made available to the system in a well-structured format. In other cases when the data is not directly entered in the system, techniques must be used to identify the structure that will help in providing the functionality for organizing and accessing the data. Multimedia information retrieval techniques, discussed in this chapter, are all about defining structure that must be used to organize and access the data and applying techniques for data analysis that will help in extracting this information from the data and storing it.

CLASSIC INFORMATION RETRIEVAL AND SEARCH

As introduced earlier, information retrieval primarily addresses techniques for searching content in text documents. In its early stages, it was predominantly concerned with printed documents. During that time, human-generated index terms were commonly used to match relevant content (compare also the end of this book). With the arrival of the Web, each node on the Web was considered a document and all these documents were connected on the Web. For searching documents, the concept of keywords evolved to replace indexing terms. Keywords were considered important words used in documents. Techniques were developed to detect these words in documents and automatically prepare indices that contained a number of keywords in each document. Initially, these words, their frequencies in a document, and the uniqueness of their usage in general were used to search for documents. As search evolved and users required better approaches, many other characteristics, such as headings, anchor texts, and the link structure of the Web, were used to index and search for documents. In this section, we will discuss basic concepts from information retrieval and how some of those are applied in search approaches. Many of these concepts are slowly being extended to index and search multimedia documents. In Figure 15.3, we show the basic architecture of a search approach. This general

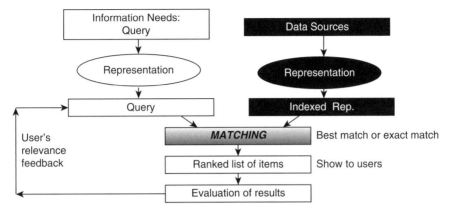

Figure 15.3. An information retrieval system must convert all documents into their logical representation and index them. For each query, appropriate documents are retrieved using their logical representation and a ranking algorithm.

diagram could be applied to any search problem. Let us discuss information retrieval using some basic blocks from this architecture.

In a classic information retrieval (IR) scenario, the searchable data is available as a collection of documents. The information retrieval system's task is to identify all documents that will be relevant in the context of a search query. To facilitate retrieval, each document is represented in a structured form that will allow matching. As discussed previously, structuring of data helps in organization and indexing, resulting in efficient searches. Because natural language text is not structured data, we need to represent each file in a structured data form that could be indexed and searched. *Logical representation*, commonly called a *logical view*, is used to represent the document or the original source using the data that captures the essence of the document from the perspective of search. One defines or designs a logical representation based on the types of searches that users of the system should perform. A logical representation is designed by considering:

- Attributes or features that can be used by users to define their problem.
- The system can automatically extract those attributes and features from data sources.

One uses representation to index documents by essentially creating an indexed representation of these features and linking those to original documents. In IR systems, words are used as logical representation because:

- words are understood by people; and
- words can be indexed using very simple text-processing techniques.

A user articulates his information need as a query in the form of a keyword or some combination of words. All queries must be articulated using the same logical representation the system uses. In some cases, the user's representation may not be exactly at the same level. In those cases, the system should translate the user query to the IR system such that the IR system gets the query in the same logical representation. The query in logical representation is matched with the indexed representation of the documents. The matching process could be very simple, as in just finding a simple term, or could be very complex, as we will see in multimedia cases in some of the following sections. Based on the result of matching, the IR system may find many documents that may satisfy the need of the user to a varying degree. Unlike database systems where search is binary, IR systems do not provide direct records that give users the answer, but they provide sources where the information could be found. Thus, the result of matching only indicates that a particular document may satisfy the user's information need.

The list of documents that satisfy user needs may be presented to the user. In many cases, this list may be long and it may not be a practical idea to present the complete list. In such cases, the list should be ranked based on the relevance of the document to the information need and only a subset of higher-ranked documents should be presented to the user. The user may look at the list and may provide feedback to the system in terms of which documents are relevant to the information need and which are not. This information provided by the user, commonly called *relevance feedback*, may be used by the system to modify the query and reused to get a new list from the system.

For evaluating the performance of a search system, two commonly used measures, discussed in more detail in Chapter 17, are recall and precision. *Recall* characterizes how effective the system is in finding all relevant answers among those that could be considered relevant in the whole document space. *Precision* is the measure of accuracy of results among all those that are presented as relevant answers. Precision gives us an idea of how effectively the system distinguishes between correct and wrong answers.

Because a query may result in many documents and the results are presented in a list, it is essential to decide in which order the documents should be listed in the results. Most people only see items at the top of the list. Ranking algorithms assign ranking to the result; the list contains documents in decreasing value of their ranks. The rank of a document can be judged based on many factors such as:

- number of times the keyword appears in the document;
- position and fonts used for the word (in header, boldface, size); and
- the popularity of the document as reflected by the number of times the document was opened after the search.

The rank can also be assigned using a weighted combination of factors. On the Web, a very particular ranking algorithm has become common, which we explain in detail in the next section.

Page Rank: Determining Importance of a Document Node

A very important component in ranking results is the importance or popularity of the document (which can be anything, such as a video or a Web page). To determine the importance or popularity of a page, an image, or a video, one may derive inspiration from a commonly used idea best manifested in academic circles in the form of citations. One may consider citations and links in Web pages as similar in that they both point to a source that

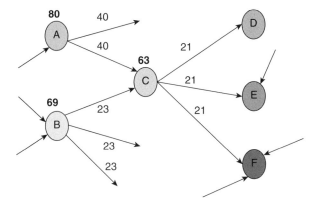

Figure 15.4. The pageRank of the node C is determined by the weights of the incoming edges from nodes A and B and is distributed equally among the nodes it points to.

is considered relevant and important. A document is considered more popular depending on the number of people referring to the document and on the importance of people referring to the document.

If one could develop an approach that considers all links in all documents, in the case of the Web all pages, and develop an approach that could consider this *link graph* to assign a numerical value of importance to each page, then we could consider the numeric values representing the relative importance of each page. Let us understand this idea using the following example.

The Web has its link structure reflected by connections of each node to other nodes using links. Consider a node C. The importance of this node is determined by the incoming links to this node and the source nodes of those links. In this case, the weights of the incoming nodes are forty and twenty-three and are added to assign the node C the page rank of sixty-three. Because the node C points to three different nodes (D, E, and F), each link gets the weight of twenty-one by equally dividing the page rank among all outgoing links from it.

This process of assigning page rank to each node by summing up weights of all incoming links and distributing this among all outgoing links is applied to all nodes on the Web, By creating an adjacency matrix to represent the link structure of the Web and applying eigenvector analysis, computer scientists have developed computational approaches to compute the page rank of each node on the Web.

Unindexed Search: TF/IDF

Another very popular technique for searching through documents is called TF/IDF. It was originally developed for text retrieval, but research has shown its applicability to multimedia data. TF/IDF stands for term frequency/inverse document frequency. TF/IDF is a value that reflects how important a word is to a specific document versus the collection of all documents. *Frequency* is a count of how often a word appears in a specific document while the document frequency counts how often the word appears in all documents divided by the number of documents. Mathematically inverting it makes the TF and DF values multiplicable. TF and IDF are defined as follows:

$$\text{tf}(t,d) = \frac{\text{f}(t,d)}{\max\{\text{f}(w,d) : w \in d\}}$$

$$\text{idf}(t, D) = \log \frac{|D|}{|\{d \in D : t \in d\}|}$$

with

$|D|$: the total number of documents in the corpus

$|\{d \in D : t \in d\}|$: number of documents where the term t appears. If the term is not in the corpus, this will lead to a division by zero. It is therefore common to adjust the formula to $1 + |\{d \in D : t \in d\}|$.

The TF/IDF value is calculated by:

$$\text{tfidf}(t, d, D) = \text{tf}(t,d) \times \text{idf}(t, D).$$

The intuition for the approach is as follows: Let's assume we have a set of English text documents. The given user query is "the yellow submarine." The goal is to determine which text document is most relevant for the query. The TF values will be very low for all documents that do not contain all three words, "the," "yellow," and "submarine," but this still leaves too many documents. So to further distinguish them, we find out how distinctive each of the words is. This is done by the IDF. For example, the term "the" is so common that it would incorrectly emphasize documents just because they contain the article. Clearly, the word "yellow" is second and "submarine" has the highest relevance. Hence *inverse document frequency* is incorporated as a factor to diminish the weight of terms that occur very frequently in the collection and increases the weight of terms that occur rarely.

Of course, TF/IDF search is not language specific and it is also not specific to what the "words" actually are. Therefore, TF/IDF approaches have been reported to successfully work for multimedia search substituting words for pixels, features, or other units extracted from audio or visual data.

Relevance Feedback

In many cases, articulation of a query precisely to get answers from an information retrieval system is not easy. This is because the system may have only a vague idea about what a user is looking for, or the concept or information sought may be difficult to articulate exactly. For example, a user may be looking for people who look like Abraham Lincoln. How can one articulate a query to an image retrieval system to find all people who look like Abraham Lincoln? To deal with such situations, the concept of successive refinement of queries later popularized as relevance feedback was introduced. As shown in Figure 15.5, based on the query by a user, the system produces a ranked list of results. The user then can

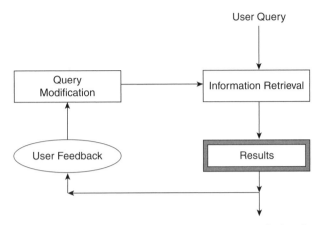

Figure 15.5. A user query may not represent what the user really has in mind. An iterative query refinement may be used to refine the results to suit user needs.

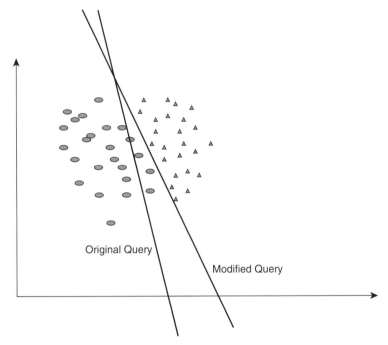

Figure 15.6. Based on the user query, the system uses a classification function that gives unsatisfactory results. User's feedback about relevance results in a modified query that gives better results.

provide explicit or implicit feedback to the system by conveying which of the results listed are not relevant to the query posed by the user. The system can then modify the query and fetch a new set of results.

One way of looking at this approach is to consider this as a simple classification problem, as shown in Figure 15.6. Based on the query by a user, the system considers all documents or images in two classes: relevant documents and not-relevant documents. The classification is done using a mathematical approach that considers different features. If the user is not satisfied with the results, then the classification function used by the user and by the system are considered different. The goal of the relevance feedback is to get more information from the user about the classification function that the user has in mind. Based on the feedback from the user, the system changes its classification function to align it better with that of the user.

The foregoing discussion using classification function works very similarly if in place of classification function, we consider a ranking function.

Image Search on the Web

Early on, most images on the Internet appeared as parts of documents. In these cases, the images could be considered secondary to the text material because images were used to provide experiential component in an otherwise text document. Searching for images on the Web started out very similar to searching for text. Images are searched on the Web using keywords. The keywords that characterize images are usually from the following:

- name of the image file;
- text on the page where the image is located; or
- tags assigned to the image.

In early systems for Web Image Search, image files were not even opened to analyze them. An image file was detected from the extension in the file name and then the search was performed using text. This approach does have limitations, but fits well with techniques used in text search. We will therefore continue this chapter by briefly describing text information retrieval.

During the past decade, many applications emerged where photos or images are the main part of the document. These applications could use text as the supporting material, but the photos are considered the main carrier of information and experiences. In such applications, techniques based on text analysis and keywords may be inadequate. In some such applications, tags have been used, but as we will discuss, the limitations of tags make them only partially useful, and other techniques, more focused on image content, are being explored.

FROM INFORMATION RETRIEVAL TO MULTIMEDIA INFORMATION RETRIEVAL

The basic structure of Multimedia Information Retrieval (MIR) is very similar to the structure of IR shown in Figure 15.3. MIR has several important differences in the components as compared to IR, however. In Figure 15.5, we show a general architecture of a MIR system. We can understand various issues related to MIR systems by considering the role and functionality of each major component as well as interactions among these components. A major challenge for building successful MIR systems is to understand not only each component, but its role and interactions in the system. The main components of a MIR system are discussed here.

Media processing to extract features: Sensors collect data, but it is unstructured. Therefore all the processing is done based on information derived from this data. In some cases, the information is at the level of the application, but in most cases, one must rely on intermediate information, commonly called *features*, as discussed in Chapter 17. In every type of signal analysis, feature selection and feature detection is one of the most important steps. Depending on the signal and the applications, different types of features may be extracted. Spectral characteristics, texture, color, and shape are all example of features.

Indexing: Organization of information means finding suitable approaches to indexing to efficiently gain access to it. In multimedia data, this becomes a serious challenge. Indexing is usually based on the extracted features. However, in most applications, one is less interested in the structure of a document than in the information derived. Current approaches to indexing are strongly influenced by the type of content. Unified indexing approaches should allow accessing information of diverse content based on information requirement. Another problem is the dimensionality of data. The number of features required for characterizing an image and other media data is very large and requires multidimensional indexing techniques.

Interaction environment: A user commonly formulates a query to the system and the system responds by providing an answer. Because we are not searching text, however, what is the query? In some cases, the user uploads example documents that contain videos or audio. In any case, the interaction environment for a multimedia-based search is more complicated than for queries based on keyboard input. To resolve this problem, systems are increasingly trying to introduce some knowledge about the state of the user and are also trying to personalize the responses to the user by using profiles and other information related to the user, as shown in Figure 15.5. Almost all mobile search systems use the location of the user as a parameter in providing search results. Use of social networks has also started playing a role in these systems. Relevance feedback has been used as a mechanism to refine the response of the system for a specific query. Thus, though most systems still utilize a simple stateless query and answer system, many applications are starting to embed search or retrieval systems in their environment to make the whole environment more interactive and contextual. Many applications are naturally designed to use an incremental approach to solve a problem. In such systems, retrieval is a component that serves in the background by bringing the right information to the user at the right instant.

In the following sections, we will try to address these important issues and direction in various MIR systems.

CONTENT-BASED RETRIEVAL

Retrieval techniques were initially developed to consider image collections. These techniques were called *content-based image retrieval* (CBIR) because they considered image characteristics for retrieving images. An image could be represented using its basic features. Commonly used basic features are color, texture, and structure or shape.

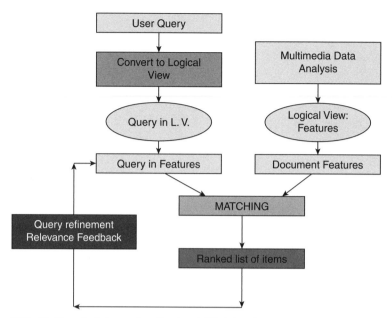

Figure 15.7. Multimedia Information Retrieval: High-level components.

We discuss these features in more detail in Chapter 17. These three attributes of an image are captured using different types of image characteristics computed using image processing techniques applied to the pixel characteristics.

The early versions of CBR used a weighted combination of the these features to judge image similarity and rank pictures. Sometimes these systems were also called Query by Image Example because the query for an image was another image.

Figures 15.6 and 15.7 show two examples of these systems. In both these figures, screenshots for a query and its results are shown. In both figures, the query image is the first image; the top left image and all images are shown in the order of their similarity to the query image from the database. The number of images in the database for these examples was about twenty thousand.

In Figure 15.6, the top right panel shows that a user could assign importance to different image features in the query.

These systems are ranking images based on similarity of visual characteristics of images; they do not have any concept of objects as we know them. Thus in Figure 15.7, one can see that most images are similar to the query image because they contain a large number of green pixels with similar textures and in the center is another object of a different color – in most cases similar to the color of the query image. The system is not trying to detect roses as in the query image, though the majority of results contain flowers, particularly roses.

Many enhancements have been made to these basic techniques. One can divide each image into multiple regions, say a 3 x 3 grid, compute these features for each region, and compare these with the corresponding ones. The similarity is then judged based on how

Figure 15.8. A screenshot showing the selected image, the weights for different features and results corresponding to this query. (See Plate VIII for color version.)

Figure 15.9. For the query related to a rose, in the top left corner as the first result, the top 50 results are shown here. (See Plate IX for color version.)

close each region is to a corresponding region. Another simple modification is to consider a color histogram prepared using only coherent colors. This is done by ignoring those pixels whose color value is different from their neighbors. This means that most noisy pixels and pixels on edges are ignored and only those pixels in homogeneous color regions are considered.

Query by Humming

Music search is similar to image search in that often music is found through metadata, for example, composers, title, and genre. Music databases like the popular Apple iTunes, for example, work exactly that way. Another strategy for music search is to use collaborative filtering. The assumption is that if someone likes a piece of music, then that person will like other pieces that other persons liked as well. Of course this, again, requires users to fill in metadata for the pieces of music. There is, however, one characteristic of music that can be exploited better than in other media: users are often able to reproduce the music or at least parts of it by singing or humming it themselves. This is exploited in music search and called Query by Humming or QbH. A QbH system takes a user-hummed melody as an input query and compares it to an existing database, returning a ranked list of music closest to the input query. These systems are most useful for portable devices with a built-in microphone, such as smartphones, allowing for faster searching through music files. Close relatives to Query by Humming systems are systems that allow the entry of the melody through a virtual keyboard, notes, or by tapping the beat. The most important problem to solve in these systems is, of course, that of the definition of closeness.

To compare melodies, so-called pitch signatures are often extracted from each piece of music and then compared with a pitch signature extracted from the query. A pitch signature is a set of pitch values (see Chapter 5) per time frame. Edit distance (see Chapter 17) is often used as a metric, that is, counting the editing steps (inserting, deleting, or replacing a note) needed for converting the query signature into each of the database pitch signatures.

Of course, this method is not perfectly accurate, but many QbH systems utilize it. Although many articles describing these systems explored the use of other features, such as beat, it is often reported that the pitch signature methods (also called melody contour) work best. As usual, we recommend digging further into the literature for details.

Retrieval Based on the Semantic Content

If the content of multimedia documents in terms of objects in it and relationships among them is somehow available, then it is possible to develop powerful retrieval techniques that could actually be called content-based retrieval. Earlier we discussed computing average attributes of pixels in a query image and using those to retrieve similar images based on those attributes. In more realistic situations, we might consider the following queries:

- Show all photos of Jay in which he is participating in a sporting activity.
- Show me all photos of Jay with Tarah in Cabo.
- Was Tarah with Jay in Paris?

These queries require recognition of objects and their relationships in photos. These queries cannot be answered without clear object models. Object recognition has been a very important research area in computer vision for about fifty years. The more general research area of pattern recognition deals with identifying patterns that may correspond to objects, concepts, or activities in data. The fundamental problem addressed in pattern recognition is: given N patterns (P1, P2, …, Pn) that are models of corresponding objects or concepts, identify which of these patterns are present in a given data set.

Clearly recognition and retrieval are not the same problem, but recognition may play a very important role in content-based retrieval. The queries listed earlier all require recognition of objects and concepts and relationships among them. This important fact has resulted in the application of several recognition techniques to detect objects and annotate images with these objects for retrieval purposes.

The first step in developing recognition approaches is to have strong models for objects. Considering the variability of objects, their appearances, and changes in appearances in images due to different viewpoints, illumination conditions, and climatic conditions, it is very difficult to create models for objects that could be used for recognition in images. The popularity of machine-learning techniques in computer vision and multimedia is primarily for simplifying the process of creation of these models that could be used in recognition.

Despite significant efforts in development of automatic recognition techniques, progress in this area has been quite slow. Because the need for organization and retrieval of images has become a real hurdle in the growth of many applications, manual and semiautomatic approaches have received significant popularity.

For music retrieval, for example, researchers began studying a semiautomatic approach for semantic music similarity under the name "Music Genome Project" around 2000; the result has been the popular Pandora music retrieval system. In this system, every song is represented by a set of about four hundred attributes, of which some of them have been extracted automatically and some of them have been extracted manually. The set consists of attributes like gender of lead vocalist, level of distortion on the electric guitar, and type of background vocals. To extract the features, often several audio technicians and musicians have listened to one song. The user selects a query song by searching the database with metadata, such as artist name. The query song's attributes are then used for a search to find similar sings in the database.

Retrieval Based on Tags

A very popular concept to emerge in many applications has been that of "tags" for multimedia content. This concept has been used in many other applications as well, including text documents. A person could assign tags to an image, video, or audio file to describe it. The tags could be objects, concepts, or names of objects or places. In fact, it could be anything that could describe the image and help in management and retrieval of the image. Because of the increasing use of multimedia in many applications, particularly in video sharing, use of these tags is quite attractive. Once these tags are decided, or manually selected, standard indexing techniques employed in information retrieval may be used.

One may use Exif data and other metadata to assign appropriate tags that may be used in retrieval. Popular systems like iPhoto use place-, time-, and face-recognition-based tags. Some common problems with manual assignment of tags that must be considered in any tag based retrieval system are:

- Tags are very subjective. A picture is usually assigned different tags by different people.
- Tags are time dependent. Depending on when tags are assigned to a picture, the tags could be very different.
- Availability of tags for pictures is random. For most photos, people do not assign tags. It is commonly observed that less than 2 percent of photos on most photo sharing sites have tags. Moreover, people do not assign tags to most photos in their own collections.

Video Retrieval

Information content in a video depends on the type of video. Most videos could be considered in one of the following classes:

- Professionally produced videos: Professionals produce videos such as TV and movies following well-defined conventions. These videos can be compared to well-authored text where there is a well-defined structure in the document starting from a book to chapters to subchapters to paragraphs and to sentences. Produced videos also have such well-defined structure.
- Semi-produced videos: Videos such as sports and seminar lectures are semi-produced. They also follow general conventions, but these are not so rigid. Signal quality is generally lower than professionally produced content.
- Consumer-produced video (aka "wild" videos): These are the videos most people create. Using a video camera, people may collect many video segments and edit them using one of the commonly available video editing systems. Most of these videos do not follow any videography rules and have low signal quality.

Video is more than just a sequence of images; it also has synchronized audio. Depending on an application, the information content in a video may be more in audio, particularly speech, more in images, or equal in both audio and images. In any case, video must be considered very differently from images or music or speech.

Suppose that we have a collection of video. The types of queries that people may ask may be:

- In how many parties was Tarah wearing a pink dress?
- Show me all romantic scenes from *Titanic*.
- Show me all stunts by Tom Cruise.
- Show me the car stunts from *Casino Royale*. What car was Bonds driving?
- List all popular romantic movies in the past decade.
- Show me all players who "pull" like Tendulkar.
- Show me all stories on BBC that talked about the psychic octopus.

All these queries require that the video is analyzed and some information is extracted. The queries may be based on

- Objects
- Activities
- Time of activity
- Similarity of activity to a given activity
- Genre of activity
- Speech
- Music
- Concepts

This may require analysis of visual characteristics, audio, and metadata related to the video. Techniques for doing that are explained in Chapter 17.

RECOMMENDED READING

Multimedia information retrieval is currently one of the most active research areas in multimedia. The growth of content in multimedia requires the development of tools to organize and index the content for rapid and relevant access. Starting in the early 1990s, this field has grown substantially. Earliest concepts in this area were introduced in Gupta, Weymouth, and Jain (1991). Research in query by pictorial example (Datta et al. 2008) started a trend that later became known as *query by content*. Despite a vibrant research community and very active pursuit, the problems have been challenging. The most fundamental issue in organizing and accessing content is the semantic gap. The semantic gap was first discussed in Santini and Jain (1998) and later popularized in "Content-Based Image Retrieval at the End of the Early Years." Many research papers are now addressing the semantic gap. Many review papers have been written in this field. Interested readers are advised to start with one of these to get a good feel of the field. A particularly influential paper seems to be "Content-Based Image Retrieval at the End of the Early Years," which summarizes research until 2000 and is one of the most cited papers. Later review papers such as Gupta and Jain (1997), Rui and colleagues (1998), and Kankanhall and Rui (2008) give a good summary of MIR research and are good complements to the earlier review presented in "Content-Based Image Retrieval at the End of the Early Years."

Query by successive refinement was introduced in Bach, Paul, and Jain (1993) and later was formalized in general cases using the concepts of relevance feedback in Kherf, Ziou, and Bernard. The concept of emergent semantics was introduced in Santini, Gupta, and Jain (2001), and is likely to attract more attention as the data size is increasing exponentially. Trends to organize personal photos using context are explored in Anguera, Xu, and Oliver (2009), Gong and Jain (2007), Liu and Özsu (2009), Exif (2002). A good summary of metadata associated with photos is in "IEEE Transactions on Pattern Analysis and Machine Intelligence," and how to use those is explored in Sinha and Jain (2008). Some researchers have started exploring concepts of visual words (Smeulders et al. 2000). One must be very careful in using words in multimedia because words in text are manually delimited and are used as defined in a dictionary. Both of these limitations are not currently valid for visual words. Use of events for unified access to multimedia was presented in Flickner and colleagues (1995) using models of events defined in Kherfi, Ziou, and Bernardi (2004).

Further Reading

X. Anguera, J. Xu, and N. Oliver. "Multimodal photo annotation and retrieval on mobile phones." Proceeding of the 1st ACM International Conference on Multimedia Information Retrieval. 2009.

J. Bach, S. Paul, and R. Jain. "An interactive image management system for face information retrieval." *IEEE Transactions on Knowledge and Data Engineering, Special Section on Multimedia Information Systems*. Publication. 1993.

K. Barnard and D. Forsyth. "Learning the semantics of words and pictures." *Proc of IEEE Intl Conf Computer Vision*, 2: 408–15, 2000.

M. Boutell and J. Luo. "Bayesian fusion of camera metadata cues in semantic scene classification." *Proc. IEEE CVPR*, 2, 2004.

M. Boutell and J. Luo. "Photo classification by integrating image content and camera metadata." *Proceedings of ICPR*, 4, 2004.

R. Datta, D. Joshi, J. Li, and J. Wang. "Image retrieval: Ideas, influences, and trends of the new age." *ACM Computing Surveys*, 40 (2), Article 5: April 2008.

Exif: Exchangeable image file format for digital cameras: Exif version 2.2. Technical report, Japan Electronics and Information Technology Industries Association, 2002.

M. Flickner, H. Sawhney, W. Niblack, J. Ashley, Q. Huang, M. Gorkani, J. Hafner, D. Lee, D. Petkovic, D. Steele, and P. Yonker. "Query by image and video content: The QBIC System." *IEEE Computer* 18 (9), September 1995.

Bo Gong and Ramesh Jain. "Segmenting photo streams in events based on optical metadata." Proc. IEEE Conf. on Semantic Computing, Irvine, CA, Sept. 17–19, 2007.

A. Gupta and R. Jain. "Visual information retrieval." *Commun. ACM*, 40 (5): 70–9, 1997.

A. Gupta, T. Weymouth, and R. Jain. "Semantic queries with pictures: The VIMSYS model." *Proceedings of VLDB'91, 17th International Conference* on *Very Large Data Bases*, Barcelona, Spain. Sept. 3–6, 1991.

Ramesh Jain. "Out of the box data engineering: Events in heterogeneous data." Keynote talk, Proceedings of International Conference on Data Engineering, Bangalore, India, March 2003.

M. S. Kankanhalli and Y. Rui. "Application potential of multimedia information retrieval." *Proc. IEE*, April 2008.

M. L Kherfi, D. Ziou, and A. Bernardi. "Image retrieval from the World Wide Web." *ACM Computing Surveys*, 36 (1): March 2004.

Ling Liu and Tamer M. Özsu, eds. *Encyclopedia of Database Systems*. New York: Springer. 2009.

Y. Rui, T. S. Huang, M. Ortega, and S. Mehrotra. "Relevance feedback: A power tool in interactive content-based image retrieval." *IEEE Trans. Circ. Syst. Video Technol.*, 8 (5): 644–55, 1998.

Simone Santini, Amarnath Gupta, and Ramesh Jain "Emergent semantics through interaction in Image Databases." *IEEE Transactions on Knowledge and Data Engineering*, Summer 2001.

Simone Santini and Ramesh Jain. "Beyond query by example," IEEE Second Workshop on Multimedia Signal Processing, Redondo Beach, CA, pp. 3–8, December 7–9, 1998.

P. Sinha and R. Jain. "Classification and annotation of digital photos using optical context data." Proceedings of the 2008 international conference on content-based image and video retrieval, ACM (2008): 309–18.

P. Sinha and R. Jain. "Semantics in Digital Photos: A contextual analysis." Proceedings of the 2008 IEEE International Conference on Semantic Computing, IEEE Computer Society (2008): 58–65.

Arnold Smeulders, Marcel Worring, Simone Santini, Amarnath Gupta, and Ramesh Jain "Image Databases at the end of the Early Years" *IEEE Transactions on Pattern Analysis and Machine Intelligence* 23 (1), January 2001.

G. Utz Westermann and Ramesh Jain. "Towards a common event model for multimedia applications," *IEEE Multimedia*, January 2007.

EXERCISES

1. What is the fundamental difference between structured, semistructured, and unstructured data? Give an example of each type of data in its native form.

2. Can unstructured data be searched? What should one do to make unstructured data searchable?

3. What is the logical view (or logical representation) of data? In an information retrieval system, what are important requirements of the logical view?

4. Why are keywords used as the logical view of data in search systems? Do you think keywords will also be important for image search? Why?

5. What is inverted file structure in the context of an information retrieval system? Why is it so popular? Can you think of some other mechanism to replace it?

6. Why are ranked lists used in information retrieval systems?

7. What is page rank? How does it help in search? How does it assign importance to a specific document?

8. Can you extend the concept of page rank to multimedia information retrieval? How?

9. What is TF and what is IDF? What information do they capture relevant to search? How are they used in search?

10. In retrieval, what is more important, recall or precision? Why?

11. Suppose that you developed a search algorithm. You want to characterize this using some objective measure. Can you use precision and recall for that? How? Please give concrete steps, if necessary.

12. What is relevance feedback? Why is it needed? How does it work? Give an example of a relevance feedback system.

13. Give examples of features used in image retrieval systems. Why are features used in these systems?

14. Do regular image features satisfy requirements of a logical view that could be used in image information systems? Why?

15. Give example of features used in audio retrieval systems. Why are features used in these systems?

16. Do regular image features satisfy requirements of a logical view that could be used in audio information systems? Why?

17. Give example of features used in speech retrieval systems. Why are features used in these systems?

18. What kind of queries may people ask in images, audio, and video? List five queries each that you will ask for images, audio, and video.

16 Signal Processing Primer

In Chapters 5 and 6, we described sound and light and their physical properties. In this chapter, we will discuss basic signal processing operations that are common initial steps of many algorithms for audio and video enhancement and content analysis.

SAMPLING AND QUANTIZATION

As we explained in Chapter 4, a continuous function must be converted to a discrete form for representation and processing using a digital computer. The interface between the optical system that projects a scene onto the image plane and the computer must sample the image at a finite number of points and represent each sample within the finite word size of the computer. Likewise, the sound card samples the microphone output into a stream of numbers. In other words, in both cases, the matter to work with when doing computational audio and video processing is a stream of numbers that are representative of the signal at certain spatial or temporal points.

As explained before, visual data samples in images or videos are called *pixels* (**picture** *element*); temporal image samples as part of videos are called *frame*. Audio processing jargon doesn't have a special name for audio samples, but calls sets of (converted) samples *frames*. We will assume that images are sampled on a regular grid of squares so that the horizontal and vertical distances between pixels are the same throughout the image; likewise, audio samples are obtained in regular intervals. Many cameras and microphones acquire an analog signal, which is then sampled and quantized to convert it to digital. The sampling rate determines how many samples the digital signal will have (called either *image resolution* or *acoustic sampling rate*), and quantization determines how many intensity levels will be used to represent the intensity value at each sample. Chapters 5 and 6, as well as visual and acoustic processing books (see recommended reading section), discuss the factors that should be considered when selecting appropriate sampling and quantization rates to retain the important information in digitized files. In most modern cameras, the sampling and quantizing rates are predetermined and specified as the number of pixels (as MP, or million pixels) available on the chip used in the camera. In this case, the images are directly acquired in digital form.

Acoustic and visual signal samples over time are often conceptualized in what is called *time domain*: the x-axis of a graph showing a signal this way would be time. In the frequency domain, every point of the x-axis represents a certain frequency. Visualized as a graph, the diagram would show how the signal varies over frequency. Typically, just like in time domain, the y-axis would show the energy or amplitude of the signal.

LEVELS OF COMPUTATION

An image, video, or sound file usually contains several objects. A vision application, for example, usually involves computing certain properties of an object, not the image as a whole. To compute properties of an object, individual objects must first be identified as separate objects; then object properties can be computed by applying calculations to the separate objects. For considering computational aspects of audio, visual, and multimedia processing algorithms, it helps to consider each algorithm in terms of its input-output characteristics. By considering nature and the level of these operations, it is possible to consider how best to implement these operations. Note that the output of a content analysis system, unlike that of a content processing system, is some symbolic quantity denoting identity or location of an object, for instance. The amount of data a multimedia system processes is very large, and that makes the computational requirements very demanding. Because we want to discuss characteristics of operations to predict their computational requirements, we classify the levels of operations and study their general characteristics.

Sample Level

Some operations produce an output based on only a point in an image or a sample of an audio stream. Thresholding is an example of a point operation. A thresholding algorithm produces output values that depend only on the input value for a preset threshold. Thus, if $I(x,y)$, and $O(x,y)$ are input and output signals, respectively, then for a point operation:

$$O(x,y) = f\big(I(x+k,y+l)\big)$$

meaning that in the output signal, the attribute or intensity value at a point (x,y) depends only on the attribute value at a corresponding point $(x+k, y+l)$.

Local Level

A local operation produces an output signal in which the intensity at a sample depends on the neighborhood of the corresponding sample in the input stream.

Thus, for a local operation,

$$O(x,y) = f\big(I\big[Nbr(x,y,z)\big]\big)$$

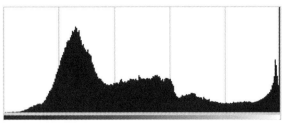

Figure 16.1. An example of a global operation: an image (left) and its histogram (right). A histogram is a plot of the number of pixels at each gray value contained in the image.

where $Nbr[x,y]$ denotes a neighborhood of sample (x,y,z). In images, the most commonly used neighborhoods are 3 x 3 windows centered around the point; in audio processing, larger windows are usually used, such as 10ms. It is possible to use larger or smaller windows depending on the operation under consideration.

Smoothing and edge detection are local operations. Because these operations require values from a neighborhood in the input image, array processors or single instruction, multiple data (SIMD) machines may be suitable for implementing these operations. In general, these operations can be easily implemented on parallel machines and can often be performed in real time.

Global Level

The output of certain operators depends on the whole file. Such operations are called *global operations*:

$$P = f\left(I\left(x,y\right)\right)$$

This operation is shown in Figure 16.1. The output of these operators may be an image or it may be symbolic output. A histogram of intensity values and the Fourier transform are global operations. We will see that most operations at higher levels are global in nature and are most expensive in terms of time requirements.

Object Level

Most applications of content analysis require properties to be computed at the object level. In acoustic processing, objects usually vary by tasks; for example, in a speaker identification system, the objects would be different speakers, while in a speech recognition system, objects could be words. In the field of computer vision, *objects* are defined as the "intuitive" objects human see. Often, size, length, average intensity, shape, frequency spectrum, texture, and/or other characteristics of an object must be computed for a system to recognize it. Many other characteristics of an object must be determined for detecting features for recognition of an object.

This leads to interesting but very difficult questions: What is an object? How do we find objects? In Figure 16.2, how many objects do we see? Some people say five, some six, and

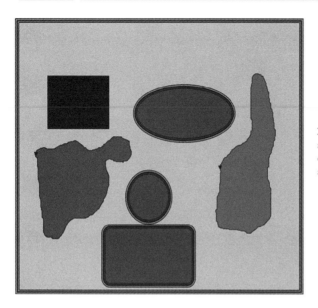

Figure 16.2. How many objects do we see in this figure? Depending on your definition of an object you may see five, six, or seven objects in this figure.

some may even say seven. All of them are right. We will see that an object is defined in a particular context. In fact, many operations in vision are performed to find where a particular object is located in an image. Objects in images pose a catch-22 situation. We must use all points that belong to an object to compute some of its characteristics, but we must use those characteristics to identify those points. We will see that significant efforts are spent to solve the *figure-ground* problem (separation of foreground pixels from background pixels) to group points into objects. To understand the contents of a signal, a content analysis system must perform several operations at the object level. More on that in the subsequent chapter. Let's start with some fundamental knowledge before introducing basic processing techniques.

THRESHOLDING

Often, we want to separate something with a property x from something else with a property y in a multimedia content processing or analysis system. This operation, which is often so very natural and easy for people, is surprisingly difficult for computers. Let us consider that we want to mark all points in an image that belong to an object of interest, commonly called *foreground*, as 1 and all other points as 0. Thus we convert an image to a binary image that gives us a mask for all object points. Such a binary image is obtained using an appropriate segmentation of a grayscale image. If the intensity values of an object are in an interval and the intensity values of the background pixels are outside this interval, a binary image can be obtained using a thresholding operation that sets the points in that interval to one and points outside that range to zero. Thresholding is a method to convert a grayscale image into a binary image so that objects of interest are separated from the

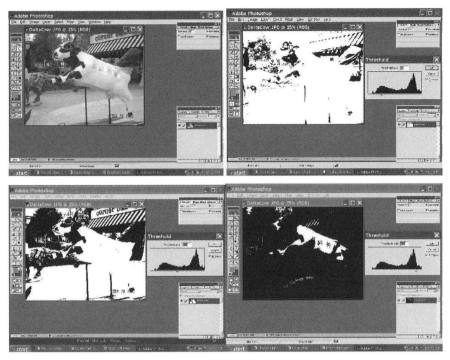

Figure 16.3. An image and several binary images obtained at different threshold values.

background. For thresholding to be effective in *object-background separation*, the objects and background must have sufficient contrast and we must know the intensity levels of either the objects or the background. In a fixed thresholding scheme, these intensity characteristics determine the value of the threshold. Let us assume that a binary image $B[i,j]$ is the same as a thresholded gray image $F_{Thr}[i, j]$, which is obtained using a threshold T for the original gray image $F[i, j]$. Thus,

$$B[i,j] = 1 \; if \; F[i, j] > T$$
$$= 0 \; otherwise.$$

If it is known that the object intensity values are in a range [T1, T2], then we may use

$$B[i,j] = 1 \; if \; T1 < F[i, j] < T$$
$$= 0 \; otherwise.$$

The results of producing an image using different thresholds are shown in Figure 16.3. Note knowledge about the application domain is required in selecting the threshold. The same threshold values may not work in a new set of images acquired under different conditions. The threshold is usually selected on the basis of experience with the application domain. In some cases, the first few runs of the system may be used for interactively analyzing a scene and determining an appropriate value for the threshold. Automatic thresholding of images is often the first step in the analysis of images in machine vision systems. Many techniques have been developed for utilizing the intensity distribution in an image and the knowledge about the objects of interest for selecting a proper threshold value automatically. Likewise, acoustic processing usually applies thresholds in time and frequency space and fails in a similar way.

LINEAR OPERATIONS

A very common type of operations useable in many situations and in many domains are the linear operations. The linear filter applies a linear operator to a time-varying input signal.

Definition 16.1: Linear Operator

Let V and W be vector spaces over the same field K. A function $f: V \rightarrow W$ is said to be a *linear operator* if for any two vectors x and y in V and any scalar a in K, the following two conditions are satisfied:

1)   Additivity: $f(x + y) = f(x) + f(y)$
2)   Homogeneity (of degree 1): $f(ax) = af(x)$.

It follows from the conditions that $f(0)=0$.

These mathematical properties have several advantages in real-world applications. For example, because of the homogeneity rule, it does not matter whether a linear filter is applied before or after amplification of a signal. The same applies for the additive mixture of two signals: the additivity makes sure that it does not matter whether the filter is first applied to each of the mixture components before the mix or after the mix to the added components. This is especially useful to generalize a one-dimensional linear filter to more than one dimension: one can just apply the operator to each dimension individually. Because of these properties, many real-world circuits and filter formulas aim to be linear. Distortions are often caused by deviations from the linearity assumption of real-world equipment, such as amplifiers (which are essentially multipliers of the signal in time space).

Linear operators are further divided into two classes: infinite impulse response (IIR) and finite impulse response (FIR) operators. In this context, operators are usually called *filters*. We therefore continue the chapter by using these two words interchangeably. FIR filters (which may only be implemented on a discrete time scale) can be described as a weighted sum of delayed inputs. If the input becomes zero at any time, then the output will eventually become zero as well, as soon as enough time has passed so that all the delayed inputs are zero, too. Therefore, the impulse response lasts only a *finite* time. In an IIR filter, the set of time when the output is nonzero will be unbounded; the filter's energy will decay but will be ever present.

The mathematical discipline behind filter design is called *linear time-invariant* (LIT) system theory. The following section discusses commonly used filters.

Common Linear Filters

Linear filters are often used to eliminate unwanted frequencies from an input signal or to select or enhance a set of desired frequencies from among many others. As the reader might already have inferred, these operations are among the most important. Common types of linear filters include the low-pass filter, which passes frequencies below a threshold; a high-pass filter, which passes frequencies above a threshold; and a band-pass filter, which passes frequencies of a band between two frequency thresholds. Similarly, preemphasis amplifies a certain band. A band-stop filter passes frequencies except a limited range; that is, it is the reverse of the band-pass filter. A special, often used, band-stop filter is the so-called notch-filter. Notch-filters have a particularly narrow stop band and are often used in audio equipment, one example being the anti-hum filter that filters electro-wire-induced humming between 59 and 61 Hz or 49 and 51 Hz (depending on the country's electrical specifications). The following example implements a typical band-pass filter:

```
// Input: 4,096 audio samples s[] sampled at 44,100Hz,
// lower boundary frequency lf, upper boundary frequency uf,
// an FFT function, an inverse FFT function (see Chapter 13)
// Output: A filtered audio signal
bandpass(s[],lf, uf, fft, ifft)
    fs[][]:=FFT(s) // convert to frequency space with block size 4,096,
            // 2nd index 0-real value, 2nd index 1 = complex value
    FOR i:=0 TO 2048: // exploit symmetry
      IF ((44100/4096)*i<lf) OR ((44100/4096)*i>hf): // bandpass
        fs[i][0]:=0
        fs[i][1]:=0
        fs[4096-i-1][0]:=0
        fs[4096-i-1][1]:=0
    s:=iFFT(fs)   // back to time space
bandpass := s[]
            Algorithm 16.1: Band-pass Filter
```

Acoustic equalizers, for example, use combinations of band-pass filters to extract individual bands that can then be amplified or suppressed according to user settings. Equalizers are part of virtually any home audio system and can be used to fine-tune the frequency spectrum of an audio signal; for example, more bass can be added and speech can be made more intelligible against background noise. The wrong settings, however, can degrade audio quality. Because the individual bands can be easily visualized using sliders, the filter is often called a *graphic equalizer*. Figure 16.4 shows a graphical equalizer that is implemented by simulating a ten-band octave filter array conforming to ISO Recommendation 266. The filters use a Gaussian curve that allows the equalizer to operate smoothly across the different bands. The center frequency occurs at the top of the Gaussian curve and is the frequency most affected by equalization. It is often notated as

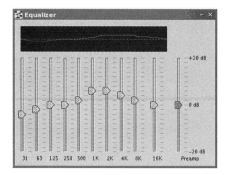

Figure 16.4. A graphic equalizer in a typical setting used for enhancing the intelligibility of speech. The numbers on the bottom show the center filter frequency in each band and the sliders manipulate the energy in each band.

f_c and is measured in Hz. The eleventh slider on the left regulates preamplification of the signal before it enters the filter bank.

NONLINEAR FILTERS

Not all operators are linear. In fact, most filters are not – but of course that does not mean that they are not useful.

One important acoustic nonlinear filter is dynamic range compression (DRC). This filter often results in surprising perceptual enhancements of the audio signal. The analog process of DRC, sometimes simply called *compression*, is not to be confused with audio compression as discussed in Chapter 12, even though DRC can lead to better data compression rates. DRC is a process that reduces the dynamic range of an audio signal; that is, it narrows the difference between high and low time levels. DRC is applied by running an audio signal through a dedicated electronic hardware unit or, nowadays, mostly through software. In the context of audio production, the hardware unit is often simply referred to as a *compressor*. A DRC is a volume control filter. Two types of compressors exist: downward compressors work by reducing loud sounds over a certain time threshold while lower amplitude sounds remain untreated. Upward compressors amplify sounds below a threshold while loud signals remain unchanged. In both cases, the dynamic range of the audio signal is reduced. DRCs are often used for aesthetic reasons or sometimes to deal with technical limitations of audio equipment, for example, to avoid clipping.

Dynamic range compression often improves the audibility of audio in noisy environments when background noise overpowers quiet sounds. In these cases, compressors are tuned so that they reduce the level of the loud sounds but not the quiet sounds, whose level can be raised to a point where quiet sounds are audible without loud sounds being too loud. Note that analog compressors always decrease the signal-to-noise ratio. While this is sometimes acceptable for human perception, it is often a problem for machine learning algorithms. Figure 16.5 shows the functionality of a typical compressor.

Building compressors, especially as analog circuits, can be complicated because they require manual fine-tuning. For example, the bend in the response curve around the threshold is usually smoothed to a rounded edge rather than kept at a sharp angle as in Figure 16.5. It is often desirable for a compressor to provide control over how quickly it acts

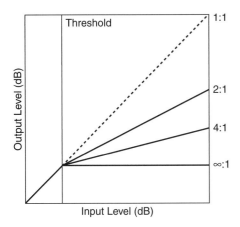

Figure 16.5. Relationship between input level, output level, and gain reduction in a set of example downward dynamic range compressors. This particular type of DRC amplifies the signal below a threshold amplitude and then dampens the signal above the threshold amplitude.

as the volume pattern of the source material that the compressor modifies may change the character of the signal quite noticeably. Some compressors therefore allow us to define an attack and a release phase similar to the attack and release phases of a synthesizer. Another difference is between peak sensing and RMS-energy sensing (compare to Chapter 14 on speech compression). A peak sensing compressor responds to the level of the input signal instantaneously while an RMS-energy compressor responds to the energy of the signal over a small time window. The second type of compressor usually resembles perception of volume more closely. Other factors include the way a compressor reacts to stereo signals or if it reacts to different subbands differently (multiband compressor). In the digital age, creating compressors no longer involves fiddling around with complicated control circuits, but tuning might still be necessary. Exercise 5 asks you to design a simple software compressor.

Downward and upward DRCs might be combined using two or more different thresholds to form a variable-gain amplifier. Figure 16.6 shows a typical signal before and after the application of a variable-gain amplifier.

Multiband variable-gain amplification is often designed to approximate the Mel or Bark curves (see Chapter 5) in order to approximate the perceptual properties of volume change in human hearing. This can be used to normalize sound files in a collection that have been recorded at different levels to about the same audible level. This function is often part of both software and hardware MP3 players.

Another set of very important nonlinear filters are resampling (subsampling and supersampling) filters. *Subsampling* (or *downsampling*) is the process of reducing the sampling rate of a signal. This is regularly done, for example, when a smaller thumbnail of an image is created or when compact disc audio at 44,100Hz is downsampled to 22,050Hz before broadcasting over FM radio. Because downsampling reduces the sampling rate, one must ensure the Nyquist sampling theorem criterion is maintained, otherwise aliasing will occur (see Chapter 4). If a signal has been recorded at a much higher sampling rate than defined by the Nyquist limit, it is very likely that the original signal will contain frequencies higher than the downsampled signal can represent. To ensure that the sampling theorem is satisfied, a low-pass filter has to be used as an anti-aliasing filter to reduce the bandwidth of

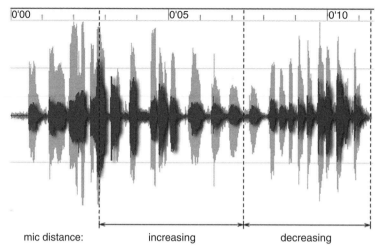

Figure 16.6. An example application of variable-gain amplifier. When the speaker turns away from the microphone, the audio gain goes down and with the mouth approaching the microphone the gain raises again (darker signal). Using DRC, the overall gain is higher and the microphone distance differences are leveled out more effectively (lighter signal).

the signal before the signal is downsampled. When downsampling by integer factors ($n =$ 2, 3, 4, etc.), all one has to do is apply a low-pass filter to the signal and then pick every nth sample from the low-pass filtered samples. When downsampling to a rational fraction m/n, the signal should be supersampled by factor m first, so that it can be downsampled by factor n in the second step.

Supersampling (or *upsampling*) is a bit more tricky. Supersampling is the process of increasing the sampling rate of a signal. For instance, upsampling raster images such as photographs means increasing the resolution of the image. Of course, objectively information cannot really be gained by algorithmic upsampling because the supersampled signal satisfies the Nyquist sampling theorem if the original signal does. So the basic supersampling algorithm is called *zero stuffing*: insert as many zeros as needed between the two original samples and then apply a low-pass filter with a threshold set at the Nyquist limit frequency of the original signal. However, more elaborate algorithms try to model the underlying continuous signal from the original samples to then sample it again at a higher sampling rate, trying to convert alias into real information. These filters are often called *interpolation filters*.

The most basic interpolation filter is the constant interpolation filter: repeat each value n times (where n is the upsampling factor) and then apply a low-pass filter. *Linear interpolation* is almost as basic: instead of duplicating each sample, assume a linear function between each of the original samples and use that to create as many new samples between the original samples as required by the upscaling factor. Generally, linear interpolation takes two data points, (xa,ya) and (xb,yb), and the interpolant is given by:

$$y = y_a + (y_b - y_a)\frac{(x - x_a)}{(x_b - x_a)}$$

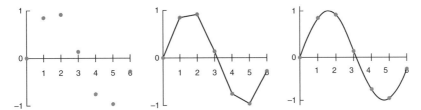

Figure 16.7. Left: original signal, middle: linear interpolation, right: polynomial interpolation. Even though the polynomial interpolation looks similar to what the original signal might have looked like, there is an infinite number of other possibilities how the original (continuous) signal might have looked like.

Because sound waves are generally sinusoidal rather than linear, these simple interpolation techniques will create (sometimes audible) artifacts. Therefore, polynomial and other nonlinear functions are often used. *Polynomial interpolation* is a generalization of linear interpolation. Generally, with n data points, there is exactly one polynomial of degree at most $n-1$ going through all the data points. However, calculating the interpolating polynomial is computationally expensive compared to linear interpolation. Suppose that the interpolation polynomial is in the form

$$p(x) = a_n x^n + a_{n-1} x^{n-1} + \ldots + a_2 x^2 + a_1 x + a_0$$

We want $p(x)$ to interpolate all data points. In other words:

$$p(x_i) = y_i \text{ for all } i \in \{0, 1, \ldots, n\}.$$

By substituting equation $p(x)$, we get a system of linear equations in the coefficients a_k, which in matrix form reads:

$$\begin{bmatrix} x_0^n & x_0^{n-1} & x_0^{n-2} & \ldots & x_0 & 1 \\ x_1^n & x_1^{n-1} & x_1^{n-2} & \ldots & x_1 & 1 \\ \vdots & \vdots & \vdots & & \vdots & \vdots \\ x_n^n & x_n^{n-1} & x_n^{n-2} & \ldots & x_n & 1 \end{bmatrix} \begin{bmatrix} a_n \\ a_{n-1} \\ \vdots \\ a_0 \end{bmatrix} = \begin{bmatrix} y_0 \\ y_1 \\ \vdots \\ y_n \end{bmatrix}.$$

Gaussian elimination can solve this system of equations. Figure 16.7 compares the three approaches for a sample signal.

Because of the computational complexity of polynomial interpolations, *spline interpolation*, which implements piecewise polynomial interpolation with low-degree polynomials, is often used to interpolate vector graphics efficiently. In audio processing, *polyphase filters* are more common; they help avoid aliasing and further distorting the signal by upsampling or downsampling. Polyphase filtering divides the signal into different subbands, which are treated independently. Using the critical subbands (see Chapter 13), for example, can reduce the effects of audible aliases.

FILTER BY EXAMPLE

Especially for noise reduction, it is often desirable to eliminate a very specific part of the signal that is not necessarily constant in frequency range or might not be sinusoid. For example, when digitizing a CD from an old vinyl record, the scratches of the pickup might cover a range of frequencies so large that using a band-stop filter might distort the signal significantly. Therefore, a common technique to eliminate such noise is to perform the digitization normally, create a noise fingerprint based on a region of otherwise silent parts of the source, and then apply a technique called *spectral subtraction*. Spectral subtraction works under the assumption that noise has been added to the signal and therefore subtracts the noise fingerprint from the actual signal in frequency space. In other words, both the noise fingerprint and the signal are converted to frequency space and then the energy values of the noise fingerprint are subtracted from the signal. Often the noise fingerprint is preamplified or reduced depending on the situation. The signal might then be converted back to time space. The popularity of spectral subtraction is due to its relative simplicity, ease of implementation, and effectiveness, especially in cases where complicated but constant noise patterns make filtering with band-stop filters cumbersome. Figure 16.8 shows the effect of spectral subtraction. The downside of spectral subtraction is, of course, that it can seriously distort the signal and is not applicable in all cases.

Another commonly used approach to reducing noise based on an example signal is the *Wiener Filter*, proposed by Norbert Wiener in 1949. Its purpose is to reduce the amount of noise present in a signal by comparison with an estimation of the desired noiseless signal. The other filters discussed in this chapter are designed to produce a desired frequency or amplitude response. However, the Wiener Filter takes a different approach: it assumes knowledge of the spectral properties of the original signal and the noise. Wiener Filters are characterized by the assumption that the signal and (additive) noise are a stationary

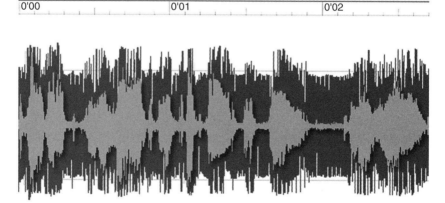

Figure 16.8. Three seconds of a speech signal (time space) with a 100Hz-sine-like humming before (dark) and after spectral subtraction (light). Humming is a frequent audio distortion when recording in situations that require long wires.

linear stochastic process with known spectral characteristics and known autocorrelation and cross-correlation. Now the Wiener Filter seeks the linear filter whose output would come as close to the original signal as possible using the least mean-square error as optimization criterion. The input to the Wiener Filter is assumed to be a signal $s(t)$ corrupted by additive noise $n(t)$. The output $s^\wedge(t)$ is calculated by means of a filter $g(t)$ using the following convolution:

$$\hat{s}(t) = g(t) * \left[s(t) + n(t) \right]$$

The error is consequently defined as:

$$e(t) = s(t) - s^\wedge(t)$$

which can be formulated as the quadratic error:

$$e^2(t) = s^2(t) - 2s(t) * s^\wedge(t) + s^{\wedge 2}(t)$$

By applying the convolution theorem and other math, one can formulate the underlying optimization problem in frequency space as follows:

$$G(s(t)) = |X(s(t))|^2 / ((|X(s(t))|)^2 + (|N(s(t))|)^2) \tag{8.6}$$

where $X(s(t))$ is the power spectrum of the signal $s(t)$, $N(s(t))$ is the power spectrum of the noise, and $G(s(t))$ is the frequency-space Wiener Filter. If the shape of $N(s(t))$ is known, an arbitrary optimization algorithm may be used. In practice, the main problem is that accurate estimates of $N(s(t))$ do not exist. Therefore, often $N(s(t))$ is simply assumed constant at the level of the signal-to-noise ratio. The following pseudo-code implements the calculation of a simple Wiener Filter this way:

```
// Input: A signal S[], an SNR snr, and a fingerprint P[]
// Needs: FFT function fft(), inverse FFT function ifft()
// Output: Wiener Filter F[]
Wienerfilter(S,snr)
  const:=1/(snr*snr)
  fft_F:=[][] // real part in fft_F[][0], imaginary in fft_F[][1]
  fft_S[][]=fft(S) // real part in fft_S[][0], imaginary in fft_S[][1]
  fft_P[][]=fft(P) // real part in fft_P[][0], imaginary in fft_P[][1]
  FOR i:=0 to length(fft_P):
    denominator:=fft_P[i][0]*fft_P[i][0]+fft_P[i][1]*fft_P[i][1]+const
    fft_F[i][0]:=fft_P[i][0]*fft_S[i][0]+fft_P[i][1]*fft_S[i][1]
    fft_F[i][1]:=fft_P[i][0]*fft_S[i][1]-fft_P[i][1]*fft_S[i][0]
    fft_F[i][0]:=fft_F[i][0]/denominator
    fft_F[i][1]:=fft_F[i][1]/denominator
  F:=ifft(fft_F)
  WienerFilter:=F
```

Algorithm 16.3: Wiener Filter

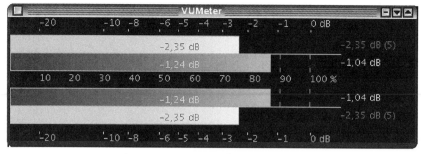

Figure 16.9. A screenshot of a typical (software) VU meter. This view shows a VU meter in stereo mode with a mono signal fed in. The inner bars show the average gain while the outer bars show the peak gain. Clippings are counted and displayed in red next to the peak gain meter.

GRAPHICAL FILTERS

Some filters can be useful in practice even without changing the input signal. One of the most frequently used examples of such a filter is the *VU meter*. A VU meter is often included in audio equipment to display the signal level in so-called volume units (which are proportional to the energy of the signal). VU meters try to reflect the perceived loudness of the sound by measuring the volume slowly, averaging out peaks and troughs of short duration. VU meters are standardized by IEC 268–10:1974. Figure 16.9 shows a typical VU meter that displays both the peak signal and the average signal level. It also counts clippings (when signals reach more than 98 percent of the maximum allowed range). The average gain level is measured by calculating the root-mean-square value of a time window of 250ms. The value ages with the last three measurements. The ideal recording maximizes the average signal without causing overrun.

NOTIONS FOR VISUAL FILTERS

In the following, we discuss notions and filters that are specifically used in images and videos, but are rarely applied to acoustic signals.

Neighbors

A pixel in a digital image is spatially close to several other pixels. In a digital image represented on a square grid, a pixel has a common boundary with four pixels and shares a corner with four additional pixels. We say that two pixels are 4-neighbors if they share a common boundary. Similarly, two pixels are 8-neighbors if they share at least one corner. For example, the pixel at location [i,j] has 4-neighbors [i + 1,j], [i -1,j], [i,j + 1], and [i,j -1]. The 8-neighbors of the pixel include the 4-neighbors plus [i + 1, j + 1], [i + 1, j – 1], [i-1, j + 1] and [i -1, j -1]. A pixel is said to be 4-connected to its 4-neighbors and 8-connected to its 8-neighbors (see Figure 16.10).

A similar notion exists for audio. Sometimes, audio samples are not only considered in time neighborhoods (which, as we already know, are actually called *windows*), but

F	B	E
C	P	A
G	D	H

Figure 16.10. The four- and eight-neighborhoods for a rectangular image tessellation. Pixel [i, j] is located in the center of each figure. For point P, its four-neighbors are A, B, C, and D, and its eight-neighbors will additionally include E, F, G, and H.

considered connected to other channels, for example, when a microphone array has been used for recording. Samples are usually connected across similar points in time.

Path

A path from the pixel at $[i_0, j_0]$ to the pixel at $[i_n, j_n]$ is a sequence of pixel indices $[i_0, j_0]$, such that the pixel at $[i_k, i_k]$ is a neighbor of the pixel at $[i_{k+1}, i_{k+1}]$ for all k with $0 \sim k \sim n - 1$. If the neighbor relation uses 4-connection, then the path is a 4-path; for 8-connection, the path is an 8-path. Simple examples of these are shown in Figure 16.10. The set of all 1 pixels in an image is called the *foreground* and is denoted by S.

Connectivity

A pixel *p* in S is said to be *connected* to *q* in S if there is a path from *p* to *q* consisting entirely of pixels of S. Note that connectivity is an equivalence relation. For any three pixels *p*, *q*, and *r* in S, we have the following properties:

1. Pixel *p* is connected to *p* (reflexivity).
2. If *p* is connected to *q*, then *q* is connected to *p* (commutativity).
3. If *p* is connected to *q* and *q* is connected to *r*, then *p* is connected to *r* (transitivity).

Connected Components

A set of pixels in which each pixel is connected to all other pixels is called a *connected component*.

Background

The set of all connected components of *S* (the complement of S) that have points on the border of an image is called the *background.* All other components of *S* are called *holes.*

Let us consider the simple picture shown in Figure 16.11. How many objects and how many holes appear in this figure? If we consider 4-connectedness for both foreground and background, there are four objects that are one pixel in size and there is one hole. If we use 8-connectedness, then there is one object and no hole. Intuitively, in both cases we have an ambiguous situation. To avoid this and similar awkward situations, different connectedness should be used for objects and backgrounds. If we use 8-connectedness for *S*, then 4- connectedness should be used for *S*.

One of the most common operations in vision systems is finding the connected components in an image. The points in a connected component form a candidate region for representing an object. As mentioned earlier, in computer vision most objects have surfaces. Points belonging to a surface project to spatially close points. The notion of spatially close is captured by connected components in digital images.

A component labeling algorithm finds all connected components in an image and assigns a unique label to all points in the same component. Figure 16.11 shows an image and its labeled connected components. In many applications, it is desirable to compute characteristics (such as size, position, orientation, and bounding rectangle) of the components while labeling these components. The following pseudo-code shows how such a search is implemented.

```
// Input: Image I where pixels p at coordinates (x,y)
// are marked either '1' or '0'.
// Output: A set C with |C|=k of a set of pixel coordinates (x,y)
connected_component(I):
k:=0
Forall p in I:
   If p==1:
     Start a new component C[k]
     Start an empty queue Q. Put p in Q.
        Until Q is empty Do:
          Take the pixel p' at the head of Q and add it to C[k]
        p':=0
          Put all immediate neighbors of p' in Q if their values are '1'
     Close C[k]
     k:=k+1
connected_component := C
```

Connected component operations can also be used on audio signals when the signal is represented as a spectrogram. In other words, by using a spectrogram, acoustic signals can be treated like an image!

Finding Edges and Regions

The most difficult part of region processing is to actually find the regions. There is an abundance of machine vision techniques approaching the problem. This is an active area of research. Our goal here is to provide understanding of basic concepts related to region finding and edge detection.

There are two approaches to partitioning an image into regions: region-based segmentation and boundary estimation using edge detection. Ideally, a region should be bounded by a closed contour, but in many cases using current techniques this is not the case. In principle, region segmentation and edge detection should yield complementary

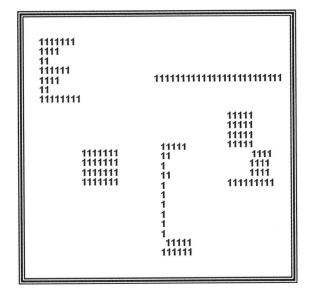

Figure 16.11. A binary image with seven four-connected and five eight-connected regions (connected components).

results. Unfortunately, in real images, because of noise and other factors, neither region segmentation nor edge detection provides perfect information.

Regions

Pixels must be assigned to regions using criteria that distinguish them from the rest of the image and help in separating objects from each other and from the background. Two very important principles in segmentation are *similarity* and *spatial proximity*. Two pixels may be assigned to the same region if they have similar characteristics and if they are close to one another. For example, a specific measure of similarity between two pixels is the difference between the intensity values, and a specific measure of spatial proximity is Euclidean distance. The principles of similarity and proximity are derived from the knowledge that points on the same object will usually project to pixels in the image that are spatially close and have similar intensity values. We can group pixels in an image using these simple assumptions and then use domain-dependent knowledge to match regions to object models. In simple situations, segmentation can be done with thresholding and component labeling; complex images may require more sophisticated techniques to assign pixels to regions that correspond to parts of objects.

Region Segmentation

Let's discuss the process of region formation, or segmentation, more precisely. Given a set of image pixels I and a homogeneity predicate $P(.)$, find a partition S of the image I into a set of n regions

$$\bigcup_{i=1}^{n} R_i = I.$$

The homogeneity predicate and partitioning of the image have the properties that any region satisfies the predicate

$P(\sim)$ = True for all R_i, and any two adjacent regions cannot be merged into a single region that satisfies the predicate

$P(\sim UR_j)$ = False.

The homogeneity predicate $P(.)$ defines the conformity of all points in the region to the region model.

The process of converting an image into a binary image is a simple form of segmentation where the image is partitioned into two sets corresponding to objects and background. The algorithms for thresholding to obtain binary images can be generalized to more than two levels. To make segmentation robust to variations in the scene, the algorithm should select an appropriate threshold automatically by analyzing image intensity values in the image. The knowledge about the intensity values of objects should not be hardwired into an algorithm; the algorithm should use knowledge about the relative characteristics of intensity values to select the appropriate threshold. This simple idea is useful in many computer vision algorithms.

```
// Input: An array representing input image, I(x,y). Each element of an array has value in the
range 0..255
// Output: Output image array (o,X,y). Each element of this array is binary.
Initialize O(x,y) to 0.
Prepare histogram of I(x,y).
Compute/get Threshold value, T, for the image I.
   For all x,
   For all Y,
   If I(x,y) >= T
      Then O(x,y) = 1.
Output image O(x,y)
```

EDGES

An edge point represents a point that separates two regions corresponding to two different objects. Thus, an edge in an image is a significant local change in the image intensity. Algorithmically, this is usually associated with a discontinuity in either the image intensity or the first derivative of the image intensity. Discontinuities in the image intensity can be either (1) *step* discontinuities, where the image intensity abruptly changes from one value on one side of the discontinuity to a different value on the opposite side, or (2) *line* discontinuities, where the image intensity abruptly changes value but then returns to the starting value within some short distance. However, step and line edges are rare in real images. Because of low-frequency components or the smoothing that most sensing devices introduce, sharp discontinuities rarely exist in real signals. Step edges become *ramp* edges and line edges become *roof* edges, where intensity changes are not instantaneous but occur over a finite distance. Most edges in images are a combination of step and line discontinuities. In computer vision, many different approaches have been developed to deal with complex images. Here we will discuss concepts related to edge detection using a general step model.

It is important to define some terms before we discuss edge detection operators to understand precisely what they do and how their results should be analyzed.

An *edge point* is a point in an image with coordinates [i,j] at the location of a significant local intensity change in the image. An *edge fragment* corresponds to the i and j coordinates of an edge and the *edge orientation* e, which may be the gradient angle. An *edge detector* is an algorithm that produces a set of edges {edge points or edge fragments} from an image. A *contour* is a list of edges or the mathematical curve that models the list of edges. *Edge linking* is the process of forming an ordered list of edges from an unordered list. By convention, edges are ordered by traversal in a clockwise direction. Edge following is the process of searching the filtered image to determine contours.

Edge detection is essentially the operation of detecting significant local changes in an image. In one dimension, a step edge is associated with a local peak in the first derivative. The gradient is a measure of change in a function, and an image can be considered an array of samples of some continuous function of image intensity. By analogy, significant changes in the gray values in an image can be detected by using a discrete approximation to the gradient. The gradient is the two-dimensional equivalent of the first derivative and is defined as a *vector*. It is common practice to approximate the gradient magnitude by absolute values. As a very simple approximation one may consider edgeness in directions x and y as

$$E_x(x, y) = F(x + 1, y) - F(x,y)$$

$$E_y(x,y) = F(x, y+1) - F(x, y)$$

Then, the greatest magnitude is in direction

$$\theta = \tan^{-1}(E_y / E_x)$$

and the edge magnitude is

$$E_m = (E_x^2 + E_y^2)^{1/2}$$

where the angle ⟨ is measured with respect to the *x*-axis.

Note that the magnitude of the gradient is actually independent of the direction of the edge. Such operators are called *isotropic operators*.

Algorithms for edge detection contain three steps:

Filtering: Because gradient computation based on intensity values of only two points are susceptible to noise and other vagaries in discrete computations, filtering is commonly used to improve the performance of an edge detector with respect to noise. However, there is a trade-off between edge strength and noise reduction.

Enhancement: To facilitate the detection of edges, it is essential to determine changes in intensity in the neighborhood of a point. Enhancement emphasizes pixels where there is a significant change in local intensity values and is usually performed by computing the gradient magnitude.

Figure 16.12. An image and edges detected in this image.

Detection: We only want points with strong edge content. However, many points in an image have a nonzero value for the gradient, and not all of these points are edges for a particular application. Therefore, some method should be used to determine which points are edge points. Frequently, thresholding provides the criterion used for detection. Figure 16.12 shows an image and strong edges detected in this image.

SEGMENTATION USING SPLIT AND MERGE

A simple intensity-based segmentation usually results in too many regions. Even in images where most humans see very clear regions with constant intensity value, the output of a thresholding algorithm may contain many extra regions. The main reasons for this problem are high-frequency noise and a gradual transition between intensity values in different regions. After the initial intensity-based region segmentation, the regions may need to be refined or reformed. Several approaches have been proposed for postprocessing such regions obtained from a simple segmentation approach. Some of these approaches use domain-dependent knowledge, while other approaches use knowledge about the imaging process. The refinement may be done interactively by a person or automatically by a computer. In an automatic system, the segmentation will have to be refined based on object characteristics and general knowledge about the images. Automatic refinement is done using a combination of split and merge operations. Split and merge operations eliminate

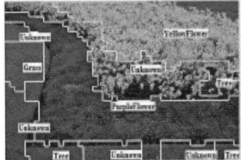

Figure 16.13. A natural scene image and its segmentation into many known components.

false boundaries and spurious regions by merging adjacent regions that belong to the same object, and they add missing boundaries by splitting regions that contain parts of different objects. Some possible approaches for refinement include:

- Merge adjacent regions with similar characteristics.
- Remove questionable edges.
- Use topological properties of the regions.
- Use shape information about objects in the scene.
- Use semantic information about the scene.

The first three approaches use only information about image intensity combined with other domain-independent characteristics of regions. The other two use domain-dependent knowledge. The literature about the segmentation of images that usually combines these techniques is vast and ever growing. Such techniques usually result in segmentation, shown in Figure 16.13. We will point to some appropriate sources in recommended readings.

Video Segmentation

Video segmentation is used in two very different senses. In computer vision and related fields, *video segmentation* is used to mean detecting meaningful objects in video. Thus, a car or a person in a sequence must be segmented based on its appearance and motion despite the fact that this object may look very different in different frames of the video. Many techniques, including motion detection, tracking, and structure from motion,

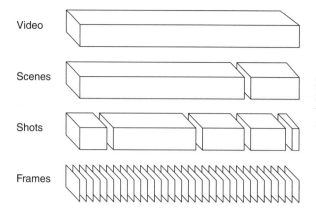

Figure 16.14. Video could be segmented starting with each frame as the basic unit and then grouping into shots, scenes, and episodes.

among others, are used for this purpose. This has been a very active research area now for several decades.

In multimedia information retrieval, these techniques play an important role, but the term *video segmentation* is used to represent structure of video, rather than content and activities in the scene the video captures. This structure is defined following concepts the video production community developed. This structure is shown in Figure 16.14.

We consider video segmentation in the sense of parsing a video rather than partitioning a scene in its individual components. The atomic unit in a video is an image frame. A video contains these frames acquired at regular intervals. The camera is either at a stationary position or in uniform motion to acquire a shot. A *shot* is a collection of frames grouped together based either on camera parameters or on some content-based criterion. For example, in a produced video, frames may be combined using many different locations of cameras. In such cases, frames from each camera may be grouped in shots. In applications like surveillance using fixed camera, a shot may contain frames related to a specific object in the camera view. A video is usually represented using one or more key frames. A *key frame* is simply a representative frame for the shot. For shots of long duration more than one key frame could be used. The next step in the segmentation is called *scene detection*. A scene in a video is a group of shots related to an event or an episode. Thus if two people are discussing, then even though the shots may represent alternating between two people, until the conversation is going on, the shots (and the frames belonging to those shots) could be considered a scene.

RECOMMENDED READING

Signal processing is its own area of scientific endeavor. It is usually studied as part of electrical engineering and falls short in most computer science curricula. If you are by any chance currently a computer science student and attending a school that has a joint electrical engineering and computer science department, use the chance to learn the basics of signal processing in the relevant classes. In our recommended reading section, we have included fundamental textbooks as well as research articles. Porat, Oppenheim, Schafer, and Buck, and Rabiner and Bernard provide textbooks on general signal processing. Williams and Taylor take an electrical engineering perspective on signal processing. It is very good to understand where the field comes from; however, it might be too technical for use as an introduction to multimedia-relevant topics. Gold, Morgan, and Ellis take a deep and thorough look at processing of audio signals in particular. Rabiner and Juang focus exclusively on speech recognition. Bovik edited an in-depth encyclopedia on image and video processing (video meaning only the visual part) that we can recommended as a textbook even though it is in the format of a reference book. Dedicated text books on computer vision include Jain, Kasturi, and Schunck and Stockman and Shapiro. The Wiener Filter and the Fourier Transform were originally described in the research articles cited in the further reading section. The standards and Web sites cited later in this chapter give examples of concrete techniques described in this chapter.

Further Reading

Al Bovik. *Handbook of Image and Video Processing*. Burlington, MA: Elsevier, 2nd edition, 2005.

Joseph Fourier. *The Analytical Theory of Heat*. Cambridge University Press. 1878. Reissued by Cambridge University Press. 2009.

B. Gold, N. Morgan, and D. Ellis. *Speech and Audio Signal Processing: Processing and Perception of Speech and Music*. Hoboken, NJ: Wiley and Sons, 2nd edition, 2011.

R. Jain, R. Kasturi, and B. Schunck. *Machine Vision*. McGraw Hill. April 1995.

C. Müller, ed. *Speaker Classification I – Fundamentals, Features, and Methods*. New York and Berlin: Springer. 2007.

Alan V. Oppenheim, Ronald W. Schafer, and John A. Buck. *Discrete-Time Signal Processing*. Upper Saddle River, NJ: Prentice Hall. 1999. pp. 468–71.

Boaz Porat. *A Course in Digital Signal Processing*. New York: John Wiley. 1997.

Lawrence R. Rabiner and Bernard Gold. *Theory and Application of Digital Signal Processing*. Englewood Cliffs, NJ: Prentice-Hall. 1975.

Lawrence R. Rabiner and B. H. Juang. *Fundamental of Speech Recognition*. Prentice Hall. 1993.

George Stockman and Linda Shapiro. *Computer Vision*. Prentice Hall. 2001.

Norbert Wiener. *Extrapolation, Interpolation, and Smoothing of Stationary Time Series*. New York: Wiley. 1949.

Arthur B. Williams and Fred J. Taylor. *Electronic Filter Design Handbook*. New York: McGraw-Hill. 1995.

Web Links

Fast Fourier Transforms, online book edited by C. Sidney Burrus, with chapters by C. Sidney Burrus, Ivan Selesnick, Markus Pueschel, Matteo Frigo, and Steven G. Johnson (2008): http://cnx.org/content/col10550/latest/.

FIR Filter FAQ: http://www.dspguru.com/dsp/faqs/fir.

STANDARDS

IEC 268-10 1974 (Peak Programm Meter, Type 1).

ISO Recommendation R. *266*-1975: Preferred frequencies for acoustical measurements.

EXERCISES

1. Implement a simple program that demonstrates the convolution theorem.
2. Smoothing a signal is a low-pass filter. Explain why.
3. Point-level and local operations are easy to compute, while global and object-level operations are usually time consuming. Why?
4. Give examples of point-, local-, global-, and object-level operations. Which of these is most useful?
5. Invent simple mathematical functions for dynamic range compression.
6. Implement a graphic equalizer as described in this chapter. Discuss how wrong application of the tool can distort the audio based on experimentation with your implementation.
7. Imagine applying a graphic equalizer to an image. Explain what would change in the image when you turn the sliders of the lower, middle, and higher frequencies up and down.
8. Older soundcards in the lower price segment often used simple averaging of the sample values for downsampling. Explain the problem with this approach.
9. Explain, using examples, why supersampling cannot win back information.
10. How can spectral subtraction work in time space?
11. Implement a Wiener Filter based on the pseudo-code presented here. How is the filter applied and what can be improved?
12. Think of a use case for a VU meter and explain how you would want it to work for this use case.
13. Usually, object-level operations are considered a bottleneck in visual computing. Why is that? What can you do to simplify object-level computations?

17 Multimedia Content Analysis

One of the biggest research questions in multimedia is how to make the computer (partly) understand the content of an image, audio, or video file. The field inside multimedia computing exploring this is called *multimedia content analysis*. Multimedia content analysis tries to infer information from multimedia data, that is, from images, audio, or video, with the goal of enabling interesting applications.

In contrast to fields like computer vision or natural language processing that adopt a restricted view focusing on only one data type, multimedia content analysis adopts a top-down viewpoint studying how computer systems should be designed to process the different types of information in a document in an integrated fashion, including metadata (for example geo-tags) and the context in which the content is presented (for example the social graph of an author). Many examples have been discussed in various chapters of this book. The top-down approach of multimedia computing mostly succeeds in solving problems with data whose scale and diversity challenge the current theory and practice of computer science. Therefore, progress is measured using empirical methods, often in global competitions and evaluations that use large volumes of data.

Given a choice of diverse data sources in a very large amount of multimedia documents, limited compute resources, and an imperfect handling of each of the sources, what is the best way of selecting data sources so that we can find a specific piece of information? For example, video is more than just a sequence of images; it also includes synchronized audio. Depending on an application, the information content in a video may be more in audio, particularly speech, more in the sequence of images, or equal in audio and images. For example, finding all parts of videos that show happy situations is an application of multimedia content analysis. Happy faces might be one way to detect that, cheerful music another, certain keywords in the description a third. In the end, the combination of cues will have the highest probability of success.

This chapter provides a short introduction to the techniques behind multimedia content analysis, which along with multimedia retrieval (discussed in Chapter 15) is one of the largest research fields in multimedia computing.

FROM MONOMEDIA TO MULTIMEDIA CONTENT ANALYSIS

Historically, even though the mathematical foundations are very similar, multimedia content analysis research seemed strictly divided according to the type of data that were to be analyzed. Therefore, many researchers work on acoustic processing, computer vision, or natural language processing. Only recently has multimodal content analysis emerged trying to merge the different types of sensory data to create unified *multi*media approaches that can benefit from the synergy of leveraging modalities in a combined way. The reason for that is the emergence of consumer-produced media.

Consumer-produced videos, images, sound, and text posts are the fastest-growing type of content on the Internet. At the time of the writing of this volume, YouTube.com claims that seventy-two hours worth of video content are uploaded to its Web site alone every minute. At this rate, the amount of consumer-produced videos will grow by 37 million hours in one year. Of course, YouTube.com is merely one site among many where videos may be uploaded, and videos are only one form of social media content. Social media posts provide a wealth of information about the world. They consist of entertainment, instructions, personal records, and various aspects of life in general. As a collection, social media posts represent a compendium of information that goes beyond what any individual recording captures. They provide information on trends, evidence of phenomena or events, social context, and societal dynamics. As a result, they are useful for qualitative and quantitative empirical research on a larger scale than has ever been possible. To make this data accessible for research, we need to automatically analyze the content of the posts.

The challenge with this data, however, is its diversity in recording quality, availability of a certain data source (does a video post have tags or not?), and other inconsistencies. For example, most videos on the social media portal Flickr.com feature heavy ambient noise, visual jitter, content editing such as subtitles and addition of music, multiple languages, and so forth. These characteristics challenge the theory and practice of bottom-up (i.e., separated by data type) content analytics because any approach targeting only one type of data (e.g., visual or acoustic or text) will a) only reach a subset of the data and b) not take advantage of cross-media redundancies that help tackle the low signal quality.

The top-down approach of multimedia content analysis, taking into account all information contained in a document, together with the field's culture of evaluating approaches on a large scale, however, seems the adequate response to the problem of handling this type of content. Having said that, multimedia content analysis also succeeds on less diverse content.

Multimedia content analysis makes use of audio, speech, image, and video content analysis rooted in the signal processing community, which is part of electrical engineering, as well as the field of statistics, which is part of mathematics. These two fields have inherited many terms that are still used. A newer field, which has grown with the popularity of the computer, is called *machine learning*. It is a subfield of statistics, combined with biology and neuroscience roots. The field of machine learning redefines many terms originally created in statistics and biology. The application of machine learning together with the foundations of signal processing to different kinds of data created the fields of audio, speech, image, and video processing, which by themselves created new terms. There are different reasons for those fields to have become separated; some are social and very pragmatic. A very important one is the amount of data to be processed. Audio and speech processing is the oldest field because computers could already process speech in the 1960s and 1970s. Image analysis is a slightly newer field, and video analysis is the newest because there is much more data to be processed. With different maturities of the fields, different generations of people have worked on the different types of data and hence, different vocabulary is used.

As discussed in the previous chapter, Multimedia *processing* techniques usually transform multimedia into other multimedia; the task of information recovery is left to a human user. Subfields include *audio, image,* and *video processing.* The processing fields study topics such as signal enhancement, compression, and correcting blurred or out-of-focus images. In general, they study the process of signal formation using different devices and how to improve quality of those signals to make them closer to the physical phenomena they represent. In some cases, the goal is to enhance the objects they represent.

Machine vision algorithms take images as inputs but produce other types of outputs, such as representations for the object contours in an image. Thus, emphasis in machine vision is on recovering information automatically, with minimal interaction with a human. Image processing algorithms are useful in early stages of a machine vision system. They are usually used to enhance particular information and suppress noise.

Computer graphics generates images for a given model using geometric primitives such as lines, circles, and free-form surfaces. Computer graphics techniques play a significant role in visualization and virtual reality. Because computer graphics is the synthesis or creation of images, in the early days, there was not much relationship to content analysis. However, recently the field has grown closer to machine vision.

Speech analysis extracts information from speech signals similar to machine vision from images and videos. Subfields include speech recognition, which tries to transcribe human speech into readable text; speaker identification, verification, recognition, and diarization, which try to analyze spoken language regarding the speakers contained; and other speech-based signal analysis schemes.

Speech synthesis is the acoustic counterpart to computer graphics. Similar to computer graphics and machine vision, the fields have commonalities even though exactly reverse.

Music analysis and synthesis are the corresponding tasks of speech analysis and synthesis, except for music. Music analysis often tries to detect notes and other musical factors.

Acoustic event detection is the field of detecting nonspeech, nonmusic events. While there is good reason to speculate that in the future people will be interested in more than just events (but also background noise, etc.), currently no strong generic computer audition field exists.

Pattern recognition classifies numerical and symbolic data using models, generally statistical models, for recognition of objects. Many statistical and syntactical techniques have been developed for classification of patterns for various applications. Techniques from pattern recognition play an important role in machine vision for recognizing objects. In fact, many machine vision techniques rely on *machine learning* algorithms to learn particular object or concept models and then to recognize them. Machine learning techniques are direct derivatives of pattern recognition approaches. In pattern recognition, the models for objects were assumed to be available, while machine learning assumes that enough data sets are available so that using computational approaches, the system can develop models for the objects to be recognized and then use those models for classifying objects.

Artificial intelligence is concerned with designing systems that are intelligent and with studying computational aspects of intelligence. Artificial intelligence is used to analyze scenes by computing a symbolic representation of the scene contents after the images have been processed to obtain features. Artificial intelligence may be viewed as having three stages: perception, cognition, and action. Perception translates signals from the world into symbols, cognition manipulates symbols, and action translates symbols into signals that effect changes in the world. Many techniques from artificial intelligence play important roles in all aspects of visual information processing.

Semantic computing, including *semantic Web research*, is concerned with systems based on expert knowledge. Decision making usually requires knowledge of the application or goal. Emphasis in multimedia content analysis systems on maximizing automatic operation means that these systems should use knowledge to accomplish this. The knowledge the system uses includes models of features, image formation, models of objects, and relationships among objects. Without explicit use of knowledge, content analysis systems can be designed to work only in a very constrained environment for very limited applications. To provide more flexibility and robustness, knowledge is represented explicitly and used by the system. In many cases, such knowledge is made available from the context in which these systems work. In Chapter 19, we will discuss how such models could be used effectively.

Psychophysics, along with cognitive science, has studied human perception for a long time. Many techniques in machine vision and speech analysis are inspired by what is known about human perception. In fact, many researchers in computer vision and acoustic analysis are more interested in preparing computational models of human perception.

Note that this classification is only a rough guideline. It is under constant flux and often, the most productive research projects and applications are those that cross the lines between established fields. Moreover, today, the processing capabilities of modern computers allow us to think about approaches that analyze multimedia multimodaly, that is, processing audio, images, motion, and metadata synergistically. As already explained, a combined processing promises improved robustness in many situations and is closer to what humans do: the human brain takes into account not only patterns of illumination on the retina or periods of excitation in the cochlea; it also combines different sensory information and benefits from past experience. Humans can use context information and fill in missing data by associating parts of objects with already learned ones.

SETUP OF A MULTIMEDIA CONTENT ANALYSIS EXPERIMENT

The basic workflow of a typical experimental setup for multimedia content analysis is that of a machine learning approach, as illustrated in Figure 17.1. The reason for that is that nearly all content analysis algorithms these days rely on statistical processing that includes or is similar to machine learning.

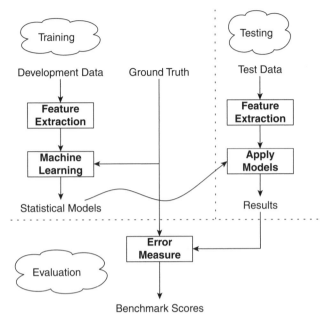

Figure 17.1. Typical work flow of content analysis.

Using training data, relevant features are extracted and passed to a machine learning algorithm. These algorithms are usually methods derived from mathematical statistics and produce statistical models. These are basically sparse representations of the data that allow thresholding of any kind. To train the models, the right answers have to be provided, which are given in the ground truth data. This is usually metadata created by human annotators. Currently common algorithms include Gaussian mixture models, neural networks, support vector machines, k-nearest neighbors, Bayesian networks, and hidden Markov models. We will describe the basic ideas of some of these algorithms later in this chapter. Feature extraction methods are usually derived from signal processing or electrical engineering. We will describe common features later.

In testing mode, the statistical models are then used to perform the actual content analysis task. The test data is run through the same feature extraction process. The results are either used for the actual application or compared against the ground truth to benchmark the quality of the algorithm.

Here is an example: Let's assume we want to detect the gender of a speaker by their voice. The development data consists of samples of female and male speech from humans of different ages uttering different text. From the raw audio files, features are extracted that try to reduce the amount of raw data while emphasizing speaker characteristics (features are further explained in Chapter 16). These are then used to train a statistical model for the two classes. In testing mode, a random audio snippet containing speech and undergoing the same feature extraction is then presented to the model for classification. The output may be used for finding out when to stop training the model. In evaluation mode, however, the quality of the classification is measured by comparing the classification results with the ground truth for many test cases and counting the number of right and wrong classifications. In our example, an error might be expressed as percentage of the wrongly classified test samples versus the total number of test samples.

Unsupervised machine learning, as opposed to supervised learning, omits the training step and statistical models are created on the fly using the test data. This is performed by trying to cluster data points into categories based on preselected properties. Evaluation is performed in a similar way.

FEATURES

The features used as input for machine learning algorithms are different for each data type because the sensor output differs per data type. Microphone output is different from camera output, for example. We begin our discussion of multimedia content analysis by discussing commonly used features in different modalities. You will see that many of these features show similarity to the information reduction approaches in the compression chapters (see Chapters 11–14). This is not a coincidence because the main function of features is to reduce the amount of information to be processed in further steps by stripping off irrelevant bits.

Energy/Intensity

The most frequently used and at the same time most basic audio feature is energy, often also called *intensity*. The most common form of energy features for content analysis is obtained by taking the root-mean-square x_{rms} if the n samples x_i:

$$x_{\text{rms}} = \sqrt{\frac{1}{n} \sum_{i=1}^{n} x_{i^2}} = \sqrt{\frac{x_{1^2} + x_{2^2} + \ldots x_{n^2}}{n}}. \tag{17.1}$$

Intensity can also be used for visual content. For example, brightness can be measured by measuring the energy over a sample of luminance values.

Acoustic Pitch

We described the calculation of pitch in Chapter 14. While pitch alone is rarely used directly for content analysis (unless the goal is to extract pitch), pitch is used as a basis for many features and therefore very important. In speech, detecting voiced and unvoiced regions has high value because unpitched regions in many domains more likely contain noise. The ratio between pitched and unpitched regions (in time) is called the *harmonicity-to-noise ratio* or HNR. HNR can be used as one feature to classify musical instruments. It can also be used for detecting a speaker's age as HNR is age dependent; older speakers have a "rougher" voice, that is, less harmonicity. Often HNR is approximated using a threshold on the zero-crossing rate of the signal (i.e., the number of times the signal changes sign).

Acoustic Long-term Average Spectrum (LTAS)

The Long-term Average Spectrum (LTAS) is often used as a feature in speaker identification. It can also be used to classify different recording environments. The LTAS is not a single value but a feature vector. To obtain the LTAS, one calculates the FFT of a signal (see Chapter 13) and averages the energies in each band over a reasonable amount of time (typically a couple of seconds).

Formants

Formants are the distinguishing or meaningful frequency components of human speech and of human singing. The information humans require to distinguish among vowels can be represented purely quantitatively by the frequency content of the vowel sounds. The formant with the lowest frequency is called f_1, the second f_2, the third f_3, and so on. Usually, f_1 and f_2 are enough to disambiguate a vowel. These two formants determine the quality of vowels in terms of the open/close and front/back dimensions. Thus the first formant, f_1, has a higher frequency for an open vowel (such as [a]) and a lower frequency for a close vowel (such as [i] or [u]); and the second formant, f_2, has a higher frequency for a front vowel (such as [i]) and a lower frequency for a back vowel (such as [u]). Vowels will almost always have four or more distinguishable formants; sometimes they have more than six. Formants are often measured manually as an amplitude peak in the frequency spectrum of the sound, using a spectrogram. In music processing, formants refer to a peak in the sound envelope and/or to a resonance in sound sources, notably musical instruments, as well as that of sound chambers.

Different algorithms are available to track formants. A common way of doing it is to resample the audio signal to a sampling frequency to twice the value of the maximum expected formant (which varies by sex and age; for a young child it could be up to 5,500Hz). Then, LPC coefficients are calculated (see Chapter 14) and searched for local maxima close to the expected frequency ranges of the formants. Figure 17.2 shows a visualization of some of the features discussed thus far, including formants.

Linear Prediction Coefficients (LPC)

The LP coefficients originally developed for speech compression and discussed in Chapter 14 are an often used feature for various speech tasks, such as speech recognition. The coefficients as well as the residual capture the characteristics of different aspects of the signal. LPCs are usually computed on small windows of the signal, for example, 10–30ms. A small window like that is usually called a *frame*. A frame is the smallest unsplittable unit of analysis.

More frequently used than LP coefficients, however, are the MFC coefficients, which are so important that we describe them in their own section.

Mel Frequency Cepstral Coefficients (MFCCs)

Human perception is different across different media. However, it is not clear if the computer should simulate this distinction. Clearly, when machine learning accurately

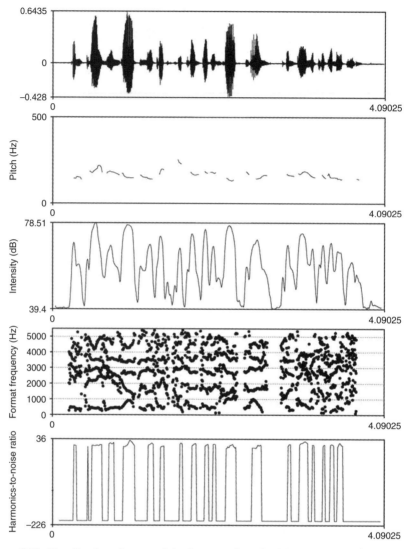

Figure 17.2. Visualization of some of the features described in this section (from IEEE TASLP article, coauthored by me).

models the human brain, then it would make sense, for example, to quantize sensor output logarithmically (see Chapter 12). However, because current machine learning algorithms are mostly statistical methods, it is not clear if this is beneficial. Nevertheless, some features, such as the Mel Frequency Cepstral Coefficients (MFCCs), do incorporate human perceptual properties. In the case of speech signals, MFCCs work remarkably well and are the most frequently used features for any speech analysis tasks, such as speech recognition, speaker identification, or language identification. Take a look at Figure 17.3, which shows the steps involved in the generation of MFCC features as a diagram.

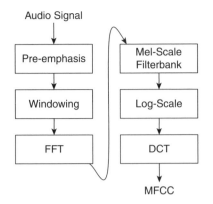

Audio Signal

Pre-emphasis

Windowing

FFT

Mel-Scale
Filterbank

Log-Scale

DCT

MFCC

Figure 17.3. The steps involved in calculating MFCCs.

MFCCs are commonly derived as follows:

- Perform a preemphasis of the signal.
- Take the Fourier Transform of a windowed excerpt of a signal, typically 10–30ms.
- Map the powers of the spectrum obtained onto the Mel scale (see Chapter 14) using triangular overlapping windows.
- Take the logarithm of the powers at each of the Mel frequencies (see Chapter 14).
- Take the Discrete Cosine Transform (see Chapter 13) of the list of Mel log powers, as if it were a signal.

The following pseudo-code implements the triangulation-shaped Mel-filter:

```
// Input: samplingrate sr, number of Fourier bins nf, number of Mel-scale coefficients nm
// Output: A Mel-scale filterbank Matrix M for convolution with an audio signal.
melfilter(sr, nf, nm)
  nyq := sr/2
  nyq_mel := 2,595 * log10(1 + nyq/700.)
  M[nf][nf] := new_zero_matrix()
  FOR i:=0 TO nf-1:
    f := i * nyq / nf
    f_mel := 2,595 * log_10(1 + f/700.)
    m_idx := f_mel/nyq_mel*nm
    j=floor(m_idx)
    M(j+1,i) = m_idx-j
    M(j+0,i) = 1.0-m_idx+j
  melfilter := M
```

The last DCT step might seem odd to the reader because it means to transform a frequency-space-based signal into frequency space. In fact, that's exactly what's being done, and the original creators found this so interesting that they named it *cepstrum* as a word play that exchanges a couple of characters from the word *spectrum*. The reason for doing this is that the values obtained in the Mel-frequency spectrum are still quite self-correlated and also often still too high-dimensional for processing (depending on the window of the FFT). So, to further abstract the signal into lower dimensionality, the DCT is used to decorrelate and then reduce the information further, for example, to twelve dimensions (a typical value for speech recognition).

Often, acoustic analysis is performed using "12 dimensional MFCC with delta and delta-deltas." This means a twelve-dimensional DCT is performed as the final step and then the differences between the twelve values (deltas) are computed and the differences between the deltas are also computed (delta-delta). This is to approximate the MFCCs and their first and second derivates. For speaker recognition and diarization, often nineteen or twenty-two dimensional MFCCs are computed as the higher dimensions are said to contain more speaker and channel information. The implementation of MFCC calculation is left as an exercise.

Visual Texture

Humans use common visual attributes to describe and understand objects and concepts in images. Psychologists have widely studied these attributes to understand how human visual processing works and is applied in image understanding and image retrieval systems.

One important attribute is texture. Texture is characterized by the spatial distribution of gray levels in a neighborhood. Thus, texture cannot be defined for a point. The resolution at which an image is observed determines the scale at which the texture is perceived. For example, when observing an image of a tiled floor from a large distance, we observe the texture formed by the placement of tiles, but the patterns within the tiles are not perceived. When the same scene is observed from a closer distance, so that only a few tiles are within the field of view, we begin to perceive the texture formed by the placement of detailed patterns composing each tile. For our purposes, we can define *texture* as repeating patterns of local variations in image intensity, which are too fine to be distinguished as separate objects at the observed resolution. Thus, a connected set of pixels satisfying given gray-level properties that occur repeatedly in an image region constitutes a textured region. A simple example is a repeated pattern of dots on a white background. Some prominent textures are shown in Figure 17.4.

One approach to measure and characterize texture is commonly called *Tamura textures*. This approach defines six textural features: coarseness, contrast, directionality, line-likeness, regularity, and roughness. These features correspond well to what humans usually use to characterize textures and have become popular.

Coarseness has a direct relationship to scale and repetition rates and is considered the most fundamental texture feature. An image contains textures at several scales; coarseness aims to identify the largest size at which a texture exists, even where a smaller micro texture exists.

Contrast aims to capture the dynamic range of gray levels in an image, together with the polarization of the distribution of black and white.

Figure 17.4. Prominent textures. The first two show regular structure, while the third one shows a texture that is characterized by its statistical characteristics.

Directionality is a global property over a region. The feature described does not aim to differentiate between different orientations or patterns, but measures the total degree of directionality.

Tamura Image is a notion where we calculate a value for the three features at each pixel and treat these as a spatial joint coarseness-contrast-directionality (CND) distribution, in the same way that images can be viewed as spatial joint RGB distributions. We extract color histogram-style features from the Tamura CND image, both marginal and 3D histograms. The regional nature of texture meant that the values at each pixel were computed over a window.

Color Histograms

In many applications, color histograms represent either an object or an image. The color histogram is used to represent variations in color in the region. Color and the notion of different color spaces have been discussed in Chapter 6. Because a color pixel has three values corresponding to the three color components, the histogram may be a three-dimensional histogram. If each color is represented using 256 values, then one needs a histogram with 256 x 256 x 256 bins. To simplify computations, one may consider the intensity ranges for each component to be represented as four bins such that bins 0, 1, 2, and 3 contain ranges of values corresponding to (0 to 63), (64 to 127), (128 to 191), and (192 to 255), respectively.

This will reduce the total color space to sixty-four bins (4 x 4 x 4). One can prepare and represent an image using such a histogram. These steps are shown here:

```
// Input: A set of sample values S
// Output: A set of histogram values H
buildhist(S)
  H := []
  foreach p in P:
    H[p] := H[p]+1
buildhist := H
```

Color histograms have been used in many stages in image processing and in many applications. One common use for which most people who use digital cameras have seen such histograms employed is color normalization. Color histograms are used in image retrieval to compare two images. Histogram features have also been used for indexing images for retrieval. Suppose one is given two images, I_1 and I_2, and their histograms are H_1 and H_2. To compare these images, one can use a distance measure between the two histograms. Two popular distance measures are the well-known L_1 and L_2 distance measures. These result in the distance between two images based on their histograms as,

L_1 distance:

$$D_{H12} = \Sigma | H_1(i) - H_2(i) |$$

and L_2 distance:

$$D_{H12} = \Sigma (H_1(i) - H_2(i))^2$$

One may also consider quadratic distance between two histograms. Consider that each histogram is a vector and consider that there is a matrix C (N x N) that gives similarity of each color i with color j. Then we define quadratic distance between two histograms as:

$$D_Q (H_1, H_2) = (H_1 - H_2)^t\, C\, (H_1 - H_2)$$

As is clear, this formulation allows us to consider the similarity of individual colors and hence some subjective elements may be introduced easily in this formulation. There are better measures to compare histograms. Perhaps the best measure is the so-called Earth Mover's distance, which is, however, computationally expensive to calculate (for more information, see fupraveerther reading). Another one is the Kullback-Leibler Divergence (KL-Divergence):

$$D_{KL}(H_1 \| H_2) = \sum_i \ln\left(\frac{H_1(i)}{H_2(i)}\right) P(i). \tag{17.2}$$

Histograms can also be used as features with the distance function being automatically learned by supervised or unsupervised learning. After all, that's why they are mentioned in this section.

SIFT

Recognition of objects under different illumination conditions and from different perspectives, including viewpoints in which the object maybe partially occluded, has posed a challenging problem in object recognition. To enable recognition under different illumination conditions and under different perspectives, researchers explored the use of salient feature points called *interest points*. These points were commonly used in matching of stereo images and in motion analysis. Their effectiveness in object recognition was found to be very limited.

A very popular approach for matching an object's image from different perspectives in images under different transformations is called *scale-invariant feature transformation* (SIFT), proposed by David Lowe. It extracts SIFT features on an object for recognition and uses them as a fingerprint to find similar objects in other images. Each feature represents a vector of interest points that are invariant to image translation, scaling, and rotation. SIFT vectors are also partially invariant to illumination changes and are robust under local geometric distortion. These vectors are very effective in matching images of the same object under all these transforms. Figure 17.5 shows an example. We refrain from putting pseudo-

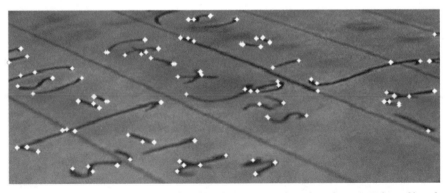

Figure 17.5. Example of SIFT features: The above image is reduced to a number of key feature points that are scale and rotation invariant.

code for the generation of SIFT features as there are currently several competing methods in research, some of which are patented. We therefore refer the reader to the further reading.

SIFT features are local features in an image and hence are very useful in many applications beyond object recognition. SIFT features have been used in many applications including tracking objects, activity recognition in video, robot localization, panorama stitching, and indexing for image retrieval. All these applications are possible because SIFT represents local characteristics and these characteristics are independent of the perspective of the camera and the position and orientation of objects. Their use during the past decade for diverse applications has demonstrated their robustness.

GIST

As discussed earlier, computations in an image could be at the local level as well as at the global level. SIFT features are local features, and a configuration of SIFT features is very useful in different applications because these local features are invariant to different image transformations. On the other extreme are applications in which one is more interested in the gist of an image. The *gist* of an image is the impression that one may get about the scene content without a detailed analysis of the image. For example, one recognizes a forest before recognizing what kind of trees are in the forest. Similarly, one can easily recognize a city scene before recognizing the type of buildings or cars in the city. Based on this observation, it seems possible to recognize the type of a scene before or even without recognizing the objects in it.

This insight suggests that it may be possible to use global features or a combination of different types of global features to recognize the type of a scene. This was formalized and proposed as a set of GIST features by Oliva and Torralba. Many variants of GIST features have been proposed and applied for recognition of scenes of different types. GIST features are computed without any form of segmentation of the image. These features capture a set of perceptual dimensions such as naturalness, openness, expansion, roughness, and ruggedness. A scene can be classified using these perceptual features. Figure 17.6 shows the idea. Again, we refer the reader to the further reading as the generation of GIST features is still a matter of research.

Researchers have demonstrated that GIST features can be used to determine the types of the scene and then other approaches can be applied for recognizing specific objects in the scene. In this respect, one may consider that GIST features are used to determine the context that could in turn be used to recognize specific objects in a scene.

Optical Flow

Image flow, commonly called *optical flow*, is the velocity field in the image plane due to the motion of the observer, the motion of objects in the scene, or apparent motion, which is a change in the image intensity between frames that mimics object or observer motion. Image flow carries valuable information for analyzing dynamic scenes. Several approaches

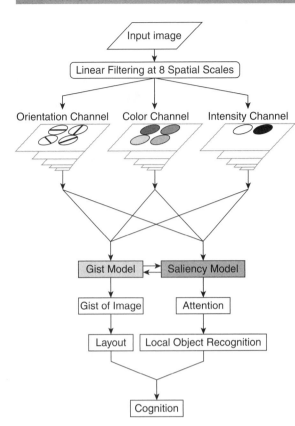

Figure 17.6. Idea of the generation of GIST features. Graphics by the original authors.

for dynamic scene analysis have been proposed that assume that image flow information is available. These computational approaches can be classified into two general categories: feature based and gradient based. If a stationary camera is used, most of the points in an image frame will have zero velocity. This is assuming that a very small subset of the scene is in motion, which is usually true. Thus, most applications for image flow involve a moving camera.

Although image flow has received a significant amount of attention from researchers, the computing techniques developed for image flow do not produce detailed results of the quality that will allow the valuable information to be recovered. Image flow computations have found applications in compression techniques where one does not require the flow vectors at the same precision level as for recovering dynamic information. One of them is explained in Chapter 12.

Flow vectors are values that can be fed into supervised and unsupervised learning techniques to help characterize the movement of the camera or the observed scene. Because of their use in compression and the unavailability of fast and accurate optical flow estimators, it is common to use the motion vector contained in compressed videos (as a result of the motion compensation) directly as a feature. Using these so-called compressed domain features is very efficient as the optical flows is only estimated once.

SUPERVISED LEARNING

Given a set of features from any modality, the next step is modeling them so that one can abstract from features and make decisions for unseen multimedia content. In the following, we will discuss common supervised learning techniques often used in multimedia. Supervised learning uses a so-called development set to learn a model for the mapping of sample values to classes (classification task) or a model for sample values to a continuous range (regression task). A typical classification task is the answer to the question "does this portion of audio contain speech?" or "which digit can be seen in the picture?"; a typical regression task is "what are the geo-coordinates of the position of the camera in this image?" The list of presented algorithms here and the explanations are not exhaustive. As explained earlier, machine learning is its own field and interested readers are invited to explore the further reading section for further reading.

K-Nearest Neighbors

The most basic learning technique, which can almost not be called a learning technique, is nearest neighbor search. Let's assume one has a data set with a number of samples in an N-dimensional space, for example, 8 x 8 binarized scanned digits (compare also the first example in Chapter 11). Each sample is labeled, that is, we know to which class it belongs. A nearest neighbor search assumes that the data set spans an N-dimensional space.

Now, given a new sample without a label, that is, from the test data, we search the development data for samples with low distances from the sample. We then take the labels of the k samples with lowest distances and vote: the label that is in the majority wins. Obviously, with $k=1$ the decision is always clear and also it is usually a good idea to choose an odd number for k even though, depending on the number of classes, this will not always guarantee an unambiguous decision. A rule of thumb is that $k=1$, $k=3$, or $k=5$ are good numbers. If these often result in too many different candidate labels to make a decision, either the distance metric or the k-nearest neighbor algorithm is the wrong choice. Nearest neighbor search with $k=1$ was also referred to as the *post office problem*, referring to an application of assigning a residence to the nearest post office (see further reading).

The following pseudo-code describes a k-nearest neighbor search with an arbitrary distance metric.

```
// Input: A number N of labeled samples S with label set L,
// k number of neighbors to take into account,
// f distance function,
// x, a sample to be classified
// Output: A label for x
k-NN(S, L, N, k, f, x)
    D := [] // array of distances with length = k
    I := [] // array of indizes to neighboring samples with length k
    C := [] // array of counts for a label
```

```
FORALL d IN D // initialize all distances to infinity
  d := +infinity
FORALL c IN C // initialize counts to zero
  c:=0
FOR i:=0 to N
  distance := f(x,X[i])
  FOR j:=0 TO k-1
    IF (distance<D[j])
      D[j]:=distance
      I[j]:= i
FOR i:=0 TO k-1
  C[L[I[i]]]++ // increase count for label
Y:=max_index(C) // Take the label with the maximum count,
        // note: decision might be ambiguous
k-NN := Y
```

Obviously, the quality of the classification results will depend on many factors, including the chosen distance metric, which determines when two samples are considered similar. Also, it can be shown that under a broad set of conditions, as dimensionality increases, the distance to the nearest data point approaches the distance to the farthest data point. Therefore, higher-dimensional data usually require different techniques. More important, the algorithm does not create a generalized model for the classes; that is, a small cluster of outliers can decrease the quality of the classification result. Also, the k-NN algorithm requires comparing the test sample with each sample in the training set, which can be quite computationally expensive. These thoughts lead us to the next algorithm.

K-Means and K-Gaussians

We presented the k-Means algorithm in Chapter 12 as a vector quantization algorithm. By keeping the labels intact, k-Means can be a good solution to reducing the size of the development set for k-NN as comparing to the means instead of the whole data will reduce the number of comparisons. Also, the means can be seen as abstract representation of the data in that they represent more than one individual value and therefore make the comparison less prone to classification errors due to outliers. K can be chosen to match the number of classes in the development set or increased for finer granularity.

When using the means to model data, it is often desired to have an indication of the variance of the represented cluster as well, that is, how close to the mean is the typical sample in the cluster. Also, as can be observed in nature, often cluster values have the typical bell-curve shape. Therefore, a very frequent way of modeling data beyond k-Means is modeling it with k-Gaussians. A function f for a Gaussian is defined as

$$f(x) = \frac{1}{\sqrt{2\pi\sigma^2}}\, e^{-\frac{(x-\mu)^2}{2\sigma^2}}, \tag{17.3}$$

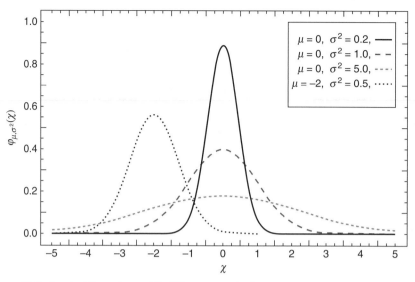

Figure 17.7. A set of Gaussians with different μ and σ2.

with μ being the mean and σ^2 the variance. Figure 17.7 shows the typical bell-shaped curves for different means and variances.

Modeling data with k-Gaussians only requires a slight modification of the k-Means algorithm: after the means have been determined, the variance σ^2 has to be calculated. This can be done by interpreting the sample values as observations as defined by probability theory. The Gaussian function becomes a probability density function:

$$f\left(x; \mu, \sigma^2\right) = \frac{1}{\sqrt{2\pi\sigma^2}} e^{-(x-\mu)^2/(2\sigma^2)}, \quad x \in \mathbb{R}. \tag{17.4}$$

and the set of samples are interpreted as values of a discrete random variable X. The variance

$$\sigma^2 = \sum_{i=1}^{n} p_i \cdot (x_i - \mu)^2 \tag{17.5}$$

with probability mass function $x_1 \mapsto p_1, \ldots, xn \mapsto pn$.

To classify a test sample, the probability of the sample belonging to each of the k-Gaussians is calculated and the Gaussian with the highest probability is chosen. The pseudo-code for calculating k-Gaussians in analogy to k-Means is left as an exercise.

Mixture Models

More often than not, clusters do not exactly adhere to the Gaussian function. For example, when there are two or more "bumps," the distribution is multimodal. This is especially the case when clusters are the mixture of two or more independent components. For example, a color model for face images might consist of the mixture of a model for skin, a model for hair, a model for lips, and a model for eyes. Obviously, different components will have different importance values, which can be expressed by weighting the individual components. In general, a probability mixture model f_X is defined as a weighted sum of its component distributions:

$$f x (x) = \sum_{i=1}^{n} a_i f_{Y_i}(x) \tag{17.6}$$

with X being a discrete random variable and a mixture of the n-component discrete random variables Y_i for some mixture proportions $0 \le a_i \le 1$ where $a_1 + \ldots + a_n = 1$.

Like k-Gaussians and k-Means, a Gaussian mixture model can also be learned by expectation maximization (EM). EM is an iterative method for finding most likely parameters for models (when probabilistic models are used, the likelihood is maximized). The algorithms alternates between the so-called expectation step (E-Step), which estimates the expected likelihood given the current model, and a maximization step (M-Step), which computes new parameters given the current memberships, maximizing the expected log-likelihood found on the E-Step. These new parameter estimates are then used to determine the distribution of the memberships in the next E-Step. This is repeated until the system converges based on an evaluation metric or a fixed amount of iterations. The mixing coefficients a_i are the means of the membership values over the N data points:

$$a_i = \frac{1}{N} \sum_{j=1}^{N} y_{i,j} \tag{17.7}$$

The model parameters f_{Y_i} are calculated by using the data points x_j that have been weighted using the membership values. For example, for a Gaussian, μ is calculated using:

$$\mu_i = \frac{\sum_j y_{i,j} x_j}{\sum_j y_{i,j}}. \tag{17.8}$$

The implementation of Gaussian mixture model training is left as an exercise. The concept of Gaussian mixture models is rather straightforward; at the same time, Gaussian mixture models are a very powerful concept used in many places in multimedia research, especially in visual and acoustic object recognition (e.g., in interactive image segmentation and speaker identification). In practical approaches, the number of Gaussians per cluster, the number of clusters (unsupervised case), and the number of training iterations and/or the convergence criterion are important factors that have to be empirically determined. Using too few Gaussians may make the likelihood estimation poor and therefore not work well for discriminating among the different clusters on the test data. Using an unlimited number of clusters or Gaussians in a mixture model allows modeling an arbitrary distribution. However, using too many Gaussians results in so-called over-fitting of the data; for example, when each data point is represented by its own Gaussian, the models are too specialized and not useful for representing the unknown test data. In other words, there is a trade-off between the number of parameters that should be used to describe the model given the number of training samples and the complexity of the distribution: too few parameters result in a bad model; too many parameters result in a bad abstraction. Chapter 17 describes the Bayesian Information Criterion, which is one way of objectively approaching the trade-off.

Artificial Neural Networks

An *artificial neural network* (ANN), often simply called *neural network* (NN), is another statistical modeling technique. The name stems from its motivational background of trying to simulate some of the structure and/or functional aspects of biological neural networks. ANNs usually consist of an interconnected group of components (often called artificial neurons), each of which simulates one function. The artificial neurons, that is, the functions, are connected in layers with each group of neurons feeding its output to a corresponding neuron in the next layer. In the end, the goal is to model a function f:X->Y, with X being the input data and Y typically being a desired regression or classification output. In most cases, an ANN is an adaptive system that learns its structure from the training data by assigning weights to the connections and parameters of the neuron functions. The most common type of ANN used in practice is the so-called multi-layer Perceptron (MLP). A multi-layer Perception is an ANN composed of many interconnected Perceptrons.

A *Perceptron* is a basically threshold function that maps its input x (a real-valued vector) to an output value $f(x)$ (a single binary value) across the matrix.

$$f(x) = \begin{cases} 1 & \text{if } w \cdot x + b > 0 \\ 0 & \text{el se} \end{cases} \tag{17.9}$$

where w is a vector of real-valued weights and is the dot product (which computes a weighted sum); b is the so-called bias, a constant term that does not depend on any input value. So the value of $f(x)$ (0 or 1) is used to classify x as either a positive or a negative instance. If b is negative, then the weighted combination of inputs must produce a positive value greater than $|b|$ to push the classifier neuron over the zero threshold. Perceptrons take multiple inputs x_i by summing them together:

$$f(x) = f(w_0x_1 + w_1x_1 + w_2x_2 + \ldots + wmxm) + b)$$

As can be seen, a single Perceptron can divide the input space into two areas, for which one area is classified as one and the other as zero. The division is a line in two dimensions, an area in three dimensions, and a hyperplane in any higher dimensionality. The Perceptron is therefore said to be *linearly separating* the space. The following algorithm can be used to train the parameters w and b given a set of input points and a set of classification labels for the input points (training data).

```
// Input: Training data with n samples x[i] and desired output labels l[i]
// Output: Perceptron parameters w[i] and b
p_learn(x[i],l[i], n)
```

```
Initialize the w[i] and b randomly by
setting w[i][t] (0<=i<=n) to be the weight at iteration t, and
b to be the bias in the output node, and
w[0]:= -b, and x[0]:=1, and
settting w[i][0] to small random values.
t := 0
DO
     FOREACH sample x[i]
   // calculate output
       output[t]:=
    (w[0][t]*x[0][t]+w[1][t]*x[1][t]+...+w[n][t]*x[n][t])+b
  w[i][t+1]:= w[i][t]+gamma*(l[i] – output[t])*x[i][t]
       // where 0<=gamma<=1 is a value to slow down the adaption rate
     t := t+1
  UNTIL t>threshold
p_learn := (w[i],b)
```

Practically, two problems have to be addressed for Perceptrons to be applicable to everyday classification problems. First, the Perceptrons have to also separate spaces that are not linearly separable, but require more complicated function. Second, the weights and biases should be tuned automatically based on a training set. The following paragraphs will explain how to do both; however, the theory of artificial neural networks is an ongoing field of research and many other networks exist in addition to the basic ones presented here. See further reading for more details.

To separate input space into more than two classes and also to separate a problem space using more than linear separation, several Perceptrons are connected allowing piecewise linear approximation of the separation function. A so-called multilayer Perceptron (MLP) is a feed-forward artificial neural network model that maps sets of input data onto a set of appropriate output. It is a modification of the standard linear Perceptron in that it uses three or more layers of nodes (so-called neurons) that are interconnected; that is, the output of the neurons in one layer feeds the inputs of the neurons in the next layer. The typical structure looks like the one sketched in Figure 17.8.

The input layer is the layer of nodes receiving the input directly. The output layer is the layer that outputs the functions directly. The so-called hidden layer is the layer in between. One can show that an MLP with three layers can approximate any function given enough neurons in the input, output, and hidden layers. Figure 17.8 shows an example of an MLP calculating the binary XOR function. For solving multimedia classification problems, many more hidden nodes are needed. A practical rule of thumb is that the number of total parameters in a neural network should be about 1 per 10–20 parameters to be learned.

While the network in Figure 17.8 is still straightforward to design manually, MLPs with hundreds or thousands of hidden layers are not. Therefore, different ways of learning the weights are based on training data. The most well-known algorithm is called *back-propagation*. The idea is that the weights are learned by calculating the output given the

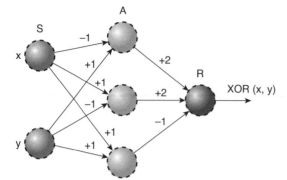

Figure 17.8. A Multilayer Perceptron (MLP) for calculating the binary function XOR. The numbers on the edges define the weights w. The bias $b=0$.

current weights and then calculating the difference between the output and the training data. When doing this for many samples, one can extrapolate an error function given the weights and then tune the weights following the gradient of that error function to a minimum. To calculate the gradient, both the error function and the Perceptron function must be differentiable. Therefore, mean-square error is often used to compare output and training data and the Perceptron function is often replaced with the so-called soft-max function, which is defined as:

$$p_i = \frac{\exp(q_i)}{\sum_{j=1}^{n} \exp(q_j)}, \tag{17.10}$$

with p_i being the values of an output node, $q_{i,j}$ the net inputs to the output nodes, and n the number of output nodes. It ensures all of the output values p are between zero and one, and that their sum is one. This also makes it easier to interpret the outputs of a node as probabilities.

The following constitutes pseudo-code for the backpropagation algorithm:

```
// Input: An MLP network with hidden and input weights wh and wi,
// Training data T
// Output: A network with new weights
backprop(network(w[i]),T)
  Initialize the weights in the network randomly
  DO

      FOREACH sample e in T
        output := compute_output(network,e) // forward pass
      mse := mean-square error (T[e] – output) at the output layer
      gradient := mse * e
        FOREACH wh in the hidden layer:
      Compute delta(wh) // backward pass
      wh := wh – gradient
        FOREACH wi in the input layer:
```

```
            Compute delta(wi) //backward pass
            wi := wi – gradient
         UNTIL mse<threshold
      backprop := network
```

Support Vector Machines

Another approach to solving the supervised classification problem is called the *support vector machine* (SVM). Like neural networks, this is more a class of algorithms rather than a single one and they are constantly evolving. Therefore, the reader is, again, strongly encouraged to follow the most recent literature on this field of specialization. Like the multilayer Perceptron, an SVM performs classification by constructing an N-dimensional hyperplane that optimally separates the data into two categories:

$$f(x) = \begin{cases} 1 & \text{if } w \cdot x + b > 0 \\ 0 & \text{el se} \end{cases} \tag{17.11}$$

Not only is this equation familiar, SVMs are closely related to neural networks: an SVM using a sigmoid kernel function is equivalent to a two-layer MLP. In contrast to MLPs, SVMs regularly solve only two-class problems. The following paragraphs explain the main concepts.

The goal when using an SVM is to find the optimal separation with a hyperplane that discriminates two clusters of input data in such a way that the sample within one category of the target outcome is on one side of the plane and cases with the other category are on the other size of the hyperplane. The vectors closest to the hyperplane are called the *support vectors* as they define the separation margin: SVM analysis finds the hyperplane that is oriented so that the margin between the support vectors is maximized. Figure 17.9 illustrates the idea based on a two-dimensional example.

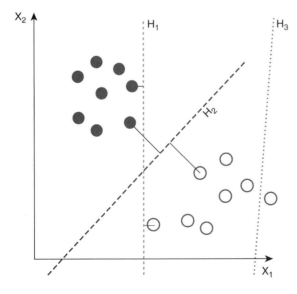

Figure 17.9. Different (hyper-)planes in space. H_3 does not separate the space correctly. H_2 and H_1 do, but only H_2 maximizes the margin between the two classes (and the support vectors).

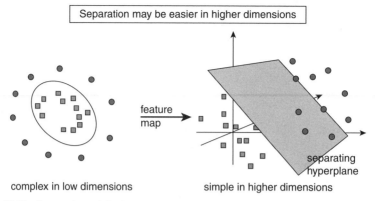

Figure 17.10. Separation of the input space is always easier in higher dimensions.

A simple two-dimensional case can be solved using dynamic programming or the Perceptron learning algorithm. However, as explained earlier, often data is not linearly separable. While MLPs implicitly learn to fold the input space when training the hidden layer of the network, SVMs use a different trick: they use a so-called kernel function to manipulate the input values so that they may be separated by a hyperplane. In other words, rather than seeking a nonlinear separation function, they transform the value space to be linearly separable. A major trick is to increase the dimensionality of the input space. This trick *always* allows one to find a linear separation if the dimensionality chosen is high enough. Figure 17.10 illustrates the idea.

Mathematically, a kernel can transform any algorithm that solely depends on the dot product between two vectors. Wherever a dot product is used, it is replaced with the kernel function. Thus, a linear algorithm can easily be transformed into a nonlinear algorithm. In practice, many kernel mapping functions may be used and finding the right one can be tricky. However, a few kernel functions have been found to work well in a wide variety of applications and seem to predominant in scientific literature. The most simple of them is the linear kernel:

$$K(x, xi) = x_i^t x, \tag{17.12}$$

with x_i being the input values. The two most frequently used are probably the polynomial kernel

$$K(x, x_i) = (1 + x_i^T x/c)^d, \tag{17.13}$$

and the radial basis function (RBF) kernel

$$K(x, x_i) = \exp\left(-\|x - x_i\|^2 / \sigma^2\right), \tag{17.14}$$

where d, c, and σ are constants. If one chooses a sigmoid function as kernel, such as

$$K(x, x_i) = \tanh\left(k\ x_i^T x + \theta\right),\tag{17.15}$$

with k and θ being constants again, one can emulate an MLP (as outlined earlier).

Finally, to allow for some flexibility in separating the categories, SVM models can have a cost parameter C that controls the trade-off between allowing training errors (e.g., allow some points to be wrongly classified) and forcing rigid margins. This is called *soft margin classification*. Increasing the value of C increases the cost of misclassifying points and forces the creation of a more accurate model that may not generalize well.

What we need now is an algorithm to train an SVM. In general, all it involves is solving the following optimization problem. As explained so far, a general SVM can be expressed as

$$u = \sum_i \alpha_i y_i K(\vec{x_i}, \vec{x}) - b\tag{17.16}$$

where u is the output of the SVM, K is the kernel function that measures the similarity of a stored training example x_i to the input x, $y_i \in \{-1,1\}$ (given by the training labels) is the desired output of the classifier, b is a threshold or bias, and a_i are weights that blend the different kernels. Training therefore consists of finding the weights a_i, which is usually expressed as a minimization of the following formula:

$$\min_\delta \Psi(\alpha) = \min_\delta \frac{1}{2} \sum_{i=1}^{N} \sum_{j=1}^{N} y_i y_j K(\vec{x_i}, \vec{x_j}) \alpha_i \alpha_j \sum_{i=1}^{N} \alpha_i,\tag{17.17}$$

subject to constraining the range of the weights and the constraint that

$$\sum_{i-1}^{N} y_i \alpha_i = 0.\tag{17.18}$$

The most common algorithm to solve the problem is the so-called sequential minimal optimization (SMO) algorithm, invented by John C. Platt (see references). The main idea behind the algorithm is, again, to break up the large problem of optimizing the margin into a number of smallest possible problems, thereby achieving a O(n log n) runtime. The algorithm is described in pseudo-code in the original reference.

Temporal Modeling

The machine learning algorithms described so far try to classify or model particular patterns or samples of data independent of each other. Especially when handling multimedia data, however, it is very often the case that a particular sample depends on the previous samples. For example, when parsing the English language in the form of text or speech, the probability of a vowel following a "y" is much higher than the probability of a "j" following a "y." These kind of temporal dependencies can be modeled in several ways, including with ANNs and working with combination of features. However, the most common way in literature is the use of a Markov chain, more particularly the use of a hidden Markov model (HMM).

A *Markov chain* is a stochastic model that assumes the Markov property, which is that the conditional probability distribution of future states of the process depend only on the present state. In other words, given the present, the future does not depend on the past. Generally, this assumption enables reasoning and computation with the model that would otherwise be computationally intractable. A hidden Markov model (HMM) is a Markov chain for which the state is only partially observable; that is, observations are related to the overall state of the system, but they are typically insufficient to precisely determine the state. A typical problem is that one is given a sequence of observations and has to compute the most likely corresponding sequence of states. Let's walk through an example.

Assume you have a set of videos and the task is to detect which scenes of the videos are violent and show a gun fight and which scenes show thunderstorms. Of course, we are dealing with real-world data, so sometimes a video shows both and sometimes a video does not contain a full visual of the scene or omits sounds (e.g., by overlapping with music).

The choice of whether it is a thunderstorm or gunfight depends on visual and acoustic detectors. Because the visual detector is not very good at detecting the large variety of guns, the choice is to mostly rely on the acoustics and to detect explosion-like sounds. While it is easy to detect sudden, loud sounds, the distinction between thunder and a gunshot can be quite hard to discern. Therefore we use a temporal model to see if the booms are classified either as gun shots or as thunder depending on whether a visual detector can observe lightning.

To do this, we need to collect enough statistics up front to be able to generalize to arbitrary videos. Using human experts, we manually annotate an equal number of videos from both categories, "thunderstorm" and "gunfight," with the two sound categories "gunshot" and "thunder" and the visual category "lightning."

Based on this annotation, we now calculate the frequency of the occurrence of the events in the videos. We divide the frequencies by the total number of events to obtain probabilities. Figure 17.11 shows the resulting graph with the probabilities. For example, we now know that in 70 percent of the cases, thunder is followed by lightning, which is then followed by thunder with 90 percent chance (unless the video ends prematurely). Also, in 60 percent of the cases, another gunshot follows a first gunshot until the video ends.

Given this data, we can now train the acoustic and the visual classifier, for example by using an ANN based on MFCC and energy features for acoustic classification and an SVM based on color histograms for the visual classifier. Using testing with the annotated data, we observe that the acoustic classifier has a classification accuracy of 85 percent and the visual classifier has a classification accuracy of 93 percent.

To understand how an HMM helps with temporal modeling, let us consider this example: our classifiers output the following sequence: boom/boom/lightning. The question now is: What sequence of thunder or gunshots would most likely explain these observations?

This is very frequent problem, especially when modeling language. An analog for speech recognition would be: given the observation of the likelihoods for certain phones, what is the probability of the speaker having uttered word x?

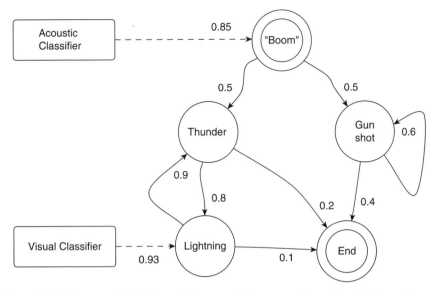

Figure 17.11. An example HMM modeling event given acoustic and visual observations.

Given an HMM, the answer to this problem is given by a very popular algorithm, named after its creator Andrew Viterbi, the so-called Viterbi algorithm. The idea behind the algorithm is that it builds a graph of all possible state transitions. Then, the path with the maximum probability is chosen, the so-called Viterbi path. The following pseudo-code shows the algorithm:

```
// Input: A sequence of observations obs[], hidden states hstates[],
// start_p is the start probability, transp[] and emit_p[] the transition
// and emission probabilities, respectively.
// Output: The output probability of the most likely path.
viterbi(obs, hstates, start_p, trans_p, emit_p)
graph = []
   path = []
   // initialize
   FOR y IN hstates
      graph[0][y] = start_p[y] * emit_p[y][obs[0]]
   FOR t:=1 TO LENGTH(obs)
      newpath = []
      FOREACH y IN hstates
      prob := max([(V[t-1][y0] * trans_p[y0][y] * emit_p[y][obs[t]])
            over all y0 in hstates
      graph[t][y] = prob
   prob := max((V[LENGTH(obs) – 1][y]) over all y in hstates
viterbi := prob
```

We leave it to the reader to play around with the model and determine the answer.

UNSUPERVISED MODELING

All the methods explained so far assumed the presence of training data. Sometimes, however, training data are not available or it is not practical to ask users to provide them. Still, it might be desirable to label multimedia data according to their similarity. This is called *clustering*, and examples of clustering were explained in Chapter 12: the k-Means and x-Means algorithms are perfectly suitable for these tasks.

Often, however, because of the type of data one is dealing with, it is desirable to use the same machine learning algorithm one would use in the supervised case, for example, when certain machine learning methods have proven to work well with a certain type of feature. Fortunately, all one has to do is to replace the error function, which is based on comparison with ground truth training data in the supervised case, with a similarity function for the unsupervised case. The following pseudo-code illustrates Gaussian mixture model training for the unsupervised case:

```
// Input: A sequence of n samples x[], a number of clusters k
// Needs: k-Means, Gaussian function f(x,mu,sigma), sum()
// Output: k parameter triples (a[],mu[],Sigma[]) that describe k
// weighted Gaussians
GMM_train(x[],k)
Initialize a[],mu[],Sigma[] by using k-Means clustering
Initialize probabilities p[][]:=0
iter:=0;
DO

    // E-Step
    Compute probabilities p[i][j]:=(a[j]*f(x[i],mu[j],Sigma[j]))/
            (sum(a[j]*f(x[i],mu[k],Sigma[k])))
        for all elements in x[i:=0..n] and all clusters j:=0..k.
    // Needs to be stored in an n x k matrix. Each individual cell of this
    // matrix corresponds to probability that x_i belongs to the Gaussian
    // distribution specified by mu[k],Sigma[k].

    // M-Step
        Update the weights a[j]:=sum(p[i][j]/n) for j:=0..k
        Update the centroids mu[j]:=sum(x[i],p[i][j])/sum(p[i][j])
        for j:=0..k
        Update the co-variances
        Sigma[j]:=sum(p[i][j]*(x[i]-mu[j])(x[i]-mu[j]))/sum(p[i][j])
        for j:=0..k
    iter++;
WHILE (iter<threshold)
GMM_train := (a[],mu[],Sigma[])
```

A typical general pattern for unsupervised training is bottom-up and top-down agglom-erative hierarchical clustering. One way to think of the concepts is to think of them as sort-ing algorithms: a divisive approach can be implemented recursively like quicksort. An agglomerative approach is comparable to bottom-up mergesort. So in general, for divisive segmentation/clustering we start at the top with all frames in one cluster. The cluster is split using a flat segmentation algorithm. This procedure is applied recursively until the algorithm determines no further splitting is necessary or each frame is in its own single-ton cluster. Top-down clustering is conceptually more complex than bottom-up clustering because we need a second, flat clustering algorithm as a "subroutine." However, it has the advantage of being more efficient if we do not generate a complete hierarchy all the way down to individual document leaves. Different algorithms are used in different situations. So again, we suggest further study of machine learning literature.

The following pseudo-code exemplifies bottom-up clustering for a generic similarity metric:

```
// Input: A sequence of samples[] (e.g., audio),
// a minimum number of frames for each model segment length,
// a similarity metric as a function,
// a threshold
// Output: A sequence labels[]
Divisive clustering(samples, segment length, metric(),threshold)
    IF #samples<window length:
      return
    run metric() over segments of samples of segment length
    determine maximum max for all windows
    IF max>threshold:
      split at sample s with metric() result m
      run divisive clustering() for samples before s
      run divisive clustering() for samples after s
      FOREACH segment seg:
        Using metric() compare seg with other segment
        IF results<threshold:
          give same label to seg and other segment
    ELSE:
      return
divisive clustering:=labels
```

The reader may ask what a suitable implementation for the metric is. Again, this depends on the nature of the problem and the underlying data. If an obvious measure cannot be found analytically (which is the case for most practical multimedia problems), only empirical measurement can quantify the quality of an approach (see next section on error measurements). Nevertheless, some metrics seem to have predominant status in the research community, such as the Minkowski metric and the two special cases of the Manhattan distance and the Euclidean distance. These were introduced for histogram comparison in this chapter. In mathematics, the Euclidean distance or Euclidean metric is the "ordinary" distance between two points that one would measure with a ruler, and is given by the Pythagorean formula. The Manhattan distance name alludes to the grid layout of most streets on the island of Manhattan, which causes the shortest path a car could take between two points in the borough to have length equal to the points' distance in taxicab geometry.

In probabilistic algorithms, entropy (as defined in Chapter 11) is often used as a metric of homogeneity inside a distribution. Derived from that, mutual information is another one often used to find out how dependent two random variables X and Y are on each other.

$$I(X;Y) = \sum_{y \in Y} \sum_{x \in X} p(x,y) \log \left(\frac{p(x,y)}{p_1(x)p_2(y)} \right), \tag{17.19}$$

where $p(x,y)$ is the joint probability distribution function of X and Y, and $p_1(x)$ and $p_2(y)$ are the marginal probability distribution functions of X and Y, respectively. Other metrics include KL-divergence, the Bayesian Information Criterion (see Chapter 18 on compression), and others. Again, we recommend studying the further reading and related work around the particular problem. Sometimes, distance metrics get invented or rediscovered around an idea because the current ones do not work as well for a specific problem.

ERROR MEASUREMENT AND EVALUATION

As explained earlier in the chapter and described in Figure 17.1, the error of a machine learning approach is quantified by comparing the output of the algorithms or systems against ground truth, usually human annotations. As could be seen from the example in temporal modeling, the statistical approaches rely heavily on the collection of frequencies, which in order to be generalizable should be collected from very large sample sizes. This is one reason multimedia content analysis researchers welcome the advent of the Internet and embrace "Web-scale" challenges. With the reliance on numbers comes the importance of error measurement to track progress and compare different approaches.

Over the years, different error metrics have established themselves in the multimedia research community. This section will explain some of them. Just like similarity metrics, classification, and clustering methods, error metrics should be chosen wisely based on the task that is to be accomplished. A wrongly chosen error metric might lead to a system being optimized toward a wrong goal. Some systems can use standard error metrics, like the following; others require specialized metrics.

Accuracy

The easiest way to measure error is to classify the output labels into wrong labels and correct labels based on ground truth. The number of wrong labels is then divided by the number of total labels. The quotient may then be expressed as a percentage. However, when

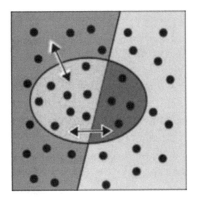

Figure 17.12. Recall/Precision and F-Measure depend on the outcome of a query in relation to all relevant documents and the nonrelevant documents. The oval depicts the outcome of the query; the correct results are green, the wrong results are red. In this picture from [cite Wikipedia], precision is visualized by the horizontal arrow and recall by the diagonal arrow.

a more specific distinction than wrong and false is needed, this metric may fail short of being intuitive. Often, several numbers are then used.

Precision/Recall

Another widely used statistical error metric is precision/recall. It is often used in multimedia information retrieval. *Precision* is the number of relevant documents retrieved by a search divided by the total number of documents retrieved by that search. *Recall* is the number of relevant documents retrieved by a search divided by the total number of existing relevant documents (which should have been retrieved). Formally:

$$\text{precision} = \frac{\left|\{\text{relevant documents}\} \cap \{\text{retrieved documents}\}\right|}{\{\text{retrieved documents}\}} \tag{17.20}$$

$$\text{recall} = \frac{\left|\{\text{relevant documents}\} \cap \{\text{retrieved documents}\}\right|}{\{\text{relevant documents}\}} \tag{17.21}$$

Figure 17.12 depicts the idea.

Outside information retrieval, the notion is usually used in a generalized manner: precision for a class c is the *number* of true positives (i.e., the number of items correctly labeled) divided by the total number of elements labeled as belonging to the class (i.e., the sum of true positives and false positives, which are items incorrectly labeled as belonging to the class). Recall is defined as the number of true positives divided by the total number of elements that actually belong to the class (i.e., the sum of true positives and false negatives, which are items which were not labeled as belonging to the positive class but should have been). Formally:

$$\text{Precision} = \frac{tp}{tp + fp} \qquad \text{Recall} = \frac{tp}{tp + fn} \tag{17.22}$$

with *tp*, *fp*, *tn*, *fn*, denoting true positive, false positive, true negative, and false negative, respectively. A precision 1.0 for a class C means that every item labeled as belonging to class C does indeed belong to class C (but does not indicate anything about the number of items from class C that were not labeled correctly). A recall of 1.0 means every item from class C was labeled as belonging to class C (but indicates nothing about how many other items were incorrectly also labeled as belonging to class C). Therefore, the two numbers give a better indication of how a certain algorithm attacks the problem. Sometimes, for example, one might want to find only certain items but we should be sure that the answer is correct. This means we want high precision and low recall. When we want many positive results but don't care about them all being correct, high recall and low precision is the goal. Of course, high precision and high recall are almost always desirable in theory but usually hard to achieve in practice.

F-Score

For some problems and for comparative reasons, a single number, instead of two, might be desirable. Therefore researchers created the so-called F-score that combines precision and recall using the harmonic mean:

$$F = 2 \cdot \frac{\text{precision} \cdot \text{recall}}{\text{precision} + \text{recall}} \qquad (17.23)$$

The F-score has often been criticized as counterintuitive because too much information is abstracted away into a single value when in fact sometimes only the histograms of the classes are a real indication of the error behavior of an algorithm.

ROC/DET Curve

Plotting the fraction of true positives versus the fraction of false positives is called *receiver-operator-characteristics*, or the ROC curve. The so-called equal error rate (EER) is the point at which true positive and false positive errors are equal. In general, the algorithm with the lowest EER is most accurate. However, often it might be desirable to choose a different operation point based on precision and recall that is more suitable for the application. Another variation of the ROC curve is the so-called DET curve. A *detection error trade-off curve* (DET) is a graphical plot of false reject (miss) rate versus false positive rate. In contrast to the ROC curve, *x*- and *y*-axes are scaled nonlinearly by their standard normal deviates, yielding to the curves themselves appearing more linear than typical ROC curves. Figure 17.13 shows the two curve variants side by side.

Word Error Rate/Edit Distance

As a final example of an application-specific error metric, we present the word error rate (WER) that measures the accuracy of a speech recognition system. The general

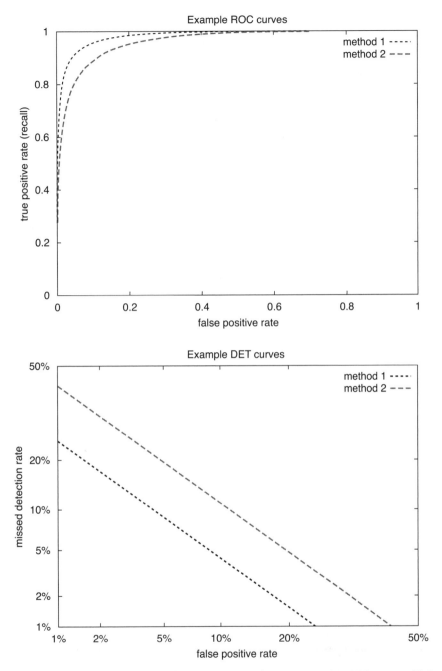

Figure 17.13. Left: Two detectors (binary classifiers) compared with ROC curves. Right: The same classifiers compared with DET curves.

difficulty f measuring the performance of a speech recognition system is that the recognized word sequence can have a different length from the ground truth word sequence.

The problem is approximated by first aligning the recognized word sequence with the reference (spoken) word sequence using dynamic string alignment. Word error rate can then be computed as:

$$WER = \frac{S+D+I}{N} \tag{17.24}$$

with S being the number of substitutions, D the number of deletions, I the number of insertions, and N the number of words in the reference. One problem with using a simple formula such as this, however, is that no account is taken of the effect that different types of errors may have on human perception and the intelligibility of the result; for example, some errors may be more disruptive than others and some may be corrected more easily than others. As explained earlier, this is a general problem with error metrics and optimizing exclusively by reducing a certain number. The formula is pretty general, though, and can also be used to measure how much two typed documents differ or how well an optical character recognition approach works.

FINAL REMARKS

At this point, we want to remember that this and the next chapter deal with statistical methods. While highly popular and effective, there are many things that need to be done properly, otherwise these methods fail. Moreover, often the methods work really well in the training phase but when applied in a real-world scenario they perform poorly, potentially causing last-minute disappointment.

Correlation versus Cause

One needs to remember that all statistical methods only work on statistical correlation, disregarding causality. So when features are trained into a model to "recognize" an object, it is a misnomer. Models are trained to compare values based on an observed distribution. If the object in question tends to correlate with a feature that has nothing to do with the object but follows the same or similar distribution, it is easy to assume the "recognizer" works even though it learned the wrong cues. A popular story in the community is that of a team of researchers who claimed to have the perfect detection algorithm for "friendly versus hostile tanks." The impressive results were soon invalidated when it was found that all the images featuring friendly tanks were taken during the day and all the images of unfriendly tanks were taken at night. In the end, the system turned out to be a day and night detector based on brightness.

Bias and Sparsity

This brings us directly to issue number two: data selection. Obviously, data should be selected in a way that all samples represent the data well in terms of dependency to the problem to be modeled and independency to any other problem. In our tank detection example, daylight, indoor/outdoor, environmental details, or whether the object is static should be made independent factors by having enough samples from all these different conditions in there. Alternatively, filters and feature transformations may take care of that. However, it is better to not rely on that as filters are hard to design and might introduce another error source. The variable we want to model, of course, should be represented well; that is, in the best case, all different outcomes of that variable are seen and the distribution of all the factors that determine the model of the variable is the actual distribution in the world. For example, when wanting to determine the geo-location of a video, we should train on enough videos from all the area we are searching in and the videos should cover the area completely and in a uniform distribution. Of course, the best case never happens, and data bias is one of the largest problems encountered in pretty much any machine learning task. If bias comes together with a data sparsity problem (i.e., there is not enough data to train on), it is almost unfeasible to try a statistical approach and it becomes important to add context (see Chapter 19) and other knowledge to the problem.

Data Collection and Annotation

So let's assume we know we have a data sparsity and bias problem. One way to solve that is to collect more and different data. Sometimes that is easy by crawling from the Internet, most often it is not. When crawling the Internet, it is easy to violate terms of services for Web sites or infringe on copyright violations. More often than not, however, crawling does not even solve the problem as the data needs to be checked manually or annotated with ground truth. Human annotation is not perfect either: annotators make mistakes, are not accurate, or simply do not agree. Especially for tasks that are more subjective (for example, emotion detection), it is very important to have multiple persons annotate the same sample and then calculate the annotator agreement. Samples with disagreement should be put aside. Sometimes joint machine learning and human annotation might help. For example, when human annotators check and correct a machine algorithm's output, it might be easier to achieve better results faster. In multimedia data, often the problem is what to annotate: only the audio track, only the visual part, both of them together or independently? This is a difficult question, but if in doubt, an experimental annotation has to be conducted that allows decisions based on annotator agreement and final performance of the trained models.

Domain Independence

With data collection and annotation being hard, it is often too easy to fall into a data sparsity and bias trap. However, sometimes the problem can be solved by restricting oneself to a certain domain and trading off generalizability versus feasibility. For example, if one trains a person detector only on broadcast news videos, it might be easier to collect and annotate data just for that special case. However, in the end, one cannot assume that the model trained for the task generalizes to more than the broadcast news domain. It might, but this has to be evaluated carefully before claimed or assumed. Another issue having to do with generalization is that training data must at all cost be separated from testing data. It is very likely that excellent results can be achieved if the training data is used for tuning the model as well as for evaluation of the performance of the model. It is equally likely, though, that given new data, the performance will be very poor. Ideally, testing data should never be used for tuning or testing, but only for evaluation at the end. Different sets of testing data can increase the likelihood of a better modeling result. Another set of trouble regards assumption: it is easy to restrict oneself to certain scenarios or restrictions in the training set and then assume they will always be there. It is very important to be conservative about assumption and when using them, document them well.

Undermodeling and Overtraining

The opposite of data sparsity is model sparsity. If there are not enough free variables in the model to capture all the nuances and angles of the data, then presenting all that data to the model is most likely a waste of CPU time. For example, if you took the ANN example of Figure 17.3 and tried to tune the parameters with backpropagation for a face detector on one hundred fifty thousand videos – it for sure would not work! All the ANN can do is separate the space for a Boolean function. Different models have different optimal numbers of parameters and training iterations. It is very important to consider the number of parameters and training iterations with regard to the data presented to the model and also the classification task to be solved. If too many variables are used for too little data, overtraining might result: the model learns the examples "by heart" and is later unable to generalize to unseen samples. For example, instead of learning two classes, a model with way too many variables might learn the IDs of the samples.

Significance of Results

In the end, it is very important to constantly check against potential problems as outlined in this section. Small improvements on too little data might be random, results in restricted domains not generalizable, and knowledge gained from modeling on a certain training set not applicable to other cases. When the goal is to create a system that works, it should be trained with diverse and large data sets, tested in different domains and with real users. The same is true for scientific experiments: Systems should be open, compared to other systems on the same data and all experiments reproducible by other researchers. Deriving from a set of independently created systems that perform well on various data sets, it might be possible to generalize conceptual methodological knowledge that contributes to scientific progress in the field.

The next chapter will present examples of prototypical monomedia and multimedia content analysis systems.

RECOMMENDED READING

The principles of statistics of machine learning and distance measures go way back before the days of multimedia computing. Therefore, we decided to include the classic book by Donald Knuth even though it is not considered part of this domain. Classical machine learning and content analysis books include Duda and Hart, Russell and Norvig, and Witten and Frank. Rojas wrote a very legible book on artificial neural networks, especially explaining backpropagation in a very graphical way. Other literature included is original research articles that describe aspects of what we touched on in this chapter. Many of them we referenced in the chapter text.

Further Reading

L. E. Baum, T. Petrie, G. Soules, and N. Weiss. "A maximization technique occurring in the statistical analysis of probabilistic functions of Markov chains." *Ann. Math. Statist.*, 41 (1): 164–71, 1970.

Kevin Beyer, Jonathan Goldstein, Raghu Ramakrishnan, and Uri Shaft. "When is 'nearest neighbor' meaningful?" *Int. Conf. on Database Theory.* 1999.

Arthur Earl Bryson and Yu-Chi Ho. *Applied Optimal Control: Optimization, Estimation, and Control.* Blaisdell Publishing Company or Xerox College Publishing. 1969. p. 481.

Richard O. Duda, Peter E. Hart, and David G. Stork. *Pattern Classification.* New York: Wiley Interscience, 2nd edition, p. 680.

B. S. Everitt and D. J. Hand. *Finite Mixture Distributions.* Chapman & Hall. 1981.

Y. Freund and R. E. Schapiro. "Large margin classification using the perceptron algorithm." *Proceedings of the 11th Annual Conference on Computational Learning Theory* (COLT '98). ACM Press. 1998.

M. J. Hunt. "Figures of merit for assessing connected word recognisers." *Speech Communication*, 9: 239–336, 1990.

Donald Knuth in *The Art of Computer Programming*, volume 3. 1973.

S. Kullback and R. A. Leibler. "On information and sufficiency." *Annals of Mathematical Statistics*, 22 (1): 79–86, 1951.

D. G. Lowe. "Distinctive image features from scale-invariant keypoints." *International Journal of Computer Vision*, 60 (2): 91–110, 2004.

J. B. MacQueen. "Some methods for classification and analysis of multivariate observations." 1. *Proceedings of 5th Berkeley Symposium on Mathematical Statistics and Probability.* University of California Press. pp. 281–97, 1967.

M. L. Minsky and S. A. Papert. *Perceptrons.* Cambridge, MA: MIT Press. 1969.

Aude Oliva and Antonio Torralba. "Building the gist of a scene: The role of global image features in recognition." In *Progress in Brain Research*, vol. 155. Ed. Martinez-Conde, Macknik, Martinez, Alonso, and Tse. New York: Elsevier B. V. 2006.

John C. Platt: "Fast training of support vector machines using sequential minimal optimization." In *Advances in Kernel Methods: Support Vector Learning*, 185–208. Boston, MA: MIT Press. 1999.

J. R. Quinlan. "Induction of decision trees." *Mach. Learn.*, 1 (1): (March 1986), 81–106.

J. R. Quinlan. *C4.5: Programs for Machine Learning.* New Jersey: Morgan Kaufmann Publishers. 1993.

Raul Rojas. *Neural Networks: A Systematic Introduction.* Berlin: Springer. 1996.

Frank Rosenblatt. "The Perceptron: A probabilistic model for information storage and organization in the brain." *Cornell Aeronautical Laboratory, Psychological Review*, 65 (6): 386–408, 1958.

Y. Rubner, C. Tomasi, and L. J. Guibas. "The earth mover's distance as a metric for image retrieval." *International Journal of Computer Vision*, 40 (2): 99–122, 2000.

Stuart J. Russell and Peter Norvig. *Artificial Intelligence – A Modern Approach,*. Essex, UK: Prentice Hall, 3rd edition, 2009.

Gideon E. Schwarz. "Estimating the dimension of a model." *Annals of Statistics*, 6 (2): 461–4, 1978.

A. J. Viterbi. "Error bounds for convolutional codes and an asymptotically optimum decoding algorithm." *IEEE Transactions on Information Theory*, 13 (2): 260–9, April 1967.

Joe H. Ward. "Hierarchical grouping to optimize an objective function." *Journal of the American Statistical Association*, 58 (301): 236–44, 1963.

B. Widrow and M. A. Lehr. "30 years of adaptive neural networks: Perceptron, madaline, and back-propagation." *Proc. IEEE*, 78 (9): 1415–42, 1990.

I. H. Witten and E. Frank. *Data Mining: Practical Machine Learning Tools and Techniques*. Burlington, MA: Morgan Kaufman. 2005.

EXERCISES

1. Describe how the GMM implementation presented earlier needs to change for supervised learning.
2. Discuss usability implications for applications that use machine learning based on supervised versus unsupervised training.
3. Implement the backpropagation algorithm and use it to train an MLP to learn the XOR function.
4. Use k-NN and GMMs to classify digits (see mm-creole.org).
5. Provide example multimedia tasks of when you think k-NN, GMMs, ANNs, and HMMs might provide good results. Why do you think so? Can you test it?
6. Assuming k-NN gives excellent classification accuracy, does it still make sense to use other techniques? Why (not)?
7. So-called confidence values provide a means to estimate how certain a classifier is of a decision. This is often desirable when integrating different media so the different decisions can be weighed against each other. Discuss ideas on how to come up with confidence values.
8. Explain strategies for the combination of different media based on GMMs, ANNs, and decision trees.
9. Explain visually how an HMM can help in speech recognition.
10. Provide four examples of applications that require low/high precision/recall (respectively).
11. Provide two examples where word error rate does not reflect perceptual error.
12. Explain what happens when models overfit or underrepresent. Discuss strategies to avoid these problems.
13. Create a program that calculates MFCC features and visualizes them. Input different audio events and note how the features change.

14. How can you classify textures? Give some classes and list features that could be used for such a classification.

15. What is optical flow? How can this be used in multimedia analysis?

16. When a camera is moving, all points in the image plane are moving. How can you determine moving and stationary objects in such a case?

18 Content Analysis Systems

In the previous chapters, we looked at low-level methods for multimedia content analysis and audio/visual processing. This chapter explores some of the bigger building blocks and applications of content analysis. Many of these single-media content analysis systems can be used alone, be modified for multimedia content analysis, or integrated within a bigger multimedia content analysis system. This chapter is designed as a short overview of how typical visual, speech, and music analysis systems work by describing on a high level which signal processing and machine learning techniques are typically used. Note that all of the systems presented here will only approximate a solution and to achieve high accuracies, they will still require a significant amount of engineering. To go beyond a certain accuracy, more research is needed, which might redefine how typical systems work in the future (thus potentially making our descriptions obsolete). However, as outlined in the previous chapter, it is possible to take error into account on a higher level and integrate several less accurate systems into one more accurate system, especially when multiple media are taken into account.

SPEECH ACTIVITY DETECTION

A fundamental task in the analysis of an audio signal is to separate human-uttered language from the remaining signal. This function is needed in almost any task that works with language, including speech compression. Typically, however, the methods used in speech compression that detect speech regions in an audio stream are not nearly as accurate. Some of them were discussed in Chapter 14, including energy thresholding and voiced/unvoiced detection. The biggest challenge with any of the basic methods is the distinction between speech and noise with similar characteristics. Therefore, an approach that usually works better is to build a classifier and train models based on audio files that contain speech with similar characteristics as the speech to be detected and other models on noise with similar characteristics as the noise to be distinguished from speech. A simple approach is to train two sets of Gaussian mixture models based on twelve-dimensional MFCC features that include energy and delta, and delta-delta coefficients. The decision is usually made on a frame-by frame basis. An HMM in combination with the Viterbi algorithm (see Chapter 17) can then be used to make an optimal decision for a larger region of the audio stream or file. By training many hours of data into the models, current speech activity detectors (often also referred to as *speech/nonspeech detectors*) obtain accuracies of up to 98 percent when the characteristics of the training data match those of the evaluation data, for example, models trained on broadcast TV and applied to broadcast TV or models trained on telephone speech and used in similar phones. The development of a simple model-based speech activity detector is left as an exercise.

LARGE VOCABULARY AUTOMATIC SPEECH RECOGNITION

Speech recognition engines are usually quite large. While small vocabulary speech recognition is used for command and control, for example, for telephone centers, and is pretty much a standard product in industry, state-of-the-art speech recognition engines for large sets of vocabulary and conversational speech contain the work of many researchers. As a consequence, complete speech recognizers barely exist in universities that only deal with certain aspects of the task. It is a domain of companies and research institutes. For that reason, and because large vocabulary automatic speech recognition (LVASR) is the most important field in speech processing research, we provide a rough overview of the functionality of an automatic speech recognizer.

Feature Extraction

Speech recognition usually starts with several layers of signal processing (e.g., preemphasis, windowing, short-term spectral analysis and filtering, and so on). The predominant features used for speech recognition are MFCCs. For special purposes, such as high-noise ASR, other features have been designed such as the so-called PLP and RASTA features, which are described in research papers listed in the references cited at the end of this chapter.

Speech Activity Detection

As with most other speech tasks, the first step is speech activity detection as described previously.

Feature Normalization

After features have been extracted and nonspeech is eliminated, the next goal is to make the features invariant to anything but the spoken words. Remember that MFCCs are used for various acoustic content analysis tasks. Ideally, we want to eliminate any statistical dependency on the speaker or the channel (microphone, room reverberation). Therefore, many techniques exist to normalize features; some are very basic, like Gaussianization, some of them are pretty advanced like vocal tract length normalization (VTLN). *Gaussianization* takes a set of audio features and normalizes them so that the histogram of the values forms roughly a Gaussian. This is similar to image histogram equalization (which is changing the samples underlying a histogram to result in a histogram with equal distribution; that is, all bins have the same value) except the target function is a Gaussian rather than a flat distribution. VTLN is further described in the further reading cited at the end of this chapter.

Recognition

Now that the audio is filtered so it contains only speech and features that are invariant to everything but the actual spoken words, one uses a classifier, such as a GMM, to compare the spoken words on different levels (using different window lengths) to the recorded and annotated words in our acoustic models. Usually, a large number of Gaussians that are used in combination to generate likelihoods for particular speech sounds in context are employed. The parameters of this acoustic model are then altered further for testing by incorporating one of several related methods for adaptation, for instance, maximum likelihood linear regression (MLLR) (see further reading). The models are often then trained in a new pass of discriminant learning using techniques like minimum phone error training. In the end, the idea is to recognize "a" by comparing it to all instances of "a" stored in our acoustic model. It is considered an "a" if it is very close to all the other instances of "a" and not so close to any other acoustic element, such as "e" or "o." Using different window lengths, one can compare on the sub-phoneme, phoneme, syllable, and word levels.

Decoder

Once small-scale recognition (e.g., phonemes, syllables, etc.) is done, the next goal is to glue the pieces together using a so-called language model. The entire acoustic likelihood estimation subsystem is used in combination with a language model probability estimation, which has been trained in a supervised fashion on a large number of words; additionally, there are usually multiple sources of word prediction information (such as large quantities of written text and smaller amounts of transcribed spoken words). Usually, HMMs are used to model phoneme and word sequences. For each acoustic instance the recognizer usually outputs a set of alternatives with probabilities, which are used as observations in the HMM. The language model chooses the most likely combination of phonemes, syllables, and words, according to the recognizer output. A very hard problem is to handle words that are not part of the language model and usually result in high error rates as surrounding words are also affected.

Textual Postprocessing

Once decoding is done, processing has to be done that may take into account prosody, speech pauses, and other hints to detect sentence boundaries so that punctuation decisions can be made. Also, named entities should be detected so that capitalization works.

This description of automatic speech recognition only conveys the general idea of this class of systems. It shows, however, how the different content analysis and machine learning techniques presented in the previous chapter work together. Speech recognition systems usually contain many signal processing, classification, temporal modeling, and other content analysis tricks that work together.

OPTICAL CHARACTER RECOGNITION

The visual equivalent to acoustic speech recognition is optical character recognition (OCR). Special-purpose optical character recognition software uses specialized codes that are easier to recognize. On the other end are handwritten character recognition systems, which are still heavily researched. The following outlines a typical document OCR approach:

Binarization

Because colors and even gray levels are unimportant for character recognition, the first step in OCR is usually the binarization of the image, that is, converting the image to black and white.

Rectification

Images of text might have been scanned in at an angle or even when scanned in straightly, pages bend toward the center of a book (just verify with the one you have in hand). This means that lines need to be rectified to make the text lines sit at a perfect horizontal angle. Geometric transformation that assume perfectly straight lines for text are often pretrained and then applied to the image. This step is similar to the feature normalization step in speech recognition.

Recognition

Now that the lines are rectified, the characters can be recognized by comparison to pretrained characters. Before this can be done, character locations are identified by applying a connected component analysis and then fitting bounding boxes around the components. The character in each bounding box can then be recognized. Often a k-NN approach is applied to compare the characters to a database of pretrained characters. This step is equivalent to the acoustic model recognition in speech recognition.

Decoder

In analogy to speech recognition, in OCR a decoder is applied to take advantage of a language model. Individual character recognitions might have failed, but higher accuracies can be achieved assuming that combination of characters exists as words in a database and that combination of words forms proper sentences. Like in speech recognition, HMMs are used to model character and word sequences. For each character instance, the recognizer usually outputs a set of alternatives with probabilities, which are used as observations in the HMM. The language model chooses the most likely combination of characters according to the recognizer output.

Although systems are widely deployed on a commercial basis, their accuracy is still not perfect and depends heavily on the quality of the document. High-contrast paper documents with clear horizontal lines of text can be better recognized than documents with lower contrast, stains, and page rips, folds, or bends. Similarly, subtitles in videos can be recognized quite well when they consist of white text in black boxes. Other text, such as running text or text embedded in the video image, is much harder to recognize as the text has to be detected first and often rectified. Like speech recognition, character recognition is highly language dependent. Latin and Chinese characters (Kanji) are obviously recognized in a different way and different amounts of work exist to do so. For more exotic languages, like Tibetan, very little software exists compared to that for English. Like speech recognition, the edit distance (word error rate) as described in the previous chapter is a standard metric to evaluate such systems.

SPEAKER RECOGNITION

Speaker recognition is the general term used for acoustic content analysis tasks where the system is to find the identity of the speaker automatically. This task has various real-world applications, including forensic analysis, door opening systems, and multimedia retrieval. Depending on the application, there are various "guises" of speaker recognition. Perhaps the most natural form is that of speaker identification, which is to identify the speaker from a spoken utterance, given the set of possible speakers of that utterance. However, in practical situations, it hardly ever occurs that the set of possible speakers is limited; usually there needs to be some verification that the speaker is one of the set. Of course, this has to be done after we detect that the audio segment in question is actually speech. Allowing for the possibility of out-of-set speakers is termed *open-set speaker identification* and requires that internal similarity scores have some form of "absolute" meaning so that a score can be thresholded and a hypothesized speaker can be rejected if the score is too low. This capability of rejecting an unknown speaker is so important that it has been the main focus in speaker recognition methods and their performance evaluation. For nondiscriminative modeling, the open-set speaker recognition problem can be generalized to the speaker detection task, where the task is to decide whether a target speaker uttered a given speech segment. As this general task is at the basis of many different application scenarios, we will use the speaker detection task (equivalent to one speaker open-set identification) as the prototype task in this description.

Universal Background Model

To cope with the open set problem, a universal background model (UBM) is used that represents the speech of "all" possible speakers. It is essentially a GMM consisting of many Gaussians; typical figures are 512–2,048 (traditionally, the number of Gaussians are chosen as powers of two). A UBM is used as the denominator in determining a likelihood ratio, representing the likelihood of the "alternative speaker" in speaker detection; that is, it is used to normalize the score by determining whether the likelihood score the GMM obtained is typical of a match or might be equally found in two random similar but different speakers. Of course there is no way to represent all possible speakers, yet thousands of speakers are used to train the UBM.

In addition to normalizing the score, UBMs are often used as the starting point for modeling a specific speaker, which can be found by adapting the UBM using limited amounts of speech from a specific speaker. It is often the displacement of the centers of the Gaussians that are used to completely characterize a speaker.

General Architecture

There is a specific training, or enrollment, phase of a speaker and a testing phase; we can differentiate between the common parts and the training/testing specific parts of the architecture. The common processing steps for a given speech segment are:

1. Speech activity detection
2. Feature extraction, usually MFCCs
3. UBM index generation: This step computes the contribution to the UBM likelihood of every Gaussian component, for every frame of the speech segment. Then the indices of the N top-most contributors are extracted. The idea is that these five are enough to compute the likelihood of the frame accurately.
4. Supervector generation: Using the top-N Gaussians per frame in calculation, the means of the UBM can be adapted to maximize the a-posteriori likelihood of the speech segment (so-called MAP adaptation). The shift in means can be said to represent the speaker of the speech segment. A per-dimension scaling of this displacement using the prior and variance parameters of the UBM and concatenation of the scaled displacement vectors into a so-called supervectors allows a geometric interpretation of this space. A speech utterance is represented as a point in this space, and when points lie close together, we consider it more likely that the same speaker uttered the speech.

The steps specific to training are:

Model generation: There are two distinct classes of modeling used in speaker recognition: generative and discriminative. For a generative model, the MAP-adapted GMM is the model – the important parameters are the (unscaled) means of the Gaussians. Alternatively, a discriminative model can be formed by using a support vector machine (SVM). Additional to the target speaker, for which the model is to be trained, many nontarget (i.e., "background") speakers are used to compare the target speaker to. As described in Chapter 17, the SVM tries to maximize the margin between the target speaker and the background speakers. That is, it tries to position a hyperplane in supervector space that has a maximum distance from the target speaker. The SVM model now is characterized by the normal n of this separating hyperplane and an offset; 500–2,000 background speakers are used typically.

Evaluation Metrics

Applications in speaker detection range from target-sparse applications in intelligence (finding the few utterances from a target speaker in a very large database of recordings) to target-rich applications such as access control (finding the presumably very few break-in attempts in long sequences of genuinely authorized speakers). In a detection trial, the prior probability of a target speaker plays a crucial role. However, these priors cannot be determined by the speaker recognition technology itself, and are given by the application. Therefore, the framework in which a speaker recognition system is evaluated is by a defining a cost function:

$$C_{det} = C_{miss}P_{tar}P_{miss} + C_{FA}(1 - P_{tar})P_{FA}$$

Here, the application-specific cost parameters C_{miss} and C_{FA} determine the expected costs made in decision errors. The error rates P_{FA} and P_{miss} indicate the probability of a miss (a not-detected target trial) and a false alarm (a falsely detected nontarget trial), and must be determined in an evaluation of the system. It can be seen that the target prior to P_{tar} governs the cost function.

SPEAKER DIARIZATION

The goal of speaker diarization is to segment a single-channel audio recording into speaker-homogeneous regions and cluster these, with the goal of answering the question "who spoke when?" Figure 18.1 illustrates the idea. The task could also be understood as temporal speaker tracking and is a rough equivalent to face tracking in the visual domain (see later in the chapter). Speaker diarization has a large set of possible and actual applications. Usually, it is employed as a front-end (also called upstream) application for different higher-level tasks, such as speech recognition; meeting, seminar, or broadcast news navigation; or even dominance detection (based on clues such as who speaks most, who interrupts whom).

In contrast to speaker recognition or identification, speaker diarization attempts to use no prior knowledge of any kind. This usually means that no specific speaker models are trained for the speakers to be identified in the recording. In practice, this means a speaker diarization system has to answer the following questions:

- What are the speech regions?
- How many speakers occur in the recording?
- Which speech regions belong to the same speaker?

Therefore, a speaker diarization system conceptually performs three tasks: first, speech activity detection; second, detect speaker changes to segment the audio data; third, group the segmented regions into speaker-homogeneous clusters. Some systems unify the two last steps into a single one; that is, segmentation and clustering is performed in one step. Over the years, the speech research community has developed many different algorithms.

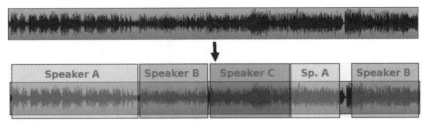

Figure 18.1. The task of speaker diarization is to determine "who spoke when" without any prior knowledge about the content of the audio track.

Many state-of-the-art speaker diarization systems use a one-stage approach, that is, the combination of agglomerative clustering with the Bayesian Information Criterion (BIC) and the Gaussian mixture models of frame-based cepstral features. This approach is described as follows.

The audio track is usually processed as MFCC features. A speech activity detector is used to filter out regions that do not contain speech. The nonspeech regions are excluded from the segmentation and clustering. The algorithm is initialized using a much higher amount of clusters than speakers expected in the audio track. Let this number be k. An initial segmentation is generated by randomly partitioning the audio track into k segments of the same length. Using the initial segmentation, k Gaussian mixture models are trained. A minimum duration (typically 2.5 seconds) is assumed for each speech segment. A majority vote is then used to combine the individual decisions. The algorithm then performs the following loop:

Re-Segmentation: Compute the likelihoods with respect to each Gaussian mixture model and vote to determine the assignment of each minimum duration segment to a particular model.

Re-Training: Given the new segmentation of the audio track, train new Gaussian mixture models for each of them.

Cluster Merging: Given the new Gaussian mixture models, try to find the two models that most likely represent the same speaker. This is done by computing the BIC score of each of the models and the BIC score of a new GMM trained on the merged segments for two clusters. If the BIC score of the merged Gaussian mixture model is smaller than or equal to the sum of the individual BIC scores, the two models are merged and the algorithm loops at the re-segmentation step using the merged Gaussian mixture model. If no pair is found, the algorithm stops.

To use the so called Schwarz Criterion or Bayesian Information Criterion (BIC), one has to assign a probability to each data point belonging to a GMM. We call the Gaussian models M, so that M_j is the j-th model (derived from the j-th mean). BIC is then defined as:

$$BIC(M_j) = i_j(D) - \frac{P_j}{2} \cdot \log R \qquad (18.1)$$

where l^j(D) is the log-likelihood of the data according to the j-th model, and p_j is the number of parameters in M_j (in our case, the number p_j is the sum of the k-1 class probabilities,

MK mean coordinates, and one variance estimate). R is the total number of data points that belong to the mean under consideration. BIC is a score, which basically favors the model with the minimum number of parameters. In other words, if our two newly introduced means represent the data equally well as one mean, we don't need to introduce two new means.

The output of a speaker diarization system consists of metadata describing speech segments in terms of starting time, ending time, and speaker cluster name. This output is usually evaluated against manually annotated ground truth segments. A dynamic programming procedure is used to find the optimal one-to-one mapping between the hypothesis and the ground truth segments so that the total overlap between the reference speaker and the corresponding mapped hypothesized speaker cluster is maximized. The difference is expressed as diarization error rate, which is defined by the U.S. National Institute of Standards and Technology (NIST). The diarization error rate (DER) can be decomposed into three additive components: misses (speaker in reference, but not in hypothesis), false alarms (speaker in hypothesis, but not in reference), and speaker errors (mapped reference is not the same as hypothesized speaker). The difference is expressed as DER, which is defined as follows:

$$DER = \frac{\sum_{\theta=1}^{\partial} \mathrm{dur}(\delta).(\max(N_{no}(s), NArp(s)) - N_{correct}(s))}{\sum_{i=1}^{\partial} \mathrm{dur}(s) - N_{ne} \int} \qquad (18.2)$$

with S being the total number of speaker segments where both reference and hypothesis files contain the same speaker pair(s). It is obtained by comparing the hypothesis and reference speaker turns. The terms $N_{ref}(s)$ and $N_{sys}(s)$ indicate the number of speakers speaking in segment s, and $N_{correct}(s)$ indicates the number of speakers that speak in segment s and have been correctly matched between reference and hypothesis. Segments labeled as nonspeech are considered to contain zero speakers. DER is usually expressed in percentages. When all speakers and the nonspeech in a file are correctly matched, the error is zero percent.

Speaker diarization is currently an area of research. Different approaches are investigated, including methods that incorporate spatial information such as video images or the time delay of arrival from different microphones.

FACE DETECTION AND FACE RECOGNITION

The visual equivalent to speaker identification and diarization is face recognition and face detection. For humans, faces of people are one of the most important visual objects. Many applications require detecting and recognizing people in images. Object recognition has been a popular topic in computer vision research since its early days when automatic techniques were of interest in robotic applications. As the number of consumer-produced photos increased, the importance of faces as a significant object increased. During the past decade, face detection and face recognition has become a dominant task in photos. Most digital cameras, including mobile phone cameras, now have an automatic face detection algorithm that draws a rectangle around every face that is detected in a photo.

Face detection is different from face recognition. *Face detection* identifies a human face and marks the location by drawing a rectangle around it. Face detection algorithms usually mark all human faces in an image. *Face recognition* detects the presence of a specific person, say John Doe, in images. Face detection identifies a human face while face recognition identifies a specific person's face. Face detection techniques have matured to the point that they are commonly used, but face recognition remains a challenging application.

Face detection algorithms usually use a set of features related to faces, such as patterns of vertical and horizontal lines, eye ovals, and skin color detectors. A given image is first transformed into these features. Common learning techniques are then used to classify regions of images into faces or not faces. Often a window-sliding technique is employed; that is, the classifier is applied to rectangular portions of an image, sliding through all locations at different scales. The image rectangular areas that qualify are marked as faces. One of the most commonly used face detectors was developed by Viola and Jones (see further reading). This detector uses features similar to Haar Wavelet basis functions for efficient computation and a variant of the AdaBoost learning algorithm to model and detect faces in images. Because of its efficient implementation, it has become one of the most popular face detectors. Most face detection techniques are very effective in recognizing frontal faces. For faces in unusual orientations or in nonfrontal positions, the results of these techniques degrade rapidly. Error in face detection is usually measured in precision/recall (for the detection of the faces) and then in Euclidean distance (for the position of the face). More information on face detectors can be found in the further reading references listed at the end of this chapter.

ACOUSTIC EVENT DETECTION

Acoustic event detection (AED) identifies different acoustic events inside an audio stream. The task is inherently harder than speech activity detection because the different event classes can have severely different or similar properties. Often it is hard to model varying durations (even inside the same class of events) and, of course, it is not guaranteed that the sound for a particular event is not a subset of another one (this is a similar problem as in entropy-based compression; see Chapter 11). AED systems are therefore trained on a case-by-case basis with many hours of data. They are very similar to speaker recognition systems and baseline approaches use Gaussian mixture models (GMMs) combined with hidden Markov models (HMMs) using a universal background model (UBM). However, recent research has shown that so-called supervector methods can improve event detection. Recent approaches of acoustic event detection therefore compute the mean and standard deviations of the feature trajectories and use these statistics as input features for a support vector machine (SVM). This "GMM-SVM" approach combines the discriminative properties of SVMs with the ability of GMMs to deal with variable length sequences. One can use a linear kernel derived from Kullback-Leiber distance for this:

$$K_{\text{lin}}(s_a,s_b)=\sum_{i=1}^{M}\left(\sqrt{w_i}\sum_i^{-\frac{1}{2}}\mu_i^a\right)\left(\sqrt{w_i}\sum_i^{-\frac{1}{2}}\mu_i^b\right)^t \tag{18.3}$$

where s_k is a GMM supervector obtained by pooling together all the Gaussian means μ_{ki} of a means-only MAP-adapted GMM for the sequence k. Σ_i and w_i are the original weight and covariance of each Gaussian on the UBM model used for adaptation. A more detailed description of the approach can be found in the articles referenced.

VISUAL OBJECT RECOGNITION AND TRACKING

The visual equivalent to acoustic event detection is visual object recognition, the most important field of computer vision. Many research approaches exist and their accuracy depends on various factors. Face detection and character recognition has already been described. General object recognition in images currently often uses SIFT features (see previous chapter) in combination with other features. Unfortunately, the problem is so hard and solutions are so diverse that we are unable to describe a typical approach in this chapter. We need to refer the reader to the references.

In videos, further assumptions can be made, for example object persistency (an object cannot vanish and come back unless occluded by another object). In the following, we will therefore outline common visual video analysis techniques that can be used in addition to object recognition techniques.

The input to a dynamic scene analysis system is a sequence of image frames taken from a changing world. The camera used to acquire the image sequence may also be in motion. Each frame represents an image of the scene at a particular instant in time. The changes in a scene may be due to the motion of the camera, the motion of objects, illumination changes, or changes in the structure, size, or shape of an object. It is usually assumed that the changes in a scene are due to camera and/or object motion, and that the objects are either rigid or quasi-rigid. The system must detect changes, determine the motion characteristics of the observer and the objects, characterize the motion using high-level abstraction, recover the structure of the objects, and recognize moving objects. In applications such as video editing and video databases, it may be required to detect *macro* changes in a sequence. These changes will partition the segment into many related segments exhibiting similar camera motion or a similar scene in a sequence.

A scene usually contains several objects. An image of the scene at a given time represents a projection of the scene, which depends on the position of the camera. Four possibilities exist for the dynamic nature of the camera and world setup:

1. Stationary camera, stationary objects (SCSO)
2. Stationary camera, moving objects (SCMO)
3. Moving camera, stationary objects (MCSO)
4. Moving camera, moving objects (MCMO)

For analyzing image sequences, different techniques are required in each of the afore-mentioned cases. The first case is simply static scene analysis. Many applications require information extracted from a dynamic environment; in some cases, a vision system must understand a dynamic process from a single viewpoint. In applications such as mobile robots or autonomous vehicles, a vision system must analyze an image sequence acquired while in motion. Recovery of information from a mobile camera requires different techniques than those needed when the camera remains stationary. A sequence of image frames offers much more information to aid in understanding a scene, but significantly increases the amount of data to be processed by the system. However, research in dynamic scene analysis has shown that the recovery of information in many cases is easier in dynamic scenes than in static scenes. In dynamic scene analysis, SCMO scenes have received the most attention. In analyzing such scenes, the goal is usually to detect motion, to extract masks of moving objects for recognizing them, and to compute their motion characteristics. MCSO and MCMO scenes are very important in navigation applications. MCMO is the most general and possibly the most difficult situation in dynamic scene analysis, but it is also the least developed area of computer vision.

Change Detection

Detection of changes in two successive frames of a sequence is a very important first step for many applications. Any perceptible motion in a scene results in some change in the sequence of frames of the scene. Motion characteristics can be analyzed if such changes are detected. A good quantitative estimate of the motion components of an object may be obtained if the motion is restricted to a plane that is parallel to the image plane; for three-dimensional motion, only qualitative estimates are possible. Any illumination change in a scene will also result in changes in intensity values, as will scene changes in a TV broadcast or a movie. Most techniques for dynamic scene analysis are based on the detection of changes in a frame sequence. Starting with frame-to-frame changes, a global analysis of the sequence may be performed. Changes can be detected at different levels: pixel, edge, or region. Changes detected at the pixel level can be aggregated to obtain useful information with which the computational requirements of later phases can be constrained. We discuss different techniques for change detection. We will discuss one of the simplest yet most useful change detection techniques, *difference pictures*. In a special case, this technique is called *background subtraction*, when one of the frames is known to be the background because in that case the resulting difference pictures show areas corresponding to moving objects. The most obvious method of detecting change between two frames is to directly compare the corresponding pixels of the two frames to determine whether they are the same. In the simplest form, a binary difference picture $DPjk(x, y)$ between frames $F(x, y, j)$ and $F(x, y, k)$ is obtained by:

$$DPjk(x, y) = 1 \text{ if } |F(x,y,j) - F(x,y,k)| > T$$
$$= 0 \text{ otherwise}$$

where T is a threshold.

In a difference picture, pixels that have value one may be considered the result of object motion or illumination changes. This assumes that the frames are properly registered.

A straightforward, domain-independent method of comparing regions in images is to consider corresponding areas of the frames. These corresponding areas may be the super-pixels formed by pixels in non-overlapping rectangular areas comprising m rows and n columns. The values of m and n are selected to compensate for the aspect ratio of the camera. A frame may be partitioned into disjointed super-pixels or use a local mask and compare the intensity distributions. One such method is based on comparing the frames using the likelihood ratio computing over such super-pixels or windows. Thus, we may compute

$$\lambda = \frac{\left[(\sigma_1^2 + \sigma_2^2)/2 + (\mu_1 + \mu_2)/2\right]^2}{\sigma_1^2 + \sigma_2^2} \tag{18.4}$$

(where μ and σ^2 denote the mean gray value and the variance for the sample areas from the frames, and then use

$$\text{DPjk}(x, y) = 1 \quad \text{if } \lambda > T$$

$$= 0 \quad \text{otherwise.}$$

The likelihood ratio test works quite well for most real-world scenes. In Figure 18.2, we show two frames of a sequence and the difference pictures for those. This figure shows the first frame in which it is known that none of the moving objects are there and the second frame is a normal frame. As can be seen, by considering the first frame as the one containing only the static components or the background, a simple subtraction mechanism, commonly called *background subtraction*, gives the shape and location of all moving objects.

Object Tracking

In many applications, an object must be tracked over a sequence of video frames. If only one object appears in the sequence, the problem is easy to solve. In the presence of many objects moving independently in a scene, tracking requires the use of constraints based on the nature of objects and their motion. Because of inertia, the motion of a physical entity cannot change instantaneously. If a frame sequence is acquired at a rate such that no dramatic change takes place between two consecutive frames, then for most physical objects, no abrupt change in motion can be observed. The projection of a smooth three-dimensional trajectory is also smooth in the two-dimensional image plane. This allows us

Figure 18.2. Background subtraction results in detection of only moving objects.

(a) A frame showing background in a scene.

(b) A later frame that has some moving objects.

(c) A difference of frame a and b shows the masks of moving objects.

to make the smoothness assumption in images. This property is used to formulate *path coherence*. Path coherence implies that the motion of an object at any point in a frame sequence will not change abruptly. We can combine the solution of the correspondence problem for stereopsis and motion. The following three assumptions help in formulating an approach to solve the correspondence problem:

- The location of the given point will be relatively unchanged from one frame to the next frame.
- The scalar velocity of a given point will be relatively unchanged from one frame to the next.
- The direction of motion of a given point will be relatively unchanged from one frame to the next frame.

We can also use the smoothness of image motion in monocular image sequences. Based on such assumptions, many computational approaches have been developed to track object or points on objects in videos. For example, compressed domain optical flow features have been used quite intensively in the MPEG-4 research community. This is a very important research area, and research has resulted in a rich set of techniques for different applications.

MULTIMEDIA CONTENT ANALYSIS SYSTEMS

As outlined in the previous chapter, multimedia content analysis follows a top-down approach, exploiting every possible cue in different media, with the goal of achieving higher accuracies on more diverse data. Sometimes this can be achieved by integrating two or three single-media systems like some of those described earlier, and sometimes it requires changing one of the systems and adding a second media stream at a feature or model level. Very often, though, combining systems is nontrivial and requires research. That's why the area of multimedia content analysis is currently a very active field of research. Depending on an application, the information content in a video may be more in audio, particularly speech, more in the sequence of images, or equal in audio and images. Sometimes a single media analysis approach will do a better job; sometimes a multimedia approach will outperform.

Multimedia content analysis research is currently driven by questions that are almost impossible to solve using single media approaches. The following are examples of concrete tasks typically evaluated in competitions and evaluations:

- Geo-location estimation: How can we estimate the geo-location of a scene shown in a particular video based on audio, visual cues?
- Video concept detection: How can we search and find videos by concepts rather than objects? For example, how can we search videos for "children catching a ball" or "birthday parties"?
- Video copyright detection: Is a video uploaded to social media infringing on the copyright of another video because a particular protected video sequence, image, or music piece was used?

- Semantic similarity detection: Do these two videos show about the same content?
- Video content detection: Select videos from social network portals that show violence or offending scenes.

Coming back to our initial example in Chapter 17 of detecting happy situations, happy faces might be one way to detect that, cheerful music another, certain keywords in the description a third. In the end, the combination of cues will have the highest probability of success. The question of how to combine the media is a matter of research, though, as different detectors have different accuracies and different semantic strength. A hard-to-detect happy face might be faked while a single user comment tagging the scene as "happy" might just do the trick. It is often said an "image is worth more than a thousand words." This is true if and only if the image can be interpreted and we often see the reverse in content analysis: tags and text are worth more than the perceptual media (compare also Chapter 15). The next chapter is therefore dedicated to alternatives to pure content analysis approaches.

RECOMMENDED READING

Many of the acoustic systems outlined here are described in more detail in Gold, Morgan, and Ellis. Bunke and Wang provide an overview of optical character recognition. Vision algorithms are described in detail in Simon. As usual, we also included original research papers in the literature, which allow readers to dive deeper into the details of the systems described in this chapter. This selection provides only an incomplete time snapshot of some works. We highly encourage the reader to go deeper on his own.

Further Reading

Xavier Anguera Miro, Simon Bozonnet, Nicholas Evans, Corinne Fredouille, Gerald Friedland, and Oriol Vinyals. "Speaker diarization: A review of recent research, audio, speech, and language processing." *IEEE Transactions*, 20 (2): 356–70.

James Bergstra, Michael Mandel, and Douglas Eck. "Scalable genre and tag prediction with spectral covariance." *Proceedings of the 11th International Conference on Music Information Retrieval (ISMIR)*, pp. 507–12, August 2010.

K. Boakye, B. Trueba-Hornero, O. Vinyals, and G. Friedland. "Overlapped speech detection for improved speaker diarization in multiparty meetings." *Proc. ICASSP*, 4353–6.

Horst Bunke and Patrick Shen-pei Wang. *Handbook of Character Recognition and Document Image Analysis*. Singapore: World Scientific. 1997.

S. S. Chen and P. Gopalakrishnan. "Clustering via the Bayesian information criterion with applications in speech recognition," *Proc. IEEE International Conference on Acoustics, Speech and Signal Processing*, vol. 2. Seattle. WA. pp. 645–8.

J. Cohen, T. Kamm, and A. Andreou. "Vocal tract normalization in speech recognition: Compensation for system systematic speaker variability." *J. Acoust. Soc. Am.*, 97 (5): part 2, pp. 3246–7, 1995.

G. Friedland, O. Vinyals, Y. Huang, and C. Mueller. "Prosodic and other long-term features for speaker diarization." *IEEE Transactions on Audio, Speech, and Language Processing*, 17 (5): 985–93, July 2009.

B. Gold, N. Morgan, and D. Ellis. *Speech and Audio Signal Processing: Processing and Perception of Speech and Music.* Hoboken, NJ, John Wiley & Sons, 2nd edition. 2011.

Hayley Hung, Dinesh Jayagopi, Chuohao Yeo, Gerald Friedland, Sileye Ba, Jean-Marc Odobez, Kannan Ramchandran, Nikki Mirghafori, and Daniel Gatica-Perez. "Using audio and video features to classify the most dominant person in a group meeting," *ACM International Multimedia Conference: Proceedings of the 15th international conference on multimedia*, pp. 835–8.

Martha Larson, Mohammad Soleymani, Pavel Serdyukov, Stevan Rudinac, Christian Wartena, Vanessa Murdock, Gerald Friedland, Roeland Ordelman, and Gareth J. F. Jones. "Automatic tagging and geotagging in video collections and communities," *Proceedings of the 1st ACM International Conference on Multimedia Retrieval*, Trento, Italy, pp. 51:1–51:8, 2011.

Simon J. D. Prince. *Computer Vision: Models, Learning, and Inference.* Cambridge: Cambridge University Press, 1st edition.

J. Ramirez, J. M. Girriz, and J. C. Segura. "Voice activity detection: Fundamentals and speech recognition system robustness." In *Robust Speech Recognition and Understanding.* Ed. M. Grimm and K. Kroschel, 460. Vienna. pp.1–22, *I-Tech*, June 2007.

S. Tranter and D. Reynolds. "An overview of automatic speaker diarization systems." *IEEE TASLP*, 14 (5): 1557–65, 2006.

D. A. van Leeuwen and M. Konečný. "Progress in the AMIDA speaker diarization system for meeting data." In *Multimodal Technologies for Perception of Humans: International Evaluation Workshops CLEAR 2007 and RT 2007.* Baltimore, MD, May 8–11, 2007, Revised Selected Papers. Berlin, Heidelberg: Springer-Verlag, 2008, pp. 475–83.

P. A. Viola and M. J. Jones. "Robust real-time face detection." *IJCV*, 57 (2): 137–54, 2004.

S. Wegmann and L. Gillick. "Why has (reasonably accurate) automatic speech recognition been so hard to achieve?" *Tech. Report, Nuance Communications*, http://web.mit.edu/kenzie/www/wegmann/wegmann_gillick_why.pdf, 2009.

EXERCISES

1. Implement a simple speech activity detection as described in this chapter. Use available corpora from the Internet to train your Gaussians. Measure the classification error with a) different set of parameters when training the Gaussians b) the number of Gaussians c) when testing on the training set d) when testing on a different audio corpus.

2. Discuss possibilities to extend a speech recognition system with video analysis. When do you expect your multimodal system to work well?

3. List three possible distortions in scanned book pages and discuss how you would filter them.

4. Explain how you would like to change the behavior of a speaker identification system for these applications: video retrieval, biometric authorization, a game that gives you a score based on how well you imitate a celebrity's voice.

5. Describe an alternate clustering algorithm for speaker diarization that starts with one cluster and splits subsequently. Analyze the runtime for the algorithm presented in this chapter and your new one.

6. In the segmentation/clustering algorithm presented in this chapter, the clusters are said to be "purified" in each step by merging two clusters according to the BIC.

Provide a colloquial explanation for how this "purification" works. Explain possible problems.

7. Perform the following experiment: Ask a co-student/coworker to find a video on the Internet in a language that you do not speak and where you do not know the participants. It should contain a conversation of several minutes with at least four speakers (a foreign talk show might be a good choice). Do not watch the video, only listen to the audio and perform manual speaker online diarization by saying "speaker 1" "speaker 2." Let your coworker/co-student rate you: How good are you at assigning the right speakers in a normal and in an overlap situation? How does the situation improve once you look at the video?

8. Pick one of the audio analysis tasks described earlier. Explain typical expected problems when performing the task as presented here in the following data domains: recorded voice-over IP phone conference, a board meeting recorded with a microphone array, a conversation recorded with a cell phone in a car, a recorded theater performance, broadcast news, an air-traffic control session, a microphone mounted onto a surveillance camera.

9. Define a difference picture. Where can a difference picture be used?

10. Differencing or background subtraction based on simple differencing may not be robust. What would you do for robust background subtraction?

11. What is a correspondence problem in motion analysis? Where is it used?

12. What important physical attribute of moving objects do you use in visual tracking of objects?

19 Content and Context

In the previous chapters, we described many signal processing and content analysis techniques. However, the content of an image or audio file does not alone determine its meaning and impression on the user. In this chapter, we will therefore describe other factors that are very important to consider in multimedia computing: the set of surrounding circumstances in which the content is presented, otherwise known as *context*. Context is often neglected in academic work because it can be leveraged in many ways in multimedia systems and is often so effective that the content analysis approach becomes secondary. So let us first find out what context really is.

Almost two centuries ago, George Berkeley asked: If a tree falls in a forest and no one is around to hear it, does it make a sound? *Sound* is often defined as the sensation excited in the ear when the air or other medium is set in motion. Thus, if there is no receiving ear, then there is no sound. In other words, perception is not only data – it is a close interaction between the data, transmission medium, and the interpreter. This is shown in Figure 19.1.

Multimedia communication and computing is fundamentally related to the perception problem. In any perception problem, three components must be considered.

- The data acquired for an environment
- The medium used to transmit physical attributes to the perceiver
- The perceiver

Characteristics of each of these must be considered in designing and developing a multimedia system. It has been very well realized, and rigorously articulated and represented, that we understand the world based on the sensory data that we receive using our sensors and the knowledge about the world that we have accumulated since our birth. Both the data and the knowledge are integral components of understanding.

Let us revisit multimedia computing from the fundamentals. Where does multimedia data come from? Why do we even need multimedia? What is the multimedia content problem?

Multimedia data, such as visual (photos and video), aural, and other sensory data are captured for an event that unfolds over time. Each medium represents a particular physical spatiotemporal attribute of the event. An event represents changing

Figure 19.1. Perception requires a source, a medium, and a perceiver.

relationships among objects and these are captured by different media. The data captured by any kind of sensor really represents these spatiotemporal physical attributes of the environment. Objects are part of the environment, and their physical attributes are captured by the media.

Each sensor only captures one type of physical attribute from the perspective afforded from its physical location, including its orientation. Multiple sensors could be combined to create the composite data representing a synchronized signal obtained from these sensors. Thus, one uses appropriate number and types of sensors to capture all attributes of the event that may be of interest in a particular application. Multimedia is the right approach to capture event information and experiences because each medium captures only one physical attribute and, taken as a whole, the multimedia stream is capable of combining the correlated and complementary information from individual streams to provide more holistic information and experience than possible using any one medium. None of the individual medium, including the most powerful human sense of vision, can capture holistic experience in most applications. Humans have many senses and combine them to experience events in the real world (see also Chapter 8).

Of equal importance is the fact that each sensor captures data about the environment from its position and perspective. If its position or perspective is changed, then the data and experience also change. For interpretation of the data, one must know the position and perspective. Moreover, many sensors, like cameras, have several other parameters (focal length, aperture diameter, flash, etc.) that determine the capture of the data, and hence they are very important in understanding and analyzing the experience represented by the data.

The most important component in multimedia computing systems is the user. Each user is unique and while interacting with a system, the context may be different. Interpretation of the data is not only user dependent, but also dependent on the context of the user. If you give the same photo to different people and ask them to assign tags to represent the photo, there may be as many different tags as the number of people assigning tags. Moreover, many studies have demonstrated that if you give the same photo to the same person at two different times in different contexts, then the tags assigned are different. The concept of Rorschach tests is based on the theory that an interpretation of data depends as much or more on the person perceiving the data as on the data itself.

CONNECTING DATA AND USERS

Multimedia computing addresses a problem that many other fields like computer vision, databases, and information retrieval face: connecting data and users. As shown in Figure 19.2, data exists in many forms, ranging from bits to alphanumeric documents to photos and video. Users of the data in a modern computing environment, however, may come from different education backgrounds, cultures, and socioeconomic statuses. The challenge is to connect a user with a data source so the user can use the data he needs to solve his application. A key point to remember is that a user is never interested in what and where the data is; she is only interested in solving the problem at hand.

The major hurdle in connecting users to the data is often referred to as the *semantic gap*, usually defined as:

> *The semantic gap is the lack of coincidence between the information that one can extract from the visual data and the interpretation that the same data have for a user in a given situation.* A linguistic description is almost always contextual, whereas an image may live by itself.

To understand the semantic gap, let's consider Figure 19.3. This figure shows that the data operations in a computer start at the bit level and can be structured to represent various data concepts such as documents, images, and videos. A user, however, always starts thinking in terms of objects and events and builds other concepts based on the basic notions of objects and events. The transformation of data-level concepts such as images to user-level concepts such as objects and events is the challenge that must be solved by content analysis and used in content organization and retrieval.

DATA

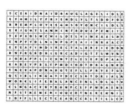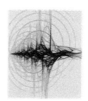

Figure 19.2. A user combines information from multiple sources, including multiple human sensors, to understand an object or event.

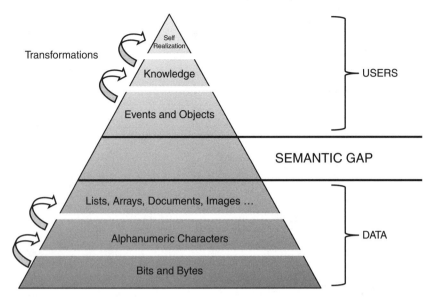

Figure 19.3. The semantic gap is created because computers operate using bits and structuring them into bytes and other structures. Humans think in terms of events and objects and build their concepts in terms of those. How we go from bits to objects and events is the gap that must be bridged to allow smooth interactions between humans and computers.

CONTENT AND CONTEXT

Content usually refers to data values in a multimedia stream, such as images or audio. It is commonly understood that we refer to substantive information perceived by a user in the data that is represented by a particular file. Content analysis and content-based retrieval represents the majority of research done in multimedia and related fields like computer vision. Thus a photo may depict a person standing near a car next to a house. The challenge content analysis faces is the famous problem of pattern recognition. In all sensory data, the problem is to segment the data into meaningful parts and to use known models of objects of interest to label all segments of an image. This is where one runs into a tricky situation: we need segments to recognize objects, but we also need objects to segment the data. It is possible to formulate this problem such that one can use models of potential objects to segment and then see how the segments best fit object recognition. One may potentially use an optimization framework to accomplish this. The problem gets complicated and almost intractable because in some cases, most notably in images, a higher-dimensional space is mapped into two-dimensional space, resulting in loss of information and making the problem impossible to solve unless some strong assumptions are made. This is the reason behind the *sensory gap*, defined as: *the gap between the object in the world and the information in a (computational) description derived from a recording of that scene.*

In many sensors, the signals from multiple objects get intermingled and combined, making it almost impossible to solve the problem. The only way to simplify the problem appears to be to use other information and to reduce the number of potential objects that could be in the data, and then check which objects are most likely to result in the signal.

Philosophers and scientists have tried to solve the mystery of human perception for several centuries and are still far from any seemingly right solution. Closer to multimedia, people have been working on image recognition and speech recognition (notice only speech recognition, not audio recognition) and are still far from solving these problems, even with the powerful computing infrastructure that we have. The successful solutions usually are for limited domains, meaning the number of objects is limited in those applications, making the problem more tractable.

Let us look at a related concept: context. *Context* is defined in standard dictionaries and reference sources as:

- the set of circumstances or facts that surround a particular event, situation, and so forth;
- the interrelated conditions in which something exists or occurs: environment or setting;
- determinant of meaning.

In technical areas, context started receiving attention during the past decade and has been receiving increasing attention. The precise definition of context is very difficult because content and context are closely related, as one could easily see from the dictionary meaning of context. Several researchers in the psychology of perception, neurophysiology, and the cognitive sciences have emphasized the role of context in understanding our environment. Clearly, a perceiver is at least as important as the data in perception. The perceiver uses extensive context in understanding signals and recognizing objects and events in it.

When using multimedia, each media data stream may act as context for another. Consider a video. It has an image sequence and an audio stream. As is easily obvious, without audio we cannot fully understand video, and without visual signal we cannot fully experience video. In multimedia, each media stream has incomplete information about the environment captured and must utilize complementary information in some other media stream to recreate the environment to understand and enjoy it.

Types of Context in Multimedia Systems

Most information systems are becoming multimedia. Data for an event is collected using many different types of sensors and is organized according to the event. This data can then be served to consumers as requested. Most users request data based on events or people or concepts. To satisfy these needs, emerging information systems are increasingly organized as shown in Figure 19.4.

The context or knowledge that could be used in analyzing data may be considered in the following different classes:

1. **Context in Content:** Relationship among different objects and even their subparts in the real world can be converted to relationships among data items and can be applied in analysis of data.
2. **Device Parameters:** Environmental parameters of the digital devices at the time of data collection play an important role in the analysis of data.

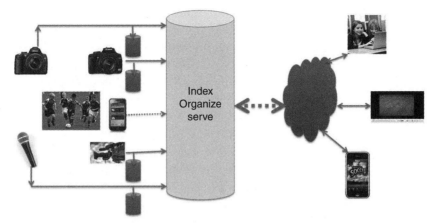

Figure 19.4. An eco-system showing creation to consumption of multimedia data. Capture depends on the location, environmental conditions, and device parameters. All data is locally stored and collectively organized and indexed for serving consumers on different devices.

3. **Data Acquisition Context:** Knowledge about the person collecting data, location, and environmental conditions at the time of data acquisition (sun angle, cloudy, rainy, night, indoor, etc.) affects the content, and knowledge of these could be used in data analysis.

4. **Perceiver:** Cognitive scientists know the importance of the perceiver. Rorschach tests are a clear demonstration of the knowledge and personality of the perceiver in interpretation of visual data.

5. **Interpretation Context:** The real-world situation in which the data is interpreted results in focus on different aspects of data. A botanist looks at a garden with different goals and interprets it differently than a person interested in enjoying the beauty of flowers.

Consider a simple case to understand how context can significantly simplify analysis: a photo is taken and needs to be interpreted. If one knows when the photo was taken and what the lighting level was in the scene, one can use appropriate parameters for segmentation and interpretation of images. Moreover, if the photo was taken in Iowa, one should not expect beaches or mountains.

In the following, we discuss the role of each of these types of context. Explicit consideration of the aforementioned classes of contexts helps analysis and management of multimedia data. We show examples of these contexts.

Context in Content

In image understanding, one starts with the intensity values at every pixel and computes edges, regions, and other features. These features are then used to find meaningful objects and events in the image. The role of context in image understanding, commonly called *computer vision*, was emphasized even in very early days by systems developed for the block worlds and those for indoor scenes like MYSYS. Waltz developed a constraint propagation framework to label junctions and understand configuration of blocks. This work was one of the earliest works in computer vision, and the one that resulted in further exploration of the role and propagation of constraint.

A very clear role of context was demonstrated in 1976 in MYSYS system, where it is stated: "In scene analysis, it is frequently impossible to interpret parts of an image taken out of context. Different objects may have similar appearances, while objects belonging to the same functional class can have strikingly different appearances (e.g., chairs). Ambiguous local interpretations must be ruled out by using contextual constraints to achieve a meaningful, globally consistent interpretation of the whole scene."

Further they said: "Scene interpretation is an attempt to explain observed sensory data in terms of prior knowledge about the depicted domain. The explanation can entail many types and levels of knowledge, some of which may be probabilistic or inconsistent. It must also allow for the likelihood that the data is noisy. For these reasons, scene interpretation is not a purely deductive problem with a unique correct solution; it is a problem that requires a search for the best or optimum explanation."

Early research in scene understanding resulted in the realization that problems in scene understanding are posed by providing (1) a set of possible assignments for each region, with associated a priori likelihoods for each assignment; and (2) a set of constraints that are derived for the types of scenes to be analyzed and that determine the a posteriori likelihood of regions.

This approach resulted in a popular framework commonly called *relaxation labeling*, which has been formalized and used in many computer vision systems. The basic idea in this approach is to utilize knowledge of local relationships among objects that may appear in a scene and use these local relationships to propagate local interpretations repeatedly to refine overall interpretations over the image. Thus one may use simple facts like "a computer monitor is on a desk," "floor is at the bottom in an image," and "desk is on the floor" in an office scene. A set of such constraints among all objects can then be used iteratively in the interpretation process. The process starts with recognizing all possible regions and assigning them all plausible levels. The relaxation process then iteratively eliminates all implausible levels. When this process terminates, each region is assigned the best possible interpretation based on the constraints, or the knowledge, available.

Relaxation processes have been defined at pixel levels. Also the relaxation processes have been developed considering a set of labels where each iteration eliminates certain labels. Another approach uses probabilistic assignment of labels by updating the probability of labels in each iteration.

Verification Vision

Another commonly used approach for recognizing objects using context is called *verification vision*. Suppose that we are given an image of an object and we need to find how many times and where this object appears in an image. Such a problem is essentially a verification problem, rather than an object recognition problem. There are many approaches for verification. One of the most popular is called *template matching*. A verification algorithm can be used to exhaustively verify the presence of each model from a large model base, but such an exhaustive approach will not be very effective. A verification approach is desirable if one, or at most a few, objects are possible candidates. If one is given contextual information, then that could be used to constrain the number of potential objects in an image. Thus, if one knows that an image was taken inside the kitchen of a Western home, then one can list the number of objects that may need to be verified; clearly an elephant or a tall banyan tree will not be in that list.

CONTEXT-ONLY IMAGE SEARCH: COMMERCIAL SYSTEMS

The most commonly used examples of use of context in search are the commercial applications of image search from any major search engine, Google, Bing, or Yahoo. These were described previously. Suppose that you search for images with keyword Obama, rose, Tendulkar, or cars. Look at the results of the image search and you will be surprised. Most of the results are correct. Surprisingly, as is well known, most of these results are obtained without even opening the image file – that is, without even looking at the content. These search systems only use the context provided to them from sources such as the name of the file containing the picture, surrounding text on the page where the picture file appears, and the topic of the page. These search engines perform much better than any content-based retrieval system that we have seen, including the ones that one of the authors was involved in developing.

DEVICE PARAMETERS

For considering a common example of device parameters, let's consider a device that most of us use regularly: a digital camera. Unlike their predecessors, modern digital cameras are more "event-capture" devices than photographic devices. Modern digital cameras have multiple sensors, including GPS to determine the location of the photograph, present on it that can capture much more information about the photo shooting event. The digital photograph is no longer just a collection of pixels; it has a host of sensory information stored as metadata. This information can be summarized if we model the digital photograph as a multilayered structure as shown in Figure 19.5. The layers are: (i) pixel/spectral layer and (ii) meta layer. The pixel layer stores information recorded by the CCD (as pixel values). The content of the image is present in this layer. The meta layer stores the contextual information about a photo shoot. The meta layer can further be divided into the following sublayers:

a. *Optical Meta Layer*. It contains the metadata related to the optics of the camera; for example, the focal length, aperture, exposure time, and so forth. These metadata store important cues about the context in which the image was shot (like the lighting condition, depth of field, and distance of subjects in the image).

b. *Temporal Meta Layer*. It contains the time stamp of the instant in which the photo was shot. The time stamp of a single image in a stand-alone environment is not informative enough. But in a collection of images (e.g., photo albums), the time difference can shed valuable light on the content of the images.

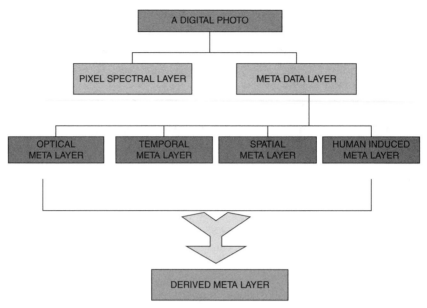

Figure 19.5. Different types of information stored with an image taken by a digital camera.

    c. *Spatial Meta Layer.* It contains the spatial coordinates of the places where pictures were shot. These coordinates are generated by the GPS systems attached to the camera. In the case of camera phones, cell tower ids help generate this data.

    d. *Human-Induced Meta Layer.* This layer contains the tags/comments/ratings people post. Community tagging (in online photo albums) or voice tagging in mobile phones help generate data for this layer.

    e. *Derived Meta Layer.* This metadata is inferred from other information by various statistical modeling approaches. The taxonomy defined here helps us to explore the information sources present in a digital camera image. The spectral, optical, and temporal layers are currently present in almost all digital photographs, while the spatial, human-induced, and derived meta layers might not be present.

Exif data is attached to all digital pictures and contains very valuable information about camera parameters used in taking photos. These parameters affect the part of the scene imaged and the intensity values of pixels, while others give very valuable contextual information about the data acquisition context.

    Sometimes the context provided by device parameters like Exif is more meaningful than context provided by the analysis of content or intensity values. Consider the photo shown in Figure 19.6. If we try to assign tags based on pixel features only, we may obtain: *scenery, trees, water,* and *wildlife.* However, tags based on Exif features give: *indoor, party, portrait,* and *group photo indoors.* Why is there a discrepancy between tags predicted by the content and the context channel? This is a photo of a photo. The image originally appeared in a magazine, and Figure 19.6 is a photo of it using a standard digital camera. Because the

Figure 19.6. What do you see in this photo? Exif parameters correctly analyze that this is a photo of a photo – this is not a photo taken in the real world.

content and context channels capture two entirely different semantics about an image, the tags are different.

Similarly, anybody, including a very effective photo interpretation system, may look at Figure 19.7 and interpret it to be a scene from China. But Exif parameters for the photo tell us without any real effort that this is a photo taken in the China Pavilion of Epcot Center.

Perceiver

Many psychological tests and even many photos that commonly appear in psychology literature show a picture to people and ask them to specify what they see in the picture. In these experiments, the goal is to know about the personal characteristics of the perceiver. These tests demonstrate that the interpretation of data depends on the perceiver. Common phrases used by people such as "Do you see what I see in this picture?" are clear indications of the well-recognized role of the perceiver. A perceiver brings general knowledge of the environment that she lives in to bear on the interpretation of the data. Because we all grew up in the physical world that we inhabit, we make several contextual assumptions about the world. Our brain automatically uses these assumptions in interpretation of data. The best example of this is visual illusions. In visual illusions, we see something that is different from objective reality. Even after measurements and knowing that what we see is not right, our cognitive system does not accept the reality. This clearly demonstrates the role of assumptions that we all use in interpretation of data. Sometimes, the interpretation of data tells a lot more about the interpreter than about the data.

Figure 19.7. Where was this picture taken? Photo interpretation will mislead that this is in China, but context correctly tells that this is taken in Orlando, Florida. GPS parameters have no difficulty in putting the photo at the right place.

Domain Knowledge

Consider Figure 19.8: What do we see in this picture? A plausible answer would be an Atomic Force Microscope image that shows the composition of a material at a cellular or atomic level. In fact, what you are seeing is a recent breakthrough in developing cost-effective chemical sensors. However, the viewer cannot understand what this is because they cannot interpret these images without context and associated knowledge, despite the fact that this image is the announcement of an important breakthrough. This example illustrates that without domain knowledge, it is almost impossible for people to analyze and understand context.

Context in Photo Management in Smartphones

The current generation of digital photos is captured by smartphones. As shown in Figure 19.9, smartphones are privy to many information sources that augment photos with lots of contextual knowledge. Let's consider scenarios where context can play a useful role for organizing photos on smartphones.

   a. Identifying people: Most consumer cameras can detect frontal faces while shooting photos. However, face recognition and assigning name tags to each individual face is an open problem. In the case of smartphones, face identification can be made easier by limiting the match search to a smaller set. Our personal calendars provide us with the names

Figure 19.8. What do we see in this picture? It depends purely on the domain knowledge.

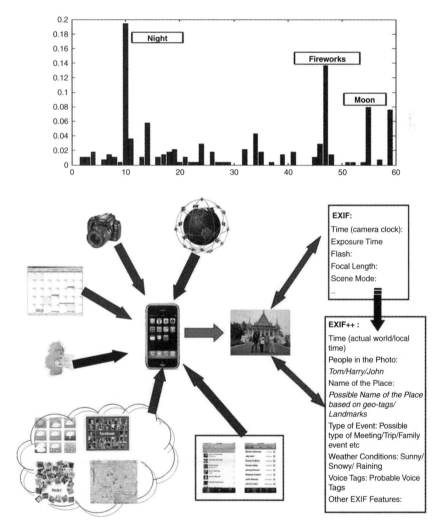

Figure 19.9. Showing how each photo by modern cameras will be augmented with very rich metadata – that we call Exif++.

of people we are meeting at any particular point in time. If a portrait or group photo was shot at a specific time, we can compare the faces appearing in the photo with the faces of people we were supposed to meet. The latter can come from any social network or photo sharing site. If we do not get a good match, the system can go through the list of recent callers and match with the faces of the callees. If not, we can go through our contact list to find a good matching face. This makes the problem much easier to solve.

b. Identifying objects: Object identification is another problem. Usually, people shoot landmarks or special objects of interest using their smartphones. The Exif information can tell us if the object of interest is indoors or outdoors. We can also estimate a possible size of the object based on the focal length, field of view, and subject distance. Geo-location will help us narrow down to a small set of important objects (e.g., landmarks or flowers or food) shot in that area. Comparison to this refined set is likely to generate much better results for object identification.

c. Event name tagging based on public/private calendars: People shoot a lot of photos at their life events, for example, parties, trips, and meetings. It is very relevant and useful to tag photos based on the events. It may be very difficult to automatically tag a photo with an event name (John's birthday) or even a generic class name (indoor party) based on pixels and Exif alone. However, personal calendars can help in such cases to properly tag using event names. Further, people often participate in public events like concerts, baseball games, parades, and so forth. There are abundant sources of event repositories on the Web. Based on a user's location information and the events taking place in the vicinity, it may be possible to predict the proper event name (e.g., Celtics versus Lakers game) with good accuracy.

RECOMMENDED READING

In human perception, Irwin Rock and Richard Gregory have strongly championed the role of knowledge in many different forms in visual perception. They believed that context plays an as important, in most cases a significantly more important, role as content. Human sensory processing uses context extensively. Several researchers in the psychology of perception, neurophysiology, and the cognitive sciences have emphasized the role of context in understanding our environment (see Winston, Rock, Gregory, Ramachandran, and Anstis). A review of context as used in different computing systems and environments is provided in Joung, El Zarki, and Jain, Berkeley, and Abowd and colleagues. All digital cameras follow a metadata standard called Exif to capture the context around photos taken by the camera. A detailed analysis of these parameters is provided in the standard itself. Sinha and Jain explore the use of these parameters to infer the class of photos. Context has been used in computer vision extensively from its early days, for example in Kittler, Freuder, Barrow and Tennenbaum, and Galleguillos and Belongie. Much of the context used in the early days of computer vision was endogenous to images. Recent use of context is exogenous to images. Many philosophers and cognitive scientists, including two of the most noted during the twentieth century, Karl Popper and Ulrich Neisser, have created models of all human actions that include context and prior knowledge about an application as an integral component of understanding data. Media processing techniques so far, however, have focused on content assuming that interpretation can be done based only on the data values. In resolving the semantic gap, an important point is the "the linguistic description is always contextual." Context in general and GPS in particular have serious privacy implications. This is discussed in Friedland and Sommer.

Further Reading

G. D. Abowd, A. K. Dey, P. J. Brown, N. Davies, M. Smith, and P. Steggles. "Towards a better understanding of context and context-awareness." *Proc. 1st Int. Symp. on Handheld and Ubiquitous Computing* (HUC '99), pages 304–7. Springer-Verlag. 1999.

H. G. Barrow and J. M. Tenenbaum. MSYS: A System for Reasoning about Scenes, Technical Report 121, AI Center SRI, April 1976.

George Berkeley, *A Treatise Concerning the Principles of Human Knowledge*. 1734. Section 45.

Cristiana Bolchini, Carlo A. Curino, Elisa Quintarelli, Fabio A. Schreiber, and Letizia Tanca. "A Data-oriented Survey of Context Models." *SIGMOD Record*, 36 (4): December 2007.

Exif: Exchangeable image file format for digital cameras: Exif version 2.2. Technical report, Japan Electronics and Information Technology Industries Association, 2002.

John E. Exner. *The Rorschach: A Comprehensive System. Vol. 1: Basic Foundations*. New York: John Wiley & Sons. 1995.

E. C. Freuder. "Recognition of Real Objects." *Vision Flash*, 33: MIT, 1972.

G. Friedland and R. Sommer, "Cybercasing the joint: On the privacy implications of geo-tagging." Fifth USENIX Workshop on Hot Topics in Security (HotSec '10) at the 19th USENIX Security Symposium, Washington, DC.

C. Galleguillos and S. Belongie. "Context based object categorization: A critical survey." Bo Gong and Ramesh Jain, "Segmenting photo streams in events based on optical metadata." Proc. IEEE Conf. on Semantic Computing, Irvine, CA, Sept. 17–19, 2007.

Richard Gregory. *The Intelligent Eye*. London: Weidenfeld and Nicolson. 1970.

Ye Sun Joung, Magda El Zarki, and Ramesh Jain, "A user model for personalization services." Third International Workshop on Context Modeling and Management for Smart Environments. CMMSE. November 1–4, 2009.

J. Kittler and J. Illingworth, "Relaxation Labelling Algorithms – a review." *Image and Vision Computing*, 1985.

Ulrich Neisser. *Cognition and Reality: Principles and Implications of Cognitive Psychology*. San Francisco: W. H. Freeman. 1976.

Karl Popper *Objective knowledge: An evolutionary approach*. Oxford: Clarendon Press, 1972.

V. S. Ramachandran and S. M. Anstis. "The Perception of Apparent Motion." *Scientific American*, June 1986.

Irwin Rock. *The Logic of Perception*. Boston, MA: MIT Press. 1985.

S. Santini and R. Jain. "Beyond Query by Example." IEEE Second Workshop on Multimedia Signal Processing, Redondo Beach, CA, pp. 3–8. December 7–9. 1998.

P. Sinha and R. Jain. "Classification and annotation of digital photos using optical context data." *Proceedings of the 2008 international conference on content-based image and video retrieval, ACM*, pp. 309–18, 2008.

P. Sinha and R. Jain. "Semantics in digital photos: A contextual analysis." *Proceedings of the 2008 IEEE International Conference on Semantic Computing, IEEE Computer Society.* pp. 58–65, 2008.

Arnold Smeulders et al. "Content-based image retrieval at the end of the early years." *IEEE Transactions on Pattern Analysis and Machine Intelligence.* December 2000.

Patrick Winston. *The Psychology of Computer Vision.* McGraw-Hill Computer Science Series. 1975.

EXERCISES

1. What is Exif? What kind of context does it capture?

2. Suppose that we want to define endogenous and exogenous contexts for a photo. List some context parameters of each of these two types.

3. With increasing use of digital photos from cameras as well as phones, it is now possible to use tags automatically assigned by the system, rather than by humans. What kind of tags would you like to see assigned to a photo when it is taken so you can retrieve it later?

4. Using Exif, photos can be assigned to certain semantic categories, even without using any intensity values. What kind of classes can be recognized using Exif? What other classes would you like to determine and what kind of metadata will help you in that?

5. Location has become a powerful data source in many applications. Is location important for classification and retrieval of images? Give some examples.

6. Some people consider time and location the two most important parameters, or metadata, for understanding photos. What do you think about this? Give your thoughts justifying your answer.

20 Future Topics

"It's hard to predict, especially the future."

This quote is often attributed to Albert Einstein, often also to Niels Bohr. Regardless of who said it, we believe it's true. However, it's also good news. It tells us two things: first, prediction is hard, not impossible; and second, we predict many things in our lives, not only what is popularly identified as "the future." Here is an example: When somebody throws a ball at you, you move your hand toward catching it and you often succeed. Martial artists train their brains to identify opponents' subtle body cues to dodge a punch. Without predicting the punch, dodging would be impossible. And it is not only hard. This anticipation capability of the brain based on sensory input is one of the unsolved topics in multimedia computing.[1]

Of course, at the end of our book we want to give a broader overview than just a very short time prediction over the next couple of milliseconds. For that to not just be a wild guess, we want to introduce a framework that has been proposed in the literature that tries to infer from the past based on the assumption that history repeats in cycles and that the cycle frequency is determined by reputation gains and losses regarding technology.

HOW TO PREDICT THE FUTURE

We believe it is important to introduce at least one framework for how to estimate the future because we think predicting the future is a very important skill for everybody, not just multimedia researchers and practitioners. It is especially important for the field of multimedia, though, because multimedia computing has always been very closely connected to user experiences and technology-driven problems.

Figure 20.1 introduces the so-called Hype Cycle. The idea is that a technology breakthrough (e.g., the invention of the digital camera) triggers a boom. The boom creates euphoria and demand for the technology, which results in people investing time and

---

[1] Most work in that topic can currently be found in the robotics community, although mostly focusing on the visual modality alone.

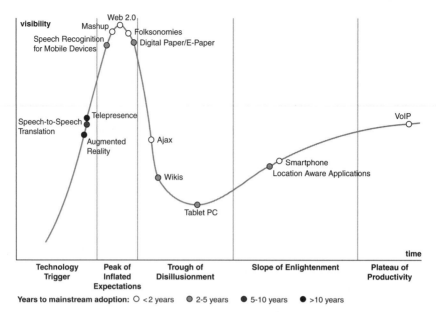

Figure 20.1. Emerging Technologies Hype Cycle 2006 (selected data points displayed only) according to Gartner, Inc.

money into it. Once euphoria has passed, the peak of inflated expectations is reached and people start to distrust the technology; the societal status of the technology enters the trough of disillusionment. Once there, it is hard work to recover. Fortunately, the model assumes that small incremental changes will then improve the reputation and visibility of the technology again and bring it into the slope of enlightenment. From there, one can reach the plateau of productivity, which allows effective work with the technology with a balanced, objective view of its limits. Most likely, the cycle will begin again once the productive phase has spawned new breakthrough results.

While this is only one narrow model of how to explain why technology history is repeating, we will use this to explain some of the aspects of why we think certain topics will hype again. The original authors of the graphics have put several technologies on the graph hypothesizing about the future of these technologies. It is interesting to look at, especially because the future has already happened and the graph is from 2006. We leave that as an exercise.

FUTURE TOPICS IN MULTIMEDIA

Concluding from what has been discussed before, future topics will most likely emerge from current and past topics by cycling through the hype cycles. So, to predict the future, it is therefore valid to take a look at current and past topics and speculate on how they might evolve based on technical progress in other fields (e.g., hardware), as well as user demand.

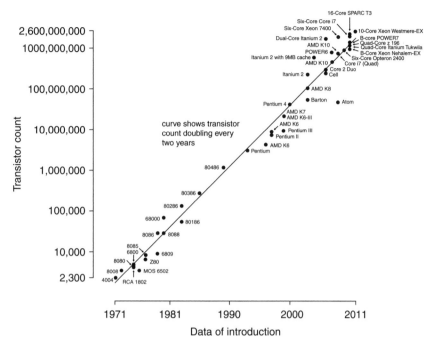

Microprocessor Transistor Counts 1971-2011 & Moore's Law

Figure 20.2. Moore's Law. Note that the law states that the amount of transistors doubles about every two years, which is only indirectly related to computational power.

More Transistors

Most books start rather than end with this: Moore's Law. Moore's Law is a rule of thumb that about every two years, the amount of transistors per chip doubles. In the past, this was equivalent to a doubling of computational power every two years (see Figure 20.2).

The fact that we talk about it in future perspectives rather than at the beginning doesn't mean it is less important. However, Moore's Law has not actually started the field of multimedia or made it feasible like with so many other areas. In fact, the increase of compute just shaped the algorithms: some algorithms that seemed infeasible are now feasible and other algorithms are forgotten because given the amount of compute, they don't make sense any more. So it is important to constantly reevaluate the state of the computer versus the decision made to do quality and quantity trade-offs. For example, nowadays, using 8 x 8 DCT blocks to do MPEG compression might actually be suboptimal given that the DCT could easily be performed on the entire frame, yielding fewer artifacts. However, when the MPEG-1 standard came out, compression in real time was only possible with specialized hardware. Also note that while the number of transistors follows an exponential curve, this only indirectly translates to computational power. In the past couple of years, transistor grows resulted in more CPU cores per chip, which means the algorithms must be effectively parallelized to benefit from Moore's Law. However, computational resources still directly increase for CPUs and memory on mobile devices because of the slight delay in development due to the mobility constraints on power and size. A third reason Moore's Law becomes less important is distributed computing (often referred to as *cloud computing*). With networks' bandwidth increasing steadily, computation can be performed "offshore," making compute resources available that wouldn't usually fit into an office or a mobile device. In conclusion, whenever thinking about a multimedia application of the future, we propose to at least take into account these three factors:

1) Moore's Law, enabling higher-density computing and more memory per chip.
2) Power and size constraints for mobile devices.
3) The possibility of distributed computing.

In fact, innovation can come from revisiting and updating old algorithms and the decisions made when developing them to the current "transistor situation."

Better Networking

Better networking is closely related to more mobility and interoperability of sensors as well as more compute. In the beginning of multimedia computing, compute was more effective than networking. This is why compression algorithms bloomed. For many things, the compression schemes of the past are now overpowered for the networks of today and one could actually save compute by using more bits of network bandwidth. Having said that, compression is still an issue when fighting latencies and also when mass consumption of data is the reality, such as in video-on-demand services. Moreover, more bandwidth enables novel applications, for example in the realm of 3D communication. Better networking coupled with better mobility allows for easier communication, a fact social networking sites widely exploit: it is now possible to casually post on the Internet (i.e., for nonbusiness purposes). The discussion here would be very similar to the "more transistor" discussion; we therefore leave it to the reader to think about the possibilities of future networking (see exercise).

More Sensors

As discussed in Chapter 4, not only will new types of sensors be developed, they will also be connected with the computer and integrated with other sensory data and, most important, become more mobile. This combination is almost a guarantee for a large variety of potential applications. It is up to the multimedia researcher and practitioner to invent them: each new sensor has its own constraints as of how its output should be compressed, analyzed, and visualized for different applications. More specifically, in multimedia we are concerned with the combination and integration of multiple sensor data. So with more sensors being developed, there is an exponential amount of combination possibilities.

In addition to new types of sensors, sensors regularly become cheaper to produce and use less power. As a result, they are more heavily integrated into mobile devices, which increase the number of potential applications in the mobile context. As an example, the recent integration of GPS sensors into cell phones has spawned a huge wave of startups making use of the location data to provide a more personalized user experience. Also, the amount of available compute resources regularly increases, which makes it possible to have more of the same sensor on one device whether it is mobile or not. For example, the single-microphone cell phone has turned into a microphone array smartphone that performs beam forming to increase the signal quality. Multiple cameras make it possible to record panoramic or stereo images even in small mobile toys. After all, humans have multiple sensors of the same type (e.g., two eyes and two ears). However, it is probably safe to say that we already have more artificial sensors than human sensors on earth – just consider your own household. When sensor readout becomes fast enough, the temporal aspect usually allows for additional impact: this is how history went from photography to video and from map services to real-time navigation. Again, the task for multimedia research is to integrate the sensors in a smart way and enable new applications.

More Mobility

In the previous paragraphs, we implied that the number of mobile devices increases steadily. However, we did so in the context of cell phones, and that is actually a bad idea because cell phones are currently decreasing the amount of mobile devices needed to perform certain tasks. In the early days of cell phones, a cell phone was just that: a mobile telephone. So people carried that in addition to other devices they might need to perform certain tasks, such as a watch (time sensor), a pocket calculator, or a dictation machine. With the advent of smartphones, many of these devices are now collapsed into one. Usually, all one needs to do is install "an app." Again, here are chances for the multimedia community as these apps, in contrast to disjoint devices, can interact with multiple sensors at once. So because we have fewer mobile devices, why do we continuously state that there are more mobile devices? First, cell phones have become ubiquitous even in regions where nobody used to have any mobile devices (e.g., India), so overall the number of cell phones per person has gone up. Second, even though mobile devices have collapsed into one, many people still have individual non–cell phone mobile devices and use them. More important, though, stationary devices have a general tendency to become mobile (the most prominent example is the phone, of course). Many desktop PCs are now substituted with laptops, in-car navigation systems are now handheld navigation systems, and the computational power of a game console can now be held in hand. Furthermore, new mobile devices with more specialized sensors are being invented. Last but not least, Terrabytes of storage have become portable, for example, calorie counters and chips in sports shoes that count steps by communicating with the cell phone, sonars for fishing, dive computers or portable projectors. While on the one hand, all of these specialized devices have a tendency to become integrated into a cell phone and therefore vanish, on the other hand, many of these devices also compete for users' attention by becoming more general. Portable game consoles now allow for Internet browsing and serve as photo and video cameras, portable MP3 players allow for gaming, and some cell phones have become so powerful they can host a Web server that serves on-demand videos. Then, of course new devices pop up that replace nonelectric mobility, for example, e-book readers, tablet computers, and electronic pens that record everything you write on a regular paper. What's more important than the quantities of these devices is the commonality of needing software that makes them operate.

When this software involves perceptual and sensory data, multimedia computing provides the methods to make them even more powerful.

Better Experience

An everlasting motivation in multimedia computing is the desire to make it "more real" and to improve the user experience. These two are not the same, but are very closely correlated. Since the early days of audio recording, making the signal cleaner was the main drive behind innovations like stereo, Hi-Fi, and, last but not least, the CD. MP3 was invented to make things sound better over the Internet. Nowadays, more loudspeakers are used to convey a spatial experience of the audio. In the visual domain, many ideas served the same purpose. For example, digital cameras got more and more Megapixels and TVs became larger and got a higher resolution. The current trend is to be also more spatial in the visual domain. Cinematic movies, TV sets, and computer games are now becoming 3D. With 3D consumption media improving in quality, the next step is surely the homemade recording of 3D and later the interactive 3D experience. As already depicted in several of the *Star Wars* movies, where different people are projected as a holography, any interactive 3D system will aim toward telepresence experience. Taking it from there, most likely other media will be made part of it, such as haptic sensors and actuators, smell, and temperature. All in all, the goal will most likely be the most real experience while at the same time making it possible to alter that experience with artificial means, for example, by adding virtual objects to the communication or adding a previously recorded snippet into a live conversation to make a person appear as if she or he was there. With higher capabilities of multimedia content analysis, these alterations of the real world become even more interesting, for example, when different background worlds can be easily superimposed or a 3D recording can be searched for various high-level aspects (such as a particular topic of conversation). Making for a more realistic experience will remain a challenge for multimedia researchers and practitioners for many more years.

More realism is one way to provide a better experience. Another way that is a challenge in multimedia computing is to provide a more personal experience. For example, users want to skip parts of videos they are not interested in. They want to get search results based on what the community they are in finds interesting (collaborative filtering) and/or only what they personally prefer. Video-on-demand sites currently spend millions of dollars to show users exactly the videos they want, exactly the trailers they want, and exactly the commercial that makes them buy products. While commercials are usually perceived as annoying, we still list targeted advertisement under better user experience because the assumption is that the right commercial will actually be perceived as informative because it presents something the user is very likely to be interested in.

Multimedia data has a disparate nature with respect to what it represents in terms of physical attributes over space and time. It is captured using different devices and, to make sense, it must be rendered using different devices. The fundamental difference in the nature and volume of data results in the storage of data using different file systems. The capture and rendering technology for each type of media also results in different type of

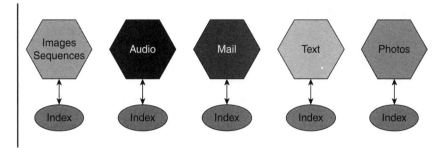

Figure 20.3. Different types of data and their indexes create isolated silos of multimedia data.

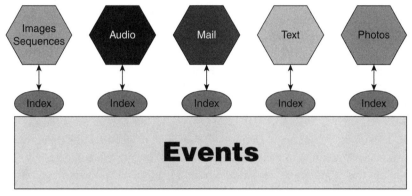

Figure 20.4. Real-world events could be used to unify different media and provide a unified framework for indexing multimedia data.

organization of data to match human perceptual perspective of that mode. This results in different approaches to indexing of the data. For example, the video may be indexed based on the time code, or frame number, while photos may be indexed based on file name of the photo, and text as page and line numbers in a document or a page. These indexes are fundamentally different and are incompatible. This creates silos among different types of multimedia data. This situation is shown in Figure 20.3.

A challenging question for multimedia research is how to break these silos to unify multimedia data. A unifying basis behind this data is not in the data but is in the real world. This data is collected for something considered important in the real world. Objects and events are complementary in modeling the real world around us. Multimedia, because of its temporal nature, is particularly important in dealing with events. Different modalities of data capture different aspects of events and objects. Because different streams of multimedia data have nothing in common except that they are all related to the same real-world event, it is natural to index them using events and their parameters. This is an effective way to unify and index the multimedia data, resulting in the situation shown in Figure 20.4. By defining an event model to represent all essential aspects of an event as well as all its associated multimedia, it is possible to create a unified approach to indexing multimedia data.

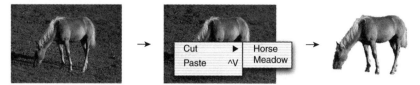

Figure 20.5. Photo editing as it should be: a semantic operation allows the user to tell the computer directly what he or she wants rather than breaking it down into a large set of tedious mini-operations.

Closely related to a more personal experience is Web sites' desire to keep users' attention. To become a great market share, a commercial Web site must make sure users stay online at the site as long as possible. Surely, this is mostly achieved by making sure the user has a perfect experience on the site in addition to the service being so essential that the user needs to spend a high amount of time on it. These and other challenges are the domain of machine learning, natural language processing, and multimedia computing and promise many problems to solve for a long time.

More Semantic

An underlying theme in many chapters in this book is that we ultimately want the computer to directly respond to high-level requests like "cut out the horse from the image and copy it into this other image" rather than having to manually perform pixel-wise selection (compare Figure 20.5).

We call operations that automatically infer the steps necessary to reach a goal based on the content of the data *semantic operations*. For semantic operations to become a reality, the computer needs to share a large amount of context with the user. Ultimately, the computer needs to share an understanding of the meaning of the data, the operation, and the user's intentions.

For example, the number of photos, videos, audios, and text descriptions of events has increased very rapidly such that the sheer volume of even personal collection of photos has become tedious to manage and maintain. As in text documents, a summary of multimedia content represents a condensed version of the information contained therein. Consider personal photos. Suppose that you go on a trip to Brazil and come back with three thousand photos. You want to share those photos with your friends and family. Would you show them all three thousand photos? In 2015, because of the easy availability of digital camera, storage, and ease in transferring those photos to your collection, you take twenty-five thousand photos. At the end of the year, you want to send a "Year in Photos" to your mother, your significant other, your best friend from childhood, your professional friends, and your cousins. How do you select twenty-five photos to represent your year in photos? These are just two simple cases of summarization of photos.

One of the most popular and frequent arts in human society has been storytelling. From oral traditions to sophisticated video production and now multimedia environments, people have used all possible technology to enhance communication of their experiences. With advances in multimedia, storytelling has taken new directions. We discussed several

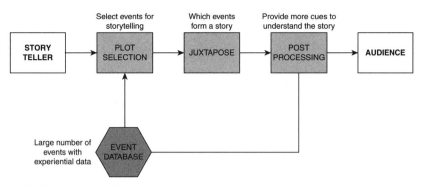

Figure 20.6. In a storytelling system, an event or a sequence of events is presented to an audience using all data that is available. The main steps in such a system, manual or automatic, are shown in this figure.

tools that one may use in storytelling in the chapter on multimedia authoring tools. In this section, we discuss techniques that will assist people in storytelling using the media that they collect. A storytelling approach could be described as the one shown in Figure 20.6.

Storytelling is based on a database of events and the experiences associated with events. A storyteller usually has a message or a perspective that she wants to convey using appropriate events and experiences associated with those. Another important factor in storytelling is the listener or the audience of the story. Events and experiences are also selected based on the audience interest and profile. Essentially, one may define storytelling as a sequence of events, and associated media, select appropriate events and for each event select appropriate media data that will maximize the message communication from the storyteller to the audience. This becomes a two-stage process. In the first stage, one selects appropriate events based on the message and then constructs a coherent story considering the profile and the level of audience.

While we believe that computers will most likely never become human enough to do so (it is also a question, by the way, if that is even a good goal), we could observe that operations have become more semantic in the past. For example, it is now possible to search for movie showtimes and the search engine presents the movie showtimes of the cinemas in your close proximity. Of course, this is enabled by the inference of your location using your IP address, wireless IDs, cell towers, or GPS sensors. But that's exactly the point: the sensors provide a context that a human would assume to be there (when one is looking for the movies at the other of the world, one usually specifies that); therefore they allow performing an operation that seems semantic as the computer does "what the user means." Apart from sensors, other enablers of semantic operations exist. Both user intention as well as context can be inferred from many sources and it is usually the combination of those. Hence, this is a topic for multimedia computing! We believe the ability to process more data in less time will allow multimedia researchers to mine large parts of the Internet for context and user intention, which is already successfully collected in social networks. It seems semantic operations go hand in hand with the demand for them. In other words, more data on the Internet will most likely provide opportunities for more semantic operations. The reason for that is it will become harder to find and use the data needed with more data being present on the Internet. For example, a simple video title search would suffice if there were only a couple hundred of videos on the Internet and the titles would be administered to be unique and descriptive by some entity. With many hours of videos uploaded to the Internet by the minute, search operations that go deeper and sift through content are in high demand. As we've argued before, only the wealth of videos will most likely enable them. Again, we believe that the combination of cues from different sources will in the end bring the most success. In other words: semantic operations are a multimedia computing challenge.

Less Privacy

The growth of multimedia as demonstrated by social networking sites such as Facebook and YouTube combined with advances in multimedia content analysis also provides novel opportunities for the unethical use of multimedia. In small scale or in isolation, multimedia analytics have always been a powerful but a reasonably contained privacy threat. However, when linked together and used on an Internet scale, the threat could become enormous and pervasive.

Imagine a future where multimedia query engines just work. You can search by topic, location, person, camera identity, or time, even when the uploader did not explicitly include such information. An unscrupulous attacker could query for videos recently recorded at resorts and then find videos taken with the same camera in nearby wealthy residential neighborhoods. This would produce an ideal hit list of targets who are likely away from home, which the thief could then refine. As reported in previous work, cybercasing already occurs, but with a multimedia query, the engine's simple methods of anonymizing posts and suppressing metadata will no longer be enough. Rather, the multimedia community needs to come up with methods to identify when information (such as the "identity" of the camera) is unintentionally leaked and develop mitigation techniques to reduce the potential harm. Here are three examples:

Person Detection: In the image realm, this is usually called *face detection*; in audio, *speaker recognition*. While the uploader can take active methods to anonymize the foreground participants if privacy is an issue (e.g., replacing their face with a black box, replacing their audio with a bleep sound), the privacy of background participants is problematic because the uploader may not care about incidental privacy breaches of the background participants.

3D Recordings: Time-of-flight cameras, light field cameras, stereo cameras, and microphone arrays are all becoming more pervasive. It is clear that similar devices will continue to be developed. Each comes with its own sets of issues and each has the potential to capture even more unwanted data.

Exotic Sensors: Everything from air pressure sensors to heart rate monitors are becoming more common, and it is likely data from these sensors will be incorporated into multimedia documents much as GPS is now. Because users often have no real notion of what is being collected or how accurate it is, they have little or no intuition of the privacy implications. A prominent historic example is GPS – only recently did the profound privacy implications of geo-tagging became commonly known.

In summary, we believe the diversity of attacks and the complexity of solving the privacy issues with multimedia content will require creative thinking of a community of researchers and therefore spawn a new field in multimedia content analysis.

Other Factors

As presented previously, many of the factors that shape the future of multimedia computing are technical. However, many factors shape the development of a field like multimedia, most importantly societal factors. As presented in the beginning of this chapter, it is the user who needs to be excited about a product or a new possibility. The user needs to adopt the technology and embrace it and the technology needs to adapt to the demands of its users. We can't emphasize enough that privacy and security concerns are an important societal issue rather than an academic hypothesis: companies get shut down, even ones with a specific technology that could have changed the course of multimedia, because a technical implementation bug made people panic.

Furthermore, the field of multimedia technology, more than other technology fields, relies on content. Movies, photographs, music, and speech are meaningless without content. Often technology gets adopted because of the specific content used. It is easy to become caught up in developing a new algorithm that will not be widely used because the content presented with it lacks wider adoption – as frustrating as that may sound.

In the end, if this continues to be true, these unpredictable factors will make it even more difficult to foresee the future of a new technology and more so of a field.

RECOMMENDED READING

In lieu of a recommended reading section, we invite you to sit back and brainstorm about the future of multimedia yourself.

Further Reading

Gartner Inc. *The Gartner Emerging Technologies Hype Cycle*. 2006.

EXERCISES

1. Evaluate the predictive power of the model in Figure 20.1 given time has past.
2. Write a paragraph about the implications of more bandwidth and cheaper network access to the field of multimedia computing.
3. What is your opinion on our statements about multimedia retrieval and online privacy? Discuss with your co-students.
4. Pick two examples of failures and successes of technologies. Find out why exactly they succeeded and why the other one failed.

Index

Aboud, G.D., 302
Absolute threshold of hearing (ATH), 165–66
Accelerometers, 30–31
Acoustic event detection (AED), 235, 281–82
Acoustic Long-Term Average Spectrum (LTAS), 239
Acoustic pitch, 238
Actuators, 28–29
AdaBoost learning algorithm, 281
Adaptive codebook, 184
Addison, Paul S., 172
ADPCM algorithm, 148–50
ADRS envelope, 47
Advanced perceptual compression
  convolution theorem, 160–61
  Cooley-Tukey algorithm, 157
  Discrete Cosine Transform (DCT), 158–60
  Discrete Fourier Transform (DFT), 156–58
  Fast Cosine Transform, 157
  Fast Fourier Transform, 157
  JPEG format and, 161–64
  MP3 format and, 168–70
  overview, 156
  perceptual video compression, 170–71.
    (*see also* Perceptual video compression)
  psychoacoustics and, 164–68
AED (Acoustic event detection), 235, 281–82
Ahmed, N., 171–72
A-law, 145–46
Algorithms
  AdaBoost learning algorithm, 281
  ADPCM algorithm, 148–50
  arithmetic coding, 135–38, 136t.11.5
  Cooley-Tukey algorithm, 157
  Huffman coding, 128–31
  k-means algorithm, 142–43
  Lempel-Ziv algorithms, 131–35
  LZ77 algorithm, 131–33, 132t.11.3
  LZ78 algorithm, 133–36, 133t.11.4
  LZC algorithm, 135
  LZW algorithm, 135

  machine learning algorithms, 235–36
  machine vision algorithms, 235
  MP3 format, 168–70
  MPEG-1 algorithm, 151–53
  Sequential Minimal Optimization (SMO)
    algorithm, 257
  Viterbi algorithm, 259, 272–73
  x-means algorithm, 143–44
Allen, J.F., 34
American National Standards Institute (ANSI), 53
Anderson, C.A., 121
ANNs (Artificial Neural Networks), 252–55
Anstis, S.M., 302
Apple, 108
Apple iTunes, 202
Application layer QoS control, 100
Approximants, 44
Arithmetic coding, 135–38, 136t.11.5
Artificial intelligence, 236
Artificial Neural Networks (ANNs), 252–55
ATH (Absolute threshold of hearing), 165–66
Attack, 47
Audio editing, 73–74
Audio processing, 235
Audio sensors, 29
Audiovisual media, 7–8
Autostereoptic displays, 59
A-weighting scheme, 37

Baars, B.J., 93
Background, signal processing and, 223–24
Bark scale, 165, 217
Barkhausen, Heinrich, 165
Barrow, H.G., 302
Bayesian Information Criterion (BIC), 252, 262,
  279–80
Belongie, S., 302
Berkeley, George, 290, 302
Bickford, A.C., 49
Big Data, 11

Binary Format for Scenes (BIFS), 171
Bing, 297
Blackstock, D.T., 48
Blu-ray format
  compression and, 124
  differential coding and, 151
  lossy compression and, 141
Body transfer illusion, 84
Bohr, Niels, 305
Books, 67–68
Botvinick, M., 84
Bovik, Al, 231
Brandenburg, K., 172
Broughton, S.A., 171–72
Bryan, K., 171–72
Bunke, Horst, 287
Bureau, M., 121
Bushman, B.J., 121

Caitlin, D.E., 25
Calvert, Gemma, 93
Cameras, 54–57
  autostereoptic displays, 59
  digital cameras, 57
  Exif format and, 24–25, 161, 298–99
  image formation, 54–56
  line of sight, 56
  moving camera, moving objects (MCMO), 282–83
  moving camera, stationary objects (MCSO), 282–83
  parallax barrier method, 59
  resolution, 56
  stationary camera, moving objects (SCMO), 282–83
  stationary camera, stationary objects (SCSO), 282–83
  television and, 56–57
  3D video, 57, 59
  video cameras, 56–57
Candelas, 52
Carryer, J. Edward, 34
CBIR. See Content based image retrieval (CBIR)
CELP. See Code Excited Linear Prediction (CELP)
Challenges in multimedia systems
  context versus content, 23–25
  semantic gap, 22–23, 25
  overview, 21
Chroma quantization, 162
CIELAB color space, 62–64
CIEXYZ color space, 63–64
Clark, A.B., 146
Classic information retrieval
  logical representation, 193–94
  Multimedia Information Retrieval (MIR) compared, 192–98
  overview, 192–94
  PageRank, 194–95
  precision, 194
  ranking, 194

recall, 194
relevance feedback, 194, 196–98
term frequency/inverse document frequency (TF/IDF), 195–96
Web Image Search, 198
Cloud computing, 11, 308
CMYK color space, 61
Codd, Edgar, 189–90
Code Excited Linear Prediction (CELP)
  adaptive codebook, 184
  bitstream, 185t.14.1
  fixed codebook, 184–85
  line spectral frequencies (LSF), 183–84
  line spectral pairs (LSP), 183–84
  overview, 182–83
Cohen, J.D., 84
Color histograms, 243–44
Color spaces, 61–64
  CIELAB color space, 62–64
  CIEXYZ color space, 63–64
  CMYK color space, 61
  RGB color space, 61
  YUV color space, 62
Color vision, 60–61
Communication
  defined, 16
  evolution of technology, 8–10, 8t.2.1
  in human society, 7–8
  overview, 25
Compasses, 30–31
Compression
  advanced perceptual compression. (see Advanced perceptual compression)
  algorithms, 128–38
  arithmetic coding, 135–38, 136t.11.5
  DEFLATE method, 133
  dynamic range compression (DRC), 216–17
  entropy and, 127
  Huffman coding, 128–31
  information content and, 125–32, 126t.11.1., 127t.11.2
  Lempel-Ziv algorithms, 131–35
  Lossy compression. (see Lossy compression)
  LZ77 algorithm, 131–33, 132t.11.3
  LZ78 algorithm, 133–36, 133t.11.4
  LZC algorithm, 135
  LZW algorithm, 135
  overview, 4, 124
  perceptual video compression, 170–71. (see also Perceptual video compression)
  run-length encoding (RLE), 124–25
  source coding theorem, 127
  speech compression. (see Speech compression)
  weakness of entropy-based compression methods, 138
Computer graphics, 235

Computing
  evolution of technology, 8–10, 9t.2.2
  expected results of computing, 11–12
  personal computers, 10–11
Connected components, signal processing and, 223
Connectivity, signal processing and, 223
Content analysis. *See* Multimedia content analysis
Content analysis systems. *See* Multimedia content
    analysis systems
Content based image retrieval (CBIR), 199–205
  overview, 199–201
  Query by Humming (QbH), 202
  semantic content-based retrieval, 202–3
  tag-based retrieval, 203–4
  video retrieval, 204–5
Content replication, 101
Content segments, 69
Context versus content
  connecting data and users, 292
  context defined, 293–94
  context in content, 294, 295–96
  context only image search, 297
  data acquisition context, 294–95
  device parameters, 297–99. (*see also* Device
    parameters)
  interpretation context, 295
  overview, 23–25, 290–91
  perceivers, 299–302. (*see also* Perceivers)
  smart phone photo management, 300–2
  types of context, 294–95
  verification vision, 296–97
Continuous media distribution services, 100–1
Contours, 227
Control theory, 25
Conventional video encoding, 170–71
Convolution theorem, 160–61
Cooley-Tukey algorithm, 157
Countermeasures regarding privacy, 118
Crocker, Lee Daniel, 151
CRT technology, 58

Data acquisition and organization in
    documents, 71–72
Data acquisition context, 294–95
Databases
  logical level of data, 190
  Multimedia Information Retrieval (MIR) and,
    189–91
  organization, storage, management, and retrieval
    (OSMR), 189–90
  physical level of data, 190
  view level of data, 190–91
Daubechies, Ingrid, 172
DCT (Discrete Cosine Transform), 158–60
Decay, 47
Decibel scale, 37
Defining multimedia systems
  audiovisual media and, 7–8
  communication in human society, 7–8
  elements of multimedia computing. (*see* Elements
    of multimedia computing)
  emerging applications and, 11
  evolution of computing and communication
    technology, 8–10, 8t.2.1., 9t.2.2
  evolving nature of information and, 11–12
  expected results of computing and, 11–12
  experiential environments and, 12–13, 14
  formal definition, 13
  multimedia aspect, 10–13
  personal computers and, 10–11
  printing press and, 7, 13
  storage and recording technology and, 8
  telegraphy and, 7
  telephony and, 10
DEFLATE method, 133
DER (Diarization Error Rate), 280
Desktop metaphor, 111, 112
Detection error tradeoff (DET) curve, 264
Device parameters, 297–99
  derived metal layer, 298
  human induced metal layer, 298
  meta layer, 297
  optical meta layer, 297
  overview, 294
  pixel/spectral layer, 297
  spatial metal layer, 298
  temporal metal layer, 297
DFT (Discrete Fourier Transform), 156–58
Dialog boxes, 110
Diarization Error Rate (DER), 280
Dictionaries, 16–17
Differential coding, 147–53
  ADPCM algorithm, 148–50
  in audio, 148–50
  in images, 150–51
  MPEG-1 algorithm, 151–53
  Paeth filter, 150–51
  PNG format, 150–51, 151t.12.1
  in video, 151–53
Digital cameras
  Exif format and, 24–25, 161, 298–99
  overview, 57
Digital television
  differential coding and, 151
  lossy compression and, 141
Digital video discs (DVDs)
  differential coding and, 151
  lossy compression and, 141
Digitization, 32–33
  discretization error, 33
  Nyquist frequency, 33
  quantization, 32
  quantization noise, 33
  sampling, 32

Diphthongs, 44
Discrete Cosine Transform (DCT), 158–60
Discrete Fourier Transform (DFT), 156–58
Discretization error, 33
Distraction, 120
Dix, Alan, 114, 121
Documents
    audio editing, 73–74
    audiovisual technology and, 68–69
    books, 67–68
    content segments, 69
    current authoring environments, 78–79
    data acquisition and organization, 71–72
    defined, 67–69
    dynamic documents, 71
    editing, 72
    elements of multimedia authoring
        environment, 75–77
    emerging multimedia editing tools, 74
    evolving nature of, 69–71
    HTML and, 78–79
    linear nature of, 69
    media asset characteristics, 75
    MPEG4 and, 79
    non-linear flow, 71
    overview, 67
    photo editing, 73, 73n.2
    Photoshop and, 79
    publishing formats, 77
    representations of multimedia documents, 77
    selection, 72
    SMIL and, 79
    spatial layout, 75–76
    stages in document creation, 71–74
    structure-based representation, 77
    synchronization, 76–77
    temporal layout, 76
    text editing, 72–73
    time-based representation, 77
    type of media and, 69–71
    video editing, 74
Dodd, George, 34
Dolby AAC, 165
Download and play, 100
Downsampling, 217–18
DRC (Dynamic range compression), 216–17
Duda, Richard O., 269
Durbin, J., 180
Durham, M., 121
DVDs (Digital video discs)
    differential coding and, 151
    lossy compression and, 141
Dynamic documents, 71
Dynamic Huffman compressors, 131
Dynamic range compression (DRC), 216–17

E-Chalk lectures, 85
Echo, 38

Edges, 226–28
    contours, 227
    detection of, 228
    edge detectors, 227
    edge fragments, 227
    edge linking, 227
    edge orientations, 227
    edge points, 227
    enhancement of, 227
    filtering of, 227
    isotropic operators, 227
    line discontinuities, 226
    ramp edges, 226
    roof edges, 226
    step discontinuities, 226
    vectors, 227
Edison, Thomas A., 39
Edit distance, 264–66
Editing of documents, 72
Einstein, Albert, 305
Elements of multimedia computing
    events, 17–18, 25–26
    experience, 15–17
    information, 15–17
    objects, 17–18, 25–26
    overview, 15
    perception, 18–19
    perceptual cycle, 19–21
EM (Expectation Maximization), 251
Enge, Per, 34
Entropy
    compression and, 127
    multimedia content analysis and, 262
Environmental sensors, 30–31
Estimation theory, 25
Euclidean distance, 261–62
Events
    as element of multimedia computing, 17–18,
        25–26
    event oriented thinking, 18
Everst, F. Alton, 48
Exchangeable Image File (Exif) format
    cameras and, 24–25, 161, 298–99
    overview, 26, 80
    privacy and, 117
    smart phones and, 302
    tag-based retrieval and, 203–4
Exotic sensors, 314
Expectation Maximization (EM), 251
Experience
    defined, 16
    as element of multimedia
        computing, 15–17
    future trends, 310–12
Experiential environments and, 12–13, 14
Explicit specification of synchronization, 90–91
Extensible Markup Language (XML), 24, 191–92
Extensible MPEG-4 Textual (XMT), 171

Face detection, 280–81
Face recognition, 117, 280–81
Facebook, 314
False creativity, 111–12
Fast Cosine Transform, 157
Fast Fourier Transform, 157
Ferreira, A.J., 172
Figure-ground problem, 212
Filter by example, 220–22
Fixed codebook, 184–85
Flash, 118–19
Flickr.com, 234
Floyd, R., 49
Fonts, 110
Formants, 45, 239
Fostering learning, 112–14
Fourier, Jean-Baptiste-Joseph, 156
Fraden, Jacob, 34
Frames, 209
Frank, E., 269
Fredric, Harris, 172
Frequency/loudness resolution, 165–66
Frequency space quantization, 162–63
Freuder, E.C., 302
Fricative consonants, 44
Friedland, Gerald, 121, 303
F-score, 264
Fundamental frequency, 47
Fundamental properties of multimedia applications
    and systems
  documents. (*see* Documents)
  multimedia systems. (*see* Multimedia systems)
  multimomdal integration. (*see* Multimodal
    integration)
  overview, 4
  privacy, 116–18
  safety, 119–20
  security, 118–19
  synchronization. (*see* Synchronization)
  user interface design principles. (*see* User interface
    design principles)
Future trends
  experience, 310–12
  mobility, 309–10
  networking, 308
  overview, 4, 305, 315
  prediction methods, 305–6
  privacy, 314–15
  semantic computing, 312–14
  sensors, 308–9
  transistors, 307–8

Galleguillos, C., 302
Gauntlett, David, 121
Gaussian Mixture Models (GMMs), 250–52, 272–73,
    274, 277, 279–80, 281–82
Gaussianization, 273–74
German Telefunken, 58

GIF (Graphics Interchange Format), 135
GIST features, 246
Gleick, James, 5, 14, 25, 79
Global level of computation, 211
Global positioning systems (GPS), 30–31
Global System for Mobile (GSM), 185–86
GMMs. *See* Gaussian Mixture Models
    (GMMs)
Gold, B., 287
Gold, Ben, 48–49
Gold, Bernard, 231
Google, 297
GPS (Global positioning systems), 30–31
Graphical filters, 222
Graphical user interface (GUI), 108, 111–12
Graphics Interchange Format (GIF), 135
Gregory, Richard, 302
GSM (Global System for Mobile), 185–86
GUI (Graphical user interface), 108, 111–12
Guild, J., 64
Gutenberg, Johannes, 7, 13, 67, 79

Haar Wavelet basis functions, 281
Haptic technology, 28–29
Harmonicity-to-Noise Ratio (HNR), 238
Harold, Elliotte Rusty, 121
Hart, Peter E., 269
Hayakawa, Samuel Ichiye, 5
HCI (Human-computer interaction), 108–9
HDTV, 59, 124
Headset microphones, 39–40
Hershenson, M., 93
Hershenson experiments, 84
Hidden Markov Model (HMM), 257–58, 272–73, 274,
    275–76, 281–82
Hipparchus, 146
HNR (Harmonicity-to-Noise Ratio), 238
Holes, signal processing and, 223–24
Holographic light sources, 64
HTML (HyperText Markup Language), 78–79
Huffman, David A., 128, 138
Huffman coding, 128–31
Huffman tree, 128
Human sensors, 28–29
Human-computer interaction (HCI), 108–9
Hype Cycle, 305–6
HyperText Markup Language (HTML), 78–79

IEC (International Electrochemical
    Commission), 37
IMA (Interactive Multimedia Association), 148
Image processing, 235
Immersive video, 105, 106
Implicit specification of synchronization, 90
Indexing, 199
Information
  defined, 16
  as element of multimedia computing, 15–17

Information content and compression, 125–32, 126t.11.1., 127t.11.2
Information retrieval
  classic information retrieval. (*see* Classic information retrieval)
  Multimedia Information Retrieval. (*see* Multimedia Information Retrieval (MIR))
Input devices, 97–98
Integrative systems approach, 1–3
Interaction environment, 199
Interactive Multimedia Association (IMA), 148
International Electrochemical Commission (IEC), 37
Interpolation
  linear interpolation, 218
  polynomial interpolation, 219
  spline interpolation, 219
Interpolation filters, 218–19
Interpretation context, 295
Intra-object specification of synchronization, 91
iPhoto, 203–4
IP Multicast, 101
Isotropic operators, 227

Jain, Ramesh, 14, 25–26, 79, 231
Jeoung, Ye Sun, 302
JFIF (JPEG File Interchange Format), 161
Johnson, Jeff, 120
Johnston, J.D., 172
Joint Photographic Experts Group (JPEG) format
  advanced perceptual compression and, 161–64
  arithmetic coding and, 135
  chroma quantization, 162
  frequency space quantization, 162–63
  linearization, 163–64
  lossless encoding, 163–64
  tiling, 162
  visual quantization and, 147
Jones, Gerard, 121
Jones, Matt, 121
Jones, M.J., 281
JPEG File Interchange Format (JFIF), 161
JPEG format. *See* Joint Photographic Experts Group (JPEG) format
Juang, B.H., 231

Kan, Min Yen, 93
Kellner, D., 121
k-Gaussians, 249–50
Kientzle, Tim, 48
Kittler, J., 302
KL-Divergence, 262
k-means, 249–50
k-means algorithm, 142–43
k-nearest neighbors, 248–49
Knoll, Thomas, 79

Knuth, Donald, 269
Kullback-Leiber distance, 282

LAB (Look-ahead buffer), 131
LAME, 168–70
Large vocabulary automatic speech recognition (LVASR), 273–75
  decoder, 274
  feature extraction, 273
  feature normalization, 273–74
  recognition, 274
  speech activity detection, 273
  textual postprocessing, 274–75
Lavalier microphones, 39–40
Layout frames, 92
Lempel, Abraham, 131, 138
Lempel-Ziv algorithms, 131–35
Lens distortion, 54
Levinson, N., 180
Levinson-Durbin recursion, 181
Life sensors, 30
Light
  additive methods, 58
  cameras, 54–57. (*see also* Cameras)
  candelas, 52
  color spaces, 61–64
  CRT technology, 58
  damage caused by, 120
  defined, 51–53
  HDTV, 59
  holographic light sources, 64
  lens distortion, 54
  lumens, 53
  luxes, 53
  measurement of, 52–53
  optics, 54
  overview, 51
  perception of, 59–61
  polarization, 52
  production of, 64
  properties of, 53–54
  recording of, 54–57
  reflection, 53
  refraction, 53
  reproduction of, 58–59
  subtractive methods, 58
  television. (*see* Television)
  wave nature of, 51–52
Line discontinuities, 226
Line spectral frequencies (LSF), 183–84
Line spectral pairs (LSP), 183–84
Linear filters, 215–16
Linear interpolation, 218
Linear nature of documents, 69
Linear operators, 214–16
Linear Prediction Coefficients (LPCs), 239
Linear Protective Coding (LPC), 175–82

analysis, 179–82
  Levinson-Durbin recursion, 181
  Magnitude-Difference Function, 178
  Magnitude-Sum Function, 176–77
  overview, 175–76
  pitch estimation, 177–79
  Schuer recursion, 181
  voiced/unvoiced detection, 176–77
  Zero-Crossing-Rate, 177
Linear quantization, 142
Linearization, 163–64
Linux, 146
Live video
  immersive video, 105, 106
  multiple camera videos produced
    as single, 103
  Multiple Perspectives Interactive (MPI) video,
    104–5
  one camera video, 103
  overview, 103
Lo, W.T., 121
Local level of computation, 210–11
Logical representation, 193–94
Lombard effect, 44
Look-ahead buffer (LAB), 131
Lossless encoding, 163–64
Lossy compression
  A-law, 145–46
  differential coding, 147–53. (*see also* Differential
    coding)
  k-means algorithm, 142–43
  linear quantization, 142
  motion quantization, 147
  μ-law, 145–46
  overview, 141
  perceptual quantization, 144–47
  sound amplitude quantization, 145–46
  vector quantization, 141–44
  visual quantization, 146–47
  x-means algorithm, 143–44
Lowe, David, 245
LPC. *See* Linear Protective Coding (LPC)
LPCs (Linear Prediction Coefficients), 239
LSF (Line spectral frequencies), 183–84
LSP (Line spectral pairs), 183–84
LTAS (Acoustic Long-Term Average Spectrum), 239
Lumens, 53
Luxes, 53
LVASR. *See* Large vocabulary automatic speech
    recognition (LVASR)
LZ77 algorithm, 131–33, 132t.11.3
LZ78 algorithm, 133–36, 133t.11.4
LZC algorithm, 135
LZW algorithm, 135

MacDonald, J., 83
Machine learning algorithms, 235–36

Machine vision algorithms, 235
Magnitude-Difference Function, 178
Magnitude-Sum Function, 176–77
Malware, 118–19
Manhattan distance, 261–62
Marsden, Gary, 121
Martinville, Édouard-Léon Scott de, 39
Masking, 166–68
Maximum Likelihood Linear Regression (MLLR), 274
McGurk, H., 83, 93
McGurk effect, 83
McKay, David, 138
McLuhan, Marshall, 13–14
Media asset characteristics, 75
Media processing to extract features, 199
Media synchronization, 102
Mel Frequency Cepstral Coefficients (MFCCs),
    239–42, 272–73, 279
Mel scale, 165, 217
Menu bars, 108
Metadata, 23–25, 117
Microphones, 39–41
  headset microphones, 39–40
  lavalier microphones, 39–40
  noise-canceling microphones, 40
  omnidirectional microphones, 40–41
  parabolic microphones, 40
  as sensors, 29
Microsoft, 108
Microsoft WMA, 165
MIDI, 48, 74
Minkowski metric, 261–62
MIR. *See* Multimedia Information Retrieval (MIR)
Misra, Pratap, 34
MLLR (Maximum Likelihood Linear Regression), 274
MLPs (Multi-Layer Perceptrons), 252–55
Mobility, future trends, 309–10
Modern video encoding, 171
Monomedia content analysis, evolution to
    multimedia content analysis, 234–36
Monophthongs, 44
Moore, Andrew, 144
Moore's Law, 307–8
Motion pictures, 7–8
Motion quantization, 147
MP3 format
  advanced perceptual compression and, 168–70
  algorithm, 168–70
  LAME, 168–70
  variable gain amplifiers and, 217
MPEG-1, 151–53, 165, 171, 307
MPEG-2, 165, 171
MPEG-4, 79, 171, 286
MPEG-7, 171
MPEG-21, 171
MPI (Multiple Perspectives Interactive) video, 104–5
Multi-Layer Perceptrons (MLPs), 252–55

Multimedia content analysis
  accuracy, 262–63
  acoustic event detection, 235
  Acoustic Long-Term Average Spectrum (LTAS), 239
  acoustic pitch, 238
  artificial intelligence, 236
  Artificial Neural Networks (ANNs), 252–55
  bias, 267
  color histograms, 243–44
  computer graphics, 235
  correlation versus causation, 266
  data collection and annotation, 267
  domain independence, 267–68
  edit distance, 264–66
  energy/intensity, 238
  entropy and, 262
  error measurement and evaluation, 262–66
  Expectation Maximization (EM), 251
  features of, 238–47
  formants, 239
  F-score, 264
  Gaussian Mixture Models, 250–52
  GIST features, 246
  Harmonicity-to-Noise Ratio (HNR), 238
  Hidden Markov Model (HMM), 257–58
  k-Gaussians, 249–50
  k-means, 249–50
  k-nearest neighbors, 248–49
  Linear Prediction Coefficients (LPCs), 239
  machine learning algorithms, 235–36
  machine vision algorithms, 235
  Mel Frequency Cepstral Coefficients (MFCCs), 239–42
  monomedia content analysis, evolution from, 234–36
  Multi-Layer Perceptrons (MLPs), 252–55
  music analysis, 235
  music synthesis, 235
  optical flow, 246–47
  overtraining, 268
  overview, 233
  pattern recognition, 235–36
  Perceptrons, 252–55
  precision/recall, 263–64
  psychophysics, 236
  ROC/DET curve, 264
  Scale-Invariant Feature Transformation (SIFT), 245–46
  semantic computing, 236
  Sequential Minimal Optimization (SMO) algorithm, 257
  setup of experiment, 236–38
  significance of results, 268
  soft margin classification, 257
  sparsity, 267
  speech analysis, 235
  speech synthesis, 235
  supervised learning, 248–59
  Support Vector Machines (SVMs), 255–57
  systems. (*see* Multimedia content analysis systems)
  temporal modeling, 257–59
  undermodeling, 268
  unsupervised modeling, 260–62
  visual texture, 242–43. (*see also* Visual texture)
  Viterbi algorithm, 259
  Word Error Rate (WER), 264–66
Multimedia content analysis systems
  acoustic event detection (AED), 281–82
  face detection, 280–81
  face recognition, 280–81
  large vocabulary automatic speech recognition (LVASR), 273–75. (*see also* Large vocabulary automatic speech recognition (LVASR))
  optional character recognition (OCR), 275–76. (*see also* Optional character recognition (OCR))
  overview, 272, 286–87
  speaker diarization, 278–80. (*see also* Speaker diarization)
  speaker recognition, 276–78. (*see also* Speaker recognition)
  speech activity detection, 272–73
  visual object recognition, 282–86
Multimedia Information Retrieval (MIR)
  classic information retrieval compared, 192–98
  content based image retrieval (CBIR), 199–205
  databases and, 189–91
  indexing, 199
  information defined, 189
  interaction environment, 199
  media processing to extract features, 199
  multimedia defined, 189
  overview, 188–89, 205–6
  Query by Humming (QbH), 202
  retrieval defined, 189
  semantic content-based retrieval, 202–3
  semi-structured data, 191–92
  structured data, 191–92
  tag-based retrieval, 203–4
  unstructured data, 191–92
  video retrieval, 204–5
Multimedia systems
  components of, 95–98
  configurations of multimedia nodes, 99
  content analysis systems. (*see* Multimedia content analysis systems)
  defining. (*see* Defining multimedia systems)
  download and play, 100
  emerging systems, 105
  immersive video, 105, 106
  input devices, 97–98
  live video. (*see* Live video)
  multiple camera videos produced as single, 103
  Multiple Perspectives Interactive (MPI) video, 104–5

networking, 98
one camera video, 103
output devices, 97–98
overview, 95, 105–6
processing unit, 96
Quality of Experience (QoE), 99
Quality of Service (QoS), 99
storage, 97
stored video, 100
streaming multimedia. (*see* Streaming multimedia)
Multimodal integration
body transfer illusion, 84
McGurk effect, 83
overview, 95, 105–6
sensor integration, 86
split attention, 84–86
uncertainty reduction, 84
ventriloquism, 83–84
Multiple camera videos produced as single, 103
Multiple Perspectives Interactive (MPI) video, 104–5
Music, 46–48
ADRS envelope, 47
attack, 47
decay, 47
fundamental frequency, 47
Music Genome Project, 203
Pandora, 203
percussion instruments, 48
Query by Humming (QbH), 202
release, 47
spectrum, 47
string instruments, 47
sustain, 47
timbre, 47
wind instruments, 47
Music analysis, 235
Music Genome Project, 203
Music synthesis, 235
Mussen, P., 121
μ-law, 145–46
MYSYS system, 295–96

Nahrstedt, Klara, 93, 106
National Institute of Standards and Technology (NIST), 280
Neighbors, signal processing and, 222–23
Neisser, Ulrich, 20, 25, 302–3
Network filtering, 101
Networking
future trends, 308
overview, 98
Nielsen, Jakob, 120–21
Nintendo, 59
Noise-canceling microphones, 40
Non-linear filters, 216–19
Non-linear flow of documents, 71
Norman, Donald A., 120

Norvig, Peter, 269
Nyquist, Harry, 33n.1, 34
Nyquist frequency, 33, 41
Nyquist-Shannon sampling theorem, 33n.1

Object-background separation, 213
Object level of computation, 211
Objects
as element of multimedia computing, 17–18, 25–26
intra-object specification, 91
object oriented thinking, 17
OCR. *See* Optional character recognition (OCR)
Offset, 131
Ogg Vorbis, 165
Oliva, Aude, 246
Omnidirectional microphones, 40–41
One camera video, 103
Oppenheim, Alan V., 171–72, 231
Optical flow, 246–47
Optics, 54
Optional character recognition (OCR), 275–76
binarization, 275
decoder, 275–76
recognition, 275
rectification, 275
Organization and analysis of multimedia content
multimedia content analysis. (*see* Multimedia content analysis)
multimedia content analysis systems. (*see* Multimedia content analysis systems)
Multimedia Information Retrieval (MIR). (*see* Multimedia Information Retrieval (MIR))
overview, 4
signal processing. (*see* Signal processing)
Output devices, 97–98
Overdriven signals, 41

Paeth filter, 150–51
PageRank, 194–95
Pandora, 203
Parabolic microphones, 40
Parallax barrier method, 59
Path, Signal processing and, 223
Pattern recognition, 235–36
Pelleg, Dan, 144
Perceivers, 299–302
domain knowledge, 300
overview, 295
smart phone photo management, 300–2
Perception
defined, 18
as element of multimedia computing, 18–19
models and, 19
perceptual cycle, 19–21
Perceptrons, 252–55
Perceptual cycle, 19–21

Perceptually encoded information
   light. (*see* Light)
   overview, 3
   sensors. (*see* Sensors)
   sound. (*see* Sound)
Perceptual quantization, 144–47
   A-law, 145–46
   motion quantization, 147
   μ-law, 145–46
   sound amplitude quantization, 145–46
   visual quantization, 146–47
Perceptual video compression, 170–71
   conventional video encoding, 170–71
   modern video encoding, 171
Percussion instruments, 48
Peregrin, Jaroslav, 25
Persaud, Krishna, 34
Person detection, 314
Personal computers, 10–11
Phonautograms, 39
Phonemes, 44
Phonograph cylinders, 39
Photo editing, 73, 73n.2
Photoshop, 79
Pitch estimation, 177–79
Pixels, 209
Platt, John C., 257
PNG. See Portable Network Graphics (PNG)
Pohlmann, Ken C., 48, 153
Polarization, 52
Polynomial interpolation, 219
Polyphase filters, 219
Popper, Karl, 25, 302–3
Porat, Boaz, 231
Portable Network Graphics (PNG)
   DEFLATE method and, 133
   differential coding, 150–51, 151t.12.1
Postscript, 118–19
Precision in classic information retrieval, 194
Princen, J.P., 172
Printing press, 7, 13
Privacy
   future trends, 314–15
   overview, 116–18
Processing unit, 96
Proprioception, 15n.1
Psychoacoustics
   absolute threshold of hearing (ATH), 165–66
   advanced perceptual compression
     and, 164–68
   Bark scale, 165
   frequency/loudness resolution, 165–66
   masking, 166–68
   Mel scale, 165
Psychological effects, 119
Psychophysics, 236
Publishing formats for documents, 77

Quality of Experience (QoE), 99
Quality of Service (QoS), 99
Quantization
   chroma quantization, 162
   digitization and, 32
   frequency space quantization, 162–63
   linear quantization, 142
   motion quantization, 147
   perceptual quantization, 144–47.
     (*see also* Perceptual quantization)
   signal processing and, 209–10
   sound amplitude quantization, 145–46
   vector quantization, 141–44. (*see also* Vector
     quantization)
   visual quantization, 146–47
Quantization noise, 33
Query by Humming (QbH), 202
Query by Image Example, 200
Questionnaires, 115
Quinton, A., 25

Rabiner, Lawrence R., 231
Radio, 7–8
Ramachandran, V.S., 302
Ramp edges, 226
Ranking in classic information retrieval, 194
Raskin, Jef, 120–21
Real Time Control Protocol (RTCP), 102–3
Real Time Streaming Protocol (RTSP), 103
Real Time Transport Protocol (RTP), 102–3, 171
Recall in classic information retrieval, 194
Receiver-operator-characteristics (ROC) curve, 264
Recursive filtering techniques, 20–21
Reflection, 53
Refraction, 53
Regions
   similarity and, 225
   spatial proximity and, 225
Release, 47
Relevance feedback, 194, 196–98
Remote controls, 110–11
Resolution
   cameras, 56
   of sensors, 32
   visual, 29
Responsiveness, 113
Reverberation, 38
RGB color space, 61
Riul, A., Jr., 34
RLE (Run-length encoding), 124–25
Robotics, 305n.1
ROC/DET curve, 264
Rock, Irwin, 25, 302
Rojas, Raul, 269
Roof edges, 226
RTCP (Real Time Control Protocol), 102–3
RTP (Real Time Transport Protocol), 102–3, 171

RTSP (Real Time Streaming Protocol), 103
Run-length encoding (RLE), 124–25
Russell, Stuart J., 269
Rutherford, E., 121

Safety, 119–20
Salomon, David, 138
Sample level of computation, 210
Sampling, 209–10
Saxe, John Godfrey, 4
Sayood, Khalid, 138
SB (Search buffer), 131
Scale-Invariant Feature Transformation (SIFT),
  245–46, 282
Scherp, A., 25
Schuer recursion, 181
Schwartz Criterion, 279
Search buffer (SB), 131
Search engines, 297
Security, 118–19
Segmentation
  split and merge, 228–30
  video segmentation, 229–30
Selection of documents, 72
Semantic computing
  future trends, 312–14
  overview, 236
Semantic content-based retrieval, 202–3
Semantic gap, 22–23, 25, 292
Semantics, 15–16, 25
Semi-structured data, 191–92
Sensor integration, 86
Sensors
  accelerometers, 30–31
  audio sensors, 29
  bias, 31
  compasses, 30–31
  defined, 28
  digitization, 32–33
  drift, 31–32
  environmental sensors, 30–31
  exotic sensors, 314
  future trends, 308–9
  human sensors, 28–29
  hysteresis, 32
  life sensors, 30
  noise, 31–32
  nonlinear behavior, 31–32
  offset, 31
  operational range, 31–32
  overview, 28
  properties of, 31–32
  resolution, 32
  saturation, 31
  sight sensors, 29
  smell sensors, 29
  tactile sensors, 28–29
  taste sensors, 29
  temperature sensors, 30
  time sensors, 31
  types of, 28–31
  weight sensors, 30
Sensory gap, 293
Sequential Minimal Optimization (SMO)
  algorithm, 257
Session Initiation Protocol (SIP), 103
Shannon, E., 127, 138
Shapiro, Linda, 231
Sharp, Helen, 121
Shirky, Clay, 79
SIFT (Scale-Invariant Feature Transformation),
  245–46, 282
Sight sensors, 29
Signal processing
  audio processing, 235
  background and, 223–24
  connected components and, 223
  connectivity and, 223
  downsampling, 217–18
  dynamic range compression (DRC), 216–17
  edges and, 226–28. (see also Edges)
  figure-ground problem, 212
  filter by example, 220–22
  frames, 209
  global level, 211
  graphical filters, 222
  holes and, 223–24
  image processing, 235
  interpolation filters, 218–19
  levels of computation, 210–12
  linear filters, 215–16
  linear interpolation, 218
  linear operators, 214–16
  local level, 210–11
  neighbors and, 222–23
  non-linear filters, 216–19
  object-background separation, 213
  object level, 211
  overview, 209, 230–31, 235
  path and, 223
  pixels, 209
  polynomial interpolation, 219
  polyphase filters, 219
  quantization, 209–10
  regions and, 225–26. (see also Regions)
  sample level, 210
  sampling, 209–10
  spectral subtraction, 220
  spline interpolation, 219
  split and merge, 228–30
  subsampling, 217–18
  supersampling, 218
  thresholding, 212–14
  upsampling, 218

Signal processing (*cont.*)
  variable gain amplifiers, 217
  video processing, 235
  video segmentation, 229-30
  VU meters, 222
  Wiener filter, 220-21
SILK, 186
Simon, J.D., 287
Singhavi, L.M., 25
Single Instruction, Multiple Data (SIMD), 211
Sinha, P., 302
SIP (Session Initiation Protocol), 103
Skype SVOPC, 186
Sliding windows, 131
Smart phones
  event name tagging, 302
  identifying objects, 302
  identifying people, 300-2
  photo management, 300-2
Smell sensors, 29
Smeudler, Arnold, 25
SMIL (Synchronized Multimedia Integration
    Language), 79
SMO (Sequential Minimal Optimization)
    algorithm, 257
So, R.H.Y., 121
Social media, 116
Soft margin classification, 257
Software evaluation through human subjects, 114
Sommer, R., 121, 303
Sony ATRAC, 165
Sound
  adaptive concatenative synthesis, 48
  A-weighting scheme, 37
  concatenative synthesis, 48
  constructive interference, 38
  damage caused by, 120
  decibel scale, 37
  defined, 36
  destructive interference, 38-39
  echo, 38
  human-created sound, 45-46
  interference, 38
  microphones, 39-41. (*see also* Microphones)
  music, 46-48. (*see also* Music)
  overdriven signals, 41
  overview, 36
  physics of, 36-37
  production of, 43
  properties of, 38-39
  psychoacoustics. (*see* Psychoacoustics)
  recording of, 39
  reproduction of, 39, 41-43
  reverberation, 38
  speakers, 41-43
  speech, 43-45, 49. (*see also* Speech)
  synthesis of, 48

  wavetables, 48
Sound amplitude quantization, 145-46
Sound pressure, 37
Source coding theorem, 127
Spatial layout of documents, 75-76
Spatial synchronization, 91-93
Speaker diarization, 278-80
  cluster merging, 279
  re-segmentation, 279
  re-training, 279
Speaker identification, 117
Speaker recognition, 276-78
  evaluation metrics, 278
  general architecture, 277
  model generation, 277
  supervector generation, 277
  UBM index generation, 277
  Universal Background Model (UBM), 276-77
Speakers, 41-43
Specification of synchronization, 90-91
Spectral subtraction, 220
Speech, 43-45
  generally, 49
  approximants, 44
  compression. (*see* Speech compression)
  diphthongs, 44
  formants, 45
  fricative consonants, 44
  limited bandwidth, 45-46
  limited variance in harmonicity, 46
  limited volume, 46
  Lombard effect, 44
  monophthongs, 44
  phonemes, 44
  spectrogram, 45
  stop consonants, 43
  vowels, 44
Speech activity detection, 272-73
Speech analysis, 235
Speech compression
  overview, 174
  CELP. (*see* Code Excited Linear Prediction (CELP))
  Global System for Mobile (GSM), 185-86
  Linear Protective Coding (LPC), 175-82.
    (*see also* Linear Protective Coding (LPC))
  properties of speech coders, 174-75
Speech synthesis, 235
Spline interpolation, 219
Split and merge, 228-30
Split attention, 84-86
SQL (Structured Query Language), 191
Static Huffman compressors, 131
Steinmetz, Ralf, 93, 106
Step discontinuities, 226
Stiles, W.S., 64
Stockman, George, 231
Stoll, G., 172

Stop consonants, 43
Storage, 97
Storage and recording technology, 8
Stored video, 100
Streaming multimedia
    application layer QoS control, 100
    content replication, 101
    continuous media distribution services, 100–1
    IP Multicast, 101
    media synchronization, 102
    network filtering, 101
    overview, 100, 106
    protocols, 102–3
    streaming servers, 101–2
Streaming servers, 101–2
String instruments, 47
Structure-based representation of documents, 77
Structured data, 191–92
Structured Query Language (SQL), 191
Subsampling, 217–18
Supersampling, 218
Support Vector Machines (SVMs), 255–57, 277,
    281–82
Sustain, 47
Synchronization
    content synchronization, 87–88
    deadlines, 91
    of documents, 76–77
    explicit specification, 90–91
    implicit specification, 90
    intra-object specification, 91
    layout frames, 92
    levels of, 90
    media synchronization, 102
    multimedia streams, run-time support for, 90
    overview, 82, 86–87, 93
    spatial synchronization, 91–93
    specification, 90–91
    temporal synchronization, 88–90
    time-dependent and time-independent media,
        run-time support for, 90
Synchronized Multimedia Integration Language
    (SMIL), 79
Systems
    multimedia content analysis systems.
        (see Multimedia content analysis systems)
    multimedia systems. (see Multimedia systems)

Tactile sensors, 28–29
Tag-based retrieval, 203–4
Tags, 24
Tamura image, 243
Task-orientation, 109–11
Taste sensors, 29
TCP (Transmission Control Protocol), 102
Telegraphy, 7
Telephony, 10

Television
    cameras and, 56–57
    communication by, 7–8
    CRT technology, 58
    differential coding and, 151
    HDTV, 59, 124
    lossy compression and, 141
    speech activity detection, 273
    visual quantization and, 147
Temperature sensors, 30
Temporal layout of documents, 76
Temporal modeling, 257–59
Temporal synchronization, 88–90
Tennebaum, J.M., 302
Terhardt, E., 172
Term frequency/inverse document frequency (TF/
    IDF), 195–96
Text editing, 72–73
"Thinking outside in," 109
3D video
    cameras, 57, 59
    damage caused by, 120
    future trends, 310
    privacy and, 314
Thresholding, 212–14
Tiling, 162
Timbre, 47
Time-based representation of documents, 77
Time sensors, 31
Tokens, 131
Torralba, Antonio, 246
Transistors, future trends, 307–8
Transmission Control Protocol (TCP), 102
Transparency, 112–13
Trash bins, 112
Turing completeness, 118–19

UBM (Universal Background Model), 281–82
UDP (User Datagram Protocol), 102
UmaSwami, 20
Uncertainty reduction, 84
Universal Background Model (UBM), 276–77, 281–82
Unstructured data, 191–92
Upsampling, 218
User Datagram Protocol (UDP), 102
User interface design principles
    Desktop metaphor, 111, 112
    dialog boxes, 110
    false creativity, 111–12
    fonts, 110
    fostering learning, 112–14
    graphical user interface (GUI), 108, 111–12
    human-computer interaction (HCI), 108–9
    menu bars, 108
    questionnaires, 115
    remote controls, 110–11
    responsiveness, 113

User interface design principles (*cont.*)
  significance of testing, 116
  software evaluation through human subjects, 114
  task-orientation, 109–11
  "thinking outside in," 109
  time of operations, 113
  transparency, 112–13
  trash bins, 112
  video surveillance tests, 114–15

Variable gain amplifiers, 217
Vector quantization, 141–44
  k-means algorithm, 142–43
  linear quantization, 142
  x-means algorithm, 143–44
Vectors, 227
Ventriloquism, 83–84
Verification vision, 296–97
Video cameras, 56–57
Video editing, 74
Video processing, 235
Video retrieval, 204–5
Video segmentation, 229–30
Video surveillance tests, 114–15
Viola, P.A., 281
Viruses, 119
Visual dictionaries, 16–17
Visual object recognition, 282–86
  change detection, 283–84
  difference pictures, 283–84
  object tracking, 284–86
  path coherence, 286
Visual quantization, 146–47
Visual texture, 242–43
  coarseness, 242
  contrast, 242
  directionality, 243
  Tamura image, 243
Viterbi, Andrew, 259
Viterbi algorithm, 259, 272–73

Vocal Tract Length Normalization (VTLN), 273–74
Voiced/unvoiced detection, 176–77
Vowels, 44
VU meters, 222

Wall, Larry, 109–10
Waltz, D.L., 295–96
Wang, Patrick Shen-pei, 287
Web Content Accessibility Guidelines (WCAG),
  120, 121
Weber-Fechner Law, 60, 145
Web Image Search, 198
Weight sensors, 30
Welsh, T.A., 138
WER (Word Error Rate), 264–66
Westermann, G. Utz, 25–26
What-You-See-Is-What-You-Get (WYSIWYG), 12
Wiener, Norbert, 220
Wiener filter, 220–21, 231
Williams, Arthur B., 231
Wilson, Jon S., 34
Wind instruments, 47
Winston, Patrick, 302
Witten, I.H., 138, 269
Word Error Rate (WER), 264–66
Wu, Dapeng, 106
WYSIWYG (What-You-See-Is-What-You-Get), 12
Wyzecki, G., 64

x-means algorithm, 143–44
XML (Extensible Markup Language), 24, 191–92
XMT (Extensible MPEG-4 Textual), 171

Yahoo, 297
YouTube.com, 188, 234, 314
YUV color space, 62

Zero-Crossing-Rate, 177
Ziv, Jacob, 131, 138
Zwicker, Eberhard, 165